To K from M
25/12/2005

The Bonnie Links of Turnberry

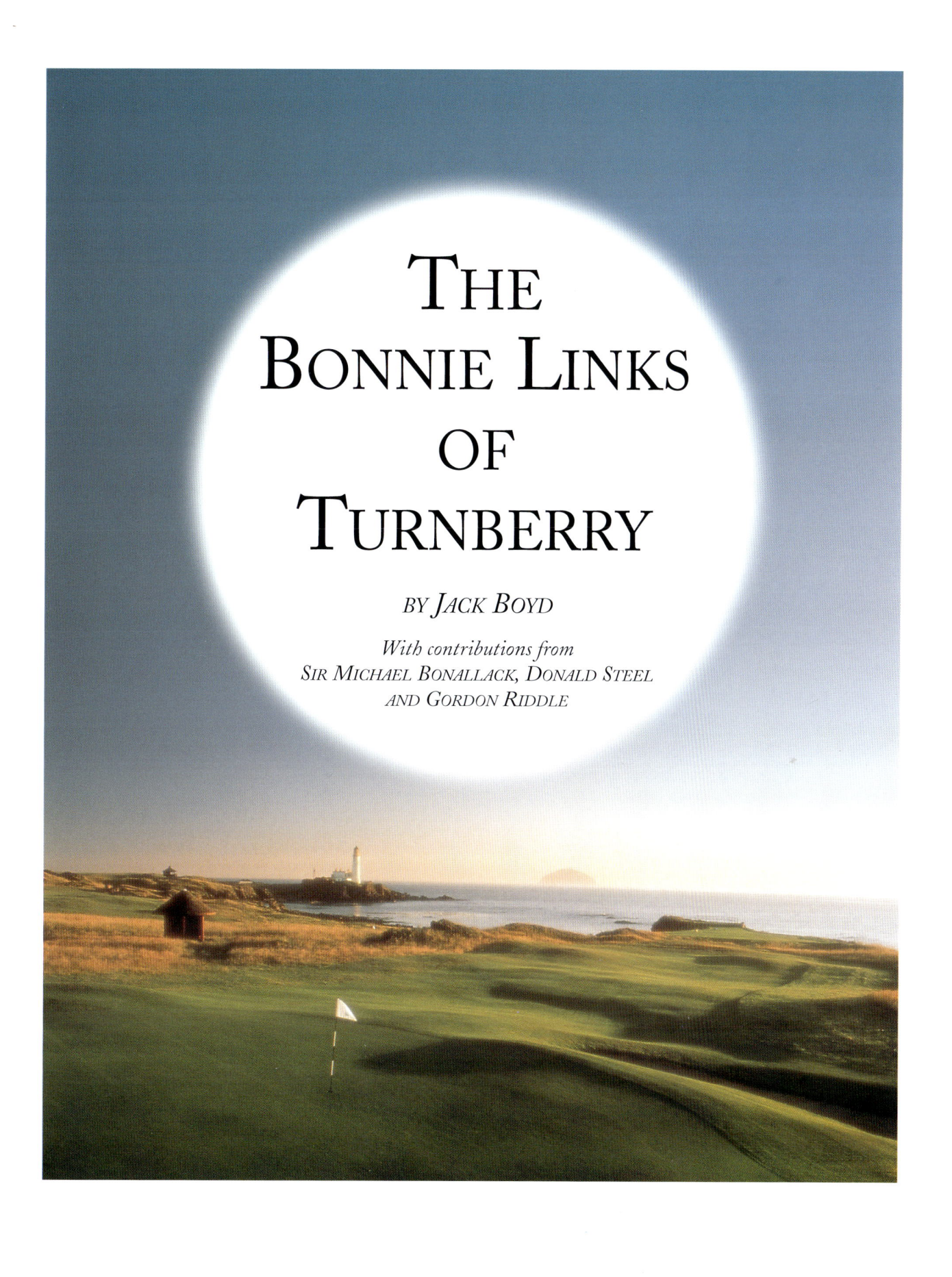

by Jack Boyd

With contributions from
Sir Michael Bonallack, Donald Steel
and Gordon Riddle

PUBLISHED BY
Turnberry Golf Club

© COPYRIGHT
*The text of book is the property of Turnbery Golf Club.
No part of it may be reproduced, in any manner whatsoever,
without the written permission of the Club.*

Author's Dedication

*To the memory of Jessie and Sally,
two wonderful brave ladies.*

Typeset in Caslon 10pt
by Fiona McColm, Advertisingworks Scotland Ltd.

Printed and bound by Adline Litho, Cumbernauld, Scotland

ISBN 0-9537811-6-X

FOREWORD

by The Marchioness of Ailsa

I was deeply touched when I was asked to write a Foreword to this book. Turnberry and the Golf Club hold a very special place in my life and in the history of the Kennedy family. My late husband's grandfather, the Third Marquess of Ailsa, Lord Archibald Kennedy, commissioned the construction of the first course in 1901 and was Honorary President of the Club for its first 43 years. His father, Lord Angus Kennedy, came home on leave from the Royal Navy in 1917 in a plane of the Royal Flying Corps which landed on a Turnberry fairway and, after the Second World War, he drove the first ball at the official re-opening of the reconstructed Ailsa Course in 1951. I myself served as Honorary President of the Ladies' Section of the club for a period of 38 years from 1962 till 1999.

I cannot claim to be a golfer of any merit and so am unable to offer an expert opinion on the golfing qualities of the courses or on the stirring golfing deeds achieved at Turnberry during the past century and which are, in any event, so well chronicled and described in the following pages. Who however, whether golfer or not, could fail to be awestruck by the majestic hotel on its hilltop and the panoramic view from there over the famous courses to the lighthouse on its promontory where land and sea meet so dramatically? Who could fail to appreciate the natural beauty of the background of the sea beyond, stretching to Ailsa Craig, Arran, the Kintyre peninsula and even the Irish Coast on a clear day? Who could fail to be moved by the story of Turnberry's phoenix-like rising again after twice being converted to a military airfield to help the war effort and at the dreadful cost of many brave young lives, whose names appear on the granite memorial on the hill overlooking the Twelfth Ailsa Green?

I have valued and enjoyed my association with Turnberry Golf Club which has been such an important element in the history and tradition of Turnberry. The telling of the Turnberry story from beginning to end in all its fascinating detail was long overdue and I congratulate the Club and the author, Jack Boyd, for undertaking this important task and producing a book to be treasured.

Author's Foreword

In November 1987 John Davidson suggested at a meeting of the Management Committee that a history of the Club should be prepared and it was reported that Past Captain David Gourlay, assisted by Bill Tait, already had this in hand. Sadly David Gourlay died in January 1988 and, although Bill Tait continued researching for the project unearthing a lot of interesting and useful material, particularly from the Scottish Record Office in Edinburgh, not much further progress was made until March 1992, when a Club History Committee was formed, comprising myself, Bill Manson, John Davidson, Alex Wilson and Bill Tait. We set about researching the Club's minutes in detail, dividing the work amongst us with each concentrating on different aspects. That year there was also an unexpected and exciting breakthrough when my representations to the Marquess of Ailsa and his Factor, David Gray, resulted in the Factor unearthing letters and other documents tied up in bundles with red ribbon and carefully indexed chronologically from 1892 till 1910. Their existence had been completely forgotten until they were discovered in a storeroom annexed to Maybole Castle by the Factor's daughter, who had been enlisted to search through old records during her university holidays. Imagine my excitement when the papers turned out to be all the incoming letters and ancillary papers received by the Factor of the time, Mr. Thomas Smith, relating to all the early proposals for a golf course at Turnberry, to the hotel being built and to the arrangements between the Third Marquess of Ailsa, the Glasgow & South West Railway Company and Turnberry Golf Club. The discovery was like finding a window with a direct view into the past and it fired my imagination and my determination to see through the whole project. I felt privileged to be the first person a century or so later to be reading the words of the many and varied people whose views, actions and decisions started off the train of events which resulted in Turnberry becoming one of the most famous and admired golf resorts in the world and the setting for some of the most important and momentous deeds in the history of the game of golf.

Initially there were discussions about who would write the proposed book, as it was not a task for a committee and the Club was not in a financial position to engage a professional writer. With the Club's minutes and the material from the Marquess of Ailsa and the Scottish Record Office, there was certainly sufficient information to make a start on the early years. On the basis that it would be helpful, even if the Club subsequently employed a professional writer or an editor, I decided in 1995 to make that start in my spare time. By late 1996 I had drafted the first two chapters and discussions had taken place with Chris Rouse, the General Manager of Turnberry Hotel, who was enthusiastic about making the history project a joint venture between the Hotel and the Club. This was agreed by the Club on the basis that the Hotel would employ professional writers to tell the story of the Hotel and of the tournaments and I would write a section about the origins and the history of the Club. By May 1997 the Hotel had engaged a professional editor to research the Hotel side, engage writers, liaise with the Club and make all the arrangements for artwork, illustrations, printing and publication. The total cost was to be borne by the Hotel, which at that time was owned by the Japanese company Nitto Kogyo. Matters proceeded on this basis and there were periodic meetings to review progress but it soon became apparent to the Club that the character of the proposed book was not what it wanted. It seemed that it was being planned as a lavish 'coffee table' style book which would be a useful marketing tool for the Hotel, while the section on the Club's history might be relegated to an appendix. In the meantime in January 1998 the ownership of Turnberry changed hands from Nitto Kogyo to the American company, Starwood, and Chris Rouse left Turnberry in June 1998. The editor experienced problems in getting confirmation from Starwood that they were going to take over the project and progress stalled. Then in January 2000 Starwood decided not to proceed. The Club immediately took a decision to go it alone and entrusted me with the daunting task of writing the book. As no history of Turnberry would be satisfactory unless it told the whole story of the place and not just the story of the Club, this involved a great deal of further research, but I found willing helpers in that task in two long standing fellow members Malcolm Wilkinson and Andrew Dinwoodie, whose assistance has been invaluable. In addition Andrew has made a very special contribution by acting as a proof reader. As a research chemist and author of scientific papers I could not have found anyone better or more qualified for that task and I am very much indebted to him for his meticulous work. Not only did he check everything from punctuation and spelling to errors and layout, he provided expert comment on content, style and indeed on every aspect of the work. Special thanks also go to another member, John McMillan, whose drawing, surveying and architectural skills were crucial to tracing the layouts of the original course and subsequent alterations and who provided the various course layout plans.

I also wish to mention the late Sally Lambie, a good friend who was a lecturer in law at Glasgow Caledonian University and co-author of a legal textbook on employment and commercial law, who kindly read over the text at every stage. Her comments, advice and support were invaluable. Another person whose help was invaluable was my secretary, Evelyn Riddick, who patiently and enthusiastically committed my handwritten text and subsequent numerous revisals to disc. A debt of gratitude is also due to D. Briggs & Co., Solicitors, Maybole, for the use of their computers and staff, entirely free of charge, and to Dave Killicoat of Maybole Historical Society for photographic work and publishing advice.

When the decision was taken in 2000 to go it alone it meant spending a considerable proportion of the Club's limited financial resources on the project and I felt a terrible burden of responsibility at having been entrusted with the task. At that point Tim Morrison lent me a copy of the book 'Golf, Scotland's Game' by David Hamilton, a Scottish surgeon and author of several books on the history of golf, who runs the award winning Partick Press, devoted to printing and publishing works on the history of sport, and suggested that I contact David for advice. He couldn't have been more helpful and I started sending him my early text for comment. It was his encouragement and enthusiasm, as well as his expert advice and suggestions, which gave me the confidence to proceed. If the book meets with his approval as a worthwhile contribution to the story of the game of golf then I will be happy. Of course I hope that it will also bring pleasure and interest to all who read it. Turnberry's was a story waiting to be told. I hope I have done justice to it.

Preface

by Alan McKinlay
Captain Turnberry Golf Club

Turnberry Golf Club is deeply indebted to the author of this book, Jack Boyd He is a local solicitor, who was born in 1933 in the small town of Maybole situated seven miles north and inland of Turnberry and who has been a member of Turnberry Golf Club for over 40 years. Educated at Carrick Academy, Maybole, and Glasgow University, after doing National Service in the Royal Air Force he came back to Maybole to practice law in 1960 and, for a period of 11 years from 1964 till 1975, he served as part-time Town Clerk for that ancient and historic burgh and its Town Council. Always keen on sport he started playing golf at Maybole municipal golf course whilst still at school, but athletics became his priority at university and he was the Scottish half mile track champion in 1958, held the Scottish Native record for that distance for many years and still holds the record for 1000 yards. His record at golf is not so distinguished but he is a very useful player and held a handicap of three for many years before two artificial hips and historical researching caught up with him. He served as Captain of the Club from 1992 till 1994 and chaired our Championship Committee for The 1994 Open. Jack has given an enormous amount of his time to researching and producing this book and his dedication has given us a book of which the Club can be proud.

The Club is also indebted to Donald Steel, Sir Michael Bonallack and Gordon Riddle for their much valued and excellent contributions and to Donald Steel and Raymond Jacobs for material and information from their personal archives.

Club histories are usually for members and about members but this book will also appeal to a wider audience as it is the story of a place and of events of historic importance and of great interest to students of the game of golf. This is not just the history of a golf club. It also throws light on many important social, political and commercial events both local and national throughout the whole of the twentieth century, as reflected in the establishment and development of a small corner of Ayrshire called Turnberry which is now known worldwide because of the game of golf. It is a story of kings, lords, railways, hotels, wars and international businesses as well as of Open Champions and ordinary club members. It is the story of a place so favoured by nature and so renowned for the sporting theatre it has inspired that, if there was ever to be a call to establish a single home for The Open, Turnberry would surely be a prime candidate.

I was tasked two years ago, along with the author and Past Captain Tim Morrison, with bringing this book to the point of publication and we are all now delighted to have achieved that goal, with the help of our fellow members Ian Brown, Alan Brown and Alex Ingram in relation to the commercial and technical aspects of the process. We can all now look forward to more relaxed games together without any questions being raised about the book's progress! I commend this book to you and earnestly hope that it will give the reader as much pleasure as we, the members, gain from our Club and our play on the magnificent Turnberry courses.

MESSAGES AND CONGRATULATIONS

On the occasion of its Centenary Turnberry Golf Club is honoured to have received the following messages and congratulations from Jack Nicklaus, Colin Montgomerie and Turnberry's three Open Champions, Tom Watson, Greg Norman and Nick Price.

'One of my greatest memories will always remain the duel against Jack Nicklaus in the 1977 Open Championship at Turnberry.'

TOM WATSON

'Given that I have always had affection for Scottish links golf, coupled with the fact that I recorded my first major championship victory at Turnberry, obviously I have a special spot in my heart for the club. Dating back to the turn of the 20th century when it became one of the first golf resorts of its kind, all the way through today 100 years later, the name Turnberry has by itself always stood for quality and success. I have often said that Turnberry is the best-conditioned Open course I ever played, and in a day and age where too many new golf courses are built in a one-dimensional fashion that only the game's most powerful golfers can play, Turnberry remains one of the best representations of what the founders of our great game envisioned. Even with all the technology that has come along in the game, Turnberry remains a thinking player's course and it takes more than length to conquer it. Although Turnberry is already one of the most famous layouts in golf, its legend will undoubtedly continue to grow for the next 100 years and beyond.'

GREG NORMAN

'I am very pleased to offer my best wishes and congratulations on the Centenary of Turnberry Golf Club.

Even though I didn't win the Open at Turnberry, the club – and particularly the Ailsa golf course – will always have a fond place in my heart, for that was the scene of one of the most exciting and enjoyable head-to-head matches in my career.

In 1977, when Tom Watson and I were paired together for the final round of the Open, we had great fun throughout an unforgettable match. Tom just played better, and I guess in the end, he was really the one who had more fun! But it was an exhilarating experience to be there, taking on that grand golf course and both playing so well that it was a shame one of us had to lose. It is probably one of the most talked-about Opens in history – even more so than any of the three I won.

I look forward to the day when I will return to that beautiful course by the sea, but until that time, I will continue to revisit Turnberry in my heart and mind and will always savor the superb experience of the game of golf at its best.

Good golfing.'

JACK NICKLAUS

'Like so many golf courses, Turnberry has seen so much drama over the years. From the three runways that were constructed on it during the Second World War, to arguably the most dramatic and famous duel in golf between Jack Nicklaus and Tom Watson in 1977. It was incredible theatre, played out on one of the most beautiful and picturesque golf courses imaginable. I also recall my phenomenal 63 that my good friend Greg Norman shot in the second round in 1986, that set up his first Open Championship win.

To me, there can be no better golfing experience than playing Turnberry on a sunny day with a gentle breeze. However, the true test is to play in the weather that the west coast of Scotland is so famous for – a 30 m.p.h. wind blowing across the Irish Sea and the temperature hovering around 5 degrees C. This is what brings out the true character of the golf course and tests any golfers mettle.

For my 40th birthday, my wife commissioned Graeme Baxter to paint the 10th hole for me from behind the green, with the Lighthouse and Ailsa Craig framing the background. A more beautiful picture is hard to find on any golf course. That painting now hangs in my study and I have the pleasure of looking at it every day I am home, and needless to say, it reminds me constantly of that Sunday in 1994 when I won The Open at Turnberry.

I have such fond memories of Turnberry, as do so many golfers who over the years have had the distinct pleasure of playing one of the greatest golf courses in the world.

Congratulations to all at Turnberry on this, your Centenary year, and as always I look forward to coming back and enjoying one of my favourite places to play.'

NICK PRICE

'I am delighted and honoured to have been asked by the Committee of the Turnberry Golf Club to contribute to their Centenary book.

Turnberry has always been, and always will be, one of my favourite places in the world. I was born in Ayrshire and it's where I learned to play and enjoy the game of golf. Indeed, much of my amateur golfing days were spent at Turnberry, a Club which now commands worldwide recognition with both the Ailsa and Kintyre courses – two truly demanding tests of links golf.

I always look forward to coming to Turnberry and try to visit as much as I can. I am extremely proud of the Colin Montgomerie Links Golf Academy, which was built in 2000, and of my continuing association with the Golf Club. In fact, on a fine, summer's evening I don't think there could be a better place to be than walking round the Ailsa course and taking in the spectacular views to the west, with the Ailsa Craig and the distant outline of the Mull of Kintyre.

I have many fond memories of playing at Turnberry as no doubt do all the past and present members of the Turnberry Golf Club and I wish them all the very best in their Centenary year and beyond.'

COLIN MONTGOMERIE

Contents

Chapter I - Historical Background
1. Birthplace of Scotland's Freedom.
2. Early Golf in South Ayrshire.
3. First Beginnings at Turnberry.
4. The Railway Connection.
5. Lord Ailsa Builds the First Course.
6. Girvan Golf Club Opens the Course.

Chapter II - The Club's Early Years
1. Formation of Turnberry Golf Club.
2. Club Affairs – 1902-1919.
3. Open Professional Tournament 1908.
4. Scottish Professional Golf Championship 1911.
5. Ladies' British Open Amateur Championship 1912.
6. International Match at Turnberry 1914.
7. Course Changes prior to The Great War.
8. The War Years.
9. Snippets from Club Minutes in historical context 1892-1914.

Chapter III - A Time for Golf then War Again
1. Club Affairs and Course Changes.
2. Ladies' British Open Amateur Championship 1921.
3. Scottish Ladies' Amateur Championships.
4. Ladies' British Open Amateur Championship 1937.
5. Second World War.
6. Snippets from Club Minutes in historical context 1920-45.

Chapter IV - Post War Turnberry 1946-1971
1. The Ailsa Course is Restored.
2. An Assessment of the Turnberry Courses – by Donald Steel.
3. The Club Survives.
4. Championships Held – 1952-1963.
5. Amateurs – v – Professionals Match 1958.
6. Amateur Championship 1961 & Walker Cup 1963 – by Sir Michael Bonallack
7. The Fewer the Better – Braemar Tournament.
8. A Period of Quiet – 1964-1971.
9. Snippets from Club Minutes in historical context 1946-1971.

Chapter V - The Modern Era Begins
1. Characters, Players and Pro-Ams 1972-1980.
2. Turnberry's Great Triumverate.
3. Big John, Rip, Tango and Others.
4. John Player Classics and Other Tournaments.
5. The 1977 Open Championship.
6. Professionals at Turnberry.
7. The Supporting Cast by Gordon Riddle.

Chapter VI - Centenary – The Closing Years
1. The Final Period 1980-2002.
2. Turnberry Ladies.
3. Trophies.
4. The Amateur Championship 1983.
5. The 1986 Open Championship.
6. The Senior British Open Championships 1987 to 1990.
7. The 1994 Open Championship.
8. The Amateur Championship 1996.
9. Weetabix Women's British Open Championship 2002.

Chapter VII - Reflections of Past Captains
1. David Logan 1980-1982.
2. Bill Judge 1982-1984.
3. Alex Todd 1984-1986.
4. Stewart Jardine 1988-1990.
5. Bill Manson 1990-1992.
6. Charlie Jack 1994-1996.
7. Jim Smith 1996-1998.
8. David McDowall 1998-2000.
9. Gordon Rodger 2000-2002.
10. Tim Morrison 2002-2003.

Appendices
1. Contemporary Description of the First Course.
2. Open Championships' Statistics.
3. Amateur Championships' Statistics.
4. Turnberry Club Captains and Champions.
5. Ladies' Section Captains and Champions.
6. Acknowledgements, Credits and Bibliography.

Chapter I

Historical Background

Kings, Lairds, Railways and Lords all play a part.

BIRTHPLACE OF SCOTLAND'S FREEDOM

TURNBERRY is now rightfully renowned for its golf courses and for the great golf championships and champions which it has produced. Not so well known though is its significant place in the history of Scotland long before the magnificent hotel or the majestic golf courses were built. According to Kevan McDowall, a local historian, the name Turnberry means 'the castle built on the stormy sharp rocky promontory' and the ruins of the ancient Turnberry Castle can still be seen on its spectacular rocky headland. The castle dates back at least to the 11th century and has associations with Scotland's hero king, Robert the Bruce. It is also the site of the famous lighthouse. As maritime traffic along the coast of Carrick increased throughout the nineteenth century, so too did the number of shipwrecks off Turnberry Point and on the Brest Rocks at the south end of Turnberry Bay, and the Commissioners of Northern Lighthouses instructed their engineers Thomas and David Stevenson, the father and uncle of the famous writer Robert Louis Stevenson, to recommend a site for a lighthouse. They recommended that it be built on Turnberry Point and it was built in 1873 on a site in the middle of the ruined walls of Turnberry Castle. There it stands today adjacent to the ninth hole of the Ailsa Course, with its silhouette and that of the historic ruined castle being a symbol known to golfers throughout the world, since it appeared on the first membership cards of Turnberry Golf Club when the Club was formed in 1902.

The Club, throughout its 100 year history, has never owned the golf course at Turnberry. For the first four of those years it was owned by the Marquess of Ailsa and for the next 96 years it has been owned by successive owners of the world renowned Turnberry Hotel. The stories of Turnberry, Turnberry Golf Club and Turnberry Hotel are inextricably linked, and the purpose of this book is to tell those stories. They are set against a background of much earlier events of immense importance in the national history of Scotland.

It was at Turnberry Castle in 1286 that the Bruce family, in the person of the future King Robert's grandfather, convened a meeting of his followers and asserted his claim to the throne of Scotland. He appealed for support to King Edward I of England, but Edward appointed not him, but John Baliol, an English puppet, as king. When even Baliol rebelled against his English master the cruel Edward marched north with his powerful army and crushed the Scots with brutal savagery, including the butchery of 17,000 men, women and children at the sacking of Berwick on Tweed.

Scotland had surely reached her lowest point of despair and shame and even her very nationhood was all but dead. Fortunately, two men led Scotland out of the ashes of shame and back to nationhood and freedom. The first was William Wallace and the second was Robert the

1902 Photograph of Turnberry Castle and Lighthouse which appears on Turnberry Golf Club's early membership cards.

Chapter I - Historical Background

Bruce who, in all likelihood, was born at Turnberry Castle. The Castle was the seat of the McDowalls, the Lords of Galloway and Earls of Carrick, and one legend tells of events said to have occurred around 1271, when Bruce's father was hunting in the area and he met Marjory McDowall, Countess of Carrick, a widow, whose husband had been killed in a crusade to the Holy Land. It is said that Marjory took a fancy to the young nobleman, made up her mind that he was going to be hers and ordered her servants to take him to Turnberry Castle. Whether it was by force or by her womanly charms, she prevailed upon him to marry her a few days later and the Ayrshire castle is the most likely birthplace of their son Robert the Bruce, later crowned King of Scotland in 1306. Legend also has it that it was at Turnberry in 1307 that Bruce launched his early struggles to free Scotland from the English tyranny. He was in hiding across the Firth of Clyde on the island of Arran with Sir James Douglas and a small band of supporters. He sent a scout called Cuthbert over to Ayrshire to

Above: 'Rock' Profile beside 10th green on Ailsa Course - romantically said to be that of Robert the Bruce.
Below: View over the whins and Firth of Clyde to the Isle of Arran from where Bruce sailed to start his campaign against the English

assess the possibility of an uprising, with orders to light a beacon on the Carrick coast if things looked favourable. Cuthbert found things anything but favourable, as the area was occupied by a strong English force under the command of Henry Percy, Lord of Northumberland, who was in occupation of Turnberry Castle. However, the story goes that some locals were burning whin bushes and when Bruce saw the smoke he mistook it for the signal and he sailed across from Arran to meet Cuthbert at Port Carrick, about two miles north of Turnberry. They resolved to attack the English under cover of dark and one by one knocked out the English outposts, but before they could reach the castle the alarm was raised and Percy was able to retreat to the safety of its thick walls. When daylight arrived Bruce and his men were gone, having withdrawn into the hills, but Percy abandoned Turnberry and retreated to Ayr, for fear of further attacks. This began Bruce's campaign to free his country, which seven years later ended with victory for Bruce and Scotland at Bannockburn.

These events are not forgotten locally, with place names such as Jameston, Douglaston, Kings Field, and of course 'Bruce's Stone', the name for the ninth hole on the Ailsa Course, all taking their names from that momentous night in the history of Turnberry and Scotland. It is a place which was destined to have many more momentous moments, not so bloody, but in their own way just as heroic. Perhaps some day the old castle and its story might even inspire a modern Scottish hero to win the greatest golf championship in the world, 'The Open', on what is one of its finest venues.

Above: Ruined gable wall of the Castle in 2002 after a century's further decay.
Below: View from 10th green of Ailsa Course which is so close to sea level that high tides of winter storms almost reach it.

Chapter I - Historical Background

Early Golf in South Ayrshire

THE early history of golf is well documented elsewhere, and everyone knows that it was so well established in Scotland in the fifteenth century, that Parliament in 1457 passed a law against participation in the sport because of its interference with the practice of archery. The oldest clubs and courses were established in the East of Scotland in the eighteenth century and it was not until a full century later that formal clubs and courses were formed in Ayrshire. Prestwick Golf Club and Prestwick St. Nicholas Golf Club were first in the area in 1851, and others followed, the principal dates being as follows:- Troon 1878; Ardeer 1880; Irvine 1887; Kilmarnock Barassie 1887; Largs 1891; West Kilbride 1893; Western Gailes 1897.

New Research – Golf in 1751

Until now only a few scattered references and folk tales allude to golf in Ayrshire prior to the nineteenth century, usually involving notable individual golfing incidents. The Laird of Bargany who had his estate about four miles north of Girvan and about the same distance inland of Turnberry and who died in 1597, was reputed to have sustained a broken nose from a hit by a golf ball struck *'on the hills of Air (Ayr) in recklessness'*. Another Laird of Bargany was noted in 1620 to have played golf on the links at Ballantrae, situated about 17 miles south of Turnberry. In Maybole, the once-important inland 'capital' of Carrick, situated 7 miles north of Turnberry, there is a description in 1683 of *'a pleasant spot enclosed with an earthen wall wherein they were wont to play football but now at Gowffe and Byasse bowls'*.

However recent original research has thrown new light on the early development of the game in South Ayrshire and events which took place very close to Turnberry. These are revealed in a recent paper compiled by David Hamilton entitled 'The Girvan Gang – Golf in Ayrshire in 1751'. Research by Professor Michael Moss of the University of Glasgow in the papers of the Kennedy family, whose estates included the lands of Turnberry, has brought to light an important letter. The letter is dated 15th February, 1751, and was written by Archibald Kennedy to Sir Thomas Kennedy:-

> *'There are grand Golf Matches at Girvan every fortnight. The parties generally are Bargandy [Bargany], Ardmillan, Penmore [Pinmore], Mr. Cathcart, the Minister and Dr. Bannerman, which occasions harmony and friendship and Sir John is the judge of fair play at that and the drinking, there are often complaints for the most part of next day of sore heads and great 'druiths' [thirsts].'*

At the time of the letter the only formally organised Scottish golf club was the Gentlemen Golfers of Leith, later called the Honourable Company of Edinburgh Golfers, a society formed in 1744. The Royal and Ancient Golf Club, at first known as the St. Andrews Society, only emerged in 1754. Yet here is evidence that at Girvan, only five miles south of Turnberry, a group of golfing cronies comprising well-off lairds and professional men, had gathered regularly to play the game of golf at least three years before the St. Andrews Society was formed, and exactly one hundred years before Prestwick, the first golf club in Ayrshire, appeared in 1851. The significance of the letter is that it challenges the generally held belief that golf in Scotland in the eighteenth century was almost exclusively an east coast game.

A Winter Game for Country Lairds

David Hamilton points out that it was already known that important and distinguished gentlemen from the west of Scotland were amongst the members of the pioneer clubs of the east coast in the eighteenth century. At that time golf was mainly a winter game, the summer being a busy time for landowners and country folk with sowing, tending, harvesting and storing crops, but in the winter many gentlemen wintered in Edinburgh for social, sporting, educational, legal and financial opportunities. There they could enjoy playing golf in congenial company at the courses on the coast near Edinburgh, where the climate was colder but drier. The excellent links land of Ayrshire stretching from as far south as Ballantrae to Irvine in the north was mostly ignored in the summer when the gentry were busy, but also in the winter when the attractions of Edinburgh beckoned.

Not all country lairds however would move east in the winter and the 1751 letter is testimony to this. For the group referred to in the letter, Girvan would have been a convenient place to gather for their games and for their socialising and drinking. It was central to their various country houses, and convenient also for the minister and the doctor. There was good links land along the coast north of the River Girvan, still occupied by part of today's municipal course, and there would be good hostelries for the eating and drinking and accommodation after the game, before returning home the next day.

Turnberry links would not have been so central or convenient for hospitality and accommodation and its development was destined to be delayed for another 150 years after the 'Girvan Gang' had enjoyed their games only five miles away.

If the Girvan group had progressed to have a more formal structure with written records and a trophy to be played for, then south Ayrshire might have spawned a club as old and important as the great clubs of the east of Scotland. As it was, a formal club at Girvan was not formed till more than 100 years later. The exact date of formation is not known but Girvan Golf Club's Cockburn Medal has been played for since 1872 and it is thought that the club may date back as far as 1860. When improved rail and road transport made it opportune for the great natural links at Turnberry to be developed for golf, it was historically fitting that Girvan Golf Club was to have an important part to play, as will be detailed later in this chapter.

Painting by an anonymous artist dated around 1740. It is entitled 'View of St. Andrews from the Old Course with Golfers' and is the earliest known image of golf being played on the Old Course. It gives some idea of how the 'Girvan Gang' might have appeared as they played their grand golf matches on the links north of Girvan in 1751.

CHAPTER I - HISTORICAL BACKGROUND

FIRST BEGINNINGS AT TURNBERRY

IN terms of the game of golf and its long history in Scotland in general and Ayrshire in particular, Turnberry was a late starter, probably due mainly to its isolation from larger communities. Even the short distance between the nearest towns of Maybole on the north and Girvan on the south would have been a considerable barrier to access before there was any public or motorised transport. In some places such as Carnoustie, Troon and St. Andrews, undoubtedly links land on the outskirts of those towns had been used unofficially by the public for many generations for the pursuit of golf prior to the formation of formal clubs, but this does not seem to have been the case at Turnberry which had no town close enough for such easy access.

The latter part of the nineteenth century was a time of unprecedented development of the game, not only in Scotland but also in the rest of Britain and abroad. Inevitably it was only a matter of time before the potential of the Turnberry area was recognised. The land at Turnberry was part of Cassillis and Culzean Estates belonging to the ancient and distinguished Kennedy family who have a long history in this part of Scotland going back to mediaeval times. The family holds the titles of Marquess of Ailsa and Earl of Cassillis and their two main residences were Culzean Castle, on the coast about four miles north of Turnberry and Cassillis House situated inland about three miles north of Maybole. Archibald Kennedy, the Third Marquess of Ailsa, (Lord Ailsa) was the incumbent when the first golfing development took place at Turnberry at the end of the nineteenth century and in the early part of the twentieth century.

First Moves Unsuccessful - 1892

The first documented proposal for golf at Turnberry came in the form of a letter, dated 30th July, 1892, from William Murray, Banker, Girvan, to Thomas Smith, Lord Ailsa's factor. He stated that there was *'a proposal to form a golf club for Girvan, Maybole and Kirkoswald on suitable links which could be got at Turnberry. The course would extend from near Turnberry Lodge farm steading to near the Lighthouse and be entirely or mostly on Mr. Bone's farm. Mr. Dick and Mr. Bone have agreed to give the use of their land; I presume Lord Ailsa will not object'*. Mr. Murray then convened a public meeting of interested gentlemen, to be held in the open air at Turnberry near Bruce's ruined castle and the lighthouse built nineteen years earlier by the Lighthouse Commissioners. It was held on Saturday, 27th August 1892, and the *Ayrshire Post*, dated 2nd September, 1892, contained the following report of the meeting:-

GOLF.

A Meeting of Gentlemen favourable to the formation of a Golf Course at Turnberry Castle, will be held at the Light House, on Saturday, 27th August Curt., at 3 p.m.

Gentlemen who intend being present will please intimate to Mr. Murray by Friday.

Girvan, 23rd August, 1892.

'A meeting was held on Saturday afternoon, at Turnberry Castle, for the formation of a new golfing club at Turnberry Links. The subject had been in consideration for some time by gentlemen in connection with the Girvan Golf Club who had visited the place and gone over the ground. It was arranged that a joint meeting of those favourable to the scheme in Girvan, Maybole and Kirkoswald should be held on the ground on Saturday to formally constitute the club. The meeting accordingly took place, and was held in the open air on Saturday afternoon on the vaulted ruins of Turnberry Castle – the castle of the Gaelic lords of Galloway, and afterwards the principal seat of the Earls of Carrick, and famous as the birthplace of King Robert the Bruce. Seated on and within these ruined walls a council was held – Mr. Marshall, schoolmaster, presiding. Mr. William Murray, Banker, Girvan, the principal promoter of the scheme, was unavoidably absent, but a letter was read from him detailing the steps taken to secure the ground. Lord Ailsa, the proprietor, gives a hearty countenance to the scheme and the arrangement made with the tenant, Mr. Bone. A letter was also read from Mr. David Andrews, Banker, Girvan, approving of the formation of the club, and promising practical support. On the motion of the Rev. S.C. Fry, Girvan, seconded by Mr. Andrew Brown, Commercial Bank, it was agreed to form the club, and the following gentlemen were appointed on interim committee to complete the arrangements:- Mr. Marshall, chairman, Mr. A Brown, secretary, Mr. Andrew Dunlop, Royal Bank, treasurer, Rev. C.S. Fry, Girvan; Mr. William Murray, Mr. David Andrews, Mr. Smith, The Castle, Maybole, the Rev. Mr. Muir, Kirkoswald; Mr.McCracken, Blackheath, London; Mr. W.C. Scott, Glasgow; and Mr. Rutherford, Edinburgh. Lord Ailsa was most heartily thanked for his kindness, and it was agreed to solicit his patronage as hon. president of the club. Mr. Eaglesham, C.E., Ayr, has agreed to prepare a plan of the ground free of charge. The committee proceeded over the proposed course. Turnberry is about equal distance from Girvan, Maybole, and Kirkoswald, and thus favourably situated for the three parishes. The ground extends for about two and a half miles along the shore of the Firth of Clyde, and embraces sufficient hazards to

Chapter I - Historical Background

make the game interesting and bring out the science and skill of the player. The course will be laid out in 18 holes, with fine drives between and splendid putting ground in the hollows. The situation is one of the finest that could anywhere be met with.'

Despite Mr. Murray's confidence about the approval of Lord Ailsa, it seems however that he may have been too presumptious and maybe also too tactless, and the Club and its proposals did not find favour with his Lordship. It is interesting to note that one reason for his Lordship being against the project was on account of it perhaps 'spoiling the only hare ground' left in the area, and it is indeed still quite common to see hares on the course. Perhaps a more diplomatic approach might have been more successful, but in any event the local interests lost the initial opportunity to establish a golf course at Turnberry. Nevertheless credit must be given to those early enthusiasts who gathered at the Lighthouse and viewed the magnificent terrain, no doubt with excited anticipation of the wonderful golfing potential and challenge it presented. They could hardly have envisaged however that they were standing on the site of what was to become the world famous and spectacular ninth hole of the Ailsa Course at Turnberry, which is now universally acclaimed as one of the finest and most scenic courses in the world. One hundred years later, in 1992, Turnberry Golf Club and Turnberry Hotel marked the centenary of this meeting by establishing an annual golf match for a handsome crystal trophy. The first match was played on the exact centenary anniversary date, 27th August 1992, and the 1892 Trophy is displayed in the clubhouse. On it are engraved the words of the original notice of the meeting.

---

128 Hope Street,
GLASGOW, 6th March, 1897.

Dear Sir,

It is proposed to form a Club for the purpose of acquiring a lease of ground at Turnberry Point, Ayrshire, and laying out a Golf Course. The Marquess of Ailsa, who is the proprietor of the ground, has been approached, and there is every reason to believe that a Lease can be got at a moderate rental.

The ground proposed to be leased extends to 180 acres or thereby, and is ample for an 18-hole course. It is bounded on the landward side by the shore road to Girvan. The turf is virgin turf. The soil consists almost entirely of sand, and, from a golfer's point of view, the ground is of the finest. Beside the road the surface is level, but becomes undulating a little way out and rolls into hills of bent grass near the beach. It breaks in places into natural bunkers, and a little stream which runs through the ground, and would have to be crossed twice, would make an excellent hazard. A stone wall which crosses the links could also be utilised as a hazard. The quality of the turf is such that little more than cutting and rolling is required to form putting-greens.

Although there is no hotel in the immediate vicinity, there are houses in the neighbourhood where golfers could be comfortably put up. The links are within half an hour's drive from Girvan Station. At no very distant time a railway will probably be constructed to Turnberry, and this would bring it within ninety minutes of Glasgow. At present it can be reached in about two hours.

A meeting for the purpose of discussing the scheme and, if so resolved, of forming a Golf Club, will be held in the **M'Kechnie Library, Girvan, on Thursday, 11th Curt., at 8 o'Clock p.m.,** at which your attendance is requested.

Kindly make the matter known to any persons likely to be interested.

Further information may be had from any of the undersigned.

DAVID ANDREWS,
Union Bank House, Girvan.

ANDREW BROWN,
Commercial Bank House, Girvan.

JOHN M. MACHARG,
69 Buchanan Street, Glasgow.

JAMES H. EDMISTON,
128 Hope Street, Glasgow.

The next recorded attempt to establish a golf course at Turnberry was on 17th July 1896, when James Edmiston, a Solicitor from Glasgow contacted Lord Ailsa's Factor on behalf of parties *'interested in forming a Limited Company to take over ground at Turnberry Lighthouse for a golf course and hotel'*. By March 1897 the proposals seem to have been modified to omit the proposed hotel and to form a golf club instead of a limited company, and the proposal was supported by David Andrews, Union Bank House, Girvan, Andrew Brown, Commercial Bank House, Girvan, John M. McHarg, 69 Buchanan Street, Glasgow, and James Edmiston. A public meeting was held in the McKechnie Library, Girvan, on 11th March 1897, and thereafter local committees were formed in Maybole and Girvan to promote and plan the project. Negotiations took place with Lord Ailsa's Factor, Thomas Smith, Esq., of The Castle, High Street, Maybole, and discussions also took place with Lord Ailsa's agricultural tenants in occupation of the land at Turnberry. The tenants however refused to negotiate terms and by July 1898, Lord Ailsa intimated that he wished the matter to 'lie over meantime'. Once again the chance of establishing a club-based golf course at Turnberry fell by the wayside.

The Turning Point

Matters then took another turn. As in many other places in Scotland and England the development of golf at Turnberry was influenced by the interest of one of the rapidly expanding railway companies, who saw commercial opportunities in providing public transport by rail and hotel accommodation, allied to golfing facilities, enabling developments to take place in areas otherwise too remote to be viable. Such a company was the Glasgow & South Western Railway Company and their plans and an agreement between them and Lord Ailsa were to play an important and crucial part in determining the shape of Turnberry's golfing future.

Culzean castle, the home of the 3rd Marquess of Ailsa, situated on a sea cliff about 4 miles north of Turnberry. The Marquess built a 9-hole golf course in its grounds in 1898, prior to commissioning Willie Fernie in 1900 to build a course at Turnberry.

Chapter I - Historical Background

The Railway Connection

ARCHIBALD Kennedy became the Third Marquess of Ailsa in 1870 at the age of twenty two and was a man of many parts with great influence in the County of Ayrshire, of which he was Lord Lieutenant from 1919 to 1936. He very successfully developed the shipbuilding and engineering company inherited from his father and established shipyards at Maidens, Ayr and Troon, expanding the company from modest beginnings at his Culzean estate. His company built steam and sailing yachts, steamers and packets ranging in size from ten to one thousand tons, and he held a Master's Certificate in navigation. His estates in Ayrshire extended to over seventy-six thousand acres and included the Lands of Turnberry. Significantly one of his other business interests was as a director of The Glasgow & South Western Railway Company and this and his keen interest in the game of golf were the catalysts which led eventually to the construction of the first golf course at Turnberry.

Maidens and Dunure Light Railway

Under the Light Railways Act of 1896 The Glasgow & South Western Railway Company applied to the Light Railway Commissioners for permission to build a line for passengers and goods, from Ayr to Girvan. Construction of this line was authorised on 30th September, 1899, by the Maidens and Dunure Light Railway Order. The Company already had great experience of the benefits which golf could bring to their business from the traffic on their line from Glasgow to Ayr. It served the many wonderful golf courses which proliferated down the Ayrshire coast after Prestwick was formed in 1851. On the stretch from Prestwick to Irvine the line, which still exists, passes by or through eleven golf courses. In that stretch of approximately twelve miles there is hardly a point where the passenger does not have a view from his window of one or more courses. The public stations at Prestwick and Troon are adjacent to golf clubhouses and Glasgow Gailes and Western Gailes shared a private station to serve both courses. Their members were mostly from Glasgow and this and the growing popularity of golf generally, boosted tremendously the traffic on the line and, no doubt also, the profits of the Glasgow & South Western Railway Company. So much so that in 1910 *Rail and Travel Monthly* magazine dubbed the railway from Glasgow to Ayr the *'Golfers Line'*.

Accordingly, with this successful and profitable experience to draw on, the directors of the Railway Company no doubt proceeded with great confidence and high expectations with their new project. Their plans were ambitious and involved constructing a single track line nineteen and a half miles long down the Ayrshire coast, at a reputed cost of one pound per inch. It was to pass through Carrick, the southern part of Ayrshire, connecting Ayr and Girvan via the villages of Alloway,

Turnberry Station looking north with part of the hotel in the background

Dunure and Maidens. En route the passengers would experience some of the finest scenery in southern Scotland, with spectacular and breathtaking sea views across the Firth of Clyde to the mountains of the Isle of Arran, to Ailsa Craig, to the Kintyre peninsula and even on clear days to the Mountains of Mourne in Northern Ireland. The exciting and far seeing business plan was to build a new luxury golfing hotel at Turnberry where it was also proposed to construct a golf course on adjoining links land already identified as superb for the purpose by the local gentlemen whose proposals for a golf course and golf club were rejected by Lord Ailsa in 1892 and again in 1897. However the Railway Company's plan did not initially find favour with all the shareholders of the Company. According to a report in the *Glasgow Herald*, of a meeting of the Company held on 5th February 1901 in Glasgow, the directors sought approval to proceed with the project and it was explained that *'the extent of the ground was 15 acres for the hotel and 175 acres for the golf course; and that the ground had been arranged for with the Marquess of Ailsa on particularly favourable terms for the company'*. Two shareholders strongly opposed the scheme and one of them spoke against it saying, *'I think it is entirely outwith the business of the company. Surely the gentlemen who play golf are sufficiently interested to make a course and erect a clubhouse for themselves. The company may as well propose to run a theatre or a football club'*. However, his amendment to refuse approval of the proposal was defeated and the stage was set for the whole project to proceed.

Agreement with Lord Ailsa

The Company went on then to promote a private Act of Parliament to obtain the necessary powers to carry out the scheme and the second schedule to that Act contained an agreement between The Glasgow & South Western Railway Company and Lord Ailsa. Before this agreement was finalised there had been a great deal of negotiation between the parties, particularly with regard to the arrangements for the construction of the golf course and control of its use thereafter. As was common in that era with large estates, Lord Ailsa's estates were *'entailed'* with the effect that no part could be sold or *'feued'* by a current proprietor without first satisfying the Court of Session that such disposal was prudent and necessary and for the benefit of future generations of the family. Feuing in Scotland was and still is a grant of the right to use and occupy a piece of land in perpetuity in exchange for an annual monetary payment called a feuduty – a sort of lease without a termination date. It was anticipated by Lord Ailsa's lawyers that such consent would be readily obtained for the feuing of the 15 acre site for the hotel and Lord Ailsa was happy enough to agree to that on terms favourable to the Railway Company. The enhanced value of his adjoining land for feuing and development would have been a powerful incentive for this arrangement. However, the lawyers advised that it would be much more difficult to obtain consent to sell or feu the larger area for the golf course. There was also the question of whether or not it was in his Lordship's interests to relinquish all control over the golf course to the Railway Company. A letter of 4th June 1900 from his Lordship's solicitors to his factor sets out the position very clearly and with great foresight and it contained the following comments and advice on the negotiations, prior to agreement being finalised, viz:-

'The Railway Company' solicitors apparently regard the golfing rights as being an appendage of the hotel, and their alterations on your notes are all directed to giving the Railway Company the control of the golf course in perpetuity and the exclusive use thereof to persons authorised by them. We did not understand that that was the intention; on the contrary we understood the course was to be for the common benefit of Lord Ailsa's friends (including the Railway Company) and the district generally, and that while for a time the Railway Company was to have, within limits, the control of the course it was

Archibald Kennedy, Third Marquess of Ailsa

Chapter I - Historical Background

ultimately to be under Lord Ailsa's control and to a certain extent for his pecuniary benefit. They contemplate a very one sided arrangement, viz.:- that the Railway Company are to get a cheap feu for their hotel, and also that they are to get control of the very valuable golfing rights, without any corresponding benefit to Lord Ailsa – indeed, as sketched, Lord Ailsa would be a distinct loser by the transaction because he would not be getting the full value for the hotel feu and he would also be getting only the present agricultural rent for the golf course, even after he had paid one half of the expense of forming it. We do not think we could advise Lord Ailsa to agree to this and even though he did we are sure neither Parliament nor the Court would sanction the permanent alienation of part of the Entailed Estates on such terms. It seems to us that Lord Ailsa could do very much better for himself. The railway will be there and a really first class golf course could be formed at comparatively trifling expense. His Lordship would be better to form the course himself; feuing would proceed exactly as in the other case, and a hotel would no doubt be built by somebody. In this way Lord Ailsa would realise his feuing project while at the same time he would retain the control of the course for the benefit of his feuars and take some personal advantage from the considerable income which we should think must eventually come from it.'

The words were prophetic and the advice was wise and the final outcome was an agreement whereby Lord Ailsa agreed to feu 15 acres of ground to the Company as a site for its hotel, in exchange for their paying him an annual

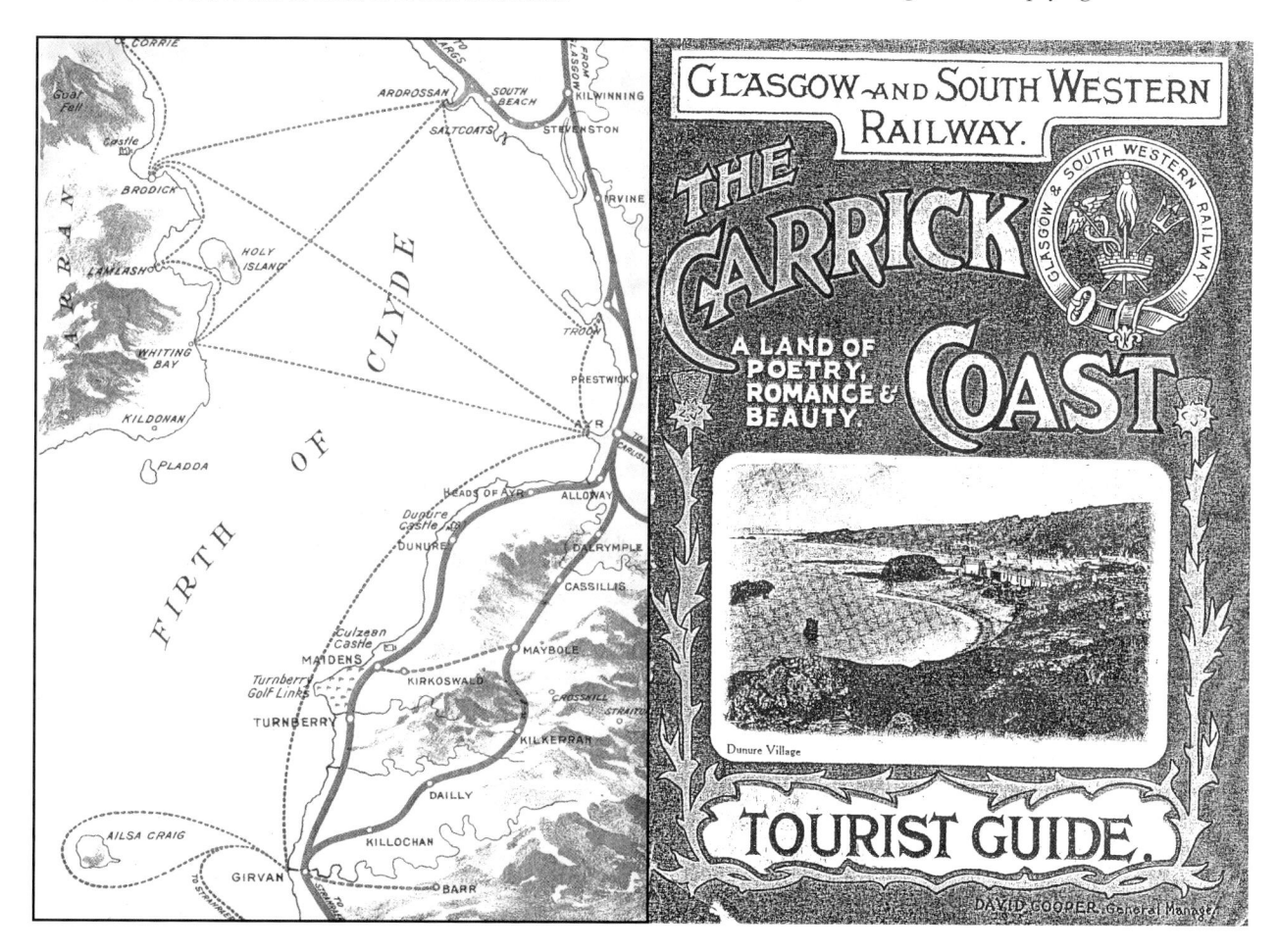

Glasgow and South Western Railway Tourist Guide Cover with map showing railway lines and ferry routes serving Ayrshire circa 1915, including the light railway from Alloway to Girvan via Turnberry. Lord Ailsa had a private station serving his castle and estate at Culzean.

13

feuduty of £6 per acre per annum. He also agreed to grant the Company *'the right and privilege in all time coming of using the links and bent hills of Turnberry, extending to 175 acres, as a golf course for the purpose of playing the game of golf thereon'*, for an annual payment of ten shillings per acre per annum, making a total annual sum of £87-10/-. In Scots Law such a right is known as a 'heritable servitude' but it usually only covers such things as a right of way for a roadway, footpath or service pipe or cable, and to grant it for a golf course was certainly unusual and notable. In exchange the Company undertook to lay out the land into a golf course at their own expense and on completion was to be entitled to use the course for its hotel guests and passengers travelling by its trains. Lord Ailsa and his family and guests were to be entitled to free use of the course and golf clubhouse, and his feuars and the general public were to be entitled to use it on payment of one shilling per day, two shillings and six pence per week or seven shillings and six pence per month or such other charges to be fixed from time to time by the Company and Lord Ailsa. The agreement did however also contain an alternative provision that Lord Ailsa could himself proceed at once to lay out and form the golf course at his own expense, but with power to the Company at any time thereafter to repay him the whole cost. Until it was repaid Lord Ailsa was to have sole rights to control the use of the course, but after repayment control would revert to the Company.

Lord Ailsa's Option

Interestingly there was a further possibility under the agreement. At any time within the period of ten years from the date of completion of the course by the Company or within ten years of the Company repaying Lord Ailsa the cost of forming the course, if it had been formed by him, Lord Ailsa was to have the option of repaying the Company one half of the cost of the formation. In the event of Lord Ailsa exercising this option he was to have the right to require the Company to transfer the golf course and the rights to play golf on it, to a joint committee. This was to be made up of three members nominated by the Company and three nominated by Lord Ailsa, with a chairman nominated by Lord Ailsa or his successors as proprietors of Cassillis and Culzean Estates. This committee would have had power to regulate play on the course by the Company's guests and travellers and by other players including club players and to fix the green fees and subscriptions at such rates as to ensure that the course would at all times be at least self supporting. The Company would still require to make the annual payment of £87-10/-, but to the joint committee instead of to Lord Ailsa. Any surplus of revenue would be divided at the end of each calendar year between the Company and Lord Ailsa in equal proportions.

As will be detailed in the next chapter, Lord Ailsa did in fact decide to form the course himself and subsequently reclaimed the whole cost, amounting to £2,018, from the Railway Company. The course was completed and opened in July 1901, but the Railway Company did not reimburse Lord Ailsa for the cost until 1906, when the new railway line and hotel were completed and opened. This left Lord Ailsa until 1916 to decide whether or not to take up the option to pay back one half of the cost and exercise his right under the agreement to assume joint control of the course and its profits. In the event he did not exercise this option, probably because his resources at that time were so stretched that he could not afford to do so. One can only guess as to how the future of the course, the hotel, the Club and the noble Kennedy family might have evolved differently if he had done so. The prospects for the economic viability of the hotel might have been less bright if Lord Ailsa had been sharing the profits from the golf course. Similar railway hotels at Cruden Bay and also at Dornoch, both on the north east coast of Scotland, did not survive, though Gleneagles did, despite difficult times in the course of its history. There again, perhaps if Lord Ailsa had retained control, Turnberry Golf Club of which he was the first President, might have assumed more influence over the management and development of the courses, or might even have had the opportunity at some point to acquire them. Such an outcome would surely not have led to the international golfing resort and spa which exists today, and one wonders if a club would have had the resources to rebuild the courses after their conversion to a military airfield during the Second World War. All of this can only be speculation and perhaps history's judgement on the actual outcome should be favourable. Despite many difficult times over the past 100 years, including the enormous disruption caused by the two world wars, the courses have survived and developed, to become amongst the most famous and revered in the world; and the hotel has grown steadily in quality and facilities to match the reputation of its renowned golfing links. The Club too has survived and prospered, guided by the sound counsels of its office bearers throughout the century of its existence, and still remains an important element in the overall success and ever growing historical traditions of Turnberry.

Chapter I - Historical Background

Timetable of the life of the Turnberry line

1906 - Light railway from Alloway to Girvan opened for goods and passengers by Glasgow & South Western Railway Company. Turnberry Hotel opened.

1923 - Glasgow & South Western Railway Company becomes part of London, Midland & Scottish Railway Company

1930 - Section of line from Alloway to Turnberry closed for passengers - then goods only.

1942 - Section of line from Girvan to Turnberry closed for passengers - then goods only.

1947 - Section from Alloway to Butlins at Heads of Ayr re-opened for passengers only.

1955 - Whole line closed except from Alloway to Butlins.

1968 - Section from Alloway to Butlins for passengers closed.

Platform and Canopy of Turnberry Hotel railway station. A covered way led from the station to the hotel. This explains why the main entrance to the hotel is at the rear and not seaward facing.

Lord Ailsa Builds The First Course

IT IS probably an ambition of every keen golfer to create a golf course from suitable virgin terrain. Lovers of the game constantly see in the countryside around them areas of land where they can envisage the potential for a beautiful new golf course or golf hole, to be appreciated and enjoyed by other golfers present and future. It is however, given to very few to realise this ambition, and moreover, to be instrumental in creating a course which would become one of the finest and most famous in the world. Archibald Kennedy, Third Marquess of Ailsa, was such a man.

Lord Ailsa

Lord Ailsa was a man of great enthusiasm and who achieved many things. Professor Michael Moss of Glasgow University Archives has kindly provided some fascinating material about his life and activities, from his researches for his recently published book on the Kennedy family. Apart from his devotion to yachts and shipbuilding and founding the Ailsa Shipbuilding Company, Lord Ailsa built a large extension to Culzean Castle and carried out many improvements to his estates. His family subsequently donated Culzean Castle and estate in 1949 to The National Trust for Scotland, to be preserved for the great benefit of the public. Fortunately he was also a keen devotee of the game of golf. He was a member of Prestwick Golf Club where the first Open was held in 1860 and was captain of that Club in 1899, despite the fact that he only took up active golf the previous year during a stay in France. Until then he had been a non-playing member of Prestwick. However in March 1898, during an extended stay in France, he became a member of Pau Golf Club at Plain de Billere, a spa town on the French side of the Pyrenees, and *'caught the bug'* for playing golf. The Pau Club had been founded in 1856 largely to meet the needs of British winter visitors and was the first golf club to be founded in mainland Europe.

French Golf Professional

His enthusiasm for the game was so great that, despite being in very difficult financial straits at that time, he engaged the professional from the French club, not only to give him golf tuition in France, but also to come to Scotland for three months in the summer and autumn of 1898 to continue the tuition at Culzean. He also intended at that time to utilize the services of the French professional to lay out the Turnberry links as a private course. However within a few weeks he changed his mind and decided instead to have a private course of 9 holes laid out in the deer park at Culzean, which would be much more convenient for practice than a course at Turnberry. By May that year he engaged Charles Hunter, the professional at Prestwick *'to settle about the putting greens'* of the new course at Culzean, and work on it began at once under the supervision of John Campbell from Kirkoswald. Some of the putting greens had been formed by June when Dominique, the professional from Pau, arrived to cut the first holes and *'complete the fitting up of the course'*. This course at Culzean was however not destined for a long life and, having been ploughed over during the first world war, it was never re-opened.

Engagement of Willie Fernie

However, it was on his land at Turnberry that he was to make a lasting contribution to the game of golf. Professor Moss writes that *'the Marquess had been regularly reminded for some time of the need either to increase the income from the estate or slash expenditure and he now hit on ways of both having his golf course and raising capital and revenue. In November 1892 he had been elected a director of The Glasgow & South Western Railway Company in succession to the Earl of Glasgow to represent the interests of the agricultural community. After the passing of the Light Railways Act of 1896, he seized the opportunity of promoting a new branch line which would run around the coast by way of Dunure, Culzean and Turnberry. Such a line would have the advantage of improving the access of the farms and fishing*

Chapter I - Historical Background

communities along the shore and hold out the possibility of holiday developments along the coast'. Most important of all of course it provided transport to Turnberry and held out the possibility of the golf boom already happening in north Ayrshire being extended on to his own estates there. As part of his business arrangement with The Glasgow & South Western Railway Company he commissioned the construction of a course there in December 1900, engaging Willie Fernie, the Open Champion of 1883 and golf professional at Troon Golf Club, to lay out a course at Turnberry and supervise its construction. It seems surprising and even difficult to believe now that the formal opening took place on 6th July, 1901, less than eight months later. However, in those days course design consisted of going over the ground and marking off the position of greens and tees, using the natural contours of the ground to obtain attractive holes and also using areas with good natural grass for the greens. The bunkers would be fairly rough and natural without any of the careful revetting of turf banks which are now the norm and require so much work on the part of the greenkeepers to construct and maintain. An exceptional example of the speed with which courses were laid out and played on is recorded in the history of another Ayrshire golf club, Kilmarnock Barassie, who acquired the land for their course on 26th September, 1894, and opened the new course for play 24 days later on 20th October, the course having been *'laid off'* by the St. Nicholas professional John Alan for a fee of 12/6d.!

The Land at Turnberry

At Turnberry the land available to Willie Fernie for the course is beautifully described in a letter, dated 6th March, 1897, circulated by the local gentlemen proposing a club and golf course at Turnberry, as follows:-

'The ground proposed to be leased extends to 180 acres or thereby, and is ample for an 18-hole course. It is bounded on the landward side by the shore road to Girvan. The turf is virgin turf. The soil consists almost entirely of sand, and, from a golfer's point of view, the ground is of the finest. Beside the road the surface is level, but becomes undulating a little way out and rolls into hills of bent grass near the beach. It breaks in places into natural bunkers, and a little stream which runs through the ground, and would have to be crossed twice, would make an excellent hazard. A stone wall which crosses the links could also be utilised as a hazard. The quality of the turf is such that little more than cutting and rolling is required to form putting-greens.'

Apart from the stone wall, which no longer exists, these features can all still be recognised today. According to the *Ayrshire Post* of 22nd March, 1901, the quality of the turf was apparently exceptional. Throughout its whole existence since, Turnberry's turf has always been recognised as exceptionally fine for a links course, while at the same time retaining the best qualities of links in respect of natural drainage, firmness and fast and true greens. The very best of the turf in 1901 was on the flatter, more inland land, which was of

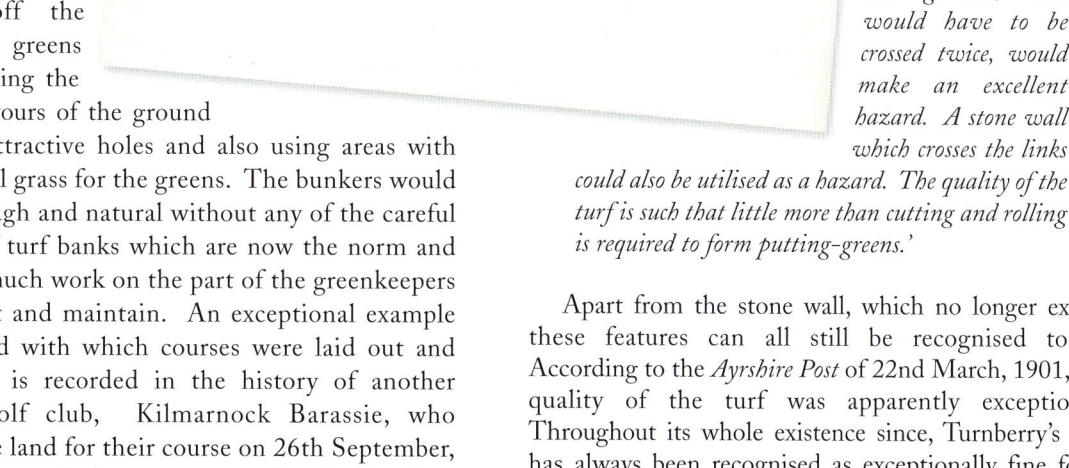

Letter from W. Fernie, headed 'Champion Golfer 1883 & Winner of 22 First-Class Tournaments - Practical Golf Club and Ball Maker', to Lord Ailsa's Factor, confirming his first visit to Turnberry to lay out a course there in 1900.

a large enough area to accommodate the whole 18 holes. However Fernie chose to incorporate some of the rougher areas amongst the dunes nearer the sea to create a more interesting and challenging course. The *Ayrshire Post* article suggested that, with the abundance of good ground available, it was probable however that alterations to the initial layout would be made and of course, that certainly turned out to be the case, as will be described later. The article is wonderfully descriptive and revealing of attitudes to the game and the courses at the turn of the century and is worth quoting in full:-

'No-one who has ever seen the ground that lies adjacent to Turnberry Castle, with an eye to golf, has been able to deny that its natural advantages for the practice of the game of golf are superlative. There is a combination of the natural qualities of golfing ground that are rarely to be met with on a true seaside course, for in addition to the prevailing characteristics of the seaside links it combines to some extent some of the best qualities of an inland course such as are to be found at Bridge-of-Weir, Greenock, and Kilmacolm, that is to say, the natural rock crops up through the turf and forms hazards at one point in the round. As for the sandhills and bent-covered hills, they are among the most formidable to be anywhere met with. But the principal and most favourable feature of the ground is the quality of the turf which covers a considerable extent of its area. This part of the ground is said to have been at one time cultivated, but that has not been for the last twenty years. It is now covered with exceedingly fine crisp turf, unmixed with other vegetable products, and almost unbroken except by a rabbit's hole here and there. This expanse of turf, which occupies an extensive flat on the landward side of the course, is perhaps the finest piece of natural turf of a similarly large extent that has ever come under the operation of a professional golfer in the laying out of a golf course for the first time. But though there was almost a large enough area of ground for 18 holes in this expanse there was too much sameness about it to justify Fernie in confining himself to it, more especially as there is a great area of ground of a quite different and more diversified description. Towards the sea there is a region of undulating bent, and beyond that and abutting on the sea beach there is an extensive range of sandhills, in addition to the rocky ground already referred to. Fernie has drawn upon them all for the formation of the course. Had he kept to the smooth ground he might have laid out the course with very

Willie Fernie (middle) who laid out the original Turnberry course in 1901 and sons Edward (left) and Tom (right) who was the professional at Turnberry from 1911 till 1926.

Chapter I - Historical Background

little trouble to himself and expense to his employer. And though some of the ground he has chosen to go through will require time, trouble and expense to make it subservient to the golfer, what he has done will meet with the general approval of golfers who came to play over the course. The ground that he has had to work upon is in extent so much beyond the requirements of an 18-hole course that it is not improbable that alterations in the present round may be made, but in the meantime he has struck a happy medium between the rough and the smooth. He has given the golfer an opportunity of tasting of the delights of long driving on the level, without a single obstruction, and he has taken him among the sandhills, where the most formidable obstacles will have to be overcome, both in driving and approaching. Roughly speaking, about one-third of the holes have been put on the smooth ground, about one-third on medium ground and about one-third on rough ground. It must be admitted that the rough ground is very rough, being simply great sandhills covered with rank bent, and some of the putting greens ought to be laid, the laying of the first being imperative, but there is an undergrowth of fine grass, which will be nursed to the surface after the bent has been cut or, still better, burned. On the smooth ground all that requires to be done to form putting-greens is to roll them. In laying out the course Fernie has not lost sight of the picturesque, and has taken the golfer along to the coast at the rocky part near the north and, where the castle and lighthouse are situated, which abounds with headlands, inlets of sea, and caves, and where commanding views of the Firth of Clyde and the links can be obtained. The southern part of the course is guarded by an enormous sand barrier, which overhangs the beach. Fernie has not been afraid to at once introduce the golfer among the sandhills. Indeed, the golfer is in among them from the first tee. He argues rightly that the player is better able to cope with them at the outset, when he is fresh, than after he is more or less fatigued by playing over half or more than half of the course.'

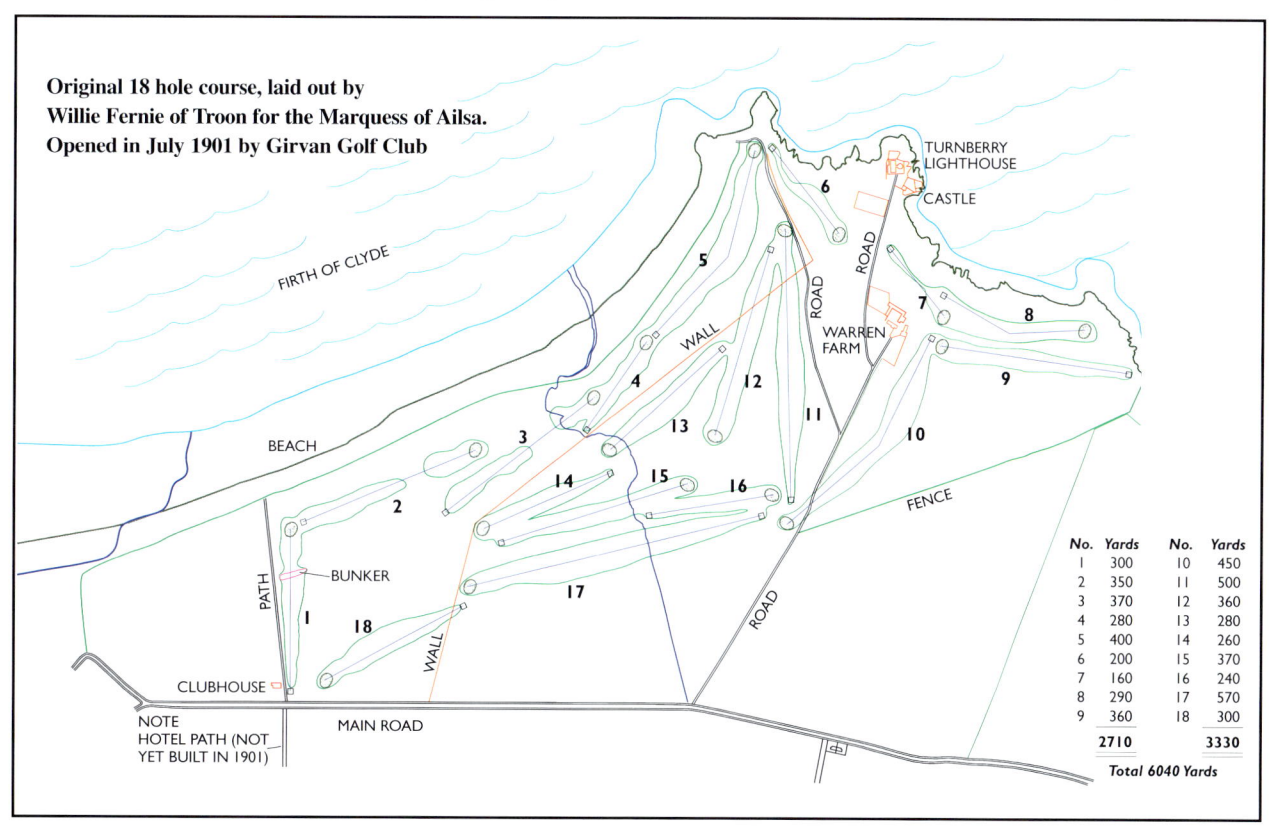

Original 18 hole course, laid out by Willie Fernie of Troon for the Marquess of Ailsa. Opened in July 1901 by Girvan Golf Club

No.	Yards	No.	Yards
1	300	10	450
2	350	11	500
3	370	12	360
4	280	13	280
5	400	14	260
6	200	15	370
7	160	16	240
8	290	17	570
9	360	18	300
	2710		**3330**

Total 6040 Yards

This plan was drawn by John McMillan, a member of Turnberry Golf Club, using written and photographic data only, but it is thought to be reasonably correct.

Layout of the First Course

No original plans showing Fernie's layout of the course have been found, but nine photographs of this original course appear in a book published in 1904 by John Latta and William Miller entitled *The Kingdom of Carrick and its Capital*. The *Glasgow Evening Times* and *Golf Illustrated* gave a full description. *(See Appendix 1)* From these photographs and this newspaper report the layout must have been approximately as shown on the plan illustrated above. One of the most notable differences from the present course was the line of the first hole, which ran from the road towards the sea, with the first green in the valley of the present fifth fairway. The second hole was played from there, blind over the high ground now occupied by the eighteenth tee, to a green in the low hollow short and inland of the present sixth green. The third green lay in the curve north of Wilson's burn with the tee on the high ground of the present seventeenth fairway and requiring a blind second shot over high ground. The fourth green seems to have been in the large hollow in front of the present eighth tee. The fifth hole was similar to the present eighth, and the sixth green was just short of the lighthouse road level with the lighthouse. The inward half meandered further inland than the present Ailsa course and a wall featured as a hazard at certain holes.

For laying out this course and superintending its construction and maintenance for a period of five years Willie Fernie's fee was £69-18/-. The total cost of forming the course and maintaining it in the period of five years from December, 1900 till 31st December, 1905 was £2,854-15/6d. These sums seem

PHOTOGRAPHS OF FIRST COURSE

'Ailsa Craig' bunker on 1st hole

1st Green and 2nd Tee

Driving from 2nd tee

20

Chapter I - Historical Background

3rd Green

15th Green

4th Green

very small by today's standards, but according to data supplied by the Bank of England and the Retail Price Index, the value of the £1 in 1900-05 was equivalent to £55.81 in 2000, making the cost of the course the equivalent of £160,000 and Willie Fernie's fee the equivalent of £3,900 in the year 2000. Fernie was possibly very satisfied with this considering that it was a part-time commission. On the other hand the outlay by the Marquess on the construction and maintenance of the golf course was very substantial and stretched his resources at a time when his income was struggling to keep up with his expenditure on Culzean Castle and his many other projects and interests. The cost can also be put into further perspective by comparing it with a membership subscription of £1-1/- in 1902 and a lowest tender of £205,000 received by Glasgow & South Western Railway in 1900, for the construction of their whole new light railway from Ayr to Girvan, including nine railway stations, sixty five bridges, varying in span from 10 to 118 feet, six culverts and two viaducts with spans of 100 and 118 feet.

Three weeks prior to its official opening on 6th July, 1901, the condition of the course was described in a letter from Robert McConnell, the Secretary of Girvan Golf Club, to Lord Ailsa's factor, as being too rough for play. By April 1903 a report to the annual general meeting of Turnberry Golf Club stated that *'when the club entered into possession in May 1902 the course was not in anything like playing order. However by the beginning of July that year a marked change for the better was noticeable. The greens were better attended to, the 'way through' the*

21

Back Tee for 6th

High forward Tee for 6th

7th Green

greens was cut, first by a reaper and then by a mower and by the month of August, the course, for a new one, was in very fair playing order'. It would seem that, with its exceptionally fine turf, cutting of the fairways was perhaps a greater task at Turnberry than on many other links courses on which the grass was less lush and more mixed with other slow growing vegetation. By August 1904, apparently there was still some dissatisfaction with the condition of the course and Robert M. Nisbett, the Secretary and Treasurer of Turnberry Golf Club, wrote to Lord Ailsa's factor requesting that various areas of rough grass be cut, particularly in front of tees and behind greens. Lord Ailsa's head greenkeeper, Andrew Page, commented on these requests in a letter to the factor, dated 11th August, 1904, which gives an interesting insight into greenkeeping practices and differing opinions of the time relating to the setting up of the course. He commented that, although his workmen agreed that the grass should be cut in front of tees and behind greens, *'Lord Ailsa and Fernie gave them peremptory orders not to do so, as it was an important part of the game to penalise bad players who do not drive off properly or overdrive when approaching the green'*. The wording may be quaint and old fashioned but the thinking of Lord Ailsa and the former Open Champion was very much in line with the strategy employed by the R. & A. and others in setting up championship courses now, to test the greatest players in the game.

Chapter I - Historical Background

Girvan Golf Club Opens The Course

THE distinction of being the first club to play the new Turnberry golf course and of holding the opening ceremony and golf tournament goes not to Turnberry Golf Club, but to Girvan Golf Club. On 25th November 1900, David Andrews, a Girvan solicitor, wrote on behalf of that club to Thomas Smith, Lord Ailsa's factor, who had his office at The Castle, Maybole. He explained that, owing to recent feuing of parts of the Girvan course, the club had determined to abandon the course as no longer suitable. The Girvan course at that time was situated at Watermouth Park on the North side of the River Girvan at Girvan harbour, but a large part of the course had been taken over for the construction of the houses, which are now found on Golf Course Road. Mr. Andrews enquired about the possibility of the club *obtaining ground at or near Turnberry or obtaining the privilege from the Glasgow and South Western Railway Company after that company acquires land, of playing over the course to be formed at Turnberry'*. At the time of this approach from Girvan, Lord Ailsa was still negotiating his arrangements with the Railway Company, which envisaged the Company eventually constructing a golf course at Turnberry. However the new railway line and hotel were then still just bold visions, and construction of the line did not start till May 1902. The hotel wasn't completed and it and the railway line didn't formally open till May 1906. In 1900 the Railway Company was not contemplating the construction of the golf course until nearer the completion of the hotel. It seems that the timing of Girvan Golf Club's proposal was opportune, because Lord Ailsa promptly replied. He indicated that, although ground could not be made available for Girvan Golf Club to make a course for themselves at Turnberry, he was prepared to proceed immediately under his agreement with the Railway Company, as described above, to form a new course and negotiate terms for its use by Girvan Golf Club, pending its acquisition by the Railway Company. By 11th December 1900 the solicitor for the Railway Company had approved of the Marquess building the course at once, and as described above, Willie Fernie, golf professional at Troon, was immediately engaged by Lord Ailsa to lay out the new course.

Terms are Agreed

By 1900 Girvan was becoming quite popular as a summer holiday resort for visitors. Its situation at the seaside, with a beach and a harbour, and its location amidst lovely South Ayrshire countryside was attractive, particularly to city dwellers from Glasgow and elsewhere. It also had a well established golf course, which was popular with visitors, and so the threat to this from housing development was a real problem, not only for the golf club, but also for Girvan's budding tourist business. It must have seemed an excellent solution for Girvan Golf Club to move to a new course at Turnberry with the prospect of there being convenient transport by way of a short five mile rail journey from Girvan to Turnberry when the new railway was completed. Terms for Girvan Club's use of the course were fairly quickly agreed with Lord Ailsa as follows:-

(1) For the privilege of playing over the course from 15th May 1901 till 15th May 1902, Lord Ailsa was to receive 80% of the club's income from annual subscriptions and the subscriptions of summer visitors.

(2) Members of the club to be restricted to persons permanently resident in Girvan.

(3) Subscriptions of members to be 10/- per annum and subscriptions of summer visitors to be 5/- per fortnight or 7/6d. per month.

The transfer of the Girvan Club to Turnberry proceeded quickly thereafter as soon as the course was ready for play, and it was Girvan Golf Club which arranged the opening ceremony, as can be seen from the following letter, dated 18th June 1901, from Robert McConnell, the Girvan Club secretary, to Lord Ailsa's factor :

*Thomas Smith, Esq.,
Maybole.*

Sir,

Turnberry Course

Special General Meeting of the Club was held last night, when your letter of 11th instant was read. The meeting considered it very satisfactory and it was unanimously resolved to remove to Turnberry at the earliest opportunity. The meeting after discussion fixed Friday, 5th July, for the formal opening of the course, play to start at 5.00 p.m. and I was desired to say that the Club would be very pleased if Lord Ailsa could find it convenient to be present at the opening on that date.

As players from this Club will be playing on the course from this date I am instructed to point out that holes should now be made in every green with a flag staff in each, and that sandboxes be placed at the teeing grounds. Then there is no entrance to the course from the Maidens Road opposite the 1st teeing ground but no doubt this will be made in due course.

I noticed when over the course last Saturday that the greens are still in a very rough condition, in fact too rough for play, and only constant work and playing on them will bring them into condition. The club is very pleased that the old toll is to be put in order, where accommodation can be had for clubs etc.

All approaches to the course are protected by barbed wire and the greens are surrounded by the same. The Club desires to state that thereby lady members are debarred from gaining access to the greens. In other courses where the greens have to be wired in, an entrance or wicket is left at each corner.

The course in time it will make one of the best and I have no doubt but that the Girvan Club will avail itself to the full of the privileges so kindly granted by Lord Ailsa.

*I am
Yours faithfully,*

Robert McConnell, Hon. Secy.

Obviously the course was still in a very rough condition and it seems that it was being grazed by sheep, which necessitated fences round the greens to protect them. It is interesting that the Girvan Club obviously had lady members and one assumes that the reason why the ladies would be debarred from the greens would be due to the difficulty of climbing over a barbed wire fence in long dresses, without showing what would in those days be considered an indecent amount of leg.

Opening Ceremony

Arrangements were duly made by Girvan Golf Club for the opening ceremony and golf tournament for the new course provided by Lord Ailsa and, at that stage, owned and controlled by him. His Lordship generously donated a gold medal to go to the winner of a handicap competition, and the event took place on Saturday, 6th July 1901. *Golf Illustrated* reported it as follows:-

> *'The important new golf links at Turnberry, adjacent to Turnberry Castle and lighthouse on the Ayrshire coast, was opened for play on Saturday, last week. The more one sees of the links serves to confirm the impression that the course will one day be among the finest in the three kingdoms.*
>
> *Fernie, the Troon professional, who laid it out under the direction and at the expense of the Marquess of Ailsa, on whose ground it is, has made it of full Championship length, and the writer knows of no links where there is such diversity of hazards, rocks coming in at the sixth, seventh, eighth and ninth holes, and the most formidable of sandhills at the first, second, third, fourth and fifth, while compensation for that is found in some of the smoothest of holes among the others. It is anticipated that the Glasgow and South Western Railway will eventually take over the links and build a hotel, the site of which has been fixed, but in the meantime the links is too far out of the beaten track, being five miles from the nearest railway station, Girvan, to become widely known until the new railway which passes close to the course and the hotel have become actual facts. Pending that, Lord Ailsa has charged himself with the upkeep of the links, and the first Club to get the rights of playing over it is the Girvan Club, whose old nine-hole course near the*

Chapter I - Historical Background

town is in course of rapid appropriation by the builder.

It was under the auspices of this Club that the course was opened on Saturday. There was a large company, including many ladies, present, and the weather could not have been finer for such an enterprise. Fernie, the Troon professional, went round the links for the first time in a three-ball match with Mr. D. McConnell and Mr. John Eaglesham, and the difficulty of the round may be inferred when it is noted that, playing a good game, the professional required 90, Mr. McConnell taking 97 and Mr. Eaglesham 105. The company were entertained to an 'al fresco' tea by the Girvan ladies.'

Mr. D. McConnell, who won the gold medal playing off a handicap of scratch, was the brother of Robert McConnell, the Secretary of Girvan Golf Club, and the medal was sent on to him at his address in London. The medal was awarded outright and unfortunately its present whereabouts is unknown.

Girvan's Tenure Short Lived

Girvan Golf Club's place in the history of Turnberry was accordingly notable and important but was destined to be short-lived. Moves were afoot in influential circles for the formation of a completely new club to be called Turnberry Golf Club, and the Girvan Club was fearful that they might lose privileges at Turnberry to the new club. Early in 1903, they applied to amalgamate with the new club, as explained later, and ceased operating as a club at Turnberry in May 1903. Fortunately however about the same time further ground was found neighbouring their old course at Girvan and a new Girvan Club re-formed there. Evidence of this appears on one of their trophies, the Cockburn Medal, which is inscribed as having been won in 1902 at Turnberry by Robert McConnell and in 1903 at Girvan by Fergus McCallum. Thus ended a local link between Girvan Golf Club and Turnberry golf course, but the important connection with Girvan has never ceased. Turnberry Golf Club has, throughout its existence, always had numerous members from Girvan, including many fine golfers and many who have served as office bearers of the Club.

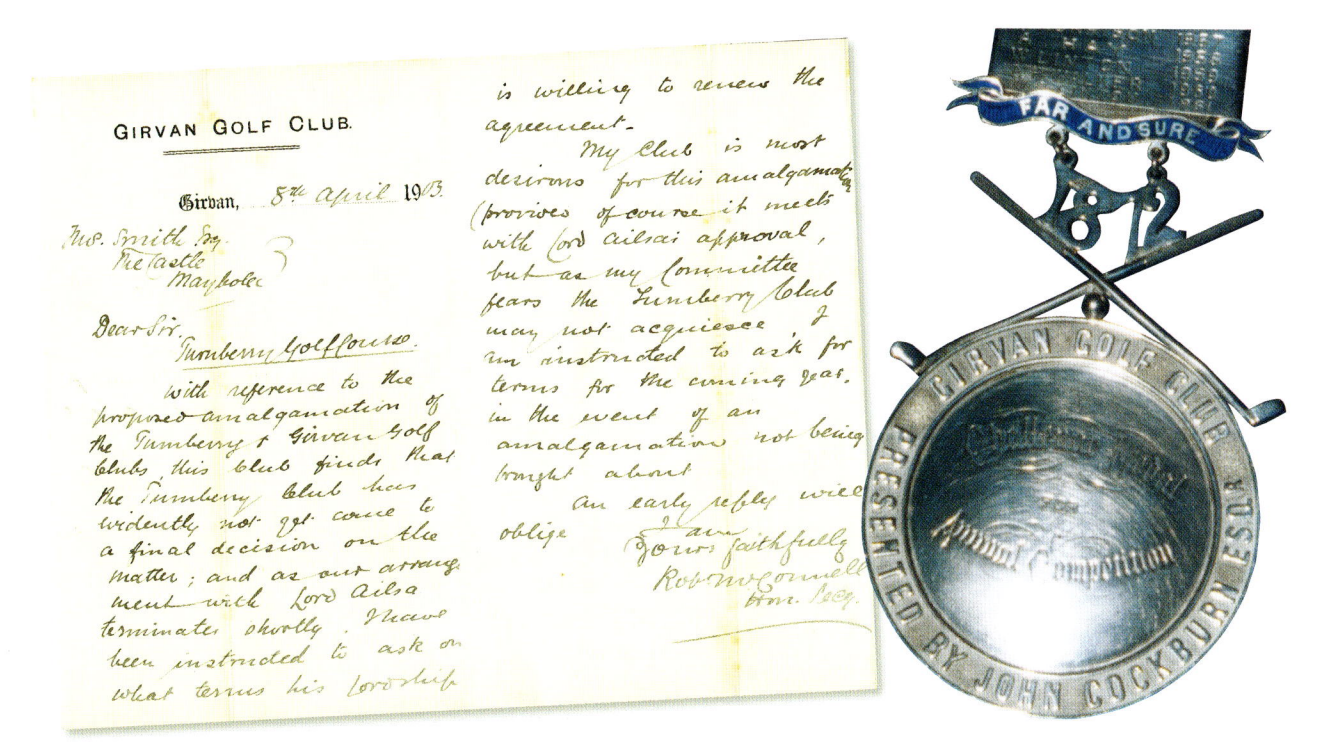

Letter from Girvan Golf Club referring to amalgamation with Turnberry Golf Club

Cockburn Medal

25

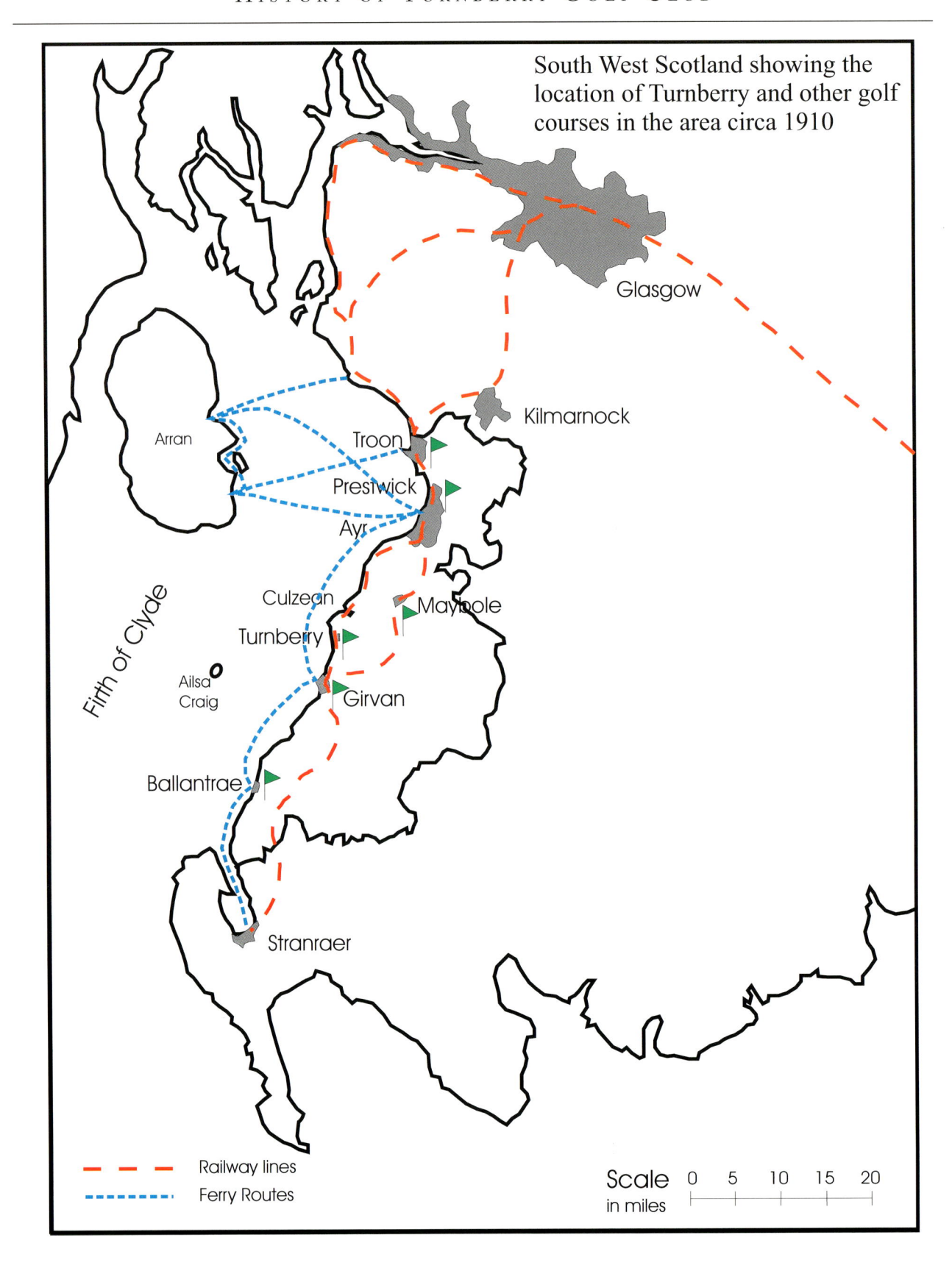

South West Scotland showing the location of Turnberry and other golf courses in the area circa 1910

CHAPTER II

THE CLUB'S EARLY YEARS

The club is formed, important tournaments are held,
but war clouds halt progress.

FORMATION OF TURNBERRY GOLF CLUB

Inaugural Meeting in Maybole Town Hall

IT was not until the Spring of 1902 that Turnberry Golf Club came into being when a meeting of gentlemen in favour of forming a golf club for the district was held on Thursday, 24th April, 1902, in Maybole. Maybole was then a small town with a population of about 5000 situated seven miles north and inland of Turnberry and historically was the capital of a district known as Carrick which stretched from the River Doon, in the north, to the River Stinchar at Ballantrae, in the south. The other main town in that district was Girvan situated on the coast five miles south of Turnberry. In mediaeval times the rich and powerful local families with estates and castles in the district, would all have had town houses in Maybole, and the district court and jail were situated there. The most powerful of these families were the Kennedys, of whom the Marquess of Ailsa was the head and who figures so much in this story of Turnberry. Their town house in Maybole was the grandest of them all. Known as Maybole Castle it still stands in the High Street to this day. At the turn of the century when the inaugural meeting of Turnberry Golf Club took place in the newly erected Town Hall of Maybole, the little town had become a busy commercial and industrial centre. Earlier in its history the main business of the town had been weaving, as a cottage industry, but by 1902 it had a thriving leather and boot and shoe industry with two leather tanneries producing the leather and four or five factories producing boots and shoes. It also had two engineering works producing agricultural implements for the busy farming industry surrounding the town and also to export throughout Britain and even abroad. Maybole, at that time, was more industrialised than its neighbour Girvan and, amongst its residents, had many influential and successful businessmen. Moreover it still housed the Factor (Estates Manager) of the Marquess of Ailsa in Maybole Castle. Girvan, on the other hand, was principally a fishing village and increasingly popular holiday resort, but did not have much industry and, consequently, not so many influential and successful business men as Maybole. Unlike Girvan, Maybole still did not have a golf course or golf club and, against

Above: Thomas Smith, Factor of the Third Marquess of Ailsa from 1879-1910, who convened and chaired the inaugural meeting of the Club held on 24th April 1902.
Below: Thomas Smith's leather bound Membership Card for the inaugural season 1902-1903.

Chapter II - The Club's Early Years

this background, the important men in Maybole saw their opportunity to form a golf club to operate at the new Turnberry course and were able to obtain the support of the Marquess and his Factor in this project. The meeting in the Town Hall was attended by 22 persons including Ex-Provost Marshall of Maybole, a local industrialist and Mr. Thomas Smith, the Factor of the Marquess of Ailsa. Mr. Smith chaired the meeting and it was resolved to form a golf club to be known as Turnberry Golf Club to play on the golf course at Turnberry *'just recently made entirely at Lord Ailsa's expense'*, under the supervision and direction of *'one of the most experienced professional golfers in Scotland, Mr. William Fernie of Troon, who was British Open Champion in 1883'*. It was explained to the meeting that, when the new light railway from Ayr to Girvan was formed by Glasgow and South Western Railway Company, that Company would take over the course and that the guests at their new hotel at Turnberry and persons travelling on their trains would have preference on the course, but that the public and the local clubs would also be entitled to use the course and that the interests of the Club would be carefully looked after. It was agreed to fix an annual subscription of One guinea with no entrance fee for the first 100 members, and the Marquess of Ailsa was proposed as Honorary President and his son, the Earl of Cassillis, as Honorary Vice-President. Following that meeting a circular was issued locally inviting gentlemen to join the new Club and by 15th May, 1902, there had been 128 applications. The first general meeting of the new Club was held on 23rd May, 1902, in the Town Hall, Maybole, when a Constitution and Rules were approved and all 128 applicants were admitted as founder members. It was agreed that 80% of the Club's income be paid to Lord Ailsa for the use of the course and the following office bearers were appointed:-

President – The Most Noble, The Marquess of Ailsa.
Vice-President – The Earl of Cassillis
Captain – J. Marshall, Esq., Laurel Bank, Maybole
Vice-Captain – John Templeton, Esq., Maybole.

Transport to the Course

The Club was up and running and no time was lost in getting down to the business of playing golf on the exciting new course. Its condition was still fairly rough and an old railway van without electricity, gas or running water served as a clubhouse. The van was provided by Lord Ailsa whose connections with the Glasgow & South West of

Above: Maybole Castle, the town house of the Third Marquess and office of his Factor.
Below: Maybole Town Hall where inaugural meeting held.

Scotland Railway Company perhaps facilitated its acquisition. At this time of course there was still no railway at Turnberry, the nearest stations being at Girvan, five miles distant, and Maybole, seven miles distant. Presumably the railway van was transported from one of these stations by road, probably on a trailer drawn by horses or by a steam locomotive. It would have been subject to the so-called 'Red Flag' acts of parliament which stipulated that three persons must be in attendance, one to steer, one to control the horses and one to go ahead with a warning red flag to avoid danger to other road users. The hill across the road from the course was still covered in rough grass and trees and no start had yet been made on the proposed new hotel or railway line. Golfers travelling from outwith the area would have been able to use the Railway Company's existing inland line to get to Maybole or Girvan. From there they and the local players from Maybole and Girvan would in the main have required private transport. Motorised vehicles for personal transport were at a very rudimentary stage in their development and would have been very few and far between. Moreover they were not reliable nor generally trusted and their speed was restricted by statute to 12 miles per hour. So transport would be mainly by horse or horse and carriage. The *Ayr Observer* in April 1902 reported that 'bus hirers' were *'to run a popular fare to the golf course at one shilling per head'* and that *'this until the railway was made would be a convenience and an inducement for summer visitors who go in for golfing'*. The buses in question would have been horse drawn at that time. 'Charabancs' which were early motorised open top buses did not make their appearance till some years later.

Opening of Turnberry Golf Club

As explained above the course had already been opened in July 1901 by Girvan Golf Club, but the new Turnberry Golf Club held a formal ceremony to mark the Club's opening on Saturday, 30th August, 1902, followed by a match between a team headed by the Captain and a team headed by the Vice-Captain, and to this day the Club holds this match annually. The 1902 occasion was reported in the *Ayr Observer and Galloway Gazette* as follows:-

OPENING OF TURNBERRY GOLF CLUB NEW RECORD BY FERNIE

The formal opening of Turnberry Golf Course took place on Saturday last. The afternoon was fine and there was a strong muster of members.

Captain Marshall, in welcoming members and friends, said – We are met today on a historic occasion in connection with the very ancient game of golf. We are here to inaugurate the latest addition to the list of golfing, and which we are proud to name "The Turnberry Golf Course". The Turnberry club has sprung into life with great rapidity, and has already attained a roll of membership that gives evidence that the "Turnberry" will soon rival the most famous clubs in Scotland. Although we only made a start a few months ago we have now a membership of fully 150, and the cry is "still they come" and no wonder. Our course has been laid out by the veteran golfer, Mr. Fernie, whom we are glad to see present. All expert golfers are already enraptured with the high excellence of the Turnberry course. Its attractions

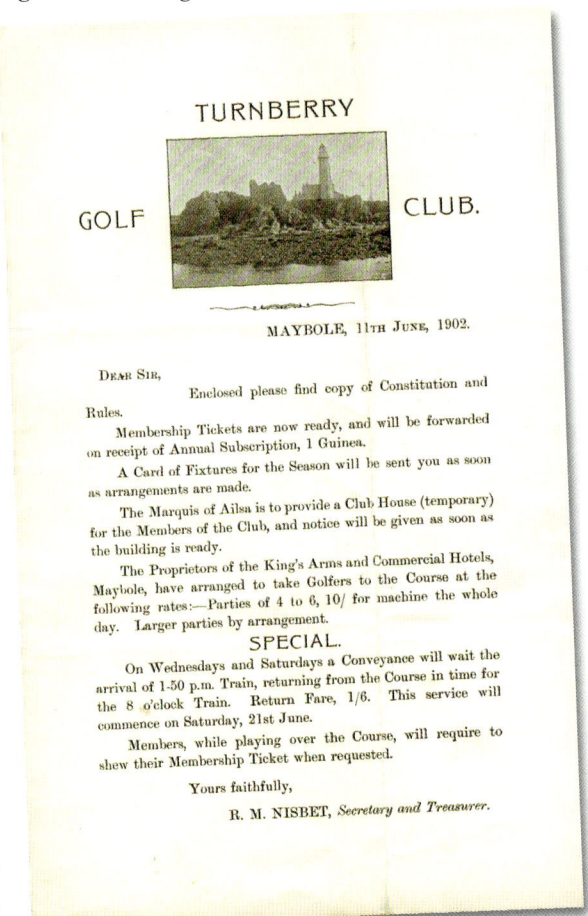

Chapter II - The Club's Early Years

are great, situated as it is under the shadow of the grand old historic castle, the birthplace of King Robert the Bruce, and within hail of the farm of Shanter, which our national poet Burns has immortalised. Our course is unsurpassed for beauty of situation and enriched by that invigorating breeze off the Atlantic. It is truly an ideal course. We are deeply indebted to the noble Marquess of Ailsa, not only for the favourable arrangement we have for the use of this course, but for the honour and prestige he has conferred upon our club by becoming our first president. We know that his Lordship is not only a keen golfer, but has always been a warm supporter of sport, both on sea and land. We may, therefore, feel assured that his Lordship will continue to further the best interests of the Turnberry Club. (Applause.) We are also highly gratified that Lord Cassillis has cheerfully consented to become our vice-president. Possibly his Lordship has resolved to beat his spear into a golf club and study the art of peace for the future. I dare say in doing so his Lordship will strive to secure the trophies of our club with all the energy he displayed in South Africa. (Applause.) I am sorry that Mr. Smith is not with us today to give us information regarding a clubhouse. I understand this matter will be attended to very soon. The probability is that the G. & S.W. Railway Coy. have great things in store for the future of golfing on the Turnberry course, and that they contemplate erecting a suitable clubhouse. I have now to thank the members of the Turnberry Club for the great honour they have conferred on me by unanimously electing me their captain. It shows that it is not necessary to be a golfer to fulfil the duties. Since receiving that great honour I have had maiden lessons, and now feel great enthusiasm in the game. I will do all in my power to further the success of the Turnberry Golf Club (Applause.)

Thereafter refreshments were served and a match followed, the teams being chosen by the captain and vice-captain, Mr. J. Templeton, J.P., and ended in a win for the captain's team by 12 holes. During the afternoon W. Fernie, (Troon) played a round with a local player, and succeeded in reducing his former record for the course, doing the round in 73. In the course of the afternoon the course was visited by the Marquess of Ailsa, president of the club, Mr. Adam Wood, Troon, Messrs. Smith and Brown, Maybole, etc. Important improvements are going on at the course, including the relaying of some of the greens and the formation of additional bunkers.

Composition of the early Membership

By January 1903 there were 159 members, who included one Marquess, one Earl, one Lord, one Rear Admiral and nine clergymen. The status or occupations of these persons are easily identified from their titles but it can be seen from other details in the records and minutes that the membership was drawn substantially from professional and business people, including local shopkeepers and people such as the postmaster, stationmaster and works managers. It did not include many ordinary working employed persons such as manual workers, labourers or employed tradesmen. This reflected the social structure of the time, when ordinary workers would not have had the time or the means to play golf, especially on a course situated in the country miles from their homes. The situation only changed radically after the Second World

Card of Fixtures of Turnberry Golf Club 1906-7

OFFICE-BEARERS.

President.
The Most Noble The MARQUIS OF AILSA.

Vice-President.
THE EARL OF CASSILLIS.

Captain.
J. MARSHALL, ESQ., Maybole.

Vice-Captain.
J. TEMPLETON, ESQ.

Committee.
Messrs J. Anderson.   Messrs A. G. Larke.
L. Baikie.   J. Rafferty.
R. Moir.   T. Smith.
T. Minto

Secretary and Treasurer.
R.M. NISBET, 1 Barns Terrace, Maybole.

List of Members.

*Those marked * are Original Members.*

*Ailsa, Marquis of, Culzean Castle.
*Agar, Alexander, Glasgow.
*Aitken, Charles K., Glasgow.
*Anderson, John, Maybole.
*Anderson, David, Maybole.
*Armstrong, Thomas, Maybole.
*Austin, R. D. J. Mein, Blackclaughrie.
Allan, Henry, Ballochmyle.
Adams, David, Maybole.

*Baikie, L. S., Kirkoswald.
*Bryan, William, Maybole.
*Blair, Commander Hunter, Blairquhan.
*Bell, Martin M., Glasgow.
*Brown, Charles W., Maybole.
*Bowman, Dr., Maybole.
*Baxter, Captain, Glasgow.
*Bonthrone, William, Maybole.
*Buchanan, D.H., Troon.
*Boyd, G. O. M., Paisley.
Brown, Nicol Paton, Glasgow.

2

*Cassillis, Earl of, Culzean Castle.
*Cameron. John, Maybole.
*Campbell, A. M., Younger of Auchmannoch.
*Carmichael, J. R., Maybole.
*Collins, Rev. Canon, Ayr.
*Crookston, James, Glasgow.
*Culver, William, Glasgow.
*Cameron, John, Ayr.
Carrick, John, Stewarton.
Crawford, John, Maybole.
Caird, Arthur, Greenock.
*Crawford, Andrew, Ayr.
Coats, Daniel, Paisley.

*Dunlop, William, Maidens.
*Dunlop, Quintin, Jr., Maidens.
*Dunlop, William, Glasgow.
*Dunlop, James, Maidens.
*Dick, Andrew, Maybole.
*Dobbie, R. M., Ayr.

Fullarton, David, Sen., Troon.
Fullarton, Robert, Troon.
Foulis, Stuart, Glasgow.

3

*Finlayson, John, Maybole.
*Gray, William, Maybole.
*Glendinning, Rev. W.D., Maybole.
*Gibson, T. H., Belfast.
*Galbraith, John, Glasgow.
*Gibson, James M., Maybole.
*Goudie, Andrew, Jr., Maybole.
*Gibb, Charles, Troon.
*Gibb, Alexander, Troon.

*Hunter, Thomas, Jr., Maybole.
*Hunter, Archibald, Maybole.
*Highet, David, Ayr.
*Houston, William, Maybole.
*Hastings, David, Maidens.
Hawkings, Ernest, London.
Hunter, James Kennedy, Ayr.

*Inglis, Dr., Maybole.

Kennedy, Lord Charles, Culzean Castle.
*Ker, Rev. William, Kirkoswald.
*Kennedy, James, Maybole, (deceased)
*Ker, F. W., Glasgow.
*Kennedy, Lord Angus, Troon.

4

*Kerr, John, Maybole.
*King, John, Glasgow.

*Larke, A. J., Prestwick.
*Logan, C., Glasgow.
*Lees, John, Maybole.
*Laidlaw, W.K., Edinburgh.
*Lobban, Alexander, Ayr.
Lockhart, George Mason, Ayr.
Lean, Daniel, Glasgow.
Lean, George, Glasgow.
Lean, Robert, Glasgow.
Lauder, Archibald, Glasgow.
Laird, William B., Irvine.
Laird, James, Glasgow.

*Marshall, John, Maybole.
*Minto, Thomas, Maybole.
*Maltman, Edward, Maybole.
*Mitchell, William, Maybole.
*Maltman, William, Maybole.
*Morton, James Mathie, Ayr.
*Moir, Robert, Maybole.
*Marshall, Peter, Glasgow.
*Muir, Rev. James, Kirkoswald.

5

*Meikle, James, Ayr.
*Mulvein, George, Maybole.
*Mitchell, Matthew, Glasgow.
*Morrison, William, Ayr.
*Morrison, J. C., Ayr.
*Murray, William, Ayr.
*Murray, John, Ayr.
*Maxwell Roabert, Maybole.
Muir, William, Pollockshields.
*M'Quiston, Thomas, Maybole.
*M'Cubbin, John, Maybole.
*M'Connell, P. A., Maybole.
*M'Kellar, Colin, Maybole.
*Maclachlan, R. P., Ayr.
*M'Quiston, Hugh, Ayr.
*M'Mikin, H. P. Sterndale, Grange, Maybole.
*M'Daniel, Rev. P., Maybole.
*M'Clymont, Rev. J. A., Aberdeen.
*M'Cubbin, William, Maybole.
*M'Bride, W .C., London.
*M'Pherson, James, Glasgow.
*M'Pherson, T. W., Glasgow.
*M'Kinnon, T. N., Kirkmichael House.

6

*M'Crorie, Wilfred, Ayr.
M'Allister, Alexander, Paisley.
M'Naughton, Norman, Hollybush.

*Nisbet, Robert M., Maybole.
*Neil, Thomas, Maybole.
*Neil, Robert, Jr., Maybole.

*Ochiltreet, J. H., Ayr.

*Porteous, James S., Maybole.
*Page, A.D., Culzean.
*Paterson, Peter, Maybole.
*Paterson, Thomas, Maybole.

Rafferty, John, Maybole.
*Rose, Rear-Admiral, London.
*Robson, Alexander, Culzean.
*Ramsay, David, Maybole.
*Ramsay, James, Jr., Maybole.
*Rodger, J. H., Glasgow.
*Reid, James, Maybole.
*Roxburgh, Robert, Glasgow.
*Rennie, Thomas, Glasgow.
*Rennie, William, Greenock.
Rowan, James G., Maybole.

7

*Smith, Thomas, Maybole.
*Swan, Rev. David, Maybole.
*Smith, Thomas, Jr., Maybole.
*Shiels, Thomas, Kilkerran.
*Strachan, Robert, Maybole.
Strain, John, Cassillis House.
Stobo, William P., Glasgow.

*Templeton, John, Maybole.
*Turner, Malcolm, Maybole.
*Templeton, James, Maybole. (deceased)
*Templeton, William, Maybole.
*Thompson, Rev. G., Maybole.
*Thomson Rev. William, Maybole.
*Templeton, W. J., Glasgow.
*Templeton, W. A., Kirkoswald.
Thomson, Thomas Frame, London.

*Wilson, J. Montgomery, Glasgow.
*Walker, R D., Ayr.
*Weir, Joseph, Ardrossan.
*Willock, Ex-Provost, Ayr.
*Willock, Fred., Glasgow.
*Watson, David Henry, Glasgow.
*Watson, David Henry, Jr., Glasgow.

8

*Wallace, H. R., Cloncaird, Kirkmichael
*Wood, Adam, Troon.
Walker, Alexander, Troon.
Wallace, Peter, Troon.

War when the membership of the Club widened to represent a much broader cross-section of society. The geographical spread of the membership was also interesting, with 70 from Maybole, 39 from Glasgow, 21 from Ayr and Prestwick, 4 from London, 1 from Aberdeen, 1 from Belfast, 9 from Troon, and 14 from other parts of Ayrshire.

There were no founder members from Girvan, no doubt due to the fact that Girvan Golf Club was already using the Turnberry course. However in February 1903 Girvan Golf Club applied to amalgamate with Turnberry Golf Club, and to have their members admitted as members of that club. Girvan indicated they had 58 members and offered to contribute a sum of £10 to Turnberry Golf Club and also their clubhouse at the Turnberry course. This offer was accepted by a Special General Meeting held on 12th March 1903 and a sweepstake competition was held to inaugurate the amalgamation. It is interesting to note that Lord Ailsa who received 80% of the annual subscriptions and payments from temporary members,

*Turnberry Golf Club - List of Members January 1903. Original founder members marked with *.*

Chapter II - The Club's Early Years

by way of rent for the use of the course, intimated through his factor that he would make no claim to receive 80% of the donation of £10 from the Girvan Club. The early minutes reveal the following information on financial matters:

(1) the rent paid by the Club for the first season (1902-03) was £182-15/-,
(2) an honorarium of 10 guineas was paid to the Honorary Secretary for his work in the first season, and
(3) the cost of printing 300 leather-bound membership cards was £4-16/4d.

On 28th August 1903, a mere 16 months from the inaugural public meeting, the membership had grown to 230, demonstrating a considerable demand for the new golf facilities at Turnberry. The membership was still principally drawn from local residents of Maybole and Girvan, but there was also a strong influx of influential professional and business people from the Glasgow area and even further afield including from Blackheath, London, Rugby, County Antrim and South Africa. Many of these were proposed or seconded by the Marquess of Ailsa. There was also established early a practice of having members from amongst the executive employees of the Railway Company as the owners of the future Turnberry Hotel. In September 1903 the club elected as honorary members the General Manager of Glasgow and South Western Railway Company, David Cooper, and five other executives being the Company's Secretary, Superintendent of Line, Goods Manager, Solicitor and Engineer.

The legal and historical status of the Club

No long term formal written lease or agreement has ever been put in place to regulate the Club's position at Turnberry, but nevertheless, for its whole history over 100 years, the Club has not only existed and thrived at Turnberry but has played a very important part in the establishment, development, and continued success of Turnberry as a world famous golfing resort and venue for important golfing tournaments, not least the Open Championship on three occasions to date. In particular the Club and its members traditionally have responsibility for crowd control and recruiting and managing voluntary and paid staff for this and other functions such as recording, scoring, couriers, leader boards, litter control. This kind of contribution has been essential and invaluable for the Open and the many other important amateur and professional tournaments held at Turnberry down the years. The importance of this has been acknowledged many times by the Royal and Ancient Golf Club of St. Andrews, and by the owners of Turnberry. Of course Turnberry has changed hands several times over its history and there is always inevitably the fear that some new owner, for purely commercial considerations, might fail to respect the history and traditions of the place, and the position of the Club within that history. Golf is part of the heritage and history of Scotland, and the co-existence of Turnberry Hotel and Turnberry Golf Club over 100 years to their mutual advantage is a remarkable and proud story.

CLUB AFFAIRS — 1902-1919

IN the period from the Club's formation till the First World War it thrived and developed, with a considerable influx of new members, including quite a number of foreign members. Many of the fine trophies now exhibited in the clubhouse were acquired, mostly by donation from members, and the competitions were keenly contested. The Club's arrangements to play the course were initially with the Third Marquess of Ailsa who owned and maintained the course until its management was taken over by the Railway Company in December 1905. The Marquess, Honorary President, and his son the Earl of Cassillis, Honorary Vice President, both regularly played golf at Turnberry and took a keen interest in the Club and its activities. The Third Marquess remained President of the Club until his death in 1938, when the Earl of Cassillis became the Fourth Marquess and succeeded him as President until his own death in 1943. When the Railway Company took over the course from the Marquess in December 1905, the Club faced successfully the first change of ownership and negotiated suitable terms for its continued use of the course. There was constant liaison and correspondence with the Railway Company and matters covered included the lease and use of the clubhouse; the administration of visiting golf tournaments to publicise and popularise the course; the maintenance and development of the courses; the subject of ladies' golf and admission of lady members; a heated debate about Sunday golf; the financial terms for the Club's use of the course; and all the other day to day matters which arose. Mr. David Cooper, the General Manager of the Railway Company, was the man with whom the Club mostly dealt. From the Club's minutes it is clear that there was a great deal of useful co-operation between the Company and the Club. Both sides fought their corners hard but fairly, to further their respective interests. Inevitably of course, over these early years there were ups and downs in the relationship with issues such as Sunday golf, lady members and charges being particularly contentious. The outcome however was generally satisfactory and beneficial to the Club, the development of the courses and the growing reputation of Turnberry as a very fine golf course and hotel resort.

The Hotel

The new hotel was designed by James Miller, an architect who had designed the Glasgow International Exhibition buildings of 1901 and who was an associate of the Royal Scottish Academy. It originally had a frontage of 300 feet and 100 bedrooms with all the principal rooms situated overlooking the sea. The main entrance was on the inland side facing Turnberry railway station and the station and

Turnberry Hotel with Club House in foreground - circa 1912. Courtesy of A.D. Henderson

Chapter II - The Club's Early Years

hotel were linked by a covered way leading through a large conservatory to the entrance lounge. Its situation is about 100 feet above sea level, commanding a wonderful view, not only of the golf courses, but also of the Firth of Clyde as it joins the Irish Sea, with Arran, Kintyre, Ailsa Craig and even the coast of Northern Ireland all visible on a clear day. An original special feature was a suite of bathrooms fitted for golfers, which included plunge baths with sprays, showers and waves and supplied with hot and cold salt and fresh water, the salt water being pumped up from the sea by means of an electric pump. The hotel had electric lighting throughout and electric clocks. In the grounds adjoining the hotel there were stables for horses and motor garage accommodation for 40 to 50 motor vehicles. A grand formal opening of both the hotel and the railway line was held in May 1906 before a large company of distinguished guests who travelled by a special train from Glasgow. On this auspicious occasion it was significant that, from all the important people present, the person called on by the chairman of the Railway Company to propose the toast of the day, was the first captain of Turnberry Golf Club, John Marshall, ex-Provost of Maybole. Mr. Marshall toasted the success of the new railway line and of Turnberry Hotel and praised the enterprise and foresight of the directors of the Railway Company. He expressed his confidence that the new line would prove successful beyond all expectations and would attract tourists *'in their tens of thousands'*. At the time that might have seemed a bit of an exaggeration, but who then could have foreseen attendances of hundreds of thousands at Turnberry's Open Championship occasions.

With the opening of the hotel the Railway Company then *'took over the sole right to manage and maintain the golf courses'*. This right was acknowledged in the Club's constitution at that time and, at the request of the Company, the constitution was also altered to decrease the maximum number of members from 500 to 350. An early bone of contention was the lack of stabling for members' horses, but the Company was adamant that stables would be provided only for hotel purposes. No doubt the Company wanted to encourage people to travel on the railway rather than by their own private transport. The terms for the use of the course by Club members remained on the same basis as it had been with the Marquess of Ailsa, namely the Club at first paid 80% of the proceeds from members' subscriptions to the Railway Company, and then in June 1911, this was increased to 85%.

The Clubhouse

The clubhouse arrangements were at first very rudimentary. When the Girvan Club commenced play on the course in early 1901, the members secured the use of an old toll house at the junction of Turnberry Road with the main road from Maybole to Girvan and within easy walking distance (about 500 yards) from the first tee. It was used for the temporary storage of clubs and still exists today, in use now as a holiday cottage. Then in June 1901, as described above, Lord Ailsa's factor arranged with the Railway Company for a *'railway brake van body'* to be delivered to the course as a temporary clubhouse. Things improved, when in January 1902 Girvan Golf Club moved to Turnberry and brought their clubhouse with them, re-erecting it at Turnberry, and providing Lord Ailsa with a key to locker No. 10 for his personal use. A description of this clubhouse is not available, but presumably it was of wooden sectional construction, for it to have been possible to move it from Girvan. When the new Turnberry Golf Club was formed in May 1902, they initially used the railway waggon as a clubhouse and then, when the Girvan Club amalgamated with the Turnberry Club, their clubhouse became the temporary

Old Toll House at Turnberry used in 1901 by Girvan Golf Club as temporary Clubhouse

home of the combined Club for just over a year, until a completely new clubhouse was erected by the Railway Company. Although the Company was not going to take over the management of the course until some years later, by August 1902 they were considering the erection of a permanent structure containing *'club and refreshment rooms, etc.'*. The committee of Turnberry Golf Club considered this *'very satisfactory, subject to a portion of the building being set aside for use by the members of the Club'*. This clubhouse was completed about a year later and a formal opening ceremony was held on 17th October 1903. It remained virtually unchanged, apart from internal modernisation, until a major alteration and extension was carried out just prior to the first Open Championship to be held at Turnberry in 1977. Some of the older members of the Club today still remember it affectionately, particularly the members' lounge bar which could only have measured about 15 ft. square. It had a brick fireplace which, in the winter, always had a warm fire blazing in it and the hearth was worn away by the studs of the shoes of generations of golfers. The bar was served through a small hatchway in a wall and the atmosphere was always warm and friendly. In such a small space the golf stories, jokes and conversation were enjoyed from side to side of the room, with everyone engaged in the general conviviality. Many of the most famous golfing personalities and players down the years, have enjoyed the very friendly atmosphere and camaraderie in that room. They all invariably received a very warm welcome. Henry Longhurst, when commentating on big events at Turnberry, was wont to visit the members' bar for *'fortification'* prior to ascending the gantry to his elevated commentary box. On one occasion his commentary and description of the event and venue was as eloquent as ever but was slightly inaccurate in that he referred to Ailsa Craig as being the Bass Rock. Perhaps the *'fortification'* that day had been over generous. Christy O'Connor, Senior, was another who liked the atmosphere and *'the crack'* in that members' lounge.

Gene Sarazen evicted

One of the older members however recalls an occasion in the 1960's when the welcome was less than hospitable. At that time the clubmistress, Mrs. McCallum, had an assistant called Nan, a rather sharp-tongued Stranraer lady who was never over-impressed or overawed by anyone, whatever their title or fame. The member had opened the door to the members' lounge and witnessed

New Club House at Turnberry opened by Marchioness of Ailsa 17/10/1903.

Chapter II - The Club's Early Years

the following dialogue between Nan and a diminutive American gentleman in plus fours:-

Nan: Ye' a member?

American: No Ma'am, A'm not a member.

Nan: If yer no' a member, Oot!

This all happened so quickly the member had no time to intervene before he realised that it was Gene Sarazen going out the door with his tail between his legs. Naturally the member made suitable apologies to the great man, who in retrospect thought the incident very amusing. Nan, though suitably reprimanded, was completely unrepentant!

Before the First World War the clubhouse was rented to the Club by the Railway Company and its use was restricted to Club members, their guests and temporary members, i.e. persons holding tickets for one week or longer period. The initial rent was £20 per annum but in April 1911 this was increased to £37 per annum in exchange for the Company carrying out various improvements to the premises. About the same time however the Company refused a request from the Club for the installation of electric light and the Club decided *'meantime to try the effect of a few good oil lamps suspended from the ceiling'*. So it was electric light and stables for the hotel patrons on the hill, but not for the members in their clubhouse at the bottom of the hill. A bit of 'upstairs-downstairs'. The clubhouse staff was employed by the Club and, from about 1906, the liquor licence was held by the Club as a bona fide club registered under the Licensing Act 1904. For this, the consent of the Company as owners was required and this was initially granted subject to the Club giving an assurance that the Club would 'drop the licence' when called on to do so by the Company. This was no doubt because the Company anticipated that, when the hotel was established, it would obtain its own liquor licence for the clubhouse and would want to benefit from any profits to be made from the sale of beverages. As it subsequently turned out the Company did not call on the Club to 'drop the licence' until very many years later, for reasons which will be explained. There are many references to requests being received by the Club from visiting groups for the courtesy of the clubhouse and these were mostly granted. It is interesting to note the names of some of the visiting clubs in the period from 1907 till 1914. At that point there were in Scotland very many clubs without a course and, for many people, such a club would be their only one:

    Ladies Golf Club of Great Britain

    Ayrshire Teachers Golf Club

    Glasgow & South Western Railway Golf Club

    The Dilettante Golf Club

    Glasgow Medical Golf Club

    Grasshoppers Club

    Ayr Cleek Club

    Directors of Glasgow Rangers Football Club

    Ayr Trinity United Friendly Church Golf Club

    Daimler Company of America

The holders of daily tickets for the course were not entitled to the 'privileges' of the clubhouse according to a committee minute in 1909. In 1916 this gave rise to correspondence in the press concerning the refusal of the clubmistress to supply tea to daily ticket holders. Although sympathetic when considering this complaint, the Club nevertheless agreed that visitors must be introduced by a member. This however may have been to comply with the terms of the Club's registration under the Licensing Acts, rather than any lack of hospitality.

From the formation of the Club until August 1903 all general and committee meetings were held in the Town Buildings, Maybole, but from September 1903 till May 1906 most meetings were held in the Kings Arms Hotel, Maybole, even though the new clubhouse opened in 1903. It seems that the early office bearers and committee members were reluctant to forego the comfort and hospitality of the ancient Maybole hostelry, which in its time had sheltered many famous travellers and guests, including Robert Burns, the national bard of Scotland, and the novelist Robert Louis Stevenson. However after May 1906, it became the practice to hold most meetings in the clubhouse, which coincidentally and fortuitously became licensed to sell liquor about the same time!

Sunday Golf

The matter of Sunday golf was an issue during this early period and representations about it were made to both the Railway Company and to the Club by the Moderator (minister) and Kirk Session (church elders responsible for spiritual matters) of the Church of Scotland at Kirkoswald, whose parish area included Turnberry. The opening of the railway, the hotel and the golf courses had brought an influx of visitors to the area, including not only golfers but also crowds of campers to Maidens, the nearby fishing village. The noisy behaviour and manners of many of these visitors, especially on a Sunday, and the act of playing golf on a Sunday, proved too much for some of the locals and a petition was handed to the management of Turnberry Hotel in 1908. The main objection was *'the flagrant desecration of the Sabbath by golfers'*, and the petition was received with sympathy by both the Company and the Club. Indeed the Club had already circularised its members in 1904 to the effect that there was to be no golf on Sundays and that the clubhouse would be closed on those days. To reinforce this rule in 1908 the Club posted a notice in the clubhouse window and the hotel put up a notice at the entrance gate of the golf course, forbidding golf on Sundays. The Church authorities were informed that it was hoped that this *'would have the desired effect in putting an end to this evil practice'*. Inevitably of course, as time passed, there was more and more pressure for Sunday golf, both from members and, for commercial reasons, from the Railway Company. By October 1913 the Company had introduced Sunday golf free for their hotel guests and Club members were up in arms. However their indignation, with a few exceptions, arose not so much from the prospect of Sunday golf as from the proposal of the Company to charge members a fee of five shillings for play on that day. At a Special General Meeting held in October 1913 Captain Richard Niven explained that he had protested strongly to the Company about their actions and he received a vote of confidence from the meeting. The Reverend James Muir endeavoured to raise the whole question of Sunday golf but was ruled out of order. The fight against the *'desecration of the Sabbath'* looked doomed. This was confirmed at the Annual General Meeting of the Club on 16th May 1914, when the Reverend Muir submitted a motion that there be no Sunday golf, but failed to find a seconder. On the question of the charge imposed on members by the Company, quite a few members threatened to resign if the Company didn't drop the charge. However the arguments of the Club and the Captain and this threat from members failed to move the Company, and all but one of the threatened resignations were withdrawn. Sunday golf and Sunday charges won the day. Nevertheless the Club continued to close the clubhouse on Sundays and no Club competitions were held on Sundays and this did not change until 1929.

Lady Members

From the outset there are references to ladies playing at Turnberry. We know that Girvan Golf Club had lady members when they opened the Turnberry course in 1901. Their secretary's letter to Lord Ailsa's factor just before the opening, expressed concern about lady members not being able to gain access to the greens over the surrounding sheep-proof fences and another letter seeks to obtain permission to sell monthly or fortnightly visitor tickets to ladies as well as to gentlemen. His comment in that letter was that *'visitors as a rule have often golfing members of both sexes in the family, and naturally they like to take their pleasure together'*.

When Turnberry Golf Club was formed on 24th April 1902 there were no lady members in the list of founding members and, when Girvan Golf Club amalgamated with Turnberry Golf Club it appears that only the gentlemen members of Girvan became members of Turnberry. However in June 1903 it was agreed between the Club and Lord Ailsa's factor that members could 'introduce a lady to join in a game of golf occasionally on the course but not when the greens are fully occupied or when matches are being played'. Essentially at that stage it was a gentlemen only club, except for lady guests of members, and possibly also ladies purchasing visitor tickets. This may have been due at least to some extent to the attitude of Lord Ailsa who, being annoyed to learn that there might be lady members amongst the first subscribers, wrote:-

> *'It will never do to start a mixed club in this way. I never heard of any such arrangement in any golf club I know of. Ladies' clubs and ladies' courses are always kept separate, and it will certainly not do with a course like the Turnberry Links to start with a mixed club. The usual thing is that ladies wishing to play may do so with their gentlemen friends being members or in some cases, ladies who have a low handicap are allowed to play a man's course by themselves on certain days, not being holidays or Saturdays.'*

Chapter II - The Club's Early Years

Further evidence of the male chauvinistic attitude of the time appears in a committee minute, dated 5th October 1907, when a letter was received from a prominent member. This complained of ladies playing on the course and not allowing those behind to play through, and suggested that a bye-law should be framed to deal with this matter. This attitude was not surprising considering that, at that time, female suffrage was still twenty years ahead and the early suffrage movement, under the leadership of Mrs. Pankhurst, was still struggling to make progress. However it was not long thereafter that the Turnberry Club admitted lady members and nowadays they have completely equal playing rights and status.

In August 1910, the Club applied to Mr. Cooper, the general manager of the Railway Company, for permission to admit lady members to the Club, but he replied that, although the Company directors had given the matter full consideration, they could not agree to the proposal. However by April 1911, the committee minutes record that Mr. Cooper intimated that a further application to allow lady members would receive his favourable consideration and certain improvements would be made to the clubhouse, provided the Club agreed to an increase in the rent for the clubhouse. The admission of lady members was agreed at the Club's Annual General Meeting that year, at an annual subscription of one guinea, the same sum as that paid by gentlemen, and the first fifty to be charged no entry money. The first lady members, twenty seven in number, were admitted on 2nd February 1912, four of whom were daughters or wives of the manse. It seems that golf was a popular sport amongst the clergy and their womenfolk in those days. On 17th August 1912 the first general meeting of the new Ladies' Section was held, presided over by Captain Niven who presented the ladies with a silver purse to be played for in their first competition. They elected their first office bearers and, on the proposal of Captain Niven, elected the Marchioness of Ailsa as their President and Lady Marjorie Dalrymple-Hamilton as their Vice-President.

At first the Ladies' Section relied on the main Club for their finances and in 1912 the Club contributed £3-3/- to the Ladies' Section for a prize fund, agreed to pay a 'privilege railway ticket' for use by their secretary and allocated a room in the clubhouse to be specially used by the lady members. Thereafter for many years the Club made annual financial grants to the Ladies' Section, starting at £2 in 1920 and rising to £20 by 1936.

Captains

During this early period the Club had four Captains. The first of these, who has already been referred to, was John Marshall of Laurelbank, Maybole, the small town seven miles to the North of Turnberry. In 1877 he took over the small existing company of Alexander Jack & Sons Ltd., which had been founded in 1852 and whose main activity was manufacturing horse drawn carts for local farmers. Under the management of Mr. Marshall the company developed rapidly and, by the early twentieth century, had diversified to produce almost every kind of implement and vehicle for the agricultural industry, supplying customers nationwide and even exporting to Canada and Australia. Mr. Marshall was elected Provost (civic head) of Maybole and served in that capacity from 1888 till 1893. He was one of twenty-two men of substance from Maybole and district who were present at the inaugural meeting of Turnberry Golf Club in April, 1902. By his own admission he was *'no golfer'*, but he must have been well regarded and was elected the Club's first Captain at the first general meeting of the Club on 23rd May 1902, and *'undertook to do everything in his power to further the Club's interests'*. He held office until 19th May 1906, his period in office coinciding with the initial period in the his-

John Marshall of Laurelbank, Maybole, the first Captain of Turnberry Golf Club 1902-1906 and Provost of Maybole 1888-1893

tory of Turnberry when the course was owned and managed by the Marquess of Ailsa, before it was taken over by the Railway Company when the hotel was completed and opened for business.

The second Captain was Major Andrew Dunlop of Girvan who held office for a year from May 1906 until May 1907, followed by David Templeton who was Captain for a further year until May 1908. Richard Niven of Airlie House, Ayr, then took over and remained Captain for fourteen years until May 1922. He developed a good working relationship with the Railway Company and his period as Captain saw the Club develop in prestige and importance and reach many important landmarks in Turnberry's development. There was a major course alteration in 1909 to provide two full 18 hole courses for the first time; important professional and amateur tournaments were held; and the Club and courses survived the disruption of the First World War. Captain Niven offered to stand down in 1920 but was unanimously re-elected on that occasion. He was a native of Glasgow but lived most of his life in Ayr. He was also a member of Prestwick Golf Club and had many other interests. He held many offices in local organisations including being President of Ayr and Alloway Agricultural Curling Club between 1901 and 1911, President of Ayr Burns Club, President of Ayr Primrose League, President of Ayr Conservative Club and President of Ayrshire Gardeners' Mutual Improvement Association. His garden at Airlie House had and still has one of the finest collections of herbaceous plants and shrubs in the county. His knowledge of horticulture came in useful at Turnberry when he was able to advise on treatment for greens and fairways. He was obviously a remarkable and outstanding captain, and his tenure of office covered a period when the reputation of Turnberry was greatly enhanced from the tournaments held. He saw the Club through the war years and demitted office after seeing Turnberry and the Club rise again stronger than ever, after holding their second British Ladies' Championship in 1921. His service to the Club was recognised after five years in office, when a complimentary dinner in his honour was held in the hotel on 17th August 1912. When he demitted office in May 1922, a presentation was made to him from a fund collected by voluntary subscription advertised in the *Glasgow Herald, Ayr Advertiser* and *Carrick Herald*, and in 1923 he was made an honorary life member.

Chapter II - The Club's Early Years

Open Professional Tournament 1908

The Turnberry links first achieved prominence in June 1908 when a remarkable professional tournament was held there. It had originally been intended to hold such a tournament to coincide with the opening of the palatial hotel by the Glasgow and South Western Railway Company two years earlier. The project was delayed however in order to secure a better entry to the tournament.

Club to organise the Tournament

The Company proposed to the Club that it would provide the prize money of £100 if the Club would *'take the tournament in hand and carry it through'*, and this was readily agreed. The Railway Company indicated that the hotel could not undertake the catering and a company from Ayr was hired to cater for members, players and the general public. Press facilities were set up at Turnberry by arrangement with the G.P.O., Edinburgh. Members of Turnberry and also from Troon and Prestwick Golf Clubs, were recruited to act as markers and stewards. Police Captain McHardy of Ayr was asked to provide a sufficient staff of police, namely 12 constables, for the two days of the competition. The Railway Company agreed to meet the cost of all these arrangements and the scene was thus set for the big event.

Many Open Champions in the Field

The Open Championship was due to be held that year at Prestwick in the week succeeding the Turnberry tournament and no doubt this helped in attracting a strong field to the Turnberry tournament. Although Braid, Taylor, Vardon and White were unable to take part, all the other leading professionals of the time were present.

1. W. Fernie.
2. H. Vardon.
3. J. Baird.
4. J. Taylor.
5. C. H. Mayo.
6. A. Simpson.
7. J. White.
8. A. Herd.
9. A. Kirkaldy.
10. B. Sayers. Junr.
11. J.H. Taylor.
12. A. Massy.
13. G. Duncan.

Most of the great golfers of that time shown above took part in the Turnberry Tournament in 1908.

HISTORY OF TURNBERRY GOLF CLUB

Chapter II - The Club's Early Years

The entry included the Frenchman Arnaud Massy of La Boulie, France, who was the reigning Open champion, having won at Hoylake in 1907, and having previously finished fifth at St. Andrews in 1905, sixth at Muirfield in 1906, and was subsequently to finish second at Sandwich in 1911 after a play-off with Harry Vardon. The field also included Tom Ball of West Lancashire who was to be runner-up in the 1908 Open at Prestwick, Willie Fernie of Troon who had won the Open back in 1883 at Musselburgh, Sandy Herd of Musselburgh the Open champion at Hoylake in 1902, George Duncan of Hanger Hill, who was to win the Open at Deal in 1920, and Ted Ray of Ganton, who was to win at Muirfield in 1912. Thirty six holes were to be played each day, the first round starting at 10.00 a.m. and the second at 1.30 p.m., with an interval of only four minutes between games, played in pairs – golf at the gallop indeed!

Massy beats the Field and the Weather

Duncan raised the hopes of the Scottish supporters with a fine 72 in the first round and this score was never bettered throughout the tournament. However it was reported that ill luck befell him at the start of his second round, although the nature of this was not specified. This took the heart out of him and at no time after that did he look like winning. Massy, as he had done at Hoylake, played magnificently in spite of very difficult conditions of wind and rain. The inward half of the course was much longer than the outward and had to be played into a strong head wind. Many a card showed 10 strokes or more of a difference between the scores for the two nines. Massy overcame the gale however with the power of his shots with the wooden clubs and, after Duncan's collapse in the second round, he led all the way, getting home by one shot from Tom Ball. Ball had a fine finishing round of 74 and was the only player to break 80 in all four rounds. He missed sinkable putts on each of the last two greens, or he might have forced a tie. In the absence of Lord and Lady Ailsa who had been invited but declined to present the prizes, they were presented by the Turnberry Club Captain, Richard Niven. The leading scores and prize money were:-

First	Arnaud Massy	(La Boulie)	(£40)
	75 74 79 80 = 308		
Second	Tom Ball	(West Lancashire)	(£20)
	79 77 79 74 = 309		
Third	Alex Herd	(Huddersfield)	(£10)
	77 78 81 77 = 313		
Fourth	Willie Fernie	(Troon)	(£5)
	81 78 80 77 = 316		
Fifth	E. Ray	(Ganton)	(£4.3s.4d.)
	81 75 88 73 = 317		
Special prize for best single round -			
	George Duncan (72)		(£5)

Golf Illustrated reported that *'at the presentation of prizes both Massy and Tom Ball declared it was one of the best links they had seen, and that is the opinion of all good players who have had a round over it. As the green becomes better known it is certain to increase in popularity. The situation is admirable; the air is bracing, and the locality is historically interesting, while all the most fastidious can desire in the way of creature comforts is to be found in the beautifully appointed Railway Hotel'.*

Turnberry was subsequently to host many more major professional and amateur tournaments but this first one set a very fine standard both in respect of the play and the organisation, and put Turnberry firmly on the map of championship courses.

SCOTTISH PROFESSIONAL GOLF CHAMPIONSHIP 1911

In June 1911 the fifth annual championship meeting of Scottish professional golfers was held at Turnberry, under the auspices of the Scottish Professional Golfers Union. The arrangements for the tournament were in the hands of Robert McConnell, Turnberry Golf Club Secretary, and Kenneth Henderson, the Secretary of the S.P.G.U. Glasgow and South Western Railway Company contributed £30 as a prize fund.

Tom Fernie the Favourite

There was an entry of 38 included among which was John Hunter of Prestwick, the winner in 1907, the first year of the championship, and R. Thomson, of North Berwick, the winner in 1908. Tom Fernie of Turnberry, the reigning champion, who had won at Montrose in 1909 and also at Lossiemouth in 1910, was favourite to win over his home course. The *Ayr Advertiser* reported that the weather on the opening day was oppressively hot and that the greens, being scorched and dry, were exceedingly tricky, making for remarkable ups and downs in the scoring from one round to another and much three and even four putting. R. Thomson, A. Kirkaldy and Ben Sayers led after the first round with 76 each, but only Thomson maintained his position and he finished second, two shots behind the winner, Edwin Sinclair from Leith, whose four round aggregate was 309. I. Kinnell of Prestwick St. Nicholas scored 75 in his last round, which was a course record for the new layout completed in 1909. Tom Fernie, the local professional disappointed his supporters, apparently due to erratic play through the green, pulling his drives and slicing his iron shots.

Surprise Winner

Edwin Sinclair's victory was a surprise, as he was not attached to any club and had never taken part in any important contest apart from competing in the Open Championship at St. Andrews in 1905. He had learned his golf at Leith Links but had emigrated to Australia in 1903 and worked out in the bush there until returning home only in February 1911. He was only one of two players in the field who scored under 80 in all four rounds, finishing with a 76, his best round, for a worthy victory. Sinclair's prize was £15, and the presentation was made by Sir John Bell of Montgreenan, Kilwinning, Ayrshire, who was introduced by Mr. Richard Niven, the Captain of Turnberry Golf Club. Sir John had been a member of the Club since 1903 and was a very prominent banker who had been the Lord Provost of Glasgow.

Early Score Card featuring a drawing of the young Tom Fernie, who became Professional at Turnberry in 1911 and who won the Scottish Professional Championship on four occasions, but not at Turnberry in 1911.

Chapter II - The Club's Early Years

Ladies' British Open Amateur Championship 1912

The Ladies Made Welcome

It was perhaps a happy coincidence or maybe it was in fact a clever strategy on the part of the Railway Company that it finally gave the Club permission to admit lady members in 1912, the year in which The Ladies' British Open Amateur Championship came to Turnberry for the first time. The first lady members were admitted in February 1912 and they must have been excited about the forthcoming championship to be held from 13th to 18th May. The match play championship itself was preceded by a preliminary stroke play competition and by ladies' international matches between teams from Scotland, England, Ireland and Wales. By November 1911 many arrangements had been made. The course was to be made available for practice by the competitors and for the international matches in the week preceding the championship. All competitors and the L.G.U. President, officials and members of the championship committee were to be made honorary members of the Club free of charge from 6th to 17th May inclusive. Non-competing lady members of any L.G.U. clubs were offered temporary membership of the Club for that period on payment of a green fee of five shillings. All gentlemen accompanying competitors were to pay the ordinary green fees – definitely a case of reverse discrimination! Exclusive use of the smoke room and adjoining dressing and drying rooms was to be given over to the ladies for the whole three week period.

Competitor in 1912 driving from the 17th tee still showing remnants of the wall which featured in the original course. Note the player's beautiful high follow through.

45

Club Prize

A championship committee was appointed to act with the L.G.U. championship committee, comprising Captain Niven, Secretary Mr. McConnel and Messrs. Willison, McCall and McCreadie, and 'the customary prize to the value of five guineas by the local club', was agreed upon. This prize was for the best scratch score for the medal round preceding the championship. There followed correspondence with the Railway Company as to who should fund this prize, the Club or the Company. Mr. Cooper, the general manager of the Company, did not think his Company could be expected to do so, but suggested, and the Club agreed, that it could be funded from the green fees of five shillings to be received from the lady members of L.G.U. clubs, subject to any surplus being given over to the Company, or any deficit being made good by the Club. Thus the difficulty was resolved by compromise, as has often since been the case, when problems inevitably arise in the relationship between the Club and the owners of Turnberry.

Entrants

The 118 entrants for the championship included several prominent players from abroad, amongst them Miss Nancy Parbury, the champion of Australia, Miss Florence Harvey, a former Canadian champion, Miss Mabel Thomson of New Brunswick and Miss E. Bauld of Halifax, Nova Scotia. There were also several former champions in the field including Miss Bertha Thomson who had won at Cromer in 1905 and Mrs. M. Ross of Royal Portrush who had won on three previous occasions when she played under her maiden name of May Heglet. Also entered were the sisters Leitch – no fewer than five of them – of whom Miss Edith and Miss Peggie were drawn against each other in the first round.

The championship had been won in 1909 and again in 1911 by a Scots lady, Dorothy Campbell, but she had emigrated to Canada and did not defend her title. It had also been won by another Scot in 1910, namely Mrs. E. Grant Suttie who was also a non-entrant on this occasion, and it had been five years in all since it had been won by an English lady. That was to be put right on this occasion when all four who reached the semi-final stage were English ladies and the winner was a worthy champion in Miss Gladys Ravenscroft of Bromborough. Miss Ravenscroft was 24 years of age and her first love at sport was hockey. However she abandoned that for golf at the age of 20. The *Ayr Advertiser* described her as being *'a typical example of the golfer girl, tall and of good physique, who quickly came to the front on the links'*.

Miss Gladys Ravenscroft, 1912 Champion, putting in the final against Miss Cecil Leitch. The referee is J. Laidlay who won the Amateur Championship in 1888 and 1891.

Chapter II - The Club's Early Years

She had distinguished herself the previous year at Portrush when she defeated Miss Cecil Leitch, who was fast becoming one of the best lady players of that era, and who subsequently won this championship on no fewer than four occasions. At Turnberry Miss Ravenscroft again beat Miss Leitch, this time in the semi-final by 1 hole and went on to beat Miss S. Temple, of Westward Ho, in the final, by 2 holes. The Club's prize for the preliminary stroke play competition was a pendant which was won by Miss Boyd of Westward Ho, with a scratch score of 85. The team championships were won by England, with Ireland second. The weather was fine for the semi-finals and final on the Friday and play was witnessed by a large gathering, amongst whom were the Marquess and Marchioness of Ailsa. Captain (later Major) Cecil K. Hutchison was another eminent spectator. He was a fine amateur golfer who represented Scotland on many occasions and reached the final of the British Amateur Championship at Muirfield in 1909 when he lost narrowly to Robert Maxwell. He served in the Coldstream Guards and played much of his golf in East Lothian and at St. Andrews. Later he worked as a golf course architect, helping James Braid in the construction of Gleneagles and reconstructing the Ailsa Course at Turnberry before World War II.

Vote of Thanks

Afterwards the Club donated a sum of one half guinea to Ayrshire Constabulary in recognition of service rendered in 'keeping the course clear' during the championship. This presumably referred to crowd control on the links. Tom Fernie was thanked for his services at the 'Ladies Tournament' and for having the greens and course in fine condition. Captain Cecil K. Hutchison was elected to honorary membership of the Club in recognition of his eminence in the world of golf and of the assistance which he had rendered during the championship.

Both the Club and the owners of Turnberry came out of the staging of the event with credit, for it was a great success and enhanced the reputation of the course which had been substantially re-designed only three years previously, as described later in this chapter.

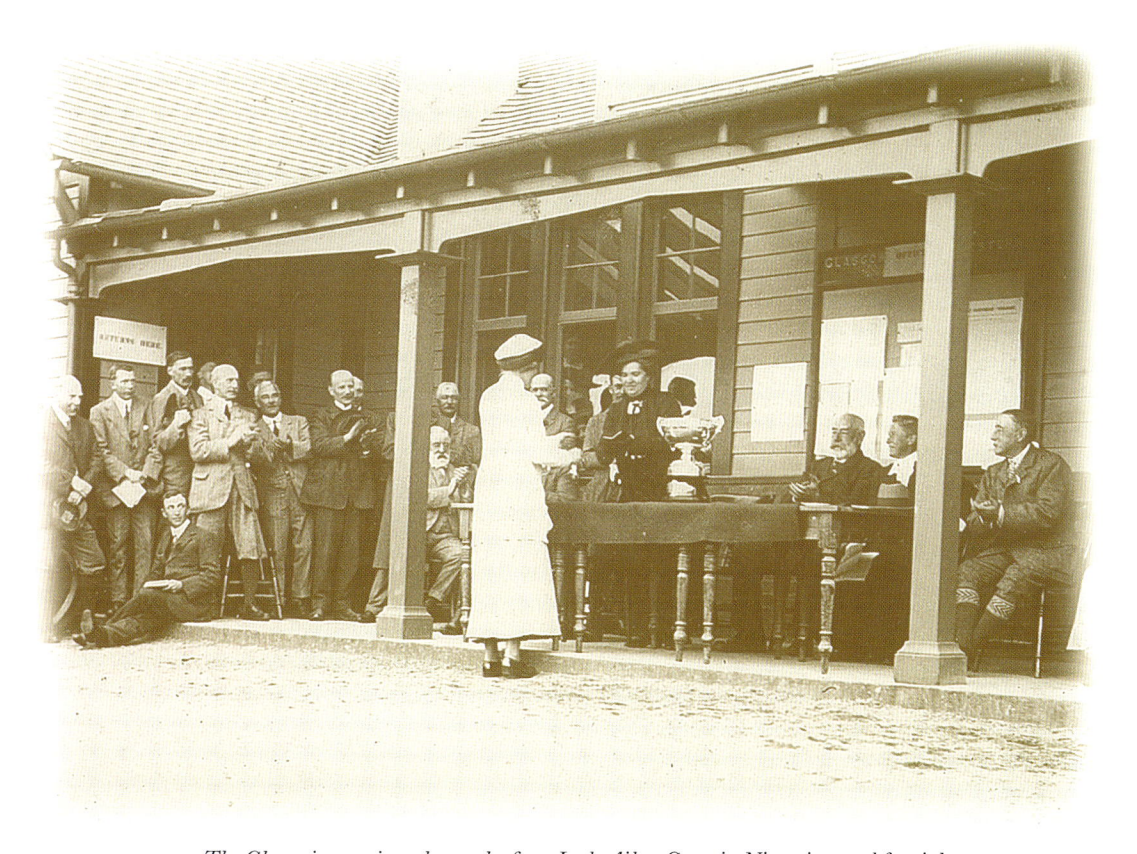

The Champion receives the trophy from Lady Ailsa. Captain Niven is seated far right.

INTERNATIONAL MATCH AT TURNBERRY 1914

In 1914 a memorable international match was held at Turnberry between England, represented by Harry Vardon of South Herts and J.H. Taylor of Mid-Surrey, and Scotland, represented by James Braid of Walton Heath and George Duncan of Hanger Hill. Remarkably it took place on a Saturday, the day after the conclusion of that year's Open at Prestwick.

The Open at Prestwick precedes the Match

The Open Championship at Prestwick that year was held in glorious weather and proved to be a fine sporting contest between Vardon and Taylor. Both of them had already won the championship on five occasions between the years 1894 and 1913, and in 1914 Vardon triumphed at Prestwick for his sixth and final win. At the presentation Taylor, in congratulating Vardon, spoke of his *'fine qualities as a man and as a golfer and conveyed the hearty congratulations of everyone in the professional ranks on his wonderful achievements'*. Such occasions and such men helped mould the best sporting traditions and fine personal conduct which were to become the hallmark of the sport of golf.

The Protagonists

James Braid had won the Open on five occasions between 1901 and 1910, and George Duncan, having been third in 1910 at St. Andrews and fourth at Muirfield in 1912, finally became Open Champion in the first championship after the war in 1920. So the match which took place at Turnberry in 1914 featured possibly the four finest golfers in the world at that time. Having played 36 holes each day at Prestwick on Thursday and Friday, the four great men moved down the coast to Turnberry and battled out a 36 hole international money match there on the Saturday. This was despite the fact that Vardon was reported to dislike playing 36 holes a day because his method of striking the ball was so accurate and repetitive that it inevitably meant that he landed in divot holes he had created in the morning! When Sam Snead heard the same tale about Ben Hogan, he said *'if Hogan was so smart, why didn't he land the ball two inches to the left of the morning divot?'* Whatever the truth or otherwise of such claims the members of Turnberry Golf Club must certainly have relished witnessing the contest in 1914, and the *Ayrshire Post* reported the match as follows:-

'The four great professionals, Vardon, J.H. Taylor, Braid and Duncan, visited Turnberry on Saturday and took part in two international matches, Vardon and Taylor representing England and Braid and Duncan Scotland. The English pair were beaten in a four-ball match in the morning by 4 holes up and 2 to play, and a foursome after luncheon was halved after a great struggle. It was by no means a pleasant day for golf; a strong wind and intermittent showers made matters distinctly uncomfortable for players and spectators alike. A large 'gallery', however, followed the play, and there was rejoicing in the Scottish camp when Braid and Duncan won in the morning. Turnberry is one of the most picturesque links on the west coast of Scotland, and, considering that there had been hardly any rain in the district for a month or so, the course was in beautiful condition. The four-ball match was very even to the turn; the Scotsmen won the 3rd hole and the rest of the holes were halved. The Englishmen were still 1 down with 8 to play, but they played the next few holes very indifferently, and Duncan and Braid won on the 16th green. The winners had an approximate better ball score of 69 to the losers one of 76. Braid and Duncan certainly played better golf than Vardon and Taylor, neither of whom had quite recovered from the tremendous strain of their great duel in the Open Championship on Friday, though indeed it was somewhat surprising that, in the circumstances, they played as well as they did. After luncheon, Vardon and Taylor played splendidly in the foursome for the first 10 holes, at which point they stood 3 up, but they lost the next 3 holes. They won the 14th, however, in a brilliant 3, and

Chapter II - The Club's Early Years

the next 3 holes were halved, but Braid came to the rescue of Scotland by holing a long putt on the last green and squared the match. Braid and Duncan had an approximate score of 78, and Vardon and Taylor 79.'

When Tom Watson won the Open at Turnberry in 1977, it was the second of five wins he was to achieve. Perhaps the ghost of Vardon returned to Turnberry to watch that victory. Watson however was not destined to go on to match the six victories of Vardon, the only golfer ever to achieve that feat.

Snow capped Arran peaks and lighthouse from behind 14th Ailsa green

Course Changes Prior to the Great War

Alterations in 1906

Willie Fernie's course layout was not destined to last long and indeed Turnberry was to be subject to numerous changes to its layout over the years. By 1906 the first major changes had taken place. The *Ayrshire Post* reported in May 1906 that a new 9 hole ladies' course had been laid out the previous winter under the supervision of the Railway Company's professional, Mr. A.N. Weir, with holes ranging in length from 156 to 285 yards. This was situated to the south of the 18-hole course, and was described as having excellent turf with sub-soil of pure sand, permitting the comfortable playing of a round after the heaviest rains. It was also reported that the main course had been considerably improved and could now be claimed as one of the finest and longest in the West. No plan of this 1906 layout is available but there is available a plan showing the layout of the ladies' course, and of the 18-hole course as at March 1908. It seems likely that this plan shows the new 1906 layouts and the names, lengths, and details of the holes of the 18 hole course were as follows:-

(1) <u>AILSA CRAIG</u> 301 yards. Par 4. From a tee close to the road beside the old clubhouse which was demolished

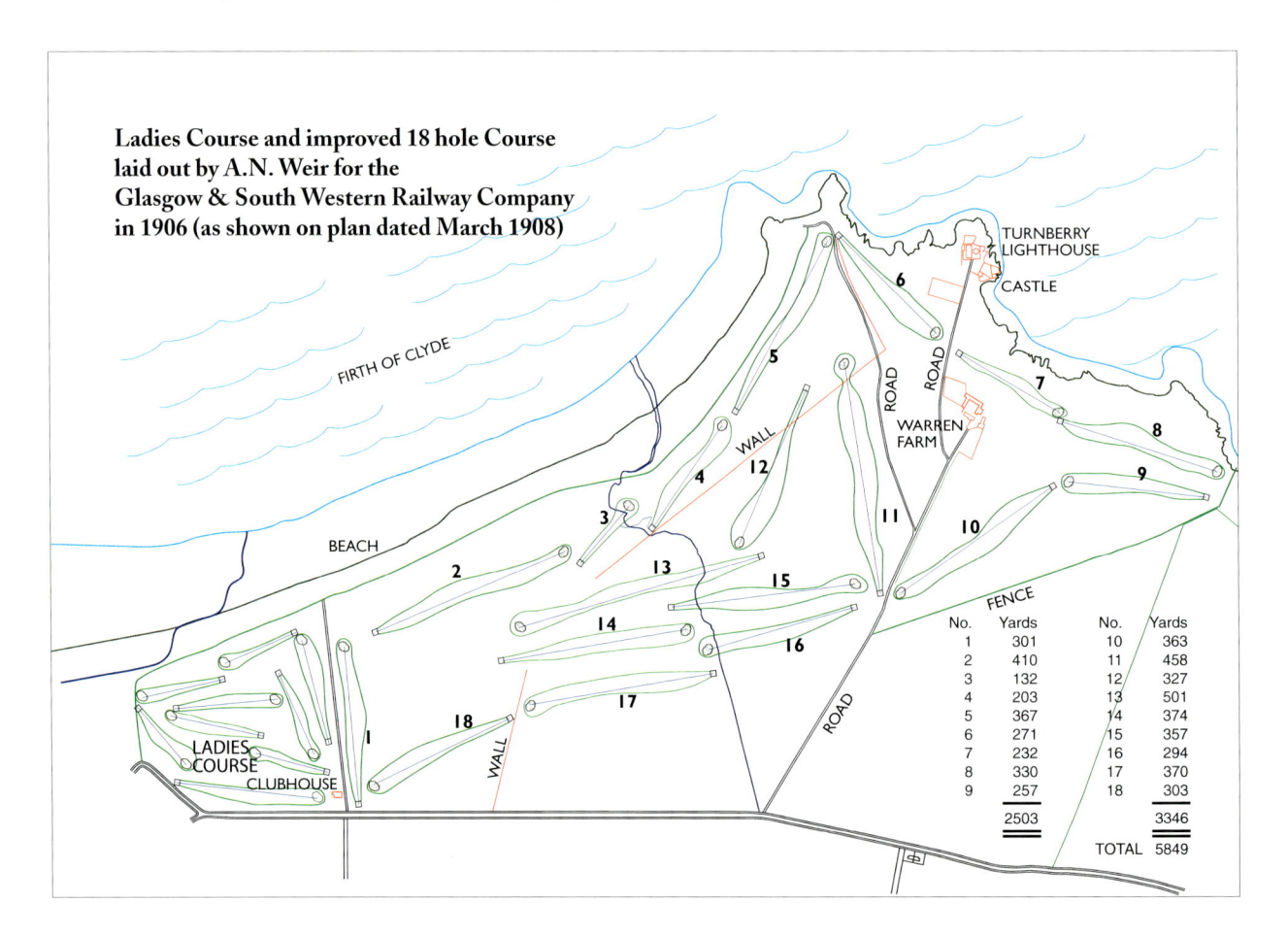

Ladies Course and improved 18 hole Course laid out by A.N. Weir for the Glasgow & South Western Railway Company in 1906 (as shown on plan dated March 1908)

No.	Yards	No.	Yards
1	301	10	363
2	410	11	458
3	132	12	327
4	203	13	501
5	367	14	374
6	271	15	357
7	232	16	294
8	330	17	370
9	257	18	303
	2503		3346
		TOTAL	5849

in 1993, it was played towards the sea across what are now the 1st, 2nd and 3rd fairways of the present Ailsa Course and then over a huge bunker, to a green situated about halfway down what is now the 5th fairway.

(2) SPION COP 410 yards. Par 4. From a tee just to the north of the Ailsa Craig green the tee shot had to be played blind over the high ground now occupied by 18th and 6th medal tees of the Ailsa Course to a green on the low ground on the inland side of the present 6th green, close to the present 17th fairway. A deep depression in the rough, which is still there, was probably a greenside bunker for this hole.

(3) PUDDOCK 132 yards. Par 3. This short hole appears to have been a blind hole to a green nestling in the curve of Wilson's Burn close to the landing area of drives from the present 7th tee. The tee was near the Spion Cop green, requiring a blind tee shot over the high ground.

(4) BENTS 203 yards. Par 3. From a tee inland of Puddock green beside a stone wall this hole required a blind tee shot to a green in the large hollow in front of the present championship tee for the 8th hole.

(5) WHAUP 367 yards. Par 4. This was similar to the present 8th hole but played from what is now the forward tee, to a green short and right of the present 8th green.

(6) LIGHTHOUSE 271 yards. Par 4. This hole was played from a tee in the area of the present forward tee for the 9th hole to a green just short of the lighthouse road, on what is now the 9th fairway.

(7) BRUCE'S CASTLE 232 yards. Par 4. Played from a tee situated on the north side of the lighthouse road opposite the Turnberry Castle to a green on the high ground of the present 10th fairway before it dips down to the present island bunker.

(8) JOHN O'GROATS 330 yards. Par 4. Played from a tee on the high ground of the present 10th fairway to a green approximately in the area of the present 11th green.

(9) BRAID SANDS 257 yards. Par 4. From a tee near the present 12th tee to a green in the area of the furthest bunker on the left of the present 12th fairway.

(10) WARREN 362 yards. Par 4. From a tee near the previous green to the area of the present 13th green.

(11) TURNBERRY 458 yards. Par 4. Very much the same as the present 14th hole but played over a stone wall across the front of the green.

(12) WALL 327 yards. Par 4. From a tee close to the present 15th green in the direction of the hotel to a green short of the burn to the west of the fairway of the 17th hole on the new Kintyre course. A stone wall had to be driven over from the tee.

(13) BURN 501 yards. Par 5. From a tee about 100 yards north of the burn on the 17th fairway of the new Kintyre course to a green near the landing area of drives from the 18th tee of the new Kintyre course.

(14) CARRICK 374 yards. Par 4. From a tee near the 18th tiger tee of the Ailsa course back to a green near the 8th green of the Academy course.

GLASGOW AND SOUTH-WESTERN RAILWAY.

THE TWO

Turnberry Golf Courses

HAVE BEEN REMODELLED UNDER EXPERT ADVISERS.

Length of No. 1 Course, 6,115 yards.
Length of No. 2 Course, 5,115 yards.

TURF UNEQUALLED ANYWHERE!

Convenient Train Service.

GLASGOW, ST. ENOCH STATION,
May, 1909.

DAVID COOPER,
General Manager.

and incorporating three new holes on the area previously occupied by the ladies' course. The new No. 2 course was constructed for the most part on the more landward and flatter portion of the land. The *Glasgow Herald* article gives a detailed description of each course and, in particular, describes the first four holes as follows:-

> *'Three fine holes have been found on the ground formerly occupied as the ladies' links. The first calls for a drive and brassey – unless for the great sloggers, who might reach the green with an iron. The second over nicely undulating ground, lies northwards, while the third is in the same direction as the first, but requires two full shots, the green being near the boundary fence. Turning again to the North two long drives should on a calm day reach the green which has hitherto served for the first hole. Against a head wind a strong tee stroke will be required to carry the hill about 150 yards in front, and in any case the hole will oftener cost five than four strokes.'*

From this it can be seen that the fourth hole was played from about the present 4th tee but the tee shot had to be played over the plateau of the present 4th green to a fairway beyond and then to a green in the valley of the present 5th fairway situated about opposite the present fairway bunkers. The 5th hole was played from new tees in the high rough ground to the left of the present 5th fairway, and the flat terracing of these can still be seen. It was played with a drive over the high ground (now occupied by the 6th and 18th tees), and then with a full shot to a new green on the high plateau near the sea (on the position of the present 6th green). The old Puddock was then played from a new tee on that plateau, as the 6th hole, and that is the hole as depicted in the painting by Drummond Fish which belongs to the Club and is displayed in the gallery of the new clubhouse. The credit for the superb siting of the present 6th green, therefore, can be awarded to A.N. Weir, the first professional, any reference to whom has often been absent from previous histories of Turnberry. At that time a substantial bridge had to be built between the new plateau green and the tee for 'Puddock', as there was a deep valley intervening.

This green was situated in the deep hollow now in front of the back tee for the 8th hole of the Ailsa course. It served as the 4th green on the original Fernie course, then became the 7th on the Weir course of 1909, but was abandoned in Hutchison's layout in 1938. This photograph shows it being played during the Ladies' British Open Amateur Championship in 1921

Chapter II - The Club's Early Years

Names of Holes of 1909 Layout

A full list of the names is not available but some of the old names survived and some new ones were added. The first three holes were new and were named respectively 'Step Ends' (an old name for the road junction just south of the course), 'Carrick Knowes' (a reference to the hilly terrain) and 'Land's End' (presumably because the green was situated at the southern west end of the course). The new fifth hole was called 'The Plateau' and the seventh in a big hollow became 'The Punchbowl'. The eighteenth remained simply 'Hame', (the Scots version of 'Home').

1962 photograph before new clubhouse, spa and golf academy were built and showing layout of 1st hole and closing holes of old Arran Course.

THE WAR YEARS

War Clouds Threaten

At the Annual General Meeting of the Club held on 15th May, 1915, it was reported as follows:- that the improvement to both courses had been steadily maintained and that they were in splendid order; that there was for the first time in the Club's history, a debit balance for the year, amounting to £66-14/- attributed to the loss of income arising from war conditions; that all club competitions had been cancelled on the outbreak of war and prize money of £12-1-6d. had been allocated to the relief of war distress, and that the Professional Tom Fernie had been at the front since Autumn 1914 and during his absence his place had been taken by his brother Harry. The committee minutes disclose that there was anxiety about meeting the Club's financial obligations to Glasgow and South Western Railway Company, as owners of the course. However an arrangement was made with the Company for such payments as were possible to be made, with any balance to be remitted as soon as the Club was in a position to do so after the war.

Despite the war the Club at first continued to function as normally as possible and as at 30th April, 1915, there were 234 gentlemen members and 54 lady members. At the Annual General Meeting held on 13th May, 1916, it was reported that the Professional Tom Fernie had been seri-

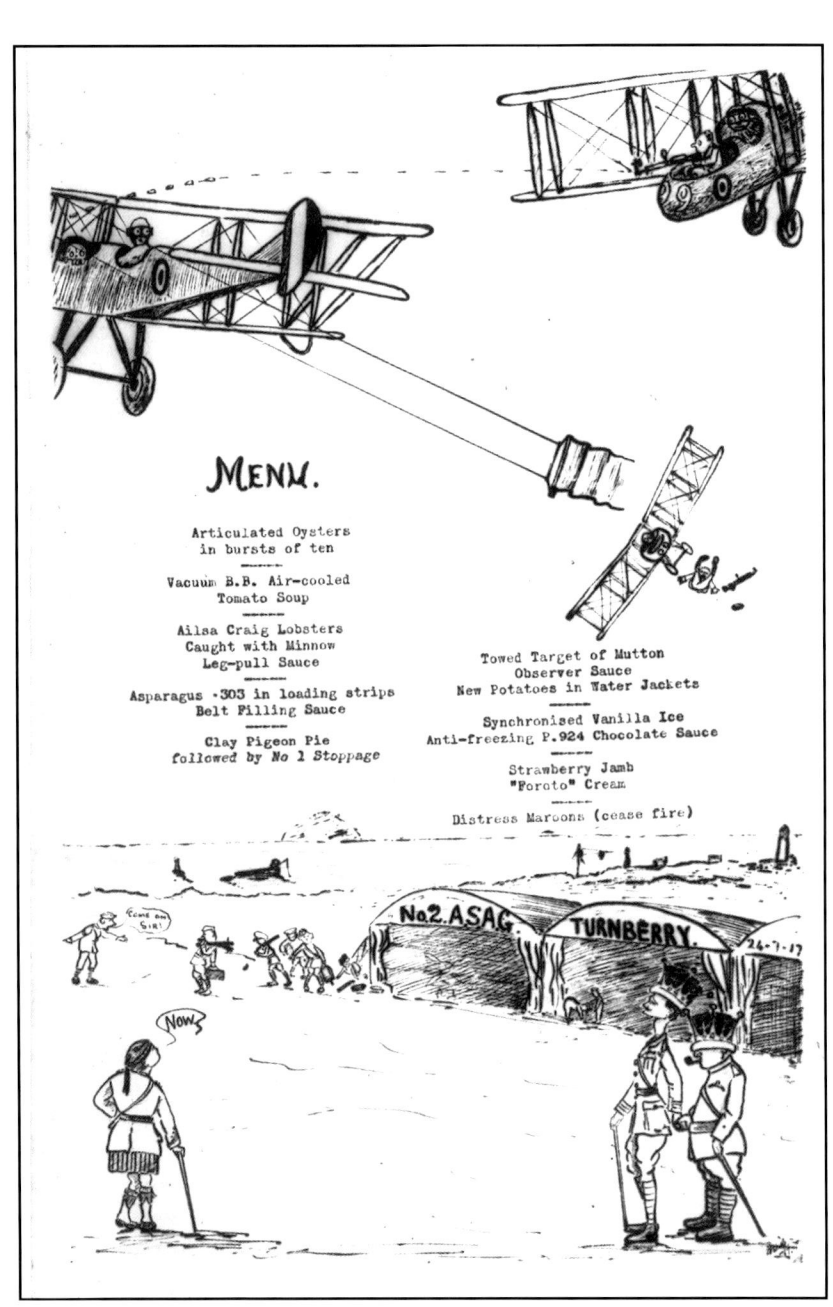

Menu of dinner of Auxiliary School of Aerial Gunnery held in Turnberry Hotel, July 1917

56

Chapter II - The Club's Early Years

ously wounded in France in early 1915 but, thankfully, was making satisfactory progress to recovery. It was proposed 'that members of the Club on active service should not be called upon to pay their subscription when serving with the colours', and this was carried unanimously. However the courses were beginning to suffer due to privations of both labour and materials caused by the war. In June 1916 Captain Niven, being a renowned amateur horticulturist, and having studied the problems, came up with some recommendations to the owners as to the following treatments which might be tried:- *A mixture of horse litter, loam and sand for top dressing; a liquid mixture of 1 to 6 parts strong sulphuric acid to water for treating fog [an undesirable coarse grass] on the greens; and either 'kiln culms' from a brewer or 'malt cummins' from a distiller as a Spring top dressing'* [waste products from beer brewing and whisky distilling].

Turnberry becomes a Flying School

However it was the war and not ingenious fertilizers which were to determine the immediate future condition of Turnberry, for in December 1916 the War Department intimated that they proposed to take over the golf courses and clubhouse, and members were asked to remove their clubs and personal belongings immediately. The clubhouse was to be used for office accommodation and as lecture and instruction rooms, with the lockers being used as *'receptacles for machine guns'!* The hotel was also requisitioned and used as an officers' mess and quarters. For the rest of the duration of the war Turnberry and the golf courses became a flying school to train pilots and observers in aerial gunnery. The personnel were mostly young volunteers recruited from other branches of the armed forces. Powered flight was in its infancy, the first flight by Orville Wright having taken place only in 1903, a mere 11 years before the war started. The planes based at Turnberry were mostly single seater fighters with open cockpits and constructed of wooden or metal frames covered with canvas. At first their only armaments were pistols carried by the pilots or shotguns carried by observers in a second cockpit. Later machine guns were mounted on top of the fuselage, but there were problems about hitting the propeller blades if the gun was fired through their arc. Sometimes, if a gun jammed, the pilot might have to stand up in the cockpit to loosen it, and if the plane banked suddenly he could easily topple out. The brave young volunteers who flew these planes knew the enormous risks involved and one such was Major J.B. McCudden who came through the ranks and earned V.C., D.S.O. and Bar, M.M. and Croix de Guerre. He was a pioneer of aerial fighting and, on operational rests from active service, he is known to have served as an instructor at Turnberry. More than 60 members of the Royal Flying Corps, who included recruits from Europe, America and Canada, lost their lives in the course of training at Turnberry during the First World War and a memorial to those who died during this period was erected on a hill overlooking the 12th Green of the Ailsa Course in 1922. After the war in 1919 the Club arranged an exhibition match between George Duncan, who was subsequently to win the Open Championship in 1920, and Tom Fernie, the Club Professional, who had just won the Scottish Professional Championship for the third time. The Club met the cost of staging the event and a collection was taken from the spectators towards the cost of the war memorial. Recent research for a book shortly to be written on Turnberry's

Crashed Bristol M.I.c single seater plane with open cockpit - Turnberry School of Aerial Gunnery 1918.

57

war-time events by Mrs. Margaret Morrell has revealed however that many names have been omitted. Hopefully this will be rectified sometime in the future.

Courses and Club Re-open

There was much resultant damage to the golf courses, but fortunately the aircraft were light and operated off grass air strips on the flatter land away from the coast, and it was possible after the war to resurrect the courses within a comparatively short time. When the war ended the Club committee reconvened in February 1919 and Captain Niven paid tribute to the several members of the Club who *'had made the supreme sacrifice'*. The Secretary reported the names of members who had died on war service were Ralph Creyke, Ralph Dubs, John Lees, William H. Graham, Hugh Wallace, Robert Inglis Junior, David Inglis and Charles Inglis. The Railway Company agreed to write off a debt of £46-2-7d. due by the Club and the Club relinquished a claim for compensation for three and a half lost playing months in Season 1916/17, in view of this 'handsome' treatment by the Company. The clubmistress Miss Robson was demobilised from the armed forces and she was re-employed at 30/- per week, a 50% increase on her pre-war wage, to take account of the higher cost of living. Tom Fernie returned as professional, having survived the war and his injuries. Number One course was re-opened in mid-April 1919 but, owing to an exceptional drought the condition of the greens rendered it impossible to hold the usual competitions that year. Nevertheless the Club showed its confidence in the future by recommending the Railway Company to offer the course for the Ladies' British Open Amateur Championship in 1920. Turnberry was back in business after its first disruption by war. It was to be another twenty years before the next such military disruption, but that was to prove a much bigger threat to the future of Turnberry as a golf course.

Participants in 1919 exhibition match at Turnberry to raise funds for war memorial for the airmen who lost their lives at Turnberry. On the left are Gordon Lochhart, an outstanding amateur and George Duncan, the Open Champion of 1920. Centre James Ferguson, the referee. On the right Tom Fernie of Turnberry, the reigning Scottish Professional Champion and Abe Mitchell a notable professional who had several high finishes in the Open

Chapter II - The Club's Early Years

Snippets from the Club Minutes in Historical Context - 1892-1919

August 1892	Meeting at the lighthouse of gentlemen favourable to the formation of a Golf Course at Turnberry Castle.
August 1892	Parliament reconvenes with Gladstone as Prime Minister and Keir Hardie takes his seat as first Labour M.P.
September 1899	The Glasgow and South Western Railway Company are authorised by the Railway Commissioners to build a railway line from Ayr to Girvan via Turnberry.
May 1900	Relief of Mafeking.
June 1900	Third Marquess of Ailsa makes an agreement with Glasgow and South Western Railway Company to provide a site for a hotel at Turnberry and for the provision of a golf course on Turnberry Links.
December 1900	Lord Ailsa commissions Willie Fernie of Troon to lay out a golf course at Turnberry.
July 1901	Formal opening of important new golf links at Turnberry under auspices of Girvan Golf Club.
December 1901	Marconi sends messages across the Atlantic by wireless telegraph.
April 1902	Turnberry Golf Club formed at a meeting in the Town Hall, Maybole, convened by R.M. Nisbett and chaired by Thomas Smith, the Factor of the Marquess of Ailsa.
April 1902	Sandy Herd wins Open with "Haskell" Rubber Ball at Hoylake.
May 1902	*Members could have the use of the railway waggon at present on the course until such time as a more suitable house should be erected.*
June 1902	Captain Marshall thanked the members of the Club for the honour they had conferred upon him in electing him Captain.
June 1902	Mr. Smith very kindly offered his office at the Castle for Committee Meetings.
July 1902	*Attention called to the lack of hooks and a pail for drinking water in the railway waggon serving as clubhouse.*
March 1903	*Agreed that the two clubs (Girvan and Turnberry) be amalgamated and that the members of the Girvan Golf Club be admitted members of the Turnberry Club.*
June 1903	First P.G.A. international match between Scotland and England at Prestwick.
April 1903	*The sketch for this Club Gold Medal was approved and the order given for Mr. Templeton to purchase it at a cost of about £7.*
June 1903	Temporary stable to be put up at early date.
June 1903	Harry Vardon wins the Open at Prestwick.
September 1903	Letter from Lord Ailsa to Club:- *'Dear Sir, I have received a letter from Mr. Cooper of G. & S.W. Railway Company, saying that the Pavilion at Turnberry is now finished and enclosing the key of the front door. Will you let me know when you propose opening it. Yours faithfully, Ailsa'.*
December 1903	Wright Brothers make first powered flight.

May 1904	Treasurer's financial statement shows the club to be in a *prosperous position notwithstanding the extra expense incurred in furnishing the Refreshment Department.*
June 1904	Jack White wins "Open" at Sandwich with total of 296 (first winning 72 hole total under 300).
October 1904	*A letter from W.A. Templeton, Kirkoswald, was read refusing to accept his prize won at the Golf Medal Meeting, as he had infringed the rule as to a lost ball.*
March 1905	*Letter read from Mr. Cooper stating that the Railway Company would take over the Golf Course on the completion of their railway.*
May 1905	*It was agreed to reduce the price of whisky sold in the clubhouse to 5p. per glass, Walker's whisky excepted; and to stock a quantity of Perrier Mineral Water.*
June 1905	James Braid wins "Open" at St. Andrews with total of 318.
July 1905	*Agreed to provide cored balls as prizes for medals.*
April 1906	San Francisco laid waste by earthquake.
May 1906	Robert McConnell of Girvan elected Secretary of Turnberry Golf Club.
July 1906	*Agreed that a golf bag rack be procured for the clubhouse, and offer of one with 12 spaces for supply, delivery and erection at a price of £1-12/6d. accepted from Messrs. Meikle of Ayr.*
October 1906	*52 applications for the post of club mistress were gone over, and Miss L. Robson of The Kennels, Culzean, was appointed.*
November 1906	Agreed to take the *Sphere, Illustrated London News, Nisbett's Golf Year Book* and *The Golfer's Handbook and Year Book* for the use of members.
January 1907	*Agreed meantime to drop consideration of installing electric light and the telephone into the clubhouse.*
May 1907	*Names to be published in clubhouse of members in arrears with subscription and struck off list.*
June 1907	Arnaud Massy wins 'Open' at Hoylake with total of 312.
November 1907	Secretary authorised to purchase a *12 inch English dial clock of best quality'* with gift of two guineas from Thomas Adams.
March 1908	*Local rules framed and approved.*
April 1908	Railway Company offers special golfer's train fare of 1/8d. return from Maybole to Turnberry to help prevent Maybole members retiring.
September 1908	Wilbur Wright breaks world flight records, flying 40 miles in 1 hour 31 minutes.
December 1908	*Clubmistress instructed to have a hot joint every Saturday for luncheon, and not required to cook food brought by members on that day.*
October 1909	Complaint that handicaps prevailing at Turnberry are lower than at other clubs.
October 1909	Report of gross abuse of privilege of cheap green fees for hotel guests – by persons simply walking through the hotel to purchase tickets.
May 1910	*Tender of £1 accepted for a "temporary wooden erection for gentlemen" on the course during a tournament.*
August 1910	Dr. Crippen arrested on board ocean liner due to "wonders of telegraphy".
April 1911	Winner of Captain's Monthly Medal disqualified for being in arrears with his annual subscription.
January 1912	Captain Scott reaches South Pole.

Chapter II - The Club's Early Years

April 1912	*The Committee feel that they have sustained a severe blow in the loss of their Secretary (Mr. Robert McConnell) who, by his straight fowardness of character, able management and great tact had rendered himself invaluable to the Club.*
April 1912	Titanic sunk by iceberg.
May 1912	*Agreed to hold an annual dinner during the winter.*
June 1912	*Secretary instructed to write to Bryant & May, of London, asking for a number of their metal stands to be used in the smoking room of the clubhouse and ordering two gross of their 'Three Lion Matches'.*
March 1913	Agreed that 3 and 4 ball matches may start at any time of day but that such matches should be cautioned to allow 2 ball matches to play through.
May 1913	The Most Noble The Marquess of Ailsa and the Right Honourable The Earl of Cassillis, were by acclamation re-elected Hon. President and Hon. Vice-President respectively.
May 1913	*Agreed that rough ground be left from about 100 yards from teeing ground.*
June 1913	Agreed to purchase a clock for the starter box *'in order that the caddies might know the time without having to peer through the window of the clubhouse'.*
October 1913	*Suggested that a stamp for stamping golf balls should be purchased.*
January 1914	*Agreed to grant honorarium of three guineas to the Professional and two guineas to the Caddie Master.*
February 1914	*Reported that Club's offer to host a qualifying round for the Open was declined by Green Committee of Prestwick Golf Club, who thought it better for qualifying rounds to be played on courses more adjacent to Prestwick.*
May 1914	*Decided it would be desirable to provide 2 step ladders 10 feet and 9 feet long by 2 feet wide for the bunker guarding the 15th green.*
May 1914	Mrs. Pankhurst arrested at Palace Gates.
August 1914	Kitchener launches army recruitment campaign "Your Country Needs You".
September 1914	Tom Fernie sent to war front and all competitions cancelled.
November 1918	Armistice signed by Germany.
February 1919	First meeting of Committee after War.
April 1919	Number One course re-opened for play.
June 1919	Treaty of Versailles signed.

History of Turnberry Golf Club

Icon of Turnberry which appears so often on television that it is sometimes privately and humorously referred to by BBC cameramen as 'TBL' ('That Bloody Lighthouse').

View of the sea and rocks beside the lighthouse, which have to be carried from the back tee to reach the 9th fairway of the Ailsa course.

Chapter III

A Time For Golf - Then War Again

Captains and Characters, Ladies' Championships Galore,
Course Changes, then War threatens Extinction

Club Affairs and Course Changes

THE report of the management committee to the Club's A.G.M. in May 1920 stated:

'After being in suspension for over two years owing to the hotel and course having been taken over by the Royal Air Force, the Club resumed possession in April 1919. At considerable expense the clubhouse was restored to its former condition and No. 1 course has now almost recovered from the effects of its occupation by the military. The greater part of No. 2 course is also open for play. Club competitions were resumed last year.'

The Club was back in business. Existing and former members as well as many new members were anxious to enjoy their favourite sport over the beautiful links whose growing charms and reputation before the war had not been forgotten.

There had been no A.G.M.s or elections of new office bearers in the three years 1916 to 1918, and the existing office bearers continued during that period. The first A.G.M. after the war was held in May 1919 and Mr. Richard Niven was re-elected Captain and Lieutenant Colonel Dalrymple-Hamilton as Vice-Captain. Mr. M.J. Finlayson, who had been acting as interim Secretary, was appointed Secretary and Treasurer to replace Hugh F. McConnell of Girvan, who had died in February 1919, having been Secretary and Treasurer since October 1912.

Fun and Games at A.G.M.

At the A.G.M. in May 1920 there were some fun and games with regard to the appointment of Captain and Secretary/Treasurer. Captain Niven said he had received a *'hint'* that he should retire and he would only continue at the unanimous request of the members. His re-election was then proposed and, as there was no amendment, it was declared unanimous. Mr. Finlayson resigned as Secretary/Treasurer and it was decided that the post be advertised at a salary of £70 per annum, with preference to be given to an ex-service man. A volunteer to be interim Secretary was called for, but everyone *'refused point blank to have anything to do with it'* and Captain Niven said he would undertake the job until a new appointment could be made. The post was duly advertised, many applications were received and a short list of three was chosen by the Club Committee. At a Special General Meeting on 12th June 1920, Mr. William Andrew Templeton was elected by ballot *'having a considerable majority over the other two candidates combined'*.

Willie Templeton

'Willie', as he was always known, was from Ayrshire farming stock. He served in the First World War and sustained serious leg and lung injuries in France, which impaired his walking abilities. This did not prevent him playing golf with a respectable handicap and a reputation for being straight down the middle and he was also a keen and noted curler. He had originally intended to enter the legal profession but the war and his injuries

Willie Templeton - Club Secretary - old photo of him in uniform.

Chapter III - A Time For Golf - Then War Again

intervened and instead he went into business as a merchant and postmaster at the sub-post office in the small village of Kirkoswald, three miles from Turnberry. He was a Justice of the Peace, dispensing justice in the local court and he also dispensed his own brand of justice at Turnberry, especially to the younger members. Campbell Hicks, who joined the Club in 1938 as an 18 year old, recalls turning up at the Club with Donald Henderson, also a new member that year, to play in their first competition. On presenting themselves to Willie Templeton for inclusion in the early draw, they were advised that they would have to wait till the next draw and that, in the meantime, they would have time enough to buy a round of drinks. They were also warned that winners of competitions traditionally bought a drink for the company. In those days it was normal for competitors to gather in the clubhouse and wait for the winner to be announced, so winning could be an expensive business!

Willie Templeton remained Secretary and Treasurer of the Club travelling between his home in Kirkoswald and Turnberry each day, until his death in September 1951. His hard-working wife looked after the village store and post office during his absences. She also operated the local telephone exchange which, in the early days, was wholly manual, requiring the operator to receive and redirect every call to its destination. Willie served under four Captains and his time in office covered periods of crisis as well as many prestigious ladies' championships and the resurgence of Turnberry after the war. He would have been involved at the time of a major problem in the relationship between the Club and the hotel in 1929/30 and also in the traumatic days of the Second World War and the difficulties of starting the Club again after the war. His wife must very often have had to hold the fort for the family business in Kirkoswald without his assistance. After his death, at the Club's A.G.M. in March 1952, Captain Oliver Hughes-Onslow referred to the great loss the Club had sustained by his death after more than 30 years of faithful services given to the Club.

Captain North Dalrymple-Hamilton

In May 1922 Richard Niven stood down after 14 years service as Captain and his place was taken by Colonel North Dalrymple-Hamilton of Bargany, near Dailly, who had been Vice-Captain for 10 years. It was his father who had donated the Bargany Cup to the Club in 1909 for competition at Turnberry by members of Turnberry, Girvan and Ballantrae Golf Clubs. His term of office lasted until May 1925 and saw the Scottish Ladies' Championship held at Turnberry for the first of no fewer than seven times. It also saw a steep rise in membership numbers to an overall 462 in 1925, including 125 ladies. The applications for membership, particularly from ladies, continued to increase at this period and in May 1926 the Railway Company agreed that the limit on membership of the Ladies' Section could be raised to 150. Despite this, by January 1928 there was a waiting list for admission to the Ladies' Section, but an application to increase the limit to 175 was turned down by the Railway Company. The total number of members at April 1929 was 519 (including 150 ladies and 50 foreign members), probably the highest number in the history of the Club.

Sir John Richmond and Colonel Bogey

During 1924 Colonel North Dalrymple-Hamilton was in ill health, it being reported in May that he was receiving treatment in a nursing home in London. He did not attend many meetings that year but in May 1925 he presided at the A.G.M. and proposed as Captain, the person who had been his Vice-Captain from 1922 till 1925, Mr. J.R. Richmond, of Blanefield, Kirkoswald. Mr. Richmond was duly elected and remained Captain until March 1936. He was later knighted for services to industry and the arts. He also received many other honours during his lifetime and his full title became Sir John Ritchie Richmond (1869-1963) K.B.E., LL.D., C.B.E. He was the elder half-brother of the first Viscount Weir, Lord William Douglas Weir, and he was a director and vice-chairman of the world famous engineering company G. & T. Weir of Cathcart (today the Weir Group). Amongst his other offices was the Honorary Presidency of Glasgow School of Art. As Vice-Captain, in February 1923, he wrote to the Club and offered a prize *'in the form of a cup, a sum of money and possibly a set of clubs'*. The offer was gratefully accepted and the Richmond Cup is still played for today in the format of a handicap stableford competition. Initially, however, it was played for as a *'bogey'* competition. Younger readers and players may never have heard of this and to them a *'bogey'* is a score of one over par at a hole. This was not always so - originally *'bogey'* was another name for par, until our American cousins changed the usage. In a *'bogey'* competition each player was in effect playing a match over 18 holes against a fictitious opponent, often referred to as *'Colonel Bogey'*, who played off scratch and scored par at every hole. The player was given his usual handicap allowance in a match play game against the Colonel and the winner of the tournament was the player who finished most holes up (or least holes down) after playing the full 18 holes.

Sir John Richmond's captaincy covered a period of change in the relationship with the hotel. From the outset the Club had fixed its own annual subscription and it had remained at one guinea for 19 years from 1902 until 1921. From this, initially Lord Ailsa, and subsequently the Railway Company, received 80%, and the Club retained the balance. The 1914-18 War upset this stability in prices and constant inflation became the norm thereafter. In 1921 the Railway Company requested the Club to double the subscription to two guineas, but settled for one and a half guineas, representing a 50% increase. A year later its share of the take was increased to 85%, and in 1924 it was again increased, on that occasion to 87½%.

Crisis in Negotiations with Hotel

In 1928 there came a major crisis in the Club's relationship with the owners of the hotel, London, Midland and Scottish Railway Company (the successors of the original Glasgow and South Western Railway Company who had built the railway line and the hotel). Although the Railway Company had from the outset owned the site of the hotel and its grounds which they had purchased from Lord Ailsa, the links land occupied by the golf courses had remained in the ownership of Lord Ailsa. Instead of outright ownership, the Railway Company only had a legal servitude right to use the land as a golf course with the necessary clubhouse. So long as this situation subsisted the Company had been content to allow fairly generous terms to Turnberry Golf Club, of which Lord Ailsa was the Honorary President and his son the Earl of Cassillis, Honorary Vice-President. Until 1928 the Club had leased the clubhouse from the Railway Company and had furnished and managed it, employed the clubhouse staff and ran the dining room and bar. Visitors could only use the clubhouse with the Club's consent. Apart from the increase in 1924, annual subscriptions had remained fairly static and were collected by the Club, which passed on the agreed percentage to the Railway Company.

In 1928, however, Lord Ailsa obviously came to the conclusion that it was in his best interests to sell the land outright to the Railway Company and the Company intimated to the Club that the conditions under which the members of the Club had the use of the clubhouse and courses would not be renewed after 30th April 1928. The Club made representations to Lord Ailsa to intercede with the Company on its behalf and was advised by his factor, Mr. Smith, that his Lordship had done his best to safeguard the interests of the Club, but could do no more. The Club was left to make the best deal it could directly with the Company and at first the prospects looked bleak. The Company was determined drastically to alter the terms for the Club and there was much consternation and speculation as to whether or not the Club could continue to operate at all under the new terms. Under the new proposals in future the Company would levy a fee of their choosing on each annual ticket holder. Even more damaging the Club would no longer

Admiral Rose (left) - a founder member and Lord David Kennedy - Vice President of Turnberry Golf Club, at the 1921 Ladies' British Open Amateur Championship.

Chapter III - A Time For Golf - Then War Again

be entitled to retain a percentage of subscriptions, and would therefore have no source of income for prizes, expenses or administration. The Club's lease of the clubhouse was to end without any guarantee as to the use of its facilities or even a room in which to hold committee meetings or an office for the Secretary. The Club would cease to hold the liquor licence, as the Company was to apply for a licence in its own name and so there would be no revenue from the bar or from catering. The new annual subscription was to be fixed at £5-5/-, with a concessionary reduction initially to £3-3/- for existing members, but no guarantee of how long such concession would continue. Despite representations for a lower rate for ladies, the same subscription was to apply to both sexes *'in view of the fact that wear and tear on courses by ladies is no less than gentlemen'*, as the Railway Company stated. No guarantee was given that the new subscriptions would include free car parking.

At a Special General Meeting on 16th March, 1929, Captain Richmond posed the question as to whether the Club should dissolve, or carry on subject to at least 75 members being prepared to continue and to pay an annual levy of 5/- to meet expenses. Mr. S. Dunn moved that the Club continue and that a plebiscite of members be held to ascertain how many would be agreeable to join on the new conditions. Mr. Charles Hunter proposed an amendment that a history of the Club since it formation and suggestions for better terms be prepared and sent to Sir Josiah Stamp, President of the L.M. & S. Hotel Services, to ask for sympathetic consideration of the Club's interests. However the motion was carried by a large majority and the result of the plebiscite was that only 143 gentlemen and 59 ladies indicated their intention to continue as members under the new terms.

Club's Position Strengthens

Events fortunately then took an unexpected turn which placed the Club in a stronger bargaining position. The Company's application to the local Licensing Court for an *'Inn and Hotel'* licence for the clubhouse was refused. The Club Committee felt it necessary to make it clear to the Company that they had in no way tried to influence the magistrates against granting the application! However the presence of Club members on the bench may not have been an insignificant factor and the Court's decision meant that the Company was forced to rely on the Club's licence again, to ensure that hotel guests and visitors could be supplied in the clubhouse with alcoholic beverages. This was done through the legal expedient of making such guests and visitors temporary members of the Club and therefore eligible to drink under the licence of a private club. The legality may have been dubious but the effect of this manoeuvre on the negotiations certainly was not. The Company had just given the Club legal notice to quit their tenancy of the clubhouse, but had quickly to rescind this and grant the Club similar arrangements to those applying in previous years.

The Club continued to lease and run the clubhouse, catering and bar and retained 12 $\frac{1}{2}$ % of the annual subscriptions. Six free guest tickets to play the course were awarded to each member and free car parking for members was agreed. On the debit side the new rate of annual subscription had to be accepted and three members of the Company were elected to serve on the Club committee, including their general manager, Mr. Arthur Towle, and the resident hotel manager. One other significant change was the opening of the clubhouse on Sundays. Until then the Club had persisted in a policy of not encouraging golf on the Sabbath and closing the clubhouse on that day.

By 15th March 1930 all these arrangements were in place and, when Captain Richmond was re-elected at the A.G.M. on that date, tribute was paid to him for *'his ability, tact and courtesy having succeeded in preserving the privileges which the Club had enjoyed for many years and steering their barque through stormy and difficult times'*. In future years, as the numbers of hotel guests and visitors grew even greater, the legality of serving them liquors under the Club's licence came more and more into question and Mr. Robert Black, a future Captain and an Ayr lawyer, is reputed to have resigned his captaincy after less than a year, as a matter of conscience and principle over this very issue.

Turnberry's Importance for Ladies' Championships

On the tournament side Captain Richmond's term of office from 1925 to 1936 coincided with a remarkable run of ladies' championships at Turnberry. No fewer than four Scottish Ladies' Amateur Championships were held there during that period, in 1924, 1930, 1933 and 1936. A further three were held at Turnberry in

1939, 1954 and 1960, making seven times in all. Add to that the Ladies' British Open Amateur Championships held there in 1912, 1921 and 1937, and it is clear that Turnberry has been a very important venue for ladies' amateur golf. Captain Richmond played an important part in the arrangements for these events and, after eleven years as Captain, his services were recognised by the raising of a fund to finance either a complimentary dinner or a presentation. Members were asked to subscribe sums of no more than five shillings and a sufficient fund was raised to present him with a set of golf clubs and leave a surplus of £6. Captain Richmond asked that this be used as a prize fund for a golf competition amongst the caddies.

Captains and Vice-Captains

For six years from 1925 till 1931 Mr. Malcolm J. Finlayson held the office of Vice-Captain. Unfortunately the minutes do not reveal any of his personal details but he was obviously well liked by the members for it is minuted that they all regretted his decision not to seek re-election and expressed their thanks to him for his valuable services in many capacities. This is no doubt a reference to him having twice filled in as interim Secretary and Treasurer, once in 1912 and again in 1919/20. It must have been rather frustrating for him to give unstinting service over so many years, but never having the honour of being appointed Captain. In this regard it was obviously no reflection on his abilities or popularity, but rather due to the long service as Captain of the very outstanding and distinguished John Richmond. Mr. Finlayson's place as Vice-Captain was taken in 1931 by J.D. Hastings Forbes, a farmer of Jameston Farm, Maidens, whose land almost adjoined the golf courses. He served for five years under the captaincy of John Richmond until he decided to retire in 1936 along with him. The Club presented him with a small gift as a token of the members' appreciation of his services.

The year 1936 saw the election of Oliver Hughes-Onslow as Captain and he remained Captain of Turnberry Golf Club for 21 years until 1957. His first Vice-Captain was John Crawford, an ex-Provost of Maybole, and the owner of a company in that town which produced boots and shoes, including custom hand-made golf shoes. Mr. Crawford died in 1939 and William McCreath, an ex-Provost of Girvan, became Vice-Captain from then until 1951.

W.L. Hope – Scottish Internatiionalist

In the Club records there is a reference to the congratulations being offered to a member by the name of W.L. Hope, for being chosen to represent Scotland. Scottish Golf Union records show that he played for Scotland against England in 1923 and also in five successive years from 1925 to 1929. During those years these matches between Scotland and England were held at the venue for the Amateur Championship just prior to the start of the Championship. The Home Internationals involving all four home nations didn't start until 1932.

Course Changes between the Wars

During the years between the wars the golf courses saw substantial changes: No. 1 course, (subsequently to be renamed Ailsa course), had re-opened for play in 1919, and fairly quickly recovered from the war disturbance; No. 2 course, (later to be renamed Arran course), took somewhat longer to be brought fully back into play and its condition was less than satisfactory. However, whereas the layout of No. 1 course remained substantially unchanged for many years thereafter, No. 2 course was completely re-designed less than two years later and the new course opened for play in June 1923. The new No. 2 course was designed by legendary golf professional and golf course architect, James Braid, and laid out under the supervision of the Turnberry professional Tom Fernie. The *Ayrshire Post* reported that a feature of the new course was the excellent layout of the greens, which all had *'big sweeping wavy 'rolls' to make putting skilful and interesting'*, and this immediately brings to mind similar characteristics of the new greens on the present Kintyre course designed by Donald Steel, and opened in 2001. The Club minutes refer to the possibility of arranging a match involving Braid and Fernie to mark the opening of the new course in 1923 but no reports can be found as to whether or not this took place. The new course was constructed by Messrs. Carters of Raynes Park and it quickly grew more popular than No. 1 course with both visitors and members and even for championships. Some of the ladies' championships were held on it including the Ladies' British Open Amateur in 1937.

In 1926, when London Midland and Scottish Hotel

Chapter III - A Time For Golf - Then War Again

Group took over Turnberry from Glasgow and South West of Scotland Railway Company, management of Turnberry became the responsibility of David Tawle, who was a keen golfer. He was the man who named No. 1 course the *'Ailsa'* and No. 2 course the *'Arran'* and he recognised the potential of the Ailsa course to become a really exceptional championship venue. To this end he commissioned Major Cecil Hutchison, one of the designers of Gleneagles Hotel courses and an honorary member of Turnberry Golf Club since 1912, to re-design the Ailsa course. The two main aims were to eliminate blind shots and increase the length of the course. Hutchison's re-designed course was completed in 1938 and Bernard Darwin, in his book *Golf between the Wars*, gave it as his opinion that Hutchison had left the course *'as pretty and charming as he found it, but in a different class as a test of golf'*. His fourth hole was indeed formidable, measuring over 500 yards long and taking in the length and contours of the present 4th and 5th holes, played as one hole! However the Second World War and the disruption of converting Turnberry to a military airfield meant that Hutchison's course was almost still-born, and had little opportunity of being tested by time or championships. The Scottish Ladies' Amateur of 1939 was the only championship played over the redesigned course and Hutchison, having died in 1941, didn't live to see the new Ailsa which was resurrected after the war.

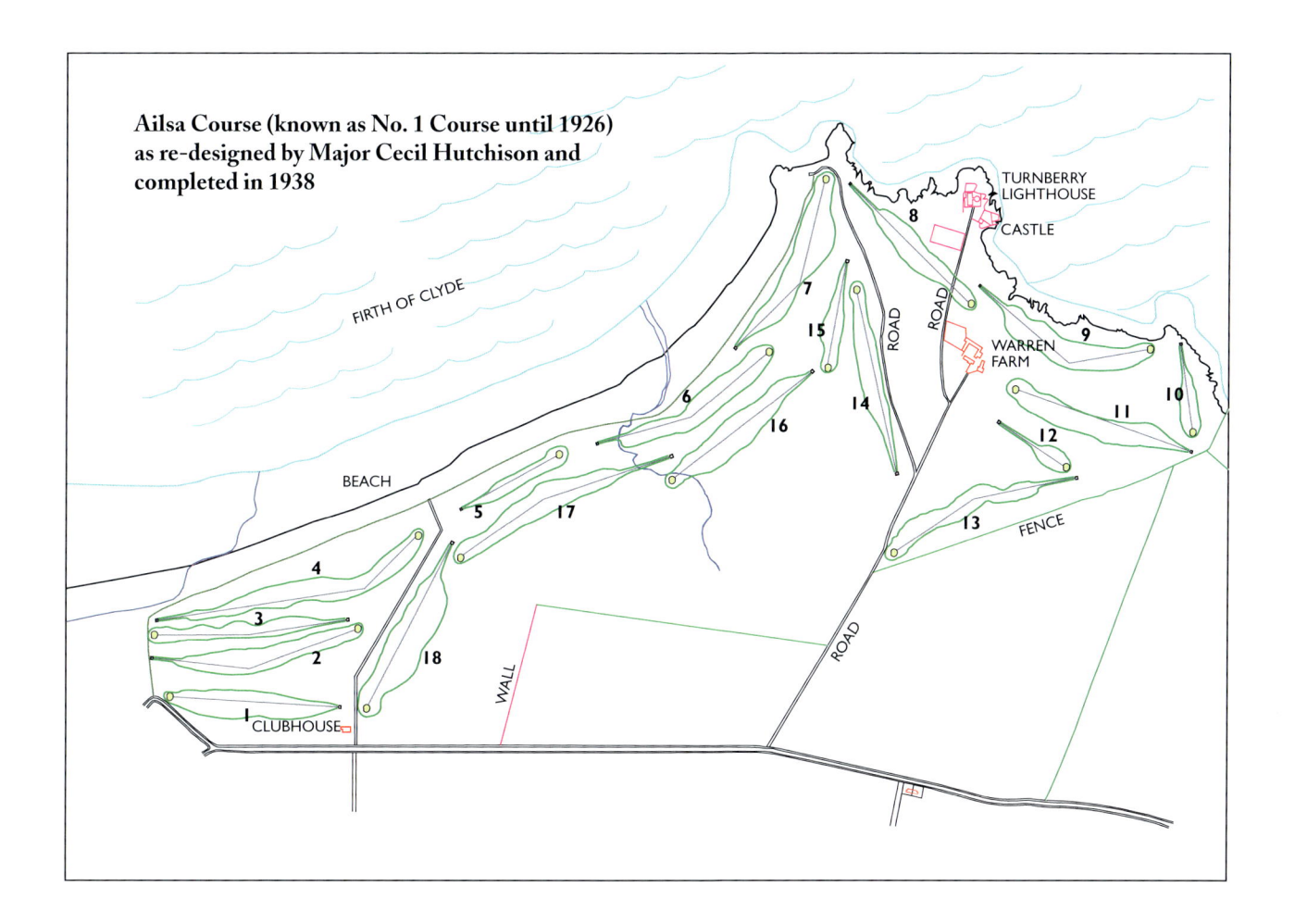

Ailsa Course (known as No. 1 Course until 1926) as re-designed by Major Cecil Hutchison and completed in 1938

Hutchison's Ailsa Course – Scorecard

Campbell Hicks, an honorary member of the Club, remembers being taken to Turnberry as early as 1936 when he was a boy of 15, by Jack Hunter and William Houston, two members from Maybole. He was allowed to walk the course with them and sometimes to play a few shots when the course was quiet. When they had finished their round he waited outside the clubhouse with a lemonade whilst the members refreshed themselves inside, no doubt with something a bit stonger. Campbell remembers Hutchison's layout of the Ailsa course well and has provided the score card of that course which is reproduced here. It shows a par of 80 and an overall length of 6615 yards, the outward half being particularly long at 3590 yards, and without a single par 3. All holes over 400 yards were classified as par 5s. At that time the stymie rule was still in force and the card is the exact width of the stymie measure of six inches. If the balls lay within that distance of each other on the green relief could be gained from the normal stymie rule of not being allowed to have an opponent's ball moved if it interfered with the line of a putt.

The names of the holes on the card show considerable changes from those of earlier layouts and for the first time the last hole was named 'Ailsa Hame'. When the Ailsa was rebuilt after the war it was all change again for the names of holes and the only old names surviving now are 'Ailsa Craig' for the first and 'Bruce's Castle' for the ninth. 'Ailsa Hame' for the last was changed in 2003 to 'Duel in the Sun', to commemorate the final day battle between Tom Watson and Jack Nicklaus in the 1977 Open.

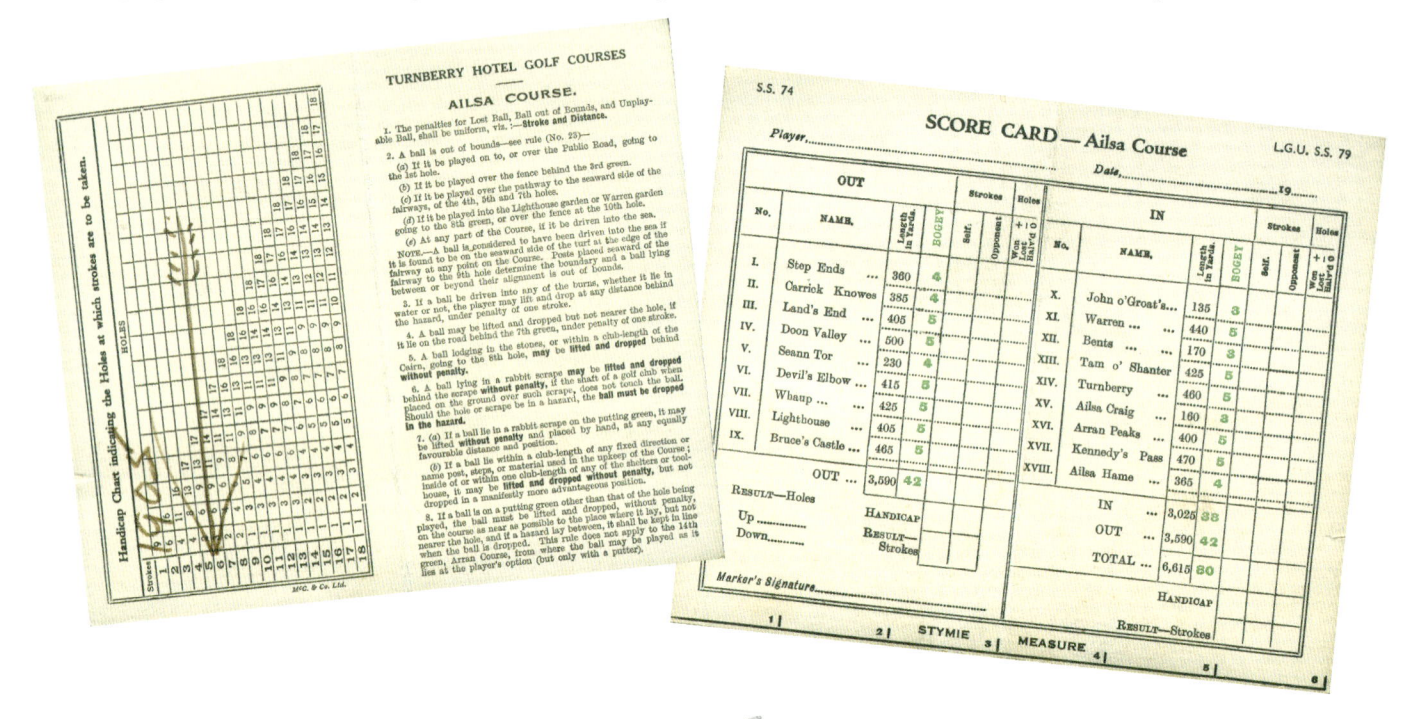

CHAPTER III - A TIME FOR GOLF - THEN WAR AGAIN

LADIES' BRITISH OPEN AMATEUR CHAMPIONSHIP 1921

HAVING hosted its first Ladies' British Open Amateur Championship in 1912 with great success, the Club lost no time after the war in pressing the Railway Company to offer the course again for this Championship. Perhaps bearing in mind the generous hospitality received from the Club in 1912, the Ladies' Golf Union readily took up the offer and agreed to hold their championship at Turnberry.

Captain Niven in Charge

The Railway Company was the sponsor of the tournament and the whole administration was carried out by the Club along with the Ladies' Golf Union. In this connection there was further discussion of a possible change in the Captaincy of the Club. Captain Niven offered at a meeting in January 1921 to resign the Captaincy which he had held since 1908. He felt it would be better to resign immediately so that his successor would have an opportunity to become acquainted with the work preparatory to and during the Ladies' Championship. Colonel North Dalrymple-Hamilton, the Vice Captain, moved that the Committee could not possibly accept this and that Captain Niven should con-

J. Jackson putting on 4th green in Ladies' British Open Amateur Championship 1921

tinue till the end of the year and take charge of the arrangements for the Championship. *'By acclamation'* this motion was agreed. Captain Niven expressed his willingness to continue and asked the Club Committee to act as a championship committee. It was no doubt fitting for the long serving Niven to finish his term in office presiding over this prestigious event. After all, his captaincy had covered every visiting tournament and match of any consequence played at Turnberry during the first 20 years of its existence.

It was arranged for the Railway Company to accommodate the competitors in its Ayr and Turnberry station hotels and to provide a special service of trains from Ayr and Girvan to Turnberry, with caddies being conveyed free of charge. Stewarding was arranged by members of the Club and of other Ayrshire clubs and the rail tickets

police were also praised for their assistance with crowd control and the Club gave them an honorarium of twenty five shillings, to be allocated ten shillings to the sergeant and five shillings each to the three constables who had been in attendance. This must have been one of the better assignments for the local constabulary!

The Course

This Championship was played on the No. 1 course (Ailsa) the layout of which had remained virtually unaltered since it was re-designed in 1909 by A.N. Weir, as already described in Chapter 2. Behind and along the seaward side of the 5th green (now the 6th) there was a deep gorge and a bridge was required to get to the next tee. This is seen in one of the photographs of the Championship

of stewards were reimbursed by the company. As in the previous championships the Club funded a prize for the winner of the preliminary stroke play event, and gave up most of the clubhouse for the use of the competitors in the Championship and in the international matches which preceded it. After the event the Club was complimented by the Ladies Golf Union and Mr. David Cooper of the Railway Company on the way in which local arrangements had been made and carried out. The

Leading Contenders

This was only the second time the championship had been held after the war. The first in 1920, held at Royal County Down, Newcastle, Northern Ireland, was won by Miss Cecil Leitch, of Carlisle and Silloth. She had also won the last championship before the war in 1914 at Hunstanton. She had a precocious talent and was a great favourite with the spectators. In 1908, as a sixteen

C. Leitch and A. Stirling crossing bridge from 5th green to 6th tee - 1921.

Chapter III - A Time For Golf - Then War Again

year old she had played in the championship at St. Andrews, and was watched and noted by Andrew Kirkaldy, who opined that she *'would be lady champion one day'*. Indeed, so impressed was he with her talent, that he even suggested that she might also win the men's title one day. Because her father was Scottish, when she was a teenager she did not qualify to play in the ladies' county team for Cumbria and, to provide her with the experience of good competition, the L.G.U. secretary, Issette Pearson, arranged for some of the best men players to take an interest in her developing talent. This led to a famous 72 hole match taking place between her and Harold Hilton in 1910 at Walton Heath and Sunningdale. She received one stroke at each of the even holes and won at the seventeenth hole of the final round, having scored a gross 76 to Hilton's 75. The match was watched by a crowd of about 3,500. During the 1920's there developed great rivalry between her and Joyce Wethered (later Lady Heathcoat-Amory), from Worplesdon.

Although Wethered was only 20 years old when she came to Turnberry in 1921, to play in the 'British Open' for the first time, she had already won the English Championship the previous year when she defeated Miss Leitch in a memorable match, despite having been six down after two holes of the second round. Wethered came from a golfing background and her brother Roger won the Amateur Championship of 1923 and was a Walker Cup golfer. Along with her brother she was taken by her parents to watch the great players, Harry Vardon and J.H. Taylor. Apparently she greatly admired the swing of Bobby Jones and she said that she tried to make her back-

11th Green of Weir's No 1 course in 1921. J. McCulloch putting against C. Leitch in Ladies' British Open Amateur Championship.

swing longer, like that of Jones. This admiration was not one-sided, for Jones admitted to admiring her swing, which he thought was the best of anyone – man or woman – he had ever seen. It must indeed have been very special, for the great Walter Hagen said she had grace, timing and touch and that the strength of her game was in its strictly feminine characteristics. In the 1920's she was the greatest British amateur lady golfer and her personal charm and wonderful sportsmanship did much to popularise ladies' golf and enhance its reputation. She won four British and five English championships and captained the Curtis Cup team in 1930.

5000 Spectators at Final

At Turnberry in 1921 there was a strong field of 113 entrants which included 11 from America, 2 from Canada and 1 from France, but the two English ladies Leitch and Wethered each came through six rounds to meet in the final. In the first round Miss Leitch beat the American star Alexa Stirling, described by *The Glasgow Herald* as being 'the most brilliant lady golfer ever from America'. There was great public interest in ladies' sport in general and in golf in particular at that time and the 36-hole final was attended by a very large crowd of spectators. It was reported in the *Ayr Advertiser* that:

'the match was played in a blaze of sunshine tempered by a slight breeze from the north-east, and before a crowd that, in the afternoon, would number about 5,000. Miss Leitch was seven up at the end of the first round and, though Miss Wethered made a gallant effort to retrieve the position in the afternoon, she lost by four and three'.

The Weetabix Women's Open Championship held at Turnberry in 2002 didn't attract any more than 5,000 spectators on its final day to watch a whole field of the

1921 Ladies' Final between Wethered and Leitch - on 10th green.

Chapter III - A Time For Golf - Then War Again

finest professional women golfers in the world. This illustrates how remarkable were the numbers which turned out in 1921 to watch just two lady amateurs battling it out in a final of the British Amateur Championship.

Amongst the spectators were Bernard Darwin, the renowned golf writer, who was made an honorary member of the Club for the duration of the Championship. Lady Ailsa, the Honorary President of the Ladies' Section of the Club, presented the trophies and medals. It sounds as if it was a most enjoyable occasion for the spectators, with the two foremost lady players of the time battling it out before an appreciative crowd – a female forerunner of another *'Duel in the Sun'* which was to take place on the same wonderful links 56 years later, between Watson and Nicklaus.

C. Leitch receiving the International Trophy won by the English team in the international matches preceding the Ladies' British Open Championship 1921. On the table is the Championship Trophy and behind the table are Captain Richard Niven and Lady Ailsa.

Scottish Ladies' Amateur Championships

BETWEEN the two world wars there were five Scottish Ladies' Amateur Championships held at Turnberry, in 1924, 1930, 1933, 1936 and 1939.

1924 Championship

The 1924 Championship was played on the Ailsa course and there were 58 entrants, including many from Ayrshire clubs, but only one from Turnberry, Mrs. W. Strain, who had a good victory in the first round, but went out in the second. The Championship was won by Miss C. Purvis-Russell Montgomery of St. Rule Club, St. Andrews, who beat Miss Hilda Cameron of Moray comfortably in the final by 5 and 4. Miss Montgomery also won the preliminary scratch medal round with a score of 84. As always at these events the Club supplied stewards and referees and made part of the clubhouse available to the ladies prior to and during the Championship.

1930 Championship

The 1930 championship was played on the No. 2 course designed in 1923 by James Braid and, by then, renamed the Arran course. *Fairway and Hazard*, a magazine for ladies' golf, reported that this course was a real test of golf and only slightly shorter, at 6000 yards, than the No. 1 (Ailsa) course, on which the 1924 Scottish Ladies' Championship and the 1921 British Championship had been played. In the hotel everything was done for the comfort of the ladies. In the evenings there were treasure hunts, dancing and bridge, and everyone thought that the British Championship should come back to Turnberry when Scotland's turn again came round. The 1930 Championship resulted in a popular victory for Mrs. Helen Holm (formerly Miss Helen Gray, a daughter of Professor Thomas Gray of Glasgow University) who was 22 years old and since her marriage, had lived and played her golf in Troon. This was her first victory, but she was to go on to win the title five times in all, the final occasion being twenty years later in 1950 when she defeated Mrs. Charlotte Beddows in the final. In between she also won the British Championship in 1934 and 1938 and played in the Curtis Cup teams in 1936, 1938 and 1948. Her opponent in the 1930 final was Miss Doris Park of Longniddry, the daughter of the famous Musselburgh golfer, Willie Park, who twice won the Open Championship. Miss Park was described as '*a frail little lady who keeps you constantly wondering how,*

Mrs Helen Holm who won her first of five titles as the Scottish Ladies' Amateur Champion, at Turnberry in 1930.

Chapter III - A Time For Golf - Then War Again

with her slight physique, she can hit the ball so far'. She battled through a tough draw, beating fine opponents in each round, including two former champions; while Mrs. Holm, playing magnificently, had a more leisurely route to the final. In the final they were all square going to the eighteenth which Mrs. Holm played brilliantly with a very long drive, a fine long iron to the green and two putts, which saw her winning the hole and the championship with a stroke to spare. The prizes were presented by Mr. John Richmond, the Captain of Turnberry Golf Club.

1933 Championship

In 1933, there were six ladies entered from Turnberry, Miss Betty Fenton, Mrs. Marjorie Milligan, Mrs. A.T. Carlow, Mrs. Agnes McCall, Mrs. W. McKay and Miss Muriel Paton. Miss Betty Fenton did best by getting to the third round. Mrs. Agnes McCall, a much loved member, who died in 1994 after over 60 years membership of the Club, reached the second round and had the pleasure of playing, though losing, to a future champion Miss Doris Park.

Contemporary Cartoon of 1933 Championship

As in 1930, the tournament was again played on the Arran Course and the Champion of 1930 and 1932, Mrs. Helen Holm, put in a staunch bid to retain the title. On the way she beat Mrs. W. Greenlees of Troon Ladies in the third round in a tight match and in the semi-final she beat the promising Miss Jessie Anderson to earn a final place against Miss Millicent Couper of North Berwick. Miss Anderson, still only eighteen years old and eligible for girls' tournaments, was the daughter of Joe Anderson, the golf professional at Perth, and this was her debut in the senior national championship. En route to the semi-final she had a great hat-trick of victories in rounds two, three and four, beating three former holders of the title, Miss A. Glover, Miss Jean McCulloch and Mrs. (One-Putt) Percy. In the match against Mrs. Percy she won the hearts of the crowd with her cheery natural demeanour, whilst at the same time showing wonderful fighting spirit coming back from three down to win, despite the brilliant putting of Mrs. Percy. The turning point was at the tenth hole where she had a long downhill putt and boldly sent the ball curling round a stymie* and into the hole, to square the match. It was nevertheless an impressive performance and she was described in *Fairway and Hazard* magazine as *'swinging the club beautifully freely when playing either a losing or a winning game, while the number of times she pitched stone dead out of a bunker was startling'*. However she met her match against Mrs. Helen Holm in the semi-final, going down by 3 and 2.

Miss Millicent Couper, the other finalist, thoroughly deserved her place in the final, having beaten two British internationalists Miss Doris Park and Miss Purvis-Russell Montgomery and a Scottish internationalist, Mrs. Kelway Bamber, in the earlier rounds. The final itself was close and keenly contested in wet dismal conditions and went to the 22nd hole after Mrs. Holm had holed out a difficult downhill four yard putt at the 18th to keep the game alive. At the final hole, the short 4th, Miss Couper played like a champion, putting her tee shot with an iron to 3 yards and holding the putt for the hole and the title.

Fairway and Hazard described the event thus:-

> *'It is only possible to describe the Scottish Championship, played over the New Course at Turnberry this year, in a series of superlatives. The entry, though smaller than usual, was of the very highest quality and the golf equally good so that the unfortunate seeker after the best match of any day was constantly being tempted away from something equally interesting by exciting news from somewhere else. The New Course is a wonderful test of golf; it was in the very pink of condition and remained so in spite of the glorious weather and*

Arran home green in 1936

* See note at foot of Page 80

Chapter III - A Time For Golf - Then War Again

blazing sun which were with us till the afternoon of the final, when it did rain. Turnberry was looking its loveliest and the sea its bluest and most inviting, though it certainly gave the hardy ones a chilly welcome.'

1936 Championship

The 1936 Championship was again held on the Arran course, as had become the custom since 1930. This was not because the ladies were being put on the easier course, for the Arran at that time was generally looked upon as the better of the two courses since its redesign after the First World War by James Braid. The reports of the Championship referred to it as 'the magnificent Arran course'. That year the champion at last was Miss Doris Park from Gullane, who had been runner-up on three previous occasions, apparently not through any lack of ability but more due to a nervous temperament. On this occasion it was reported that she showed that *'both faulty putting and treacherous nerves can be conquered'* and, in a tight final, beat Miss C. Purvis-Russell Montgomery of Elie and Earlsferry, the holder, at the 19th. Apparently Miss Montgomery was somewhat lucky in the middle of the final round, when she won the 10th hole in remarkable fashion. She had holed a yard putt and was about to concede her opponent's one foot putt when Miss Park went forward and missed it. However Miss Park recovered her nerve on the nineteenth and final green when she holed a match-winning putt of four yards.

Miss Jessie Anderson of Craigie Hill went out in the semi-final to Miss Montgomery but earlier impressed when beating Mrs. Helen Holm 6 and 5 and being level fours for the thirteen holes played. The press speculated that the title must surely be hers before long and that she might even win the British Ladies' title over the same Turnberry course the following year, a prophecy she was indeed to fulfil.

1938 Championship

In 1938 the Ailsa course had been remodelled to a design by the notable golf course architect Major Cecil Hutchison and the Scottish Ladies' Championship that year was played on it. As it turned out this was the only championship destined to be played on that particular layout, as the course was shortly thereafter substantially destroyed in the conversion of Turnberry to a military airfield for the Second World War. The final of the Championship over the remodelled Ailsa course was one of the most exciting ever and ended in victory for Miss Jessie Anderson of Craigie Hill, Perth, who beat Miss C.M. Park of Gullane at the 19th hole. Miss Anderson, who had won the British Ladies' Championship at Turnberry in 1937 over the Arran course, made her greater experience tell, holing an eight foot putt at the 18th to keep the game alive and then pitching to two feet at the 19th to take the title. A gallery, fully 500 strong, watched the final.

Mrs R.T. Peel, Scottish Ladies' Amateur Champion in 1954, who scored 67 over the Ailsa course in the first round of the final against Mrs Jessie Anderson

LADIES' BRITISH OPEN AMATEUR CHAMPIONSHIP 1937

As usual the Club was very much involved in the arrangements for the Ladies' British Open Championship, when it came to Turnberry for the third time in 1937. Captain Hughes-Onslow, Vice-Captain John Crawford, A.C. Mitchell, J.F. Courtney and R.H.U. Stevenson were appointed to the championship committee formed jointly by the Club and the Ladies' Golf Union. The Club minutes reveal that the arrangements included approval of silent 'movietones' of the championship being taken, and the appointment of programme sellers on a commission basis of 25%.

Tragic Death

The championship was played on the Arran Course which was reported to be in perfect condition and a wonderful setting for the championship. It proved a stern test for both accuracy and distance, with the hazards of whin-lined fairways, changeable winds, and slick greens getting faster every day. The championship was, as usual, to be preceded by home international matches, but only the first round of matches had been played when it was made known that 25 year old Miss Bridget Newell had died suddenly of diphtheria in Turnberry Hotel. She was one of the most prominent golfers at that time and was due to take part in the championship. When the tragic news broke the remainder of the international matches were cancelled as a mark of sympathy and by way of tribute to Miss Newell. However in the match between Scotland and England, which was played before the tragic event, Miss Doris Park showed her mettle and a sign of things to come when she overwhelmingly defeated Miss Pam Barton of England, the then current holder of both the British and the American Ladies' Championships. Miss Park, the reigning Scottish Champion, playing again the same links on which she won her Scottish title in 1936, beat Miss Barton by five and four.

Early Rounds

In the championship itself there was a very strong field with quite a number of overseas entrants, including players from America, South Africa, France and Australia. Only two Ayrshire players survived the second round, namely Mrs. Helen Holm and Mrs. W. Greenlees, two redoubtable ladies from Troon. In the third round Mrs. Holm played some great golf against the holder Miss Pam Barton, going three up at the eighth, with a score of two under fours. She was helped at the tenth by gaining a half by virtue of a stymie*, and won by four and three. In the fourth round, however, Miss Jessie Anderson, of Craigie Hill, Perth, (affectionately known to the crowd as 'wee Jessie'), was too strong for Mrs. Holm and went on playing very strongly to reach the final. Miss Doris Park, in the other half of the draw, continued to play well and to putt even better. In the semi-final she found stiff opposition against Miss Elsie Corlett, who was out in 34, but defeated nevertheless by Miss Park's deadly putter.

The Final

The final was played on a fine sunny day with a northerly wind and the morning round finished all square, Miss Park showing great determination in squaring the game after being two down to Miss Anderson. The two finalists had contrasting styles, Miss Park with a strong right hand grip under the shaft and her right arm providing most of the power and inducing tremendous top spin to the ball. Miss Anderson on the other hand employed a straight left

---

* For younger readers it should perhaps be explained that the stymie rule, which applied then, meant that, in match play, a player could not have an opponent's ball marked when it interfered with the line to the hole, but instead had to play round it or even over it with a lofted club. The latter shot required nerves of steel not only to accomplish such a delicate shot, but also to avoid damaging the green.

Chapter III - Historical Background

arm and had a beautifully balanced swing which resulted in a repetitive and confident action. In the afternoon Miss Anderson was steady as a rock but Miss Park's game and even her putting began to falter, allowing Miss Anderson to win at the 14th. It was reported in the *Fairway & Hazard* magazine that the cheering crowd entirely submerged the two finalists. Ladies' golf was a very popular spectator sport in those days, attracting thousands rather than hundreds to such an event. The magazine also reported that the trophies were presented by Captain Hughes-Onslow of Turnberry Golf Club, who made a very fine speech worthy of the occasion.

Captain Oliver Hughes-Onslow presents 1937 Championship Cup to Jessie Anderson.

Miss J. Anderson (seated left) the 1937 British Ladies' Champion, beaten semi-finalists Mrs A. McNair and E Corbett (standing) and Mrs D. Park, runner-up (seated right).

CHAPTER III - A TIME FOR GOLF - THEN WAR AGAIN

SECOND WORLD WAR

THE onset of the war in 1939 did not at first prevent the Club functioning or close the golf courses and an arrangement was made with the Railway Company for the Club to manage the courses on their behalf for the duration of the war. The report to the Annual General Meeting held on 22nd March, 1941 reveals that, as at February that year, total membership had dropped from 429 the previous year to 374, made up as follows:- Gents 232 (including 25 on war service), Ladies 98 (8 on war service), Life Member 1, Honorary Members 5, and Foreign Members 38. Then in April 1941 the Lands Office of the Air Ministry requisitioned the *'Northern portion of Turnberry Golf Links'*. Worse was to follow however when rumour had it that the Air Ministry intended also acquiring the remainder of the golf courses. The Railway Company was asked by the Club to make representations to the Air Ministry for the courses to be spared, as their *'loss would be greatly felt by golfers all over'*. The Company replied that there was nothing it could do except to *'endeavour to protect the interests of the hotel and courses generally, without of course interfering in any way with the national effort'*. In August 1941 the Club's worst fears were realised when the Air Ministry requisitioned most of the remainder of the golf course ground, leaving only that part to the South of a line drawn from the clubhouse westwards to the sea. Surprisingly at the same meeting at which this was intimated applications for membership were submitted and accepted from three ladies! There followed various meetings and discussions with the Railway Company's representatives regarding such matters as rebates in subscription, what to do with the clubhouse furniture and possible compensation claims on behalf of the clubmistress and the secretary. Also, more importantly, the Club sought assurances that 'in the event of the golf courses being re-opened, Turnberry Golf Club would be recognised by L.M.S. Railway Company'. The not entirely reassuring reply which was received from the Company Controller stated 'I think you may take it that the Company would certainly not use this emergency as a means of doing anything as regards the Club that they would not have been entitled to do had this emergency not arisen'.

Possible Disbandment of Club

Playing facilities ceased on 31st October 1941 and the holders of the various trophies at that date were asked to retain them in their possession till further notice, the feeling being that they would be safer dispersed than stored in a bank in the event of air raids. As no fewer than six out of twelve trophies were held by one man, R.H.U. Stevenson, one wonders if the logic of this policy stands up to scrutiny!

On 8th November, 1941, a Special General Meeting of the Club was held, the business on the agenda being 'to consider the future of Turnberry Golf Club and whether the Club was to be disbanded or continued'. Sixty members attended and a Mr. Greenlees proposed that the Club be continued. Mr. Ashby moved an amendment that the Club be disbanded, but on a vote being taken, the motion to continue was carried by an overwhelming majority. In the meantime however the clubhouse was closed and the furniture and furnishings were sold off by public auction, fetching net proceeds of £301-14/-. The Club's lowest point had been reached, but the courses had still to face a much sterner test before they would survive their impending metamorphosis from golf links to aerodrome.

Conversion of Turnberry to a Military Airfield

In 1941 Air Vice Marshall Sandy Johnston, then a Squadron Leader, led a special mission to Turnberry to test the flying conditions and report on Turnberry's suitability as a site for a military airfield. Apparently he made several passes and sorties over the Turnberry air space in a Spitfire and also made a landing on one of the fairways in a light Miles Master personnel carrier, almost colliding in the process with the war memorial at the 12th hole. He reported against the project, but nevertheless the Air Ministry decided to proceed with the

83

construction of a military airfield at Turnberry and the resultant damage virtually destroyed the golf courses.

Turnberry military airfield was operated by the Royal Air Force and known as Training School No. 5(c) O.T.U. and the hotel itself was converted to use as a convalescent hospital for the war wounded. The main function of the Training School was to bring together pilots, wireless operators, air gunners and navigators from all corners of the Commonwealth to train for torpedo bombing. After training, most crews were sent to squadrons employed in attacking enemy shipping in the Middle East. Training involved low level flying about 60 feet above sea level at about 140 knots and firing dummy torpedoes at target ships supplied by the Royal Navy and moored in the Firth of Clyde, such as H.M.S. Cardiff, H.M.S. Guernsey and others. They primarily used ex-Bomber Command Bristol Beauforts, Handley Page Hampdens and Wellington aircraft and there were many casualties at Turnberry due to the inherent danger of the manoeuvres, mechanical failures, trainee pilot errors and the local weather. One incident is recorded when there was almost a dummy torpedo attack made by mistake on the liner Queen Mary by the Turnberry planes, as she passed down the Clyde on her wartime troop carrying duties. It is estimated by recent research that over 200 airmen died at Turnberry during the Second World War, and some of their names were added to the war memorial at the 12th hole, only a few years ago. Hopefully the remainder will be added if and when their names can be ascertained.

The extent of the disruption to the courses was vividly described by Martin A.F. Sutton of the firm of

Aerial view of main runways of Turnberry Military Aerodrome - 1945

Chapter III - A Time For Golf - Then War Again

Suttons, who reconstructed the course after the war:-

'During Hitler's ill-fated attempt to dominate the world by force of arms the glories of Turnberry had perforce to be sacrificed. To assist in ensuring the defeat of the tyrants Turnberry was converted into a large airfield, and with the completion of this work it appeared to be wholly ruined so far as any future use as a golf course was concerned. Extensive levelling operations completely flattened large areas of the course, and numerous sandhills and other unique natural features essential to a golf course were completely obliterated. Many acres of concrete and tarmacadam runways were laid, and brick and concrete huts, hangars, transformer houses and strong-points were to be found all over the area. All the turf and top soil were stripped from the fairways and the result was such a scene of desolation that it was not surprising the opinion was freely expressed that never again would Turnberry be a first-class golf course.'

By 1942 the future of Turnberry Golf Club and indeed of Turnberry as a golfing centre looked bleak and uncertain.

Snippets From Club Minutes in Historical context 1920-45

January 1920	Management of Amateur Championship assumed by R. & A.
April 1920	*'Contribution of One guinea to be sent to R. & A. Golf Club towards the expenses of running the Amateur and Open Championships.'*
April 1921	Owing to the coal strike, it was resolved *'to ask the Railway Company to provide some coals for the clubhouse during the Ladies Championship'.*
May 1921	Bernard Darwin made an honorary member during the Ladies Championship.
July 1921	Jack Dempsey knocks out Georges Carpentier in New York fight for World Heavyweight Boxing Championship.
August 1921	*'Resolved to fix the scratch score of Turnberry at 79 and to intimate this to the Secretary of the Royal and Ancient Golf Club.'*
November 1923	*'Suggested that the matter of divots not being replaced be taken up with careless players and also the caddies.'*
January 1924	Lenin dies in Moscow.
March 1924	The sum of two guineas granted to newly formed Ayrshire Professional Golfers' Association.
July 1924	*'Agreed to send a donation of £2-5/- towards the expenses of the team being sent by the R. & A. Golf Club to America to play an International Match for the Walker Cup.'*
December 1924	Circular from Royal Aberdeen Golf Club regarding benefits or otherwise of grazing sheep on golf courses remitted to Greens Committee.
September 1925	*'Agreed to have match with hotel residents.'*
September 1925	*'Agreed to have a scratch score fixed by Scottish Golf Union and to fill in a form showing the run obtained from the various shots to each hole.'*
March 1926	Letter from Silvertown India Rubber Company allowed to lie on table as their request for the names and addresses of the club's six lowest handicap players was required for a *'propaganda scheme'* the company were contemplating.
May 1926	General Strike. Government appeals to the public not to buy more than usual quantities of foodstuffs to ensure fair distribution. Turnberry Trophy Amateur Open Tournament postponed due to Strike.
May 1927	*'Motor cycles not to be parked on verandah of clubhouse.'*
May 1927	Lindbergh flies the Atlantic.
February 1928	*'The sum of Three Guineas was granted to the Ladies Section to pay their annual subscription to the Ladies Golf Union.'*
March 1929	*'Plebiscite of members to be held on radical changes proposed by L.M.S. Railway Company.'*
October 1929	Wall Street Crash.

Chapter III - A Time For Golf - Then War Again

March 1930	Captain Richmond congratulated for *'steering the Club's barque through stormy and difficult times'*.
1930	Bobby Jones 'Grand Slam' year. Wins Amateur and Open Championships of both Britain and America.
June 1931	Mr. Fisher suggested that ball lifters be placed alongside the burns for the convenience of *'players who had the misfortune to find their ball in the water'*.
February 1932	Mr. L.S. Baikie, a founder member, given life membership in appreciation of his services to the Club.
March 1933	Death reported of Richard Niven who was Captain, *'with much acceptance, from 1908 to 1922, during which time he devoted a great deal of his time and energy to the affairs of the Club'*.
March 1933	Franklin D. Roosevelt installed as thirty second President of the United States.
March 1934	Suggestion that some of large credit balance of £565-10-7d. be expended annually on a Club dinner and presentation of prizes, was ruled incompetent.
1935	Privileges of the clubhouse extended to the Ayrshire Constabulary Recreation Club for golf outing.
November 1936	*'Caddies' Competition reported popular and competitors very appreciative of Club's interest and of the many handsome prizes.'*
December 1936	Abdication of Edward VIII in favour of his brother the Duke of York.
February 1937	*'Past Captain Richmond desires unexpended balance of funds for his presentation to be devoted to prizes for Caddies' competition.'*
12th May 1937	Coronation of King George VI. Coronation Day competition at Turnberry.
August 1937	*'Letter read from Messrs. Joe Kirkwood and Walter Hagen offering to play an exhibition match at Turnberry for a flat guarantee of £75 or five shillings gate receipt basis.'*
March 1938	Letter received from Duke of Montrose proposing a match between Seniors Golfers' Society and five senior golfers from Turnberry with handicaps ranging from 4 to 14.
May 1938	Captain reported the death of The Marquess of Ailsa, Honorary President of the Club since its formation.
October 1938	Chamberlain brings back his *'Peace'* Agreement with Hitler.
October 1938	Reported that the Turnberry team of R.H.U. Stevenson and W.G. McCulloch had reached the semi-final of the Evening Times tournament *'where they were dispatched by last year's winners'*.
January 1939	Amongst members elected were The Viscount Glenapp and Allan Stevenson.
June 1939	Committee convey congratulations to J.R. Richmond, Honorary Vice President of the Club, on being made Knight of the British Empire by His Majesty the King.
September 1939	Great Britain at war with Germany.
September 1939	Winter grazing of sheep allowed on the courses, to assist food production. Ailsa course and hotel closed because of the war.
February 1940	Nurses stationed at the hotel, now in use as a hospital, to be given the facilities of the members' tea room.
October 1940	*'Suggested, in view of a likely increase in the future prices of liquors, that the Secretary be authorised to accumulate gradually a stock of whisky and gin over immediate requirements.'*

The Ailsa Course is Restored

Restoration in doubt

AFTER the war it took some time for the War Department to give up possession of Turnberry. In March 1946 Mr. Frank Hole, Chief Superintendent of LMS Hotel Services, wrote to the Club stating that the position was still obscure, as neither the hotel nor the golf courses had been derequisitioned and, although the matter was *'actively in hand'*, it was too early for him to give any definite information as to the future prospects for Turnberry. Nothing much happened for a further two years, except an indication through the new Scottish Tourist Board that negotiations were proceeding at the highest level, but that the hotel owners were not prepared to re-open without the golf course being playable. At one point there was a meeting of the directors of the Railway Company in the hotel, when it was declared that the task of restoring the courses was too formidable and that Turnberry was finished as a golfing centre. Fortunately Frank Hole, as well as being a keen golfer, was also a man of vision and it is he who is generally credited with persuading the powers that be that the courses could and should be restored.

The New Ailsa Course goes ahead

The railways in Britain were nationalised in 1948 and the old LMS Company, which owned Turnberry, became part of the new nationalised British Transport. In April 1948 Frank Hole advised the Club that it was the intention of the Hotels Executive of British Transport to rehabilitate the hotel and courses with the least possible delay and, by February 1949, Messrs. Suttons of Reading were invited by the Hotels Executive to prepare a scheme for the reconstruction of the Ailsa Course. Suttons were specialists in grass seeds and turf formation who had already been involved in advising, constructing or providing the seeds for nearly 150 golf courses and course extensions in the United Kingdom and throughout the world. Accordingly they were well qualified for the job. We know from Martin Sutton of that company, in his account in their 1950 *Turf for Sport* publication, that he and his team spent a full week with Mr. Mackenzie Ross, of Edinburgh, the architect appointed to design the new course. The week was employed examining the terrain, deciding on which of the remaining natural features could be utilised and which new ones could be created, computing the grass seeds and soil and turf required and in general preparing a complete scheme and programme of work. Sutton concluded his account with the following comments:-

'Links land by the sea has ever been the choice of the golfer because here a real contest is assured, not only against an opponent but against Nature herself. All the great courses in Britain are laid out on this type of terrain, and it has been the endeavour of all concerned with the reconstruction of Turnberry to transform the flat ground and reproduce natural hillocks and valleys. From the back tees the new Turnberry will be of open championship class; at the same time an alternative way of playing many of the holes has been arranged so that the course will not prove to be too difficult for the medium or long handicap player. There are but one sixth the num-

Mr. P. Mackenzie Ross, Architect of the new Turnberry

Chapter IV - Post War Turnberry 1946-1971

ber of fairway bunkers formerly present. This will ensure economy in upkeep and easier play for the long handicap men. From the normal club tees the course will measure 6,250 yards, and from the championship tees 6,700 yards.'

The comment about the number of fairway bunkers in the Mackenzie Ross course being only one sixth of those formerly present on the pre-war course will surely raise a few eyebrows. This quantifies to about 180 fairway bunkers pre-war as compared to about 30 on the new course. A feature of the bunkers at Turnberry, both pre-war and after the war, was that they were not generally built with turf revetting and the tops at the front were covered in long marram grass. It was usually preferable to land in the bunker rather than miss it narrowly but be caught up in the marram grass which fringed the top. Being in the fringe often meant that the player could, at best, only hack the ball clear and, at worst, find the ball in an unplayable lie. It was not until about 1975 that the bunkers were all redesigned with revetted faces and short grass round the fringes, and so the contestants in the Open Championship of 1977 didn't have to face such terrors.

The new Ailsa course which emerged after the Second World War rightly brought great credit to Mackenzie Ross and bears little resemblance to the original course laid out by Willie Fernie in 1901. Nevertheless some credit should be given to Fernie for having the vision to lay out the outward holes of his course along the rough dunes, bents and valleys of the coastal strip. He could instead more easily have used the flatter inland portion of the land available, where there was far better turf. Of his original course perhaps the only hole which has survived is the modern eighth which is basically very much the same as his fifth.

Donald Steel, eminent journalist, author and golf course architect, provides an expert assessment of the Turnberry courses and of their turbulent history next in this book.

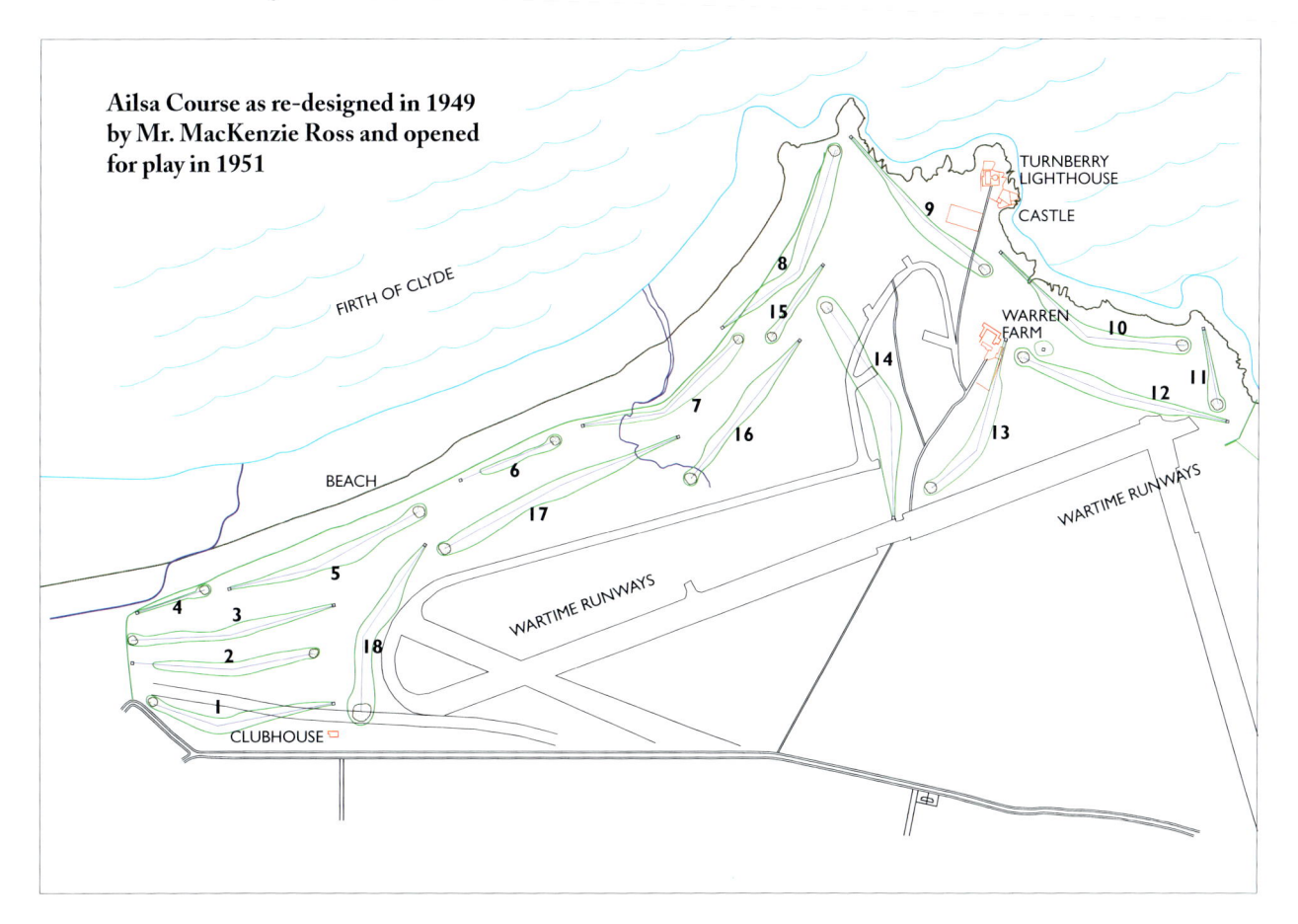

Ailsa Course as re-designed in 1949 by Mr. MacKenzie Ross and opened for play in 1951

An Assessment of the Turnberry Courses
by Donald Steel

HISTORIANS of Turnberry have had a hard time keeping pace with the extraordinary amount of upheaval, turmoil, change and costly endeavour that it has undergone in a hundred years. However, rather than classify all under the heading of misfortune, there is a powerful case to be made for the counter view. Good really has come out of evil. In the slightly adjusted words of the song, it has allowed Turnberry *'to brush itself down, dust itself off and start all over again'*.

The result has ensured that Turnberry has always been as good as new, so much better able than the majority of links to present an up-to-date challenge. Against the inexorable march in the manufacture of golfing equipment, this has been of enormous benefit but Turnberry has always been regarded in the forefront of both traditional and contemporary design.

In some respects, where Turnberry is concerned, there isn't a great deal of difference. Traditional implies the principles relating to a type of golf extolled by links courses that grows more precious not less. Contemporary is the modern interpretation of that message and the constant attempts necessary to keep it fresh although there is little recognisable about the Turnberry layout of today and the Turnberry that Willie Fernie laid out except that, understandably, the shoreline has always proved a fascination.

A plan dated April 1909 shows two courses, named rather unimaginatively, No 1 (6115 yards) and No. 2 (5115 yards) and these remained until after World War I when damage to the courses on account of conversion for military use was nothing like as extensive as it was more than twenty years later. A painting in the clubhouse gallery, dated 1920, shows Warren Farm out near what is now the 13th tee on the Ailsa with golf holes encircling it. This remained intact until World War II but, for a time after the restoration of the course in the early 1920s, the newly built No. 2 course deposed its apparent superior as the more popular for visitors and championships.

One solution, following the decision to call them Ailsa and Arran, was the revamping of the Ailsa by Major Cecil Hutchison who had assisted James Braid with the creation of Gleneagles. He eliminated a number of blind shots and added length, Bernard Darwin remarking of the Old course, as he referred to it, that *'Hutchison left it as pretty and charming as he found it but in a different class as a test of golf'*.

If its reviews were glowing, its eminence was short lived. War struck again within a year or two and, when peace came, nothing remained that was salvageable across the central heartland. Tales of the determination of Frank Hole in establishing Turnberry's future are related elsewhere but, when Mackenzie Ross had implemented his plans for the Ailsa, it placed himself and his masterpiece on the highest plane, although definite similarities ran through his thinking and that of Hutchison.

By today's numbering, there is a clear similarity in the two versions between the first three holes, holes 7 to 12, and the last three. Mackenzie Ross preserved much of the structure of the pre-war Ailsa but supplied of lot of new detail.

The reason for so saying is that aerial photographs taken in black and white of Turnberry as an airfield reveal some parts out towards what is now Ailsa's 8th green as largely untouched. When Mackenzie Ross came to assess the situation and, bearing in mind constraints on his budget, he was no doubt happy to concentrate on the worst affected areas although he would certainly have had some work to do on the untouched holes that presumably saw very little, if any, play during the war. It was the pre-war Arran that was far more badly decimated.

Nevertheless, analysis of Mackenzie Ross's work is

Chapter IV - Post War Turnberry 1946-1971

fascinating. He identified the natural contours and incorporated them as strategic allies but the fundamental truth is that he made bolder and more imaginative use of the glorious coastal stretch than anyone had done hitherto, offering a range of shot options that separates links golf from other types of course. This won the acclaim of all golfers not just the most accomplished. It soon became the course that everyone wanted to play, not just for the incredulity of seeing an example of Phoenix rising from the ashes.

As I wrote in the Open championship programme in 1977, *'Turnberry's requisitioning for a second time by the Air Ministry was certainly unfortunate and possible even a mistake. Air Vice Marshal Sandy Johnstone, then a mere Squadron Leader and, more recently, Secretary to both Glasgow and Denham Golf Clubs, was in charge of a special mission in 1941, ordered to report on Turnberry's suitability as a modern airfield.*

After a good many circuits and approaches in a Spitfire, the opinion of professional flyers, not prejudiced by their love of golf, was unanimously against the idea but either the report was blown away along the corridors of power, or else the Ministry held the belief, not unknown in government, that expert opinion is not always to be heeded.'

It may be somewhat obvious to say now that Mackenzie Ross made everyone aware of the Ailsa's glorious setting but he who dares wins and it was his decision to restore the 8th and 10th greens to the edge of the shore that captivated hearts. The back tee on the 9th was actually the later inspiration of Jimmy Alexander, Superintendent of British Transport Hotels golf courses, who redesigned the Arran, but the overall impression that Mackenzie Ross left was one of excitement, exhilaration and adventure.

It is hard to believe nowadays that the 4th and 10th greens once nestled on the water's edge before the tide retreated although there were other innovations of his that, if less glamorous, were hugely farseeing. A raised green on the 13th and a longer second shot at the 16th involving a carry over the burn called for ingenuity to conquer them. From the wartime photographs, it is easy to pick out the use made of the infamous burn on the 16th. Hutchison deserves the credit for that but Mackenzie Ross was undoubtedly a man with an eye for detail. His clever angling of the

War time aerial photographs of Turnberry as a military airfield showing many holes of the pre-war Ailsa Course largely untouched, and apparently still being cut.

— 93 —

The new 4th hole, seen from the tee site - an intriguing shot across a sandy bay. The two men in the distance are rolling the green.

5th green, for instance, illustrated his appreciation for positional play while a sharper dogleg on the 7th confirmed a desire to provide as much variety within 18 holes as possible.

Defence of links courses depends to a great degree on the wind and Mackenzie Ross preferred the near certainty of this to a minefield of bunkers. The glorious drive down the 3rd owes nothing to the presence of bunkers although it epitomises the growing strength of the test ahead. The 4th is one of my favourite short holes on any course, control, thought and guile being infinitely more important to the tee shot than muscle and might. It was the trump card of Mackenzie Ross in providing a new dimension to the Ailsa and transforming the balance of the layout, one of the pre-war samples having three short holes coming home and none going out.

In Hutchison's version of the layout, there were four holes in the stretch from the present 4th tee to the present 8th green against Mackenzie Ross's five. The main contrast was that Hutchison played a short hole after his 11th, now the 12th, and ran his 13th from a different direction to a green position roughly the same as it is today.

The unusual feature, to say the least, was that Hutchison's total of three par 3s all came on the inward nine within a cluster of six holes. It was no doubt the desire to achieve a better balance between the nines that prompted Mackenzie Ross to introduce the par 3 4th and 6th thus giving four in all. Certainly, it was an improvement particularly now in an age when shot making skills lack the ingredients that were once regarded as essential. The art of flight is invaluable on the 4th where there is no margin for error.

There is also more than a hint of death or glory about the short 15th as, indeed, there is on the 18th where cunningly placed bunkers on the left taunt those fearful of the gorse on the right. Clever bunkering is a feature of the 14th green and the second to the elevated 8th green is a test of judgement while the 9th, 10th and 12th are cracking fours. In fact, it is hard to find a weakness on a course that offers something for everyone.

Dependence on a host of statistics and a predictable, stereotyped approach renders you all at sea when the wind blows on any links. It is a vital part of their make-up but there is nothing impossible about the Ailsa if a

CHAPTER IV - POST WAR TURNBERRY 1946-1971

player's skills are well packaged. When the Ailsa deservedly graduated to the Open championship stage in 1977, Tom Watson and Jack Nicklaus unlocked its secrets in dramatic fashion. However, the other 148 were well and truly stymied by them.

One of the hallmarks of the current version of the Ailsa is that it has stood the test of time, albeit a relatively short fifty years. Additions have taken the form of a few new tees and a revision of the bunkering. Several bunkers have been added since Mackenzie Ross's day but Turnberry's chief good fortune has always been that it has had 36 holes and more lately 45 holes.

Study of the pre-1939 Arran indicates a totally different routing of the holes to the post war replacement that was opened for play in 1954. Runways destroyed the heart of the Arran whereas the coastal fringe of the Ailsa was saved. Contrary to many beliefs, the Arran was the work of Jimmy Alexander and not Mackenzie Ross.

It was built by direct labour under Alexander's supervision with all the greens, with the exception of the 1st and 18th, seeded in contrast to the Ailsa's which were turfed.

In botanical fact, it wasn't only the greens on the Ailsa that were turfed. The same treatment was afforded to the tees and fairways, using supplies from the nearby farm, a formula never before attempted in Britain and never likely to be repeated. It was a Herculean task even in an age when hand labour was more plentiful and more affordable.

All credit, therefore, to Messrs. Sutton Seeds from Reading for delivering the Ailsa miracle and to Martin Sutton, in particular, for his accurate depiction of how it came to pass. In *Turf for Sport*, a little booklet described as an Occasional Magazine for Secretaries, Greenkeepers and Groundsmen, dated Spring 1950, he itemises in great technical detail the painstaking process. As part of the historical narrative, its importance is undeniable.

'At the end of June 1949, we were informed that our scheme and estimate had been accepted and it was agreed to hold a conference at the Turnberry Hotel, itself a hospital during the war, at an early date at which a plan of campaign could be decided upon and priorities settled. This conference was duly held in the early part of August and was attended by everyone interested in any way in the project. It was arranged that an immediate start should be made with the site clearance and that following this as many putting greens as possible should be constructed and turfed during the winter of 1949-50.

The summer of 1950 was to be mainly devoted to the preparation and topsoiling of the fairways, the construction of bunkers, tees and hill work, and the completion of the remaining greens. The programme visualised the greater portion of the work being completed by September 1950, with fairway areas seeded down. It would be necessary to provide for a completely new water system with connections to all greens, and it was agreed that a new fence should be erected on the landward boundaries of the course.

Work actually commenced towards the end of

Aerodrome runway after removal of concrete and macadam. Site of the 1st fairway. (Clubhouse on left.)

— 95 —

August, 1949, and the first operation was the breaking up, excavation and removal of concrete and tarmacadam runway, and the demolition of the many buildings erected during the period of war-time occupation. The magnitude of the task can be judged from the fact that some of the runway foundations were as much as 4 feet in depth, including a 6 inch thickness of concrete.

The runways were broken up by means of concrete breakers, bulldozers, compressors, scrapers, etc. Thousands of tons of the excavated material were used to fill in large holes on various portions of the course and for the foundation of fairway hillwork, but, in addition, many thousands of tons had to be carted away by means of a fleet of lorries. It was taken to the neighbouring village of Maidens where it could be utilised to good advantage in building a new sea wall.

The removal of runways and buildings naturally left large stretches of fairway and even putting green areas utterly devoid of any trace of top soil. On the raw subsoil exposed nothing could possibly grow, and all such scars had to be made good by spreading new top soil. In the case of important areas a thickness of 9 inches to 1 foot of new soil had to be provided.

It was estimated that some 30,000 yards of top soil would be required to make good areas of demolition and to reinstate fairways from which the soil and turf had been removed. Normally the provision of such an enormous quantity of fresh soil would have been a task of some magnitude and most costly item, but it was fortunate that what we hoped would be a sufficient amount of new soil was a light sandy loam deficient in organic matter, and judged by ordinary horticultural standards, it would be considered distinctly impoverished.

It was, however, of the correct type for use in establishing a seaside golf course, and its impoverished character was ameliorated by the use of granulated peat and fertiliser. The soil varied greatly in depth and in places only an inch or two could be found. It had, therefore, to be dug out somewhat laboriously by hand, as the use of a mechanical digger would have resulted in an irretrievable mixture of soil and subsoil with disappointing results when grass seeds were sown or turf laid.

Immediately the clearance work was sufficiently under way, a commencement was made with the construction of putting greens and the preparation of fairway areas. In the construction of the

Above: Excavating concrete on the site of the approach to the 14th green.
Below: Turf being laid after the formation of the 1st green. (Ailsa Craig can be seen in the distance.)

Chapter IV - Post War Turnberry 1946-1971

greens, every possible care was devoted to making their conformation blend with that of the surrounding land. This work entailed the moving of many thousands of tons of soil sometimes as much as 4,000 cubic yards for a single green and approach. Such work was in the main carried out by caterpillar tractors and rotary scoops. The scoops were only of about 1 cubic yard capacity, as experience had shown that this size is best to deposit soil exactly where desired and to create the natural effect required.

Many fairway and approach areas were completely flat and devoid of movement, and had to be specially dealt with in order to create the beautifully undulating surface usually associated with a first-class seaside golf links. The result was obtained chiefly by use of tractors and scoops and with the occasional employment of the bulldozer.

Turf for the greens was procured from an area adjoining the site, and botanical analysis proved it to be of a most promising character which under expert treatment should work up into an excellent sward. It was composed mainly of *Poa pratensis* (Smooth-stalked Meadow Grass) with smaller proportions of *Agrostic tenuis* (Common Bent Grass), *Festuca rubra* (Red Fescue), and *Festuca capitata* (Fine-leaved Fescue). The weed content was distinctly lower than is generally the case and could mainly be dealt with by the use of Selective Weed Killers at a later date.

By the end of October [1949], such marked progress had been made that serious consideration was given to the possibility of getting nine holes ready for play by early summer of 1950. It was realised that, if this could be successfully accomplished, it would prove a tremendous asset to the famous Turnberry Hotel due to be reopened at Easter, 1950. The work would involve the turfing of some 30 acres of ground and the cutting, transportation and laying of over 290,000 turves. This immense task was successfully completed by the closing days of the old year, with every prospect that nine holes would be in a sufficiently advanced condition for play by June, 1950.

The foregoing represents a small-scale picture of all that had to be done in the reconstruction of this famous golf course. In the early days of 1950, although the back of the work had been broken, satisfying progress had been made. Much, however, still remained to be done including drainage, preparation of remaining fairways areas, construction of greens and tees, creation of artificial hillwork and similar operations. Still, it was possible to say that everything was working to schedule and there is every likelihood of the work being completed to time in the autumn of 1950.'

Above: Site preparation and turfing in progress on the 7th green.
Below: Work on the 6th green. (Hotel in background)

By Alexander's own admission, the Arran was conceived as a course of contrasting character to the Ailsa, one more suitable for the elderly. With its flat terrains and sheltered from the sea, it was a brief that could be obligingly followed but the development of the gorse that had been largely flattened during the war quickly inflated its challenge. It became a course where there was a premium on straight driving; indeed, many of the young assistants from the shop found scoring easier on the Ailsa than the Arran. Returns from the Amateur championships of 1983 and 1996, when the Arran was used as the second qualifying course, do not fully support this notion but, with a significant discrepancy in the length of the two courses, the point was well made.

With the building of the new clubhouse in 1992/93, Arran's old 1st hole, that ran parallel with the road in the opposite direction to the 1st on the Ailsa, was reduced to a par 3 but, when the hotel and course changed hands again at the end of 1998, the new owners were quick to institute radical change to the Arran – so radical, as things turned out, that it brought a change of name to Kintyre.

Their wish was to see a course of comparable challenge to the Ailsa, a marketing decision to increase the hotel occupancy rate and to take the strain off the Ailsa. It was felt that the Arran was the poor relation, a harsh judgement if viewed in the light of Alexander's original brief although understandable in commercial terms. However, the move brought the added benefit of expanding facilities in the shape of a new Academy and a short nine holes ideal for those not seeking the hefty demands of its neighbours. These were all part of the original blanket proposals.

Change to established courses is rarely far reaching. It is usually confined to a search for length and reviewing the bunkering, an exercise comprising little more than *'moving the furniture'*. What transformed the scale of change possible to the Arran was the availability of new land on Bain's Hill, land that had been acquired by Turnberry's previous owners. However, there is land and land; and Bain's Hill enjoys the most spectacular setting imaginable even by Turnberry's exalted standards. If there is a more beautiful panorama in the golfing world than that from the Kintyre's 10th tee, it has yet to emerge.

View from the 10th tee of the new Kintyre Course.

Chapter IV - Post War Turnberry 1946-1971

The elevated nature of Bain's Hill will make it prey to the weather but it gives the Kintyre a seaside flavour denied its predecessor and a series of holes that take full advantage of the nearness of the sea and changing levels. Ailsa Craig and the lighthouse provide a symbolic back cloth to many shots as well as a scenic variety between the holes unachievable amid gorse lined avenues. There was also the opportunity to hand pick which holes on the Arran to create and maintain sequence, which to sacrifice and which to modify or run together. Having Bain's Hill at the furthest point was bound to stretch the length but concern had to be focused on not over stretching it. The back nine has no let up.

Love of the Ailsa and an instinctive sympathy with links golf dictated the policy for the Kintyre's holes. Natural adornment is vastly better than artificial creation although the covering of part of the old runway network comes under the latter heading.

It was interesting that a plea at the official planning stage was lodged to make everyone aware of the runway's historical significance but the planning process was a lesson in clear thinking, trust and confidence so lacking in many parts of the world.

One aspect of the Kintyre that is uncommon in links golf is that only the 17th and 18th are consecutive holes played in the same direction. There may be no protection from the wind but adjustments in thinking and strategy are real demands even if the ability to keep the ball low is more of an asset than flying it high, an essential on so many modern courses where entrances to greens are tightly guarded and frequently only reached by lengthy carries over water or large, intrusive bunkers.

On the Kintyre, every club in the bag can be used for approaches from 100 yards. They allow free access while the areas around the greens are, in no way, restricted either, a reminder that a good deal of golf at the seaside is played along the ground or, at least, should be. A picture of the artistry and invention of Severiano Ballesteros gives a picture of squeezing the ball against the firm turf, running the ball up banks or through shallow hollows. He was the master of *'feel'*.

It is an element virtually ignored on many modern courses where golf is played more to a formula but it is not an accusation that can be levelled about Turnberry either now or when the Marquis of Ailsa set out to build a course on his own private Culzean Estate. Fate has determined that there have been many variations through the years but the latest pair of courses, the Ailsa and Kintyre, remain a splendid foil for each other, hard to beat either as harmonious neighbours or formidable battle grounds.

THE CLUB SURVIVES

War Time Office Bearers re-start the Club

AFTER the war the rejuvenation of the Club was at first left in the hands of the office bearers who had kept the Club alive during the war years and also afterwards until the course was rebuilt and opened again in 1951. They faithfully held annual general meetings in the Richmond Hall, Kirkoswald, during that period and dealt with such matters as annual financial statements, the custody of the trophies and the re-election each year of the same office bearers en bloc to hold the fort until, hopefully, the course was rebuilt. The annual financial statements were very simple, showing capital of £950 in 3% Defence Bonds and less than £100 in the bank, with the only income being the interest on the Defence Bonds and no expenditure. Nevertheless the formal meetings and the re-election of office bearers were very important because it meant that there was never a vacuum and lines of communication were kept open with the owners of the hotel. Those office bearers were Captain Oliver Hughes-Onslow as Captain, ex-Provost William McCreath of Girvan as Vice-Captain and Willie Templeton as Secretary/Treasurer. The Fourth Marquess of Ailsa who had succeeded his father as President in 1938 died in 1943, and Sir John Richmond, C.B.E., who had been elected Vice-President in 1939, continued in that capacity, the position of President being left vacant.

The Hotel re-opens

The hotel was re-opened in the spring of 1950 and nine holes of the new Ailsa course opened that summer. It was agreed between the Club and the Hotels Executive that Club members would not seek to play the nine holes until later that year, in order to make them available exclusively to hotel guests and thus assist the hotel in getting re-established. However, a few months later, members who had been on the Club's roll in 1941, were permitted to play on the course free of charge until the course was fully in play and new formal arrangements between the Club and the Hotels Executive were agreed. By May 1951 the full 18 holes of the Ailsa course were ready for play, although their condition was still rough and immature and no competitions were held that year. Indeed existing members continued to play the course free of charge until March 1952, when the Hotels Executive intimated their desire for the Club to be fully re-activated. Terms agreed for the use of the course and cloakroom facilities in the clubhouse stipulated an annual subscription of 6 guineas for gentlemen and 5 guineas for ladies, with the Club being paid back 10% of the total subscriptions to give it a working income. It was resolved to recruit new members who were to pay an entry fee of 2 guineas; membership was renewed with the Scottish Golf Union and the Ladies' Golf Union, and the first competition after the war was held on 26th April, 1952. From 1955 till 1957 ninety three new members were admitted, of whom thirty four were from Maybole, ten from Girvan, eighteen from Ayr, fifteen from surrounding villages and the rest from Glasgow area. This influx of members continued apace in the 1960's, with an increasing proportion being from Ayr, but many still being from the communities of Maybole and Girvan, whose citizens had been so influential in the affairs of the Club in its early formative years.

Normal Service resumes

After the war the clubhouse was in very poor shape, but in 1954 British Transport Hotels drew up plans for its renovation and an agreement was reached between the Club and BTH on the following matters:-

1. The Club would apply for registration under the Licensing Acts to operate a club licence to provide alcoholic refreshment to members and guests.

2. BTH would supply a steward or stewardess who would be responsible to the Club for managing the bar.

3. BTH would provide the bar stock as agents for the

Chapter IV - Post War Turnberry 1946-1971

Club as licence holders.

4. The Club would receive five per cent of the gross profit from the bar, the balance being retained by BTH to pay for the wages of the steward and the expenses of heating, lighting and maintenance of the furniture and fabric.
5. The Club would receive a 10% refund of the total revenue from members' annual subscriptions. The rates of subscriptions, visitors' fees etc. to be decided from time to time by BTH in conjunction with the Club's Committee.

The renovated clubhouse opened at Easter 1955 and the members got down to the normal activities of playing golf and enjoying the Club's social activities. After the trauma of war there was the joy of renewing old pleasures and looking forward to the future with confidence and enthusiasm.

Social Functions

In January 1954 the first dinner dance of the Club was held in the hotel and this incorporated the presentation of prizes. The idea for this came in fact from Mr. Moulin, the General Manager of British Transport Hotels, and it was taken up enthusiastically by the Club. For many years thereafter the prizes were presented at that function and not at the separate 'Smoker', as now happens. The first 'Smoker' was held in 1958 and was the occasion of a presentation being made to the retiring Captain, Oliver Hughes-Onslow. These occasions were initially called 'Smoking Concerts' at which entertainment was provided, strong drink was taken and cigars were encouraged. Smokers had not yet become social pariahs. On occasions the entertainment was provided by the members themselves, sometimes in the form of light-hearted stage sketches specially written for the occasion. Captain John Grindlay was a leading light in such ventures.

Fire on the Course

Things were not all sweetness and light however. In the Spring of 1956 two prominent members took it upon themselves to set fire to the grass and wild rose bushes on the left bank approaching the sixth hole. Reputedly the two gentlemen had suffered beyond endurance in losing balls in that area and decided to take direct action to remove the hazard. One of the gentlemen, Adam Cockburn, was subsequently to serve as Captain and the other, Dr. Scade, had served on the Club Committee for many years. They both made personal apologies for their actions and the matter was closed, without too much ill feeling and a degree of understanding.

Notable Members

During this period some notables became members. In 1959 General Dwight D. Eisenhower, the President of the United States of America, visited Culzean Castle, which had been gifted by the Fifth Marquess of Ailsa to the National Trust for Scotland in 1945. Eisenhower

President Dwight D. Eisenhower with Professional Ian Marchbank exchanging score cards after a game in 1959.

was, on that occasion, presented with the life tenancy of an apartment in Culzean Castle to mark Scotland's gratitude to him for his wartime contribution to the victory of the Allies. During his visit he played golf at Turnberry with the Club Captain Graeme McCulloch, the Turnberry Professional Ian Marchbank and Provost James Gray of Maybole, the factor of the Marquess of Ailsa and he was offered and accepted honorary membership of the Club.

In 1957 John Morton ('Morty') Dykes joined the Club at the age of 52. In 1936 he had played in the British Walker Cup team which lost 10½ to 1½ to the U.S.A. at Pine Valley, New Jersey. He and G.B. Peters halved their foursomes match with C.R. Yates and W. Emery but Dykes was beaten 8 and 7 in the singles by Yates. He gained selection for the Walker Cup team after reaching the last eight of The Amateur Championship in both 1935 and 1936. Morty Dykes was possessed of great enthusiasm and tremendous strength and stamina and his competitive golfing life spanned almost 20 years. He first represented Scotland in 1934 and between then and 1951 he represented his country 6 times and he capped his career by winning the Scottish Championship in 1951, at the age of 46.

William (Willie) John Campbell was born in Glasgow in 1906 and won the Glasgow Amateur Championship three times, in 1926, 1928 and 1932. He was runner-up in the Scottish Amateur Championship in 1934, played for Scotland on many occasions and captained the side in 1935. In 1930 he played in the Walker Cup team beaten 10-2 by the U.S.A. at St. George's, Sandwich. He joined Turnberry in 1958 and was a great friend of Stanley P. Morrison, who was Captain of Turnberry in 1965-1967. He was very fond of Turnberry and, after his death, his ashes were scattered on the ninth tee of the Ailsa course, as narrated later in the reminiscences of past-Captain C.W.F. Judge.

Officials in this Period

In March 1957 Oliver Hughes-Onslow retired from the captaincy after holding office since 1936, a period of 21 years, stating that *'he was demitting office with great regret'*. Mr. Robert Black, a solicitor from Ayr, who had served for four years as Vice-Captain, was elected Captain, and W. Graeme McCulloch, a farmer from Ballantrae and a very fine golfer, was elected Vice-Captain. Robert (Bob) Loudon, an accountant from Ayr, had taken over as Secretary/Treasurer in September 1951 and he was to hold that office for almost 22 years until March 1973, during which time he faithfully served under eight different Captains. During his time in office Bob had to weather many storms as well as many Captains. He encoun-

---

THE WHITE HOUSE
WASHINGTON

September 9, 1959

Dear Mr. Landon:

I am complimented by the action of the members of the Turnberry Golf Club Committee in extending to me an Honorary Life Membership in the Club, and I am delighted to accept.

The members of the party accompanying me, together with my friends from New York, found the Turnberry course highly interesting. We all enjoyed greatly the three rounds we had there. I hope only that I did not inconvenience the regular membership of the Club by the confusion that inevitably surrounds any attempt of mine for a "quiet" game.

I might add that Mr. Marchbanks and his assistants were extremely courteous and helpful; it was a pleasure to play with them.

Sincerely,

Dwight D. Eisenhower

Mr. Robert B. Landon
Honorary Secretary
Turnberry Golf Club Committee
10 Barns Street
Ayr, Scotland

P.S.: Thank you, too, for the tie that symbolizes my official membership.

Chapter IV - Post War Turnberry 1946-1971

'Now all you boozers take a look / here's one to grace your copy book / the Captain, Adam, James and me / having a good time drinking tea'
Left to right: J.L. Walker, J. Crosbie, Adam Cockburn and J.P.K. McDowall

tered the usual quota of awkward members and coped patiently with the difficulties which inevitably arose from time to time between the Club and the owners of the hotel. One of the responsibilities of the Secretary at that time was to organise draws to make up games for those turning up at appointed times to take part in competitions. There was one particular member who was notorious for slow play, poor golf and even worse manners, as a result of which many other members refused to play with him. Bob Loudon had a terrible time trying to get him partners and, on one occasion, having failed to get him a game, as a last resort Bob sacrificed himself and played with the obnoxious member. His thanks was a complaint made by the member to the Committee, about his being forced to play with the Secretary, *'who had played very badly'*. Bob took the matter calmly and philosophically but the Committee banned the offending member from future competitions. This was typical of Bob who carried out his duties quietly and efficiently. When he retired he was made an honorary member and presented with a gold watch by the Club. He is still remembered with affection by those who knew him.

Robert Black served as Captain for a very short time from March till October 1957, when he resigned. The minutes of the Committee note that the terms of his letter of resignation were discussed and his resignation accepted, but no hint is given of the reasons.

Graeme McCulloch was elected Captain in his place and served until 1961. His place in the history of Turnberry is narrated in the next chapter. His Vice-Captain was J.P.K. McDowall who was an insurance broker who lived in Girvan and specialised in arranging insurance for the South Ayrshire fishing fleet. J.P.K. or Mr. James (as he was often known) succeeded Graeme McCulloch as Captain in 1961, the year in which the Amateur Championship was held at Turnberry for the first time. His usual playing companions were Adam Cockburn, Jim Crosbie (often addressed as 'Captain' - a reference to his military rank) and John L. Walker from

John Grindlay - Captain 1963 - 1965

Girvan who joined the Club in the 1920s. A photograph of these four taken in 1964 by J.L. Walker is reproduced here with the rhyme written on the back and initialled 'J.L.W.'.

The 1960's started with Graeme McCulloch being asked by the Committee to continue in office as Captain for a further year till March 1961, in view of the very heavy programme which had been arranged and the fact that Vice-Captain J.P.K. McDowall had been ill and would prefer to wait another year before taking over.

The heavy programme referred to included the second visit to Turnberry of the News of the World P.G.A. Match Play Championship, the Home International Matches and the Scottish Ladies' Amateur Championship which were all played at Turnberry in 1960. Despite his indisposition the Vice-Captain, aided by the Secretary, was put in charge of the Club's contribution to the administration arrangements for those three events. In addition, when Mr. McDowall took over the captaincy in March 1961, his term of office also covered the Amateur Championship which was held at Turnberry in that year.

J.P.K. McDowall retired from the captaincy in March 1963 and his place was taken by John Grindlay, a solicitor from Maybole, who had joined the Club pre-war and had been an enthusiastic member of the Committee since 1952. He contributed greatly to establishing the very successful social events, such as the dinner dance and smoker, which became annual functions thereafter. In the 1950's and 1960's the dinner dance was very popular, with attendances of over 200 most years and as high as 360 on occasions. A modest ticket price of £1 per head in the early years perhaps contributed to its popularity and sometimes the members stretched the capacity of the accommodation and facilities of Turnberry Hotel to the limit. In some years it became necessary to arrange a disco in a separate room from the hotel's ballroom, to cater for the overspill from the main dance. The popularity of this function has continued unabated for almost half a century since the first one in 1954 and many illustrious names from the world of golf have been the Club's guests at the event.

During his vice-captaincy and his captaincy (1963-1965) John Grindlay had an interesting sequence of tournaments visiting Turnberry. The Amateur in 1961, when he was Vice-Captain, was followed by the Walker Cup and the third visit of the PGA Match Play Championship, both in 1963, and the Braemar Seven Club Tournament in 1964.

CHAPTER IV - POST WAR TURNBERRY 1946-1971

CHAMPIONSHIPS HELD - 1952-1963

Local Championships in 1952

THE new Ailsa Course had hardly had time to settle down before it was chosen as a venue for local championship events after the war. The first such event, held in 1952, was the West of Scotland Professional Championship, and this was won by one of the most outstanding and important of the post-war Scottish professionals, John Panton of Glenbervie Golf Club, near Falkirk. He and Eric Brown, of Cruden Bay Golf Club on the east coast of Scotland, north of Aberdeen, were to become dominant Scottish professionals of that era, winning many honours both nationally and internationally. Panton had already won four successive Scottish Professional Championships in the years 1948 to 1951, and so his success at Turnberry in the West of Scotland Championship in 1952 was hardly unexpected.

In an interview in April 2003, at the age of 86, John Panton recalled having taken part in an exhibition match in 1951 to mark the opening of the new course, when he partnered the Club professional Stewart McDowall against Leonard Crawley and Henry Longhurst. He also recalled a few years later playing from the new tiger tee at the 9th hole for the first time. His memory of it was that the tee at that time was only about the size of a billiard table and had no protective fence round it. There was only room for two players and he was genuinely scared of falling from the tee onto the rocks and sea below, had he lost his balance on the follow through. He also recalled that, in playing 36 holes per day in the Scottish Professional Championship in the 1950's, they would take little more time for two rounds than the modern professionals now take for one.

In 1954 the Ayrshire Amateur Championship was held at Turnberry and it was won by J.R. (Jimmy) McKay, a notable amateur who many years later turned professional and became the first professional at the municipal Dalmilling golf course.

Scottish Ladies' Amateur Championship 1954

The Scottish Ladies' Golfing Association was formed at a meeting in Turnberry Hotel in 1904 and so it was very fitting that their Jubilee Championship was held on the Ailsa Course at Turnberry in 1954. There were one hundred competitors and a celebration dinner was held in the hotel before the start of the Championship. Miss Cecil Leitch, who had won the British Ladies' Open Amateur Championship at Turnberry in 1921, was guest of honour. It was reported in *Fairway and Hazard* magazine that she stayed on to see the play and *'lent great grace and charm and an added importance to the Championship'*. Neither Miss Leitch nor the spectators were to be disappointed. The Jubilee Championship turned out to be a very happy one, blessed with superb weather and played on a course which was at its most majestic and beautiful. It will also be remembered for the very high standard of the final between Mrs. Jessie Valentine, the holder, who had already won the title four times, and Mrs. R.T. Peel of Gullane, whose best finish till then had been runner-up at her home course in 1952.

At the end of the first round of the thirty six hole final Mrs. Valentine was six holes down, despite having scored 74, which was two strokes better than the ladies' par. However this was of no avail against her opponent, Mrs. Peel, who shot a miraculous score of 67. Her figures were: Out – 4, 4, 4, 3, 3, 4, 5, 4, 5 = 36, In – 3, 3, 4, 4, 4, 2, 3, 4, 4 = 31. Her opponent could have been forgiven had she collapsed against such phenomenal scoring, but in the second round, to her credit, Mrs. Valentine continued to score par or better and managed to get the deficit back to five at the fourth. Mrs. Peel's excellent golf was, however, relentless and she finished off the match with birdies at both the eleventh and twelfth holes to win by 7 and 6, winning her first Scottish Championship with a remarkable display of fine golf.

*Mrs Peel plays a fine shot in one of the most spectacular finals on record in 1954 Scottish Ladies' Amateur Championship.
Mr Graeme McCulloch, the referee (second from left), looks on.*

Mr. Graeme McCulloch, a former Club Champion and future Captain of the Club, refereed the final and the prizes were presented by Captain Oliver Hughes-Onslow. Mrs. Dunlop-Hill on behalf of the S.L.G.A. and of the competitors, expressed thanks to both the Men's Club and the Ladies' Club for their most kind hospitality.

Scottish Professional Championships 1954 and 1959

Surprisingly, at the outset of the 1954 Championship, the professional record for the Ailsa course stood at 75 by John Panton of Glenbervie, set two years previously in the West of Scotland Championship. With Turnberry in an unusually benign mood with little wind and only a hint of rain, which went almost unnoticed, this record was soon eclipsed on this occasion.

The championship was played over two days with 36 holes played each day and, in the first round, J.S. Anderson (Bruntsfield) first lowered the record to 71, a score that was soon equalled by W.S. MacDonald of Prestwick St. Nicholas. John Panton himself scored 73 in the first round but in the afternoon he reduced the record again, this time to 68. For a time it seemed as though W.S. MacDonald would improve even on that. Standing on the seventeenth tee he needed two fours for 66, but a wayward drive and then three putts at the seventeenth cost him a 6 and he had to hole a six foot putt at the eighteenth for a four to equal the new record. MacDonald led Panton overnight by two shots, 139 to 141. Bill Henderson (Troon) retired after nine holes in the afternoon, suffering from nervous exhaustion.

On the final day MacDonald shot 70 in the morning to lead by three shots going into the final round but could only manage to score 76 in the afternoon for an aggregate of 285. Panton was more consistent, shooting two excellent rounds of 71 for a winning aggregate of 283 and his fifth Scottish title.

The Scottish Championship again came to Turnberry in 1959 and once more John Panton won the title. He left the rest of the field trailing with his four round aggregate of 282, finishing six strokes ahead of his nearest rival, Hamish Ballingall of Old Ranfurly, and eight strokes ahead of Eric Brown of Buchanan Castle. This was Panton's seventh Scottish professional title and he went on to win it an eighth time, in 1966 at Cruden Bay, when he was joint champion with Eric Brown.

Chapter IV - Post War Turnberry 1946-1971

News of the World PGA Match Play Championship 1957

Although Turnberry had become a favourite regular venue for local and Scottish Championships and also for Ladies' Championships, it had not, prior to 1957, hosted a major British professional championship, apart from the 1908 Open Professional Tournament. When the News of the World PGA Match Play Championship came to Turnberry in September 1957, it was a significant recognition of the quality of the new Ailsa course and its suitability for top events. British Transport Hotels sought and were readily granted the co-operation of the Club in running the tournament and the Club's sub-committee for this purpose comprised Vice Captain W.G. McCulloch as Chairman together with D.K. Gourlay, W.S. Linton and Secretary R.B. Loudon.

The PGA Match Play Championship had an important and distinguished pedigree. In 1903 the recently formed Professional Golfers Association announced that *'the well known newspaper, the News of the World, [has] generously offered, with a view to encouraging match play among professional golfers, the sum of £200 to be competed for at a match play tournament, limited to members of the Association'*. The first such tournament was held at Sunningdale that year and it immediately became second in importance only to the Open. At that time the top professionals played more exhibition matches than tournaments, as a regular tour had not yet by then developed. What is more there were eventually nine regional qualifying competitions which became important regular events in their own right and often included a regional championship.

These tournaments at once achieved great popularity with both the players and the public, attributed by one commentator to *'the interesting and searching nature of the test of golf'* and winning this tournament conferred great credit and fame on the player. Harry Vardon won in 1912 and declared that, in doing so, had had achieved *'one of the ambitions of my golfing life'*.

At Turnberry 64 players took part in the 43rd Championship in 1957, the first round being over 36 holes played over two days on the Tuesday and the Wednesday. On the Thursday two rounds were played each over 18 holes and on the Friday the quarter finals and semi-finals were played also over 18 holes. The 36 hole final took place on the Saturday.

Peter Thomson of Australia was a very strong favourite to take the title, having that year finished second to Bobby Locke of South Africa in the Open Championship at St. Andrews, after being the Open Champion for three successive years in 1954, 1955 and 1956. Others in the field included John Panton, the holder, Eric Brown, the reigning Scottish Professional Champion that year, Henry Cotton of England (winner of the title three times, the first being in 1929), Christy O'Connor of Ireland and T.B. Haliburton of Scotland.

On the Thursday two rounds were played in the morning and the last match out was won by Henry Cotton, after his game was allowed through by the preceding Thomson-Panton match. Thomson beat Panton 2 up and the match finished late (having taken 3½ hours). Thomson was told that the 3.15 p.m. start of his next match, against Cotton, would be delayed by 20 minutes to give him time for some refreshment. Cotton was on the tee at 3.15 p.m. and had to be dissuaded from claiming the tie due to Thomson's lateness. Thomson duly arrived at his re-scheduled time and won the match 5 and 4, watched by a crowd of 800.

Christy O'Connor receives the World PGA Match Play Championship Cup in 1957 from Robert Black, Captain of Turnberry Golf Club.

The *Glasgow Herald* predicted that the final would be between Peter Thomson and Eric Brown but in the semi-finals Thomson was beaten 2 up by O'Connor and Haliburton beat Brown at the nineteenth. The 36-hole final on Saturday was played in wind and rain but, in spite of this, the match was watched by a gallery of 1000. Only one down after 18 holes, thanks to his superior putting, Haliburton was eventually beaten by O'Connor 5 and 4. Prize money totalled £3,000 of which the winner took £750.

The *Glasgow Herald* report concluded with the following:- *'For once there appeared to be no complaints about the course where an important event was played: only the week of troublesome wind was the subject of regret. Turnberry has recovered extraordinarily from the ravages of war service'.*

News of the World PGA Match-play Championship 1960

In 1960 this important tournament returned to Turnberry for the second time. The defending champion was David Snell (Worksop) but Christy O'Connor, winner in 1957 at Turnberry, was favourite to regain the title. The first round was played in pleasant conditions of sunshine with a light wind and all of the preceding five champions came through – Ken Bousfield (Coombe Hill), John Panton (Glenbervie), Harry Weetman (Selsdon Park) and Henry Cotton, as well as Snell and O'Connor. The first round match over 18 holes between W.S. Collins (North Wales) and W.J. Brand (unattached) lasted 5 hours and 40 minutes, and went on for 13 extra holes before Collins finally won at the 31st hole. The matches on the Thursday and the Friday were played in excellent weather conditions and the *Glasgow Herald* reporter waxed lyrical about the Friday -*'Turnberry has rarely looked so magnificent: from early morning till late at night a gloriously warm sun shone and the sea has rarely looked so blue and so little affected by the wind. The weather encouraged the older of us to dispense with the normal paraphernalia of clothing which is necessary for watching golf in September'.*

Throughout the week Eric Brown, the reigning Scottish Professional Champion, had suffered from fibrositis of the neck and, in the quarter-finals against

Eric Brown plays a wood to the 3rd green in final of the News of the World PGA Match Play Championship 1960.

Panton, his driving was so erratic that only uncharacteristic errors in chipping and putting on the part of Panton gave Brown a passage to the semi-final. In this he beat Tom Haliburton at the 19th, gaining revenge for his defeat at Turnberry at the same stage in 1957. In the other semi-final the long hitting Englishman Harry Weetman beat D.C. Thomas (Sudbury).

Chapter IV - Post War Turnberry 1946-1971

The weather deteriorated for the final on the Saturday afternoon, with heavy rain starting after an hour's play. The only protection Brown had was a waterproof jacket which he wrapped round his neck and head and his lower half and legs became quickly drenched. Before the rain stopped Brown went from 1 up to 2 down by the 15th hole. In his typical never-say-die spirit Brown crashed back into the game, winning the 16th with a birdie, halving the 17th and winning the 18th by holing a tricky eight feet putt to take the match in to extra holes. They halved the 19th and on the 20th Weetman was wide left of the green with his second shot while Brown was on the green in two. Weetman chipped to six yards but Brown, leaving the pin in the hole, boldly rapped an eight yard putt which wedged between the pin and the edge of the hole. At that time there was no penalty for hitting the pin with a putt and, when the pin was gently and carefully removed, the ball fell to the bottom of the can for a winning birdie three.

Captain Graeme McCulloch presented the trophy and the winning cheque for £750.

Scottish Ladies' Amateur Championship 1960

In June 1960 the Championship came to Turnberry for the seventh time and it was notable in the early rounds for the performance of Mrs. Helen Holm (Troon). She was 53 years old and had twice been British Champion and five times winner of the Scottish title, the first being in 1930 when she beat Miss Doris Park by one hole at Turnberry. On this occasion, in the third round she had a sensational victory on the last green against Miss Belle McCorkindale (Dunaverty) who had been a finalist the previous year in both the British and Scottish Championships. Mrs. Holm had won the first of her five Scottish titles before Belle was born, but her victory over her brilliant young opponent was no fluke. Her deadly accurate short game nullified the advantage of Miss McCorkindale's powerful long game and she was round in 73 to her young opponent's 76.

The Championship was won by Miss Janette Robertson (Lenzie), the holder, who beat Miss Dorothea Sommerville (Haggs Castle) by two and one in a 36-hole final over the Ailsa Course. Miss Robertson, a Curtis Cup player, had been runner-up in 1958 at Elie when she was beaten on the last green by Miss Sommerville. She was widely recognised as a very fine golfer and her victory at Turnberry was revenge for

Eric Brown receives the News of the World PGA Match Play Championship Cup in 1960.

1958 and also confirmed her standing as Scotland's leading woman golfer at that time.

Home Internationals 1960

In September 1960 the Home Internationals were held at Turnberry and the Club hosted a cocktail party for the players and officials prior to the start of play. The Scottish team included Jimmy Walker of Irvine Golf Club and the English Team included Michael Bonallack. England won the event with Ireland second,

Scotland third and Wales last. On the final day Scotland played England and a victory would have given them a tie for the first place. The prospects looked good when the Scots won the morning foursomes 4 – 0, but in the afternoon they could only manage three wins from 10 games.

Amateur Championship 1961

Turnberry was the exciting new venue for the Championship. The fancied seeds were Joe Carr of Ireland, Jimmy Walker of Scotland, whose home club was Irvine Golf Club, just up the Ayrshire Coast, Major D.A. Blair of Nairn and Martin Christmas of West Sussex. There was interest for the Turnberry Club with three members entered, Walter Linton, Jimmy MacKenzie and Johnstone Bulloch. Walter and Jimmy got through the first round but both were narrowly defeated in the second round. Johnstone Bulloch went out in round one. Carr, Walker, Christmas and Bonallack all reached the quarter finals, with the outstanding match being that between Carr and Walker. They had played against each other on previous occasions, but Walker had never beaten the Irishman. It was a tight low-scoring match and this time Walker came out on top – at the 19th.

Another two Scots reached the quarter finals, but Innes Wright, of Aboyne lost 5 and 3 to Martin Christmas and L.S. Foster, of Prestwick lost 5 and 4 to Bonallack. In the remaining quarter final an American, R.L. Morrow, beat A.R. Dixon of Ravensworth.

In the semi-finals Walker beat Morrow at the 18th and Bonallack beat Christmas by 3 and 2, to set up a mouth-watering final full of interest for the Ayrshire golfing public. Walker's reward in any event was a place in the British Walker Cup team. The story of the final is told later in this chapter by Sir Michael Bonallack himself, the ultimate Champion.

News of the World P.G.A. Match-Play Championship 1963

The Championship was played at Turnberry for the third and last time in 1963 and Eric Brown, the defending champion, after an indifferent year, required a good performance to have a chance of a Ryder Cup place. All the leading British players, plus a South African and a Dane, were in the field of 120 who played qualifying rounds on the Ailsa and Arran courses on the Monday and Tuesday to decide the leading 64 to go forward to the match play on the Wednesday. The Glasgow Herald commented that the testing nature of the 7023 yards championship Ailsa Course was well known but that the difficulties of the 6603 yards Arran Course should not be underestimated, with its whin-lined fairways demanding consistently straight driving.

On the Monday the weather was dry and warm with a light breeze from the north, and D.J. Rees (South Herts) had a record 67 (31 inward half) over the Ailsa, while D. Miller (Stoneham) had a record 68 on the Arran. Next day, Rees added a 68 on the Arran to lead qualifiers and win the £200 prize for that stage (the championship prize was £1,250); Miller had 71 on the Ailsa. 63 players had scores of 151 or better, and the first tee was somewhat overcrowded as 9 players gathered for the sudden death play-off for the final place, which was resolved on the third hole. When the match-play started on the Wednesday, Brown was knocked out in the first round by D. Snell, the 1959 champion, and he was joined in the clubhouse by H. Weetman, P. Alliss, J.R.M. Jacobs and G.B. Wolstenholme. Next day, four Ryder Cup players – B.J. Hunt, K. Bousfield, N.C. Coles and C. O'Connor – were all beaten. In the fourth round I. Wright (unattached), the former Scottish Amateur International who had turned professional only 6 months previously, beat B.G.C. Huggett (Romford) after 5 hours 40 minutes, ending the ordeal on a grey rainy evening at the 27th hole. On the Saturday the semi-finals were played in the morning, with the final teeing off at 2.00 p.m. D.C. Thomas (Sunningdale), in the semis for the fourth time in 5 years, beat G. Will (assistant, Walton Heath) by 1 hole, while J.A. Macdonald (Bedford and Coventry) was 5 up with 8 to play against Wright, finally also winning by 1 hole. The final in the afternoon was played in a strong rain-laden south wind. Thomas' distance off the tee stood him in good stead, and he was out in 34 and 3 up. A 3 at the 10th made Thomas 4 up, then he halved the 11th and 12th, lost the 13th after a badly pulled tee shot, halved the 14th and lost the 15th to a 2 to make it 2 up; on the 16th, Thomas was home with a 4 iron and his par 4 was good enough to win the hole, the match and the Championship.

Chapter IV - Post War Turnberry 1946-1971

Amateurs -v- Professionals Match 1958

SOME of the most fascinating international golf is played in the form of team matches, with great interest and excitement aroused by those for the Ryder and Solheim cups at a professional level and the Walker and Curtis cups for the amateurs. These matches of course are either professional against professional or amateur against amateur and matches between amateur and professional teams would today seem almost too absurd to contemplate if an even contest was sought. The potential financial rewards from professional tournament golf are such that the amateur game haemorrhages most of its best players at a very early age to the professional ranks.

It is generally forgotten that such contests between the paid and the unpaid exponents of the game did take place – in 1956 at Royal Mid-Surrey, in 1957 at Lindrick and in August 1958 at Turnberry. The occasion at Turnberry is not recorded by Turnberry Hotel in the Roll of Honour of tournaments held there, but it is mentioned in the minutes of Turnberry Golf Club. In the two previous matches the professionals had won comfortably by nine games to four with two halved in 1956 and by eight games to five with two halved in 1957. At Turnberry however it was a different story. There the amateur golfers beat the professionals by nine matches to five with one halved, and thereafter there were no more such contests. This and the distinct lack of information about them in the record books almost suggests that the result at Turnberry provoked a desire to draw a veil over them.

At Turnberry, having lost the foursomes over two rounds on day one by only three matches to two, the amateurs played brilliantly on the second day to win the 36 hole singles by seven matches to two with one halved, for a clear victory by four points. It could have been worse, for Doug Sewell had been three up on Peter Alliss after 18 holes before losing and Guy Wolstenholme was dormie five up on Harry Weetman but lost the last five holes for a halved game.

Despite heavy rain there was some notable golf, not least by Reid Jack who was three down to Christy O'Connor after 21 holes, but won six of the next seven holes and went on to win by five and three, having scored five under fours for the 15 holes played in the afternoon. The other scalps claimed were those of Eric Brown by Joe Carr, Bernard Hunt by Arthur Perowne, Peter Mills by Alec Shepperson, Ken Bousfield by Michael Bonallack, John Jacobs by Michael Lunt and Harry Bradshaw by Ayrshire's own Jimmy Walker.

The professionals, who included almost the entire successful Ryder Cup team of the previous year were reported by the *Glasgow Herald* to be *'inclined to dismiss the overall defeat as having happened because, for them, there was nothing at stake'*. The verdict of the *Herald's* special correspondent was *'The truth is that in the windless weather that prevailed they were beaten by players who refreshingly were not overawed by reputations and who in a professional manner treated par as the enemy'*.

In these days of appearance money, huge prize funds and the pressures on professionals for position on the orders of merit and for Ryder Cup points, it is unlikely that such a contest will ever be held again and even more unlikely that the amateurs could emerge victorious. During the match all officials and players were made temporary members of the Club, ordinary club members acted as stewards, lady members organised the sale of programmes and Vice-Captain J.P.K. McDowall and Mr. Adam Cockburn acted as starters.

AMATEUR CHAMPIONSHIP 1961 AND WALKER CUP 1963
BY SIR MICHAEL BONALLACK

Amateur Championship 1961

PRIOR to the Amateur Championship, I had never played golf at Turnberry but after winning there the first of my five Amateurs, it will always be a place of special memories and one of my favourite golf courses in the world. Every amateur dreams of playing in the Walker Cup and winning the Amateur. In this respect I was the same as everyone else.

That particular golf season started off well for me as I had already won the Berkshire Trophy, with a record low aggregate and had tied for the *Golf Illustrated* Gold Vase. At the time these were two of the most prestigious amateur events on the calendar. I had also finished in fifth place in the Martini tournament at Sundridge Park, a Professional tournament which featured all the best home players and one or two overseas stars, including Bob Charles.

Thus I came to Turnberry in a good frame of mind, which became even better from the moment I set eyes on the magnificent golf course in its beautiful setting and checked in at the luxurious Turnberry Hotel. I had never felt more at home at any other golf event and, without being boastful, I just knew that I was going to win. In those days, the practice rounds in the Amateur were great fun, playing against old friends for the odd pound or two and then after dinner sitting down for a game or two of poker. Needless to say Joe Carr featured in both the golf and cards and, for once, I had a very successful time both on and off the golf course.

Joe was the defending Champion and as such was at the top of the draw which was seeded. I myself was at the very bottom, which meant that we could not meet until the final. That year the format of play had reverted to that used prior to 1956, with only the final being played over 36 holes, whereas for the previous five years both the quarter and semi finals had also been over the longer distance.

The golf course itself was in magnificent condition and the whole atmosphere was conducive to a very enjoyable and successful Championship.

In the first round on Monday, I played Bill Jack from Pollok and got off to a dream start, reaching the turn in one under par and finding myself five up. Pars at the next three holes saw me in the second round.

I was now playing A.J.S. McLeod from Ranfurly Castle and, after winning the first hole with a birdie, at the second I lost a hole for the first time in the Championship but then went ahead at the third to win eventually by 5/4 at which stage I was three under par.

In the third round against P.J. Binns, although I won by 6/5, it was the only match in which I was not under par for the round, finishing one over.

On the next day I got off to another good start against Bill Stewart and was five up at the turn and was level par when I won 3/2.

I knew the next match against David Frame would be difficult and, after going one up with a birdie two at the fourth, I lost the next two holes to birdies to go one down – the only time I was to be down in the whole of the Championship. However a run of pars and two birdies saw me home by 3/2.

My opponent in the last eight was somewhat of a surprise, in that Laurence Foster, at the time Secretary at Prestwick, was not in the first flush of youth but in three successive rounds had accounted for Peter Davidson, a very good player from Northumberland, John Glover, the Irish International and former Boys Champion and lastly Alex Kyle who had won the Championship himself in 1939. I think three hard matches had taken a lot out of him and I ran out a comfortable winner by 5/4 having gone out in three under par for a five up lead.

Chapter IV - Post War Turnberry 1946-1971

This brought me a semi-final clash with Martin Christmas, a very promising young golfer with a great swing and beautiful rhythm. I knew I would have to play my best to beat him. Again I got off to a great start and reached the turn five up and four under par. After winning the tenth I then lost the next three holes but steadied with a birdie at the 14th and won by 3/2.

Now I was in the final, not against Joe Carr as I had expected, but against Jimmy Walker of Irvine Golf Club, who had beaten Joe at the 19th in a marvellous match in the quarter final and had then defeated the last American Ralph Morrow in the semi-final. I knew Jimmy was a great fighter and, like myself, loved to play quickly. I also knew that the whole of Ayrshire would be cheering him on. However, when the morning arrived I was surprised and delighted to find my wife Angela, my father and a number of my friends and supporters from my home club, Thorpe Hall, had made the long overnight journey to support me.

My secret weapon that week was a new caddie, Willie Aitchison, who drove road tankers for the Coast Liner Group in the winter but, come summer, he plied his trade as a caddie. He was superb and, within the next few years carried the winner's bag in three Open Championships. The Final was played in intermittent rain and a strong breeze and in these conditions a good caddie is worth his weight in gold. Keeping the grips dry, having a dry towel and the umbrella ready at all times, makes the game so much easier for his player and Willie could not have been better at this. His yardages and judgement of distance were absolutely spot on. Some combination.

I knew a good start would be important and was delighted to find myself three under par for the first nine holes and four up. Although I lost two holes on the back nine I managed to win three others with birdies and halved the other four. I went into lunch five holes to the good, having been round in 69 in 2 hours 45 minutes. Incidentally this was the only time I played the 17th and 18th holes during the Championship.

During the break I remember enjoying my favourite *'golf lunch'* of rare roast beef and salad with French dressing, followed by a good sized helping of strawberry ice cream. This was perfectly served in the splendid large hotel dining room.

After lunch the rain persisted but I barely noticed it. You never do when you are winning. Parring the next five holes my lead had increased to six up and, although I lost the sixth and the ninth holes, four pars and a birdie at the 13th saw me win by 5/4. At that time it was the greatest moment of my life. That evening, after the presentation, all of my supporters had to return South on the sleeper, but Jimmy's friends from Irvine, who had been a wonderfully sporting crowd, invited me back to their club to the party which they had organised to celebrate Jimmy's *'victory'*. Sadly for them it was not to be, but I will never forget the kindness shown to me that night and the warmth of their welcome and of their congratulations. I eventually got to bed about breakfast time the next morning, very tired but very happy. Jimmy and I have been close friends ever since.

Walker Cup 1963

Whereas 1961 at Turnberry was a time I will always remember, the Walker Cup in 1963 was an experience I would like to forget. Once again the course was marvellous, the hotel superb and the team, which was a good one, was full of confidence. Some of us had been in the amateur team which had beaten a team of British Ryder

Michael Bonallack and Jimmy Walker at the conclusion of the final of the 1961 Amateur Championship.

Cup players in a match at Turnberry in 1958 so we were feeling very happy about our chances of beating the Americans for the first time for 25 years.

The Press too were very confident. They described the American team as lacking experience in depth because it contained a number of young players. As it turned out those young players played very well and without fear, as youth will. They blended well with players such as Billy Joe Patton, Charlie Coe, Bob Gardner and Deane Beman, playing in his third match.

The first morning did not start too well. Stewart Murray and myself playing top, got the better of Billy Joe Patton and Dick Sykes, winning by 4/3. Behind us however, Joe Carr and Charlie Green lost to Downing Gray and Labron Harris on the last green and, with Deane Beman and Charlie Coe playing well to beat Michael Lunt and David Sheahan by 5/3, it was left to Ronnie Shade and David Madeley to salvage another half point, leaving us trailing by one after this series.

Whereas the morning had not gone well, the afternoon singles could not have gone much better. Only Billy Joe Patton won for the U.S.A. whilst we won five and halved the other two matches and we actually found ourselves leading by six matches to three.

What happened overnight I am not sure, but the next morning was a disaster. Stewart Murray and myself stood at all square playing the 16th hole and, with our opponents on the green in three a long way from the hole before we had played our second shot, it looked as if we should go one up with two to play. Although at the time the press said I hit the wrong club for my second, I maintain this was not so. I was trying to play a five iron to the centre of the green, with the pin being just over the burn in the front right quarter. However, I came off the shot and cut it into the wind and, although it was flying straight at the flag, I knew that I had not hit it the way I had planned and it dropped into the burn in the deep valley in front of the green. The hole was lost and we didn't recover, going down by one hole.

1963 British Walker Cup Team
Back Row (from left to right): John Jacobs (Professional Coach), D.B. Sheahan, S.W.T. Murray, C.W. Green, M.J. Christmas, J.F.D. Madeley, A.C. Saddler, Bob Jamieson (Turnberry Professional)
Front Row (from left to right): M.S.R. Lunt, J.B. Carr, C. Lawrie (non-playing Captain), M.F. Bonallack, R.D.B.M. Shade.

Chapter IV - Post War Turnberry 1946-1971

Behind us matters were worse and, losing by 3/2, 3/2 and 3/2 in the next three games, our overnight lead vanished and instead we were one match down.

In the afternoon David Sheahan played well to beat Richard Davies and Ronnie Shade was his immaculate self in beating Downing Gray for the second day running. Our only other ray of sunshine was Sandy Saddler who halved a great match with Deane Beman. The rest of us sunk without trace.

Needless to say, the post match Dinner was not the joyous occasion we were expecting it to be some twenty-four hours earlier.

Match Results (GBI names first)

Morning foursomes – first series

1. M.F. Bonallack & S.W.T. Murray beat W.J. Patton & R.H. Sikes – 4/3
2. J.B. Carr & C.W. Green lost to A.D. Gray Jr. & L.E. Harris Jr. – 2 holes
3. M.S.R. Lunt & D.B. Sheahan lost to D.R. Beman & G.R. Coc – 5/3
4. J.F.D. Madeley & R.D.B.M. Shade halved with R.W. Gardner & E.R. Updegraff

**Morning scores –
Great Britain & Ireland 1 America 2**

Afternoon singles – first series

1. S.W.T. Murray beat D.R. Beman – 3/1
2. M.J. Christmas lost to W.J. Paton – 3/2
3. J.B. Carr beat R.H. Sikes – 7/5
4. D.B. Sheahan beat L.E. Harris Jr – 1 hole
5. M.F. Bonallack beat R.D. Davies – 1 hole
6. A.C. Saddler halved with C.R. Coe
7. R.D.B.M. Shade beat A.D. Gray Jr – 4/3
8. M.S.R. Lunt halved with C.B. Smith

**Afternoon score –
Great Britain & Ireland 5 America 1**

**Day one result –
Great Britain & Ireland 6 America 3**

Morning foursomes – second series

1. M.F. Bonallack & S.W.T. Murray lost to W.J. Patton & R.H. Sikes – 1 hole
2. M.S.R. Lunt & D.B. Sheahan lost to A.D. Gray Jr & L.E. Harris Jr – 3/2
3. C.W. Green & A.C. Saddler lost to R.W. Gardner & E.R. Updegraff – 3/1
4. J.F.D. Madeley & R.D.B.M. Shade lost to D.R. Beman & C.R. Coe – 3/2

**Morning score –
Great Britain & Ireland 0 America 4**

Afternoon singles – second series

1. S.W.T. Murray lost to W.J. Patton – 3/2
2. D.B. Sheahan beat R.D. Davies – 1 hole
3. J.B. Carr lost to E.R. Updegraff – 4/3
4. M.F. Bonallack lost to L.E. Harris Jr – 3/2
5. M.S.R. Lunt lost to R.W. Gardner – 3/2
6. A.C. Saddler halved with D.R. Beman
7. R.D.B.M. Shade beat A.D. Gray Jr – 2/1
8. D.W. Green lost to C.R. Coe – 4/3

**Afternoon score –
Great Britain & Ireland 2 America 5**

**Day two result –
Great Britain & Ireland 2 America 9**

**Match result –
Great Britain & Ireland 8 America 12**

THE FEWER THE BETTER
BRAEMAR 7 CLUB TOURNAMENT 1964

In October 1964 an interesting professional tournament was held at Turnberry. It was the Braemar Seven–Club Tournament sponsored by Braemar Knitwear Limited, an old established Scottish knitwear company from Hawick in the Borders of Scotland. Such tournaments are not uncommon at club level and indeed Turnberry Golf Club play this format for an annual Trophy donated in 1980 in memory of Bob Adamson, a keen member, who was Chief Constable of Ayrshire. However the Braemar tournament was possibly the most unusual tournament ever played under the auspices of the Professional Golfers' Association. It struck a sympathetic chord at the time with two of the most eminent golf writers, Henry Longhurst and P.A. Ward-Thomas.

A Return to Golfing Sanity

In the tournament programme Longhurst described it as an *'experimental return to golfing sanity, which surely deserves the commendation of the golfing world'*. He extolled the virtues of employing fewer clubs, arguing that the average handicap golfer in particular would probably score better with only 7 clubs than with the permitted maximum of 14. He lampooned *'the wretched golfer who knows no better, buys a huge bag to carry a full set; then cannot carry the bag, so he has to buy a perambulator in which to pull it round; and then in the U.S.A., the final lunacy of all, he has a little electric cart to carry himself as well'* – all vintage Henry. But he was not the only one to approve of the Braemar tournament. P.A. Ward-Thomas, writing in *Country Life*, welcomed it with relish saying:-

'Many years ago I went down to the West Country to see J.H. Taylor on the eve of his 80th birthday. He was in lively voice and we talked of many things, not least the modern tendency to mechanise the game, whose dignity, charm and character were, he thought, in danger. His remedy was simple, and I remember the emphasis with which he insisted that the number of clubs be reduced from 14 to seven.

To many golfers nowadays these opinions might seem to be those of an old man living in the past and regretting the present, but they held the substance of truth. The game is not the exercise of skill that it was; since the coming of steel shafts it has been easier. The golfer does not have to contend with torque and warping in the shaft, nor, to the same degree, with the feel of a club. The exactness of modern manufacturing methods ensures that clubs throughout a set are perfectly matched; their swing weight is constant; and for all practical purposes, imponderables in equipment no longer exist.

As the number of clubs increased, the variety of shots diminished and golf became a question of selecting the club rather than the type of stroke. Much of the imagination, artistry and sensitivity of touch that were essential to fashion different shots with the same club had vanished. For the modern first-class player with a grooved, repeating swing the only real problem in normal conditions is judgement of distance. The club does the work for them.

A further effect of this has been to thrust over-much emphasis on putting. This meant that even Hogan, the supreme master in the art of controlling a golf ball, was only rewarded in true measure to his skill as a striker when he putted well. In the old days a champion won by his command in every phase of the game; now even Palmer and Nicklaus, with all their power and competitive ability, could not prevail unless they were two of the world's greatest putters.

Small wonder that the golfers of old regretted the changing character of the game. When J.H. started to play, as a boy caddie at Westward Ho almost 90 years ago, he had to learn every type of shot with two or three clubs, and said that in all the years of his greatness he never carried more than seven. Although Willie Park, Open champion in the late '80s, had a full range of ten it is probable that he did not use them all in any one round: in fact the average set in those days was seven or eight.

Every winter these years there seem to be tidings of a new event for the coming season. Mostly they do not quicken anticipation, because the form of the competition so often is

Chapter IV - Post War Turnberry 1946-1971

the same old treadmill of 72-hole stroke play. It was therefore something of a relief when the Braemar company announced that they were promoting a seven-club tournament, and everyone will be interested to see what the professionals make of Turnberry next October with half their usual armoury.'

Many would still agree with the validity of the opinions expressed by Longhurst and Ward-Thomas. But such are the inherent difficulties of golf and of the challenges of the hazards provided by Nature, that it will surely remain one of the most difficult and pleasurable games in the world no matter how many or hi-tec are the clubs allowed.

Very Creditable Scoring

As it turned out the tournament proved an unqualified success, and the scores were on the whole very respectable. The winner was 29 year old Lionel Platts of Wansted with a 72 hole aggregate of 288, which carried off the first prize of £550. At that time the amateur record for the course was 72 by George McKay, a very good local player who subsequently turned professional. The professional record was 67, set the previous year, by Dai Rees, using only nine of the 14 clubs his caddie was carrying, and so the winning score of level fours for 72 holes was very respectable.

The rules of the tournament allowed the players a free choice of clubs, the selection to be declared on the first tee. A different selection could be made for each round, but the winner used the same seven clubs throughout – a driver and Nos. 4, 6, 7 and 9 irons, wedge and putter. J.R. Jacobs came second, a stroke behind, with D.C. Thomas third, a further two shots back. Jacobs revealed that he only brought seven clubs with him, to avoid any doubt about which clubs to play. They were the same as those chosen by Platts except for the choice of Nos. 3 and 5 irons instead of 4 and 6. Some notables in the rest of the field would perhaps have taken issue with the views of Longhurst and Ward-Thomas, as they did not find the task easy. Amongst them Peter Alliss and John Panton scored 297, Tony Jacklin, Harold Henning and Tommy Horton 299, Guy Wolstenholme 300, Max Faulkner 303 and Frank Rennie, the redoubtable local pro from Prestwick, scored 304.

A Period of Quiet - 1964-1971

DURING the 1950s and until 1964 the Ailsa course was in frequent demand for important tournaments and matches. In the space of seven years from 1957 till 1964 it was used for almost everything except the Open Championship itself, including the Walker Cup, the Amateur Championship, the Braemar Tournament and the Match Play Championship three times. Then, for some reason, it disappeared as a national venue for eight years until the John Player Classic was held in 1972.

Commentary at the time took the view that the reason was one of hard economics. British Transport Hotels had found that many of the single rooms in the hotel tended to be unlet for much of the year. They carried out alterations to make most rooms double, to cater for the demand from families and couples. As a consequence they developed strong holiday bookings, many of which were repeated year after year. Holding big golf events during most summer months might have meant breaking the sequence of those bookings, which might not have been easy to re-establish. Apparently there were only two months, outside the winter ones, when this did not apply – April and July. The latter was perhaps surprising but was possibly in part due to the alternative attraction for golfing families of the Open Championship which is always held in that month. In retrospect the obvious answer might have been to seek to persuade the Royal and Ancient Golf Club to hold the Open Championship at Turnberry and thus bring tremendous business in an Open year and heighten the overall fame and reputation of the resort. However, if such a strategy was even contemplated, it was not pursued or, if pursued, not successful till many years later.

Peter Ryde, writing in the *Country Life* in the late 1960s made a plea for Turnberry to be used for important events, even if it was for the kind of events where the gate was not of primary importance, such as team events like the Curtis and Walker Cups, the Home Internationals, or national amateur championships. He pointed out that Turnberry was especially suitable for such events, being able to accommodate the players, officials and others under the same roof, thus strengthening the spirit of goodwill which enhances the events. He pointed to past events at Turnberry as proof of this: *'The Walker Cup match of 1963 stays in the memory of those present, as much for the glory of the weather that preceded it and the palpable enjoyment of the Americans present, as for the sensational jolt to our chances that developed in the foursomes on the second day. The weather had been less kind for the home internationals in 1960, but Anglo-Scottish rivalry was at its friendliest peak under one roof, the subdued glee of the Scots at winning four and a half points out of five in the foursomes being matched by the moderated joy of the English at winning the first five singles and tying the match. Nor was this only true of the team events; it applied even in the Amateur, where the emphasis is on individuality, for the 1961 Amateur was one of the happiest since the war'.*

Ryde went on to complain that on a recent visit the course looked uncherished compared to its condition achieved formerly for big occasions and he commented:- *'But I cannot see a course of that stature and beauty lost to all but casual visitors and package tours without shedding a public tear in protest. Such a course, its suitability as a host to great golfing events already demonstrated, strikes me as something more than an appendage to a hotel network. Is it impertinent to suggest that its owners have an obligation to a wider public than their clients? Ailsa is an important part of our national golfing heritage. That surely should justify its being restored to a place in the golfing fixtures and, incidentally, as a household word to golfers on both sides of the Atlantic and of the English Channel'.*

The period of quiet which ensued after the Braemar Tournament in 1964 is illustrated by some entries in the minutes of the Club Committee. For instance it was reported that the usual December date for the annual dinner dance was not available in 1964 because the hotel was closing for the winter from November 1964 till February 1965. Then in June 1965 the Club Committee

Chapter IV - Post War Turnberry 1946-1971

and officials were invited to attend the filming at Turnberry of an episode of *'Shell's Wonderful World of Golf'* for television, in order to provide some *'crowd effect'*.

The Club itself was comparatively unaffected in its normal activities by the absence of tournaments. Indeed the normal golfing programme thrived, free from the inevitable interruption to play occasioned by tournaments.

In addition to the usual inter-club matches there were many special matches held, including ones against Cambridge, Oxford, Glasgow, Strathclyde and Dublin Universities and against Ayrshire County, the BBC Golf Club, and People to People Group from America. In 1972 there was a match with Royal Montreal Golf Club after which Captain R.H.U. Stevenson and Vice-Captain Tommy Armstrong were made honorary members of that Club.

It was a time of growth in the number of members, which in 1966 stood at 257 gentlemen and 51 ladies and by 1972 had risen to 333 gentlemen and 81 ladies. Social functions were well attended and the minutes mention that in 1970 there were 450 applications to attend the annual dinner dance, but only 372 could be accommodated by the hotel. To achieve these numbers the meal was buffet style and all the bars, lounges, dining room and bedrooms in the hotel were used exclusively for the function. The trophies were exhibited in the entrance hall with the list of winners, but no presentation was made.

Captains during this period were Stanley P. Morrison (1965-1967), Adam C. Cockburn (1967-1969), and David K. Gourlay (1969-1971), and R.H.U. Stevenson (1971-1973). The Vice-President since 1939, Sir John Richmond, K.B.E., LL.D., C.Bt., had died in 1963 and Oliver Hughes Onslow who had been President since 1957 died in 1972. Until the last year before he died Hughes Onslow still occasionally attended General Meetings and meetings of the Management Committee. No new Vice President or President has been elected since their deaths.

In 1965 Reginald L. Turnbull retired as Hotels Superintendent of British Transport Hotels after many years and a presentation was made to him in recognition of his good work on behalf of the Club. At that time the incumbent of the post was an ex officio member of the Club Committee. Mr. Turnbull was succeeded by Mr. F.H. Moulin.

On the golfing front Alistair Wilson and Wilson Scott were beaten finalists in the *Evening Times* Foursomes Tournament in 1968 emulating Tommy Armstrong and Walter Linton who were runners-up in the same tournament in 1960. That same year (1968) Alistair Wilson reached the last 16 of the Amateur Championship at Troon and represented Scotland in an under-25 team against a British Universities team. In 1969, along with Ruth Ferguson, he won the Worplesdon Mixed Foursomes Tournament, beating the team of Pam Tredinnick and Bruce Critchley, a Walker Cup player, in the final. Alistair's most notable achievement was possibly in 1971 when he finished runner-up to Ian Hutcheon at Leven and Lundin Links, in the Scottish Amateur Stroke Play Championship.

This period ended with great dissatisfaction about the poor condition of the courses and in October 1971 the Ailsa course was closed for repairs. One of the problems was damage caused by rabbits and Captain R.H.U. Stevenson undertook to take steps to control them.

Snippets From The Club Minutes in Historical Context - 1946-1971

March 1946	Future of Turnberry uncertain.
November 1947	Marriage of Princess Elizabeth to Duke of Edinburgh.
August 1948	British Railways nationalised.
August 1950	Members commence play again over 9 holes of Ailsa – free of charge.
April 1952	*'Agreed that first post-war competition of the Club be held on 26th April. 1952.'*
March 1953	*'Decided that prizes for trophy competitions to be vouchers for £2-2/- and £1-1/- for winners and runners-up.'*
June 1953	Hillary and Tensing conquer Everest. Queen Elizabeth II's Coronation.
May 1954	Agreed that Captain would present the prizes for the Scottish Ladies' Golf Championship.
August 1954	Bannister runs the first four minute mile.
April 1955	Sir Winston Churchill retires as Prime Minister.
May 1955	Twenty nine new members admitted.
March 1956	*'Intimated that the course had been set on fire by some members of the Club!'*
March 1957	*'Agreed on motion of Mr. Linton that knock-out ties in Club Championship be played from the back tees.'*
October 1957	British Transport Hotels intimate deep indebtedness to the Club for having P.G.A. News of the World Tournament so successfully carried through.
December 1957	Conception Golf Club from South America given permission to incorporate the 4th hole of the Ailsa in their new course.
November 1958	Captain intimates death of Andrew Scrimgeour, Head Greenkeeper, and states: *'He would be greatly missed, at all times he had given personal attention to the Club's requests in respect of the course for the members' benefit, and by his kindly courteous manner had been a good friend to the Club.'*
January 1959	The Secretary reported that the attendance at the Annual Dinner Dance was 210.
January 1959	Agreed to provide a *'Battery and Mains Portable Wireless'* for the clubhouse.
April 1959	Committee advised by Secretary that members had an enforceable right to *'every second ball'* on 1st tee.
October 1959	President of the United States of America, General Dwight Eisenhower, accepts Honorary Membership of Club.
September 1960	Turnberry Team finish runners-up in the Western Team Trophy Competition.
April 1961	*'Agreed to have a competition for pre-war members for a prize given by an anonymous donor.'*
July 1962	Letter read from Captain of Troon Golf Club thanking Turnberry for help provided at Open Championship in Troon.
November 1962	*'Resolved not to proceed with a proposal to purchase a house at Turnberry for use as club premises.'*

Chapter IV - Post War Turnberry 1946-1971

February 1963	Match versus Oxford and Cambridge University cancelled this year.	July 1969	Tony Jacklin wins the Open at Royal Lytham.
June 1963	Henry Cooper K.O.'s Cassius Clay.	June 1969	The Secretary advised that the membership at present was 329 Gentlemen, 70 Ladies and 10 Juniors.
October 1965	Henry Cotton to be guest speaker at the annual dinner dance.		
March 1966	Entrance fee for membership fixed at £5-8/- for Gentlemen and £3-3/- for Ladies.	June 1970	Tony Jacklin wins the U.S. Open.
		December 1970	'Reported 450 applications to attend annual dinner dance and agreed that two bands be engaged for the occasion.'
April 1967	'Agreed to subscribe £2 to S.G.U., for a testimonial to R.D.B.M. Shade in the form of a portrait.'	June 1971	'Decided that the foreshore did not constitute hazard at the 4th hole of the Ailsa.'
October 1966	Aberfan school disaster – 144 killed.	November 1971	'Covers provided for clubroom tables to stop noise of dominoes.'
October 1968	Dinner Dance: Agreed that trophies be shown in hotel vestibule and names of winners intimated but that no presentation be made.		

Winter panorama from beind 8th Ailsa green

One of the majestic views from the high ground of the new Kintyre course.

Chapter V

The Modern Era Begins - 1972-1980

Characters, Caddies, Classics and The 1977 Open

Characters, Players and Pro-ams 1972-1980

THE 1970s at Turnberry were busy years for the Club, the Hotel and the courses, characterised by many tournaments and events which all served to confirm Turnberry as one of the most famous names in golf. The finest and most telling accolade of all was of course the holding of The Open at Turnberry in 1977, but the period also saw two John Player Classics, a British Seniors Amateur Open, a European Open and a British Club Professionals' Championship, as well as other lesser but interesting events. The Captains of the period were all strong colourful characters, starting with David K. Gourlay who served from 1969 till 1971.

David K. Gourlay

Known to his close friends as 'Popeye', David Gourlay is still fondly remembered by the older members of the Club. He was a native of Girvan, born on 9th December 1908, and became one of that town's most popular and well-known residents. He was a printer and journalist to trade and became the owner of the *Carrick Herald*, a local newspaper, on the death of his father Thomas Gourlay in 1934. By the time he retired from the newspaper industry in 1977 he had spent 48 years with the 'Herald', 37 of them as owner and most of them as editor. His career was only interrupted during the war when he enlisted as a Royal Marine Commando and saw service in Sicily and Italy.

Golf wasn't his only sport, for he was also Girvan High School champion at both athletics and tennis and a professional footballer. While studying printing at Heriot Watt College in Edinburgh in 1926 he signed professional forms for Heart of Midlothian Football Club but he was subsequently reinstated amateur in Junior football, playing first for Shawfield and then for Glasgow Petersfield and being capped at that level for Scotland in 1930, 1931 and 1932.

David joined the Club in 1934 and was made an honorary member in 1984 after fifty years unbroken membership. He was a very useful golfer with a handicap as low as 5 in his younger days. Latterly he used to play with his feet in a hen-toed position and he would often advise this set-up for others. However this was just his incorrigible sense of humour, for the truth was that he suffered greatly from knee injuries from the football and resultant operations, and he couldn't stand any other way!

As well as serving as Captain David was always a tireless worker for the Club. It was typical of him that, when there was an unexpected vacancy for Honorary Secretary and Treasurer, he took on the job for a year in 1982-83, at the age of 73, and carried out the duties most efficiently until a more permanent appointment could be made. He died a few years later in 1987.

He was the most sociable of characters, and amongst his best cronies were James McDowall (Captain from 1961-1963) and Hamilton Mitchell (Captain from 1976-1978). Hamilton liked to tell how he had been spending the evening with 'Davie' and some other

David K. Gourlay, Captain 1969-1971

Chapter V - The Modern Era Begins - 1972-1980

bosom cronies in the Athletic Bar in Girvan, when Davie suddenly collapsed and died. Hamilton's story went that he had just bought a round of drinks and it was Davie's turn to buy the next round when the sad event intervened. Affectionately and with tongue in cheek Hamilton would say something like – *'It wasn't the first time he didn't buy his round, but sadly it was the last'*, though his actual words were much more colourful. Hamilton himself is now also gone to the great golf course in the sky and, if he's been lucky enough to team up again with Davie, no doubt they both have a chuckle over this story.

Tommy Armstrong

David Gourlay was followed as Captain by R.H.U. (Robbie) Stevenson from 1971-1973, one of Turnberry's 'Great Triumvirate' (described later), and whose successor was Tommy Armstrong who served for three years from 1973 till 1976. Tommy was one of only six of Turnberry's Captains who won the Club Championship and that was in 1958. He was, by all accounts, a very good golfer in his younger days. In 1956 he made the newspaper headlines for his performance in the third round of the British Amateur Championship at Troon when he was only beaten at the 18th by the holder of the title, Joe Conrad of Texas, U.S.A. It was reported that Tommy outplayed the brilliant American to be two up at the sixth and, with greater experience, might well have beaten him. Tommy, with his dry joky sense of humour, was a very popular Captain and, as Chairman of the Turnberry Championship Committee, ably led the Club's contribution to the organisation of the 1977 Open.

Hamilton Mitchell

Hamilton Mitchell succeeded Tommy Armstrong as Captain. He was a Girvan man and his father Robert Hamilton Mitchell was one of the very early members of the Club who was the first winner of the Bargany Cup in 1909. The family still hold a replica of the trophy which was presented along with the cup on that occasion. It was perhaps fitting that another member of the Mitchell family, Alex C. Mitchell, Hamilton's uncle, won the Bargany Cup outright in 1936, having that year won it for the third time. Fortunately and very generously Alex C. Mitchell's family, some years later, returned that fine trophy to the Club.

Hamilton was Captain during The Open Championship in 1977 but possibly his proudest golfing moment was when he had a hole-in-one at the 15th hole on the Ailsa Course in 1963, playing in a foursome with David Gourlay against Jim Grant and Andy Coulter.

Alex Scott

Alex Scott, who was Captain from 1978 till 1980, might be described as a rough diamond with a heart of gold. He was a successful self-made businessman in steel construction, in partnership with his brother Bob. Usually referred to as the 'Scott Brothers' they were intensely loyal to each other against the world, whilst at the same time capable of spectacular fraternal fights. When Alex was proposed as Vice-Captain at the A.G.M. in 1978, Jim Carrick was also nominated for the post. Hamilton Mitchell, as the new Captain just elected, was in the chair and he ruled that the vote would be by a public show of hands. Bob Scott was appointed as one of the enumerators to count the votes and the story goes that Bob was heard to mutter loudly 'It's the faces I'll be counting – not the hands'. Alex won the vote and became an enthusiastic and successful Captain for the next two years.

Noel Sturrock

There were some very fine golfers in the Club during this period, none more so than Noel Sturrock. He won the Turnberry Club Championship twice, in 1966 and 1976, and was also Champion at three other clubs, Prestwick, Barassie and West Kilbride. However it was at senior level that Noel reached national standards, winning the Scottish Seniors' Championship twice, in 1981 and 1985 and the British Seniors' Championship in 1986. At Turnberry he played often with Tommy Armstrong and with Walter Linton and Alex Thomson, two other excellent Turnberry players whose achievements are detailed in another Chapter. Sadly all three of them are now deceased and Noel was amused recently when he chanced to meet Alex Thomson's daughter Eileen, who enquired as to his health, but wondered how much longer her father would have to wait for him to re-join the old four-ball! Noel also recalled the easy informality and friendliness of golfing at Turnberry and remembers playing with Tommy Armstrong against Brian McLean and the Reverend Donald Steven, the Kirkoswald Minister. Tommy and he were 5 up by the

Vice-Captain E. I. Cullen of Turnberry Golf Club presenting the Club championship salver to Alex Thomson after he had beaten Noel Sturrock (left) in the final in 1974.

10th and Tommy advised Donald:- *'It's time you got out your prayer mat, Minister'*. Donald took no offence from the remark and, if he did offer up a prayer, it was of no avail.

British Seniors' Amateur Championship 1975

Two Turnberry members played with distinction in this Championship when it was held at Turnberry in August 1975. The tournament was played over two rounds and it was won by Harley Roberts of Stourbridge with a fine score of 139 and Jack Cannon of Irvine, a former Scottish Champion, was second with 148. Walter Linton and Allan Stevenson, both of the Turnberry Club, played in the tournament. Walter finished seventh on 152 and Allan (at the age of 67) scored 154.

Allan Stevenson

Allan Stevenson was born of farming stock at New Cumnock in 1908. As a young man of 17 he went to Glasgow to work in the Glasgow Stock Exchange. It was in Glasgow that a maiden aunt introduced him to golf. On moving back to Ayrshire as a sales representative for a coal mine he became a member of Prestwick St. Nicholas and Ayr Belleisle Golf Clubs, and played his golf with such contemporary stalwarts as Cammie Gibson, a future Scottish Amateur Champion, and Jimmy McKay, who was later to turn professional. In 1935 he opened the first shop in Ayr to specialise exclusively in sports goods, including golf equipment. The shop had an excellent workshop for the repair and customising of clubs and at one time sold much sought after putters, stamped with the name *'Allan Stevenson'*. In those days of very strict amateur rules Allan lost his amateur golfer status for a year because of a complaint that this made him a professional. Before the Second World War he was soon recognised as a very fine golfer, won many open tournaments locally and was chosen as a reserve for Scotland in 1938. In that pre-war period he received many invitations to play in exhibition matches, which included matches he played at Prestwick St. Nicholas with Henry Cotton and Jimmy Adams and at

Chapter V - The Modern Era Begins - 1972-1980

Allan Stevenson (right) during exhibition match with Henry Cotton at Prestwick St. Nicholas.

Old Prestwick with the famous cricketer Len Hutton. The Duke of Windsor was amongst the spectators at Old Prestwick.

During the war he was in the 'Observer Corps', and served on American Navy ships, identifying enemy planes and ships for battle. After the war he won a special Victory Golf Tournament at St. Andrews, which was held to celebrate the peace and he went on to win the Eden Trophy at St. Andrews in 1948, and the first Ayrshire Amateur Championship in 1950. In 1949 he won the McLeod Trophy at Old Ranfurly which at that time was an invitation tournament for international and other prominent amateurs. At the last hole in that tournament he holed a pitch for a birdie to win. As he saw the ball drop he threw his cap in the air and it landed on top of the hole, as if to seal the victory. The press made much of that incident but it was probably out of charac-

ter as he was normally a very undemonstrative man with a quiet manner. His golfing talent spoke for him and during his career he played with and became a friend of many famous golfers. Fittingly in 1949 he was capped for Scotland in the Home Internationals, played in Ireland and was partnered by another notable Ayrshire golfer J.B. Stevenson (no relation).

He was a member of Turnberry Golf Club for over 50 years and was made an honorary member. He continued to have a wonderful and lasting talent for the game into his old age and frequently scored lower than his age. One notable instance of this was when at the age of 78 he played in a Seniors pro-am tournament at Turnberry and shot 77 scratch. Bob Charles of New Zealand, a former Open Champion, who won the professional prize that day with a score not much lower, paid tribute to him in his victory speech. Particularly remarkable also was when, during his 82nd year he twice shot 64 scratch over Girvan - a remarkable feat even off the boxes and with a par of 65. He died in 1991 but is still remembered with fondness and respect as a real gentleman and an extraordinary golfer.

Charles Jack B.E.M.

The first part of the 1970s was a time of great discontent with the terms for membership and with the condition of the courses. This came to a head at a Special General Meeting on 25th October 1975 in discussions about a 25% increase in subscriptions proposed by British Transport Hotels. This was thought to be completely unreasonable and unjustified, taking into account the poor condition of the courses and clubhouse and the work done in the past and expected in the future by members in relation to the organisation of numerous visiting tournaments. The proposed increase was rejected at the meeting by a large majority and there followed negotiations which eventually resulted in a modest compromise being agreed by B.T.H., together with promises of a new clubhouse and better playing conditions.

One of the most outspoken members in this connection was Charlie Jack, a much respected member of Turnberry Golf Club from 1963 till 1990, who rendered great service to the Club as an influential member of the Management Committee. During the war he served in Burma with the rank of Major in Military Intelligence and afterwards he had a distinguished career in the police force, finishing his career as Chief Constable of Ayr Burgh Police Force from 1963 till 1967. Thereafter he was Chairman of Securicor (Scotland) Ltd. from 1971 till his death in 1990. It was in his position with Securicor that he was asked to advise an American golfer who was playing in the 1974 Open at Royal Troon on security matters. The golfer turned out to be Jack Nicklaus who had received anonymous threats on his life. Charlie spent much of that Open week with Nicklaus and they formed a firm friendship which lasted for the rest of his life.

Jack Nicklaus invited Charlie to stay with him at his home in Florida in 1974 and Nicklaus took him to several golf tournaments and included him in a golf game with the Ex-President of America, Gerald Ford. In 1975 Nicklaus asked if he would act as Tournament Director for a new company about to make a series of golfing films in the U.K. The series was called Pro-Celebrity Golf and it ran for nearly twenty years, with Charlie as its Tournament Director till his death. Most of the films were shot at Turnberry and Gleneagles with the professionals taking part including Gary Player, Greg Norman, Ian Woosnam, Lee Trevino and Sandy Lyle as well as other famous names. Over the years he met and made friends with countless celebrities from show business and sport, including Bing Crosby, Sean Connery, Ronnie Corbett, Henry Cooper, Kenny Dalgleish, Burt Lancaster and many more. His photograph album was full of all the favourite celebrities of the period. Charlie Drake addressed an autographed photo of himself *'To Charlie Jack my golfing manager who taught me to keep my glass up and my head down'*.

Charlie Jack (centre) with Sean Connery and Jack Nicklaus at Pro-Celebrity golf event at Turnberry.

Chapter V - The Modern Era Begins - 1972-1980

It was indeed fortunate for Turnberry Golf Club that, when large important tournaments came to Turnberry in the 1970s, in Charlie Jack the Club had the perfect man to take charge of crowd control arrangements. He carried out this crucial task at the John Player Classics in 1972 and 1973, The Open in 1977 and the European Open in 1979, with confident authority and efficiency. The Open in 1977 was a particularly special occasion for him when his friend Jack Nicklaus fought out the most exciting Open finish ever, losing out to Tom Watson at the final hole of their *'Duel in the Sun'*.

Pro-Am Tournaments

Turnberry entered the world of pro-am tournaments in a big way in the 1970s, starting with the Club organising its own such event for the first time in 1974. This became an annual event for many years thereafter until it was abandoned in favour of an amateur team event with members only. The problem in continuing the pro-ams arose from the difficulty of raising sufficient funds to finance the monetary prizes for the professionals. While it continued the Turnberry pro-am was generously sponsored each year by individual members without those members getting much in return except perhaps a little good publicity and goodwill, but it became more difficult each year to raise the minimum prize fund required by the P.G.A. To gain greater sponsorship would have required a more commercial approach

Bruce Forsyth, Charlie Jack, David Logan and Tim Brooke-Taylor at Turnberry Pro-Celebrity Golf.

involving sponsors being allowed to enter their own teams and that would have cut down drastically on the places available for members. The tri-am events, with all-member teams, which took the place of the pro-ams have been a notable success greatly enjoyed by the members. They usually include ancillary putting and pitching competitions, as well as a meal and prizegiving, and are a great way of getting together and fostering a good Club atmosphere.

Texaco Pro-Am 1974

Another very big pro-am event was held at Turnberry in September 1974 sponsored by the oil company Texaco. Spectator stands were erected and also a large tented village and a star-studded field of both professionals and celebrities were invited to take part in a 36 hole tournament over a Saturday and Sunday. The professionals taking part included Tony Jacklin, Bob Charles, Bernard Gallacher, Christy O'Connor, Dale Hayes and Norman Wood. The Club was invited to provide some low handicap members to take part. The fortunate ones were Bill Judge, Jack Boyd, Bob Grassom, Alex Thomson, Walter Linton and Noel Sturrock, who all enjoyed the thrill of playing before a big crowd along with top professionals. There was a banquet afterwards in Turnberry Hotel to which all the players and their partners were invited. Inscribed goblets were presented to all the amateur players and the Captain of Turnberry Golf Club, Tommy Armstrong, made an amusing speech and was congratulated for it being his silver wedding anniversary that very night.

The first prize of £1,000 went to Tony Jacklin, who won the individual tournament by six shots with rounds of 68 and 66 for 134. Norman Wood, who had been an assistant professional at Turnberry before forging a successful career as a tournament player, and Dale Hayes of South Africa were second equal on 140. In his speech, Jacklin paid tribute to the course and expressed his delight that Turnberry had at last been chosen to host the Open Championship in 1977.

Pineapple Tournament

Companies and charities at that time were realising what a wonderful sport golf was for promoting business and raising funds and several high profile pro-ams were held at Turnberry in this period. In July 1975 the Pineapple Procelam Tournament was held in aid of Cancer Relief with each team comprising a professional with three celebrities. It was sponsored by Mr. Francis 'Pineapple' Brown who had made his fortune growing pineapples in Hawaii and at the end of the tournament he presented Captain Tommy Armstrong with a beautiful silver trophy for annual competition.

On a beautiful day the crowds turned out in great numbers as much to watch a star-studded cast of celebrities as to watch the golf. Bing Crosby, at 71 years of age, was a great crowd pleaser, spending half an hour before his tee-off time signing autographs and cracking jokes. Asked why Bob Hope wasn't with him he replied *'Bob was going to come until he realised he had to pay his own air fare'!* Other stars included Don Revie, Alan Ball, Jimmy Hill, Cliff Michelmore, Arthur Montford, Stanley Baker and Christopher Lee, the last named proving himself a very fine golfer. Bing left most of the golfing to his team mates Bernard Gallacher, the fine Scottish professional from Bathgate who, many years later, was to Captain the European Ryder Cup team and Dr. David Marsh, a Walker Cup player in 1969 and 1971.

There was a prize fund of £12,000 with a top prize of £2,200, which was shared by Harold Henning of South Africa and Tommy Horton of Royal Jersey, both on three under par 68. Horton looked like winning until he came to grief in a bunker at the sixteenth by taking three shots to get out and had to sink a huge putt for a double bogey 6. Horton's team, which included the English footballer Alan Ball and Bing Crosby's son, won the team event.

Yet another of the celebrity extravaganzas, the Bob Hope Show-Am was held at Turnberry in 1980.

CHAPTER V - THE MODERN ERA BEGINS - 1972-1980

TURNBERRY'S GREAT TRIUMVIRATE

GRAEME McCULLOCH, ROBBIE STEVENSON and STANLEY MORRISON were three of the best golfers ever produced by the Turnberry Club. They were all Club champions in their younger days and later gave distinguished service as Captains of the Club. They were also all 'colourful' characters, each in his own inimitable style.

Graeme McCulloch

Graeme McCulloch was born in 1912 and, like his great friend Robbie Stevenson, was of farming stock from Ballantrae, a small fishing village situated on the coast 17 miles south of Turnberry. His father was not a golfer, but two kindly aunts were, and they introduced him to the game as a diversion to help him get over the death of his brother Noel in 1917. He learned the game on the tough narrow links of Ballantrae golf course and it was there that Graeme and Robbie first played golf together and formed a firm friendship and rivalry which was to last for their whole lives. Graeme developed a real passion for the game from the start and he soon outgrew his aunts' ability to help him develop his natural talents. At the tender age of ten he hitched a lift from Ballantrae to Girvan and took the train from there to Turnberry to play on the increasingly famous links. He was admitted as a junior member soon thereafter and his precocious talents were recognised and he was helped and encouraged by friends and members to play at Turnberry when transport allowed. When he died in 1997, aged 85, his association with Turnberry had lasted 75 of the 95 years of the Club's existence. One of his proudest possessions was a crystal rosebowl presented to him at a Past Captains' Dinner in Turnberry Hotel in 1992, to mark 70 years with the club. When he received his invitation to the dinner he explained that he would only require soft drinks at the preceding cocktail party, as he was *'try-*

Right - Captain Jack Boyd presenting Graeme McCulloch with a crystal rosebowl from the Club at the Past Captains' Dinner in 1992 - to mark 70 years with the Club.
(Left) - Robbie Stevenston (left) and Graeme McCulloch at Turnberry in 1936.

ing to bring down his lifetime alcohol consumption to above average'. The dinner that year was a particularly memorable and nostalgic occasion due to Graeme's presence. He was always known for his ready wit and sense of humour and he made a fine speech, amusing the company by admitting to having turned up in his dinner suit at the hotel a week earlier, having mistaken the date of the dinner. In true McCulloch fashion however he was unperturbed and ordered dinner at the hotel, where he was royally welcomed as an honoured guest by Luigi, the head waiter of many years, who was delighted to see him again. No doubt Luigi could remember some of Graeme's notable exploits from his younger hell-raising days, including an occasion when, for a bet, he drove a car down the steps in front of the hotel, after a particularly sociable evening.

Graeme's golfing exploits away from Turnberry are not well documented but at one time he played off plus one of a handicap and he was keenly competitive over many years, travelling all over Scotland, England, Ireland and even France to play in championships. As late as the 1970's he played in a seniors' tour in Kenya. At Turnberry he won the scratch gold medal in 1933 and 1937 and was the first winner of the Morrison Salver for the Club Championship in 1937 and the first post-war winner in 1952. He also has his name on most of the older trophies in the 1930s.

Amongst his friends he numbered the great and flamboyant American golfer, Walter Hagen, who was sometimes his guest at Ballantrae for game shooting, which Hagen enjoyed greatly. His humour at times was mischievous and he loved to discomfit his friends and opponents if they showed any weakness. One of his favourite quips, to stymie a boring tale of golf, was to say to the enthusiastic player: *'Tell me about your round, starting with your second putt at the eighteenth'*. In 1934, Captain North Dalrymple-Hamilton asked the young McCulloch to make up a four at Turnberry with the Prince of Wales and the Turnberry professional Jimmy McDowall. The Prince of Wales, who was a member at Prestwick, asked the young man why he didn't join Prestwick. He replied with tongue in cheek that he was only a poor young working farmer who would probably have to use the caddies' entrance. *'Rubbish!'* said the Prince, *'you're a good golfer and I'm not, and I come in through the main entrance'*. McCulloch did in fact become a member of Prestwick fully twenty years later and served as Captain of that club in 1972. His nickname at Prestwick was 'The Gorilla', due to his stocky build and immense power with a golf club.

Robbie Stevenson

Robbie Stevenson was born in 1910 and, like his father before him, he was a notable farmer at Balig and Corseclays farms near the village of Ballantrae, pioneering the introduction of exotic foreign breeds of cattle and new methods of crop husbandry such as the aerial sewing of turnips amongst barley. Robbie served as Vice-Chairman of the Milk Marketing Board and was a regular radio broadcaster as a panellist on *'Farm Forum'*. Ballantrae golf course was built on land which was part of the family farms and it was there that Robbie started playing golf at an early age. Like his great friend Graeme McCulloch, Robbie was a fine natural golfer, playing off scratch and plus one for many years. In 1938 he won the South of Scotland Amateur Golf Championship played over Dunskey golf course at Portpatrick and in 1938 and 1946 he won the Wigtonshire County Championship. At Turnberry he won the scratch Gold Medal four times before the war and the Club Championship in 1938 and 1940.

He joined Turnberry Golf Club in 1931 and was made an honorary member in 1977. His association with Turnberry went back even further to his childhood years. In an interview for the *Carrick Gazette* given some years earlier but published in 1994 he recalled:-

> *'My first memory of Turnberry was in 1921, when at the age of eleven years I was taken there by my father to watch the British Ladies Championship. I remember vividly watching the final between two ladies, Miss Cecil Leitch and Miss Joyce Wethered, who is now Lady Heathcoat Amory. They were playing the eighteenth hole on the Ailsa course and I remember Miss Wethered driving the green in the morning round but, despite that shot, she lost the championship.*
>
> *The Club professional in 1926 was Mr. T.R. Fernie who left Turnberry that year for Lytham St. Annes. He was succeeded by Jimmy McDowall, who was a man of great vitality. Mr. McDowall had the routine of playing two rounds every Wednesday with*

Chapter V - The Modern Era Begins - 1972-1980

the then famous ear, nose and throat specialist Dr. Forbes Walker of Ayr. They would complete the two rounds in no more than four hours and more usually in three and a half.

Captain in 1931 was Sir John Richmond with J.D.H. Forbes Vice-Captain. Turnberry Golf Club's longest serving captain was, however, Captain Oliver Hughes-Onslow who succeeded Sir John. Among the membership were G.P. Greenlaw, James Houston, Bob Mitchell, father of another captain, Hamilton Mitchell, A.C. Mitchell, now an honorary member and Stanley P. Morrison. Stanley was probably the best player that Turnberry produced who was not capped by his country. Then there was W.H. Forbes, who continued the family tradition from his uncle, J.D.H. Forbes. As well as being an accomplished golfer W.H. was also a fine tennis player and an international curler. Other members, who are now all deceased, included J.L. Walker, Duncan Colquhoun, David Gourlay, J.P.K. McDowall, Andrew McGarva, then proprietor of the King's Arms Hotel, Girvan, W.G. McCulloch of Ballantrae and T.C. Reid, who was to become president of the Scottish Football Association.

One phenomenon peculiar to Turnberry was the 'Tigers'. Under the banner 'Turnberry Tigers' a group of members each year travelled to Northern Ireland to play local clubs under the stewardship of Andrew McGarva. The event was staged as an exchange with Ulster clubs. Turnberry in those days was a far more intimate place, and that added to the attraction. The hotel was not nearly as busy and the membership was not as large as today. The result was a more friendly atmosphere. In those days none of us had much money yet we could still start out with ten bob (shillings), play a round or two, have some tea and still go home with money in our pockets. The price of a caddie when I was playing regularly was one shilling one penny, the shilling being for the caddie and the penny for the caddie-master. There was a lot more discipline in the play then. Even in the club we young ones had to be respectful to the senior members; there were certainly no first names. Golf was a sport and it was treated as such, but it was treated very seriously indeed. It was not at all unusual to see some members practice for more than an hour a day. I *think that we had much better golfers then as a result; it is certainly reflected in the handicaps and you know, in those days, Turnberry was always represented in the foremost championships. Ask me what Turnberry has meant to me. Turnberry first and foremost was always a friendly place. There was never any argument about golf despite the sense of competition. The rivalry never extended beyond the course. Another thing was that the club was not used for social climbing as happens in some other clubs. I think that is one tradition laid down in the formative years which survives today.'*

Stanley Morrison

Stanley Pringle Morrison was born on 8th July, 1900, and died on 8th September, 1971. He was educated at Glasgow High School and Glasgow University, spent his early business years with a trading house in Java and returned to Scotland in the late twenties. There he joined a whisky broking business owned and run by William Walker, J.P., who was later to become his father-in-law. He later set up his own brokerage company, joining forces with other prominent Scotch whisky brokers. The purchase of the Chivas Brothers business in Aberdeen which owned the prestigious Chivas Regal brand was a significant success and it was later sold to the Seagram Company.

S.P.M. left the industry briefly from 1948 to 1951 but then returned to it when significant opportunities arose after the war for the sale of Scotch whisky at home and abroad, especially in the U.S.A. He was possibly the pre-eminent whisky broker of his day, highly regarded for his intuitive moves. The purchase of Bowmore Distillery on the Island of Islay in 1963 proved to be an outstanding acquisition although, as he readily admitted at the time, he knew nothing about distilling whisky – preferring to drink it instead. He was one of the first to realise the potential of the Far East market for Scotch whisky, taking full advantage of that growing market in the 1960s. The industry honoured him on his seventieth birthday with a presentation dinner at St. Enoch Hotel, Glasgow.

The Club records do not show the exact date when S.P.M. joined Turnberry Golf Club but it was just after the Great War, probably in 1919. However his absence abroad on business meant that he didn't play much at

Stanley P. Morrison still swinging well in 1969.

Turnberry till about eight or nine years later. His name first appears on Club trophies in 1928 and thereafter he had a phenomenal record of winning the major trophies over a period spanning forty one years till 1969, in which year he won the Bargany Cup for the sixth time. He won the Bell Trophy, the singles match play competition five times between 1933 and 1963, the Gold Medal seven times between 1928 and 1956, the Richmond Cup five times between 1929 and 1965, the Club Championship for the S.P. Morrison Salver (gifted to the Club by himself) in 1939 and 1953 and the Ailsa Challenge Cup twice in 1928 and 1960. His record is the more remarkable since his handicap for the greatest part of that period was scratch. Moreover in the pre-war period there were plenty of low handicap players to provide competition. In addition to Robbie Stevenson and Graeme McCulloch, both off scratch or plus one, there were six other players with handicaps as low as two at some point, namely Thomas Reid, George D. Greenlaw, Alex Marr, W.H. Forbes, A.C. Mitchell and A. Stevenson, Jnr.

His wins in the Bargany Cup and Bell Trophy show that he was a formidable match player and, as late as 1965, he also won Troon Golf Club's Anderson Cup which is their individual match play competition. Unfortunately his record in open competitions and championships is not well documented but he played six times in the Amateur Championship, reaching the fourth round in 1937 when he was beaten by Dick Chapman. Incidentally on that occasion the use of fore caddies was finally banned. At Troon in 1938 he was beaten in the third round by the eventual winner Charlie Yates of America and at Hoylake in 1958 he was beaten two and one in the fourth round by Alex Kyle who went on to become the Champion. The other occasions were at Muirfield in 1932, Prestwick in 1952 and Muirfield again in 1954, when he went out in the first or second rounds.

CHAPTER V - THE MODERN ERA BEGINS - 1972-1980

126 — THE ILLUSTRATED SPORTING AND DRAMATIC NEWS—April 15, 1938

HENRY COTTON ON GOLF

I shall be writing golf in the Sporting and Dramatic each week

A Drive by Stanley Morrison

The Well-known Glasgow Amateur in Action

Captions by Henry Cotton

Special "Illustrated Sporting and Dramatic News" Photographs

1 A big, heavy fellow with a comfortable, wide stance and lovely free orthodox swing and a full pivot—club-face beautifully open.

2 Feet solidly placed and body and left side ready for the hit—the club-head already moving fast.

3 Free and solid—and what a lovely wide finish!

4 A grand finish—I like the control—and the way the hands have stayed on the club.

135

As well as being a member of Turnberry Golf Club S.P.M. was also a member of other West of Scotland Clubs including Barassie, Western Gailes, Glasgow Golf Club, Troon and Ballantrae, but his great love was Turnberry. His family had rented property on the seafront at Girvan at the turn of the century and he had many memories of the early days of Turnberry Hotel and golf courses. Moreover there was an early family association with Turnberry, as the family building business of Morrison Mason (later sold to Sir William Arrol & Co.) were the contractors who built the railway line from Alloway to Girvan via Dunure, Maidens and Turnberry for the Glasgow & South Western Railway Company and his father and grandfather were in charge of that contract. Before the Second World War he acquired a house, then called Hillfir, situated just across the public road from the first hole on the Ailsa course. He bought it from the Reid family who owned Partick Thistle Football Club whose ground was at Firhill – hence the name reversal. S.P.M. changed the name of the house to Parknasilla after the name of a village on the West Coast of Ireland where he had spent his honeymoon and, of course, played golf. The caddies at Turnberry always wanted to be part of any game which involved S.P.M. because at the end of the round they would be asked along with Tango, his regular long-time caddie, to go to Parknasilla, where the housekeeper was instructed to pour them all generous measures of whisky and beer.

S.P.M. was well known for the admirable consistency of his golf and was a stickler for the rules of the game but also at times, contentious and controversial. Sam McKinlay, the Walker Cup player and golf correspondent of the *Glasgow Herald* described him as being a *'rather rumbustious character'*. The Club minutes contain reference to more than one occasion on which S.P.M. complained or was complained against. Even when he was proposed for Vice-Captain in 1963 his good friend Tommy Girvan spoke against his election, but of course Tommy always took great pleasure in putting the *'cat among the pigeons'* on such occasions. Their friendship was not in the least disturbed by the incident and, indeed, S.P.M. respected people more if they held their ground when they disagreed with him. As Captain from 1965 till 1967 he led the Club with panache and authority.

He was a very close friend of Henry Cotton who often stayed at Turnberry during tournaments there, such as the News of the World Match Play Championship. Henry liked to practice his chipping on to the small greens of the hotel's pitch and putt course near Parknasilla and he would get S.P.M.'s sons Brian and Tim to bowl to him at a cricket net set up in the garden of Parknasilla - batting was good for his timing he would say – bowling was not. At S.P.M.'s invitation Cotton was the guest speaker, proposing a toast to the Club, at the Annual Dinner Dance and Presentation of Prizes in 1965. S.P.M. introduced him with the words *'I take great personal pleasure in calling upon one of the greatest golfers of all time to say a few words. Ladies and gentlemen, the great maestro himself. Henry Cotton'*. But the admiration was not just one-sided, for Henry Cotton used photographs of S.P.M. to illustrate one of his teaching pieces in the *Illustrated Sporting and Dramatic News*, showing a good driving technique.

In addition to his membership of the Clubs already mentioned, he was a founder member of the 32 Club, established in 1932, whose membership is by invitation only, the prerequisites for membership being to have played in the Walker Cup or for your country, to be a scratch golfer, or finally to have a cheery countenance. S.P.M. was eminently qualified under the last two headings.

BIG JOHN, RIP, TANGO AND OTHERS

THERE was a ripple of excitement round the clubhouse at Turnberry one day, as an American four ball came down the final hole with four caddies. The unusual thing was that one of the caddies was slung over the shoulder of a fellow caddie, while the other two caddies were each carrying two bags. Strong drink and a five hour round had taken its toll at the sixteenth but his comrades had come to the rescue and got him and the players home safely. It's not known what effect this incident had on the tips, but it is likely that the Americans just loved it and were as generous as usual. After all, what a story to take back to the U.S. of A.! Stories like this are part of the folklore of Scottish caddies who are a very special breed of hardy and often colourful characters who have contributed immensely to the history and success of the game of golf.

Caddies have always been an important part of the Turnberry scene and the Club minutes contain many references to them and to the caddiemaster, who also acted as the starter in the early years. Prior to the Second World War there were both men and women caddies, and one of the Club's Honorary Members, Campbell Hicks, can recall this and particularly remembers one woman caddie who had only one arm! The Club took an active interest in the caddies and their regulation and welfare and in 1907 it is recorded that the Club gave the caddiemaster an honorarium of one guinea, a sum equivalent to a member's annual subscription, and this became an annual practice for many years. In 1908 the Club adopted the following Bye-Laws for caddies:-

'1. No caddie shall be allowed on the course unless his name be registered in a book to be kept for the purpose by the caddiemaster; and all caddies must remain in the place appointed for them, unless when engaged by a player.

2. No caddie shall be employed by a player except through the caddiemaster (or in his absence the professional) to whom the charge of one shilling for eighteen holes (which includes the cleaning of the clubs) is to be paid. The charge for cleaning clubs only is $^1/_2$ pence per iron club. No payment is to be made direct to a caddie, except when he is engaged for two rounds, when sixpence shall be paid for lunch.

3. No caddie shall enter the clubhouse on any pretext whatever.

4. The duties of a caddie shall include the following:-

   a. to tee the player's ball when required
   b. to watch its flight, and find it for the players
   c. to replace and press down with the foot any turf cut out in the course of the game
   d. to give information regarding direction and distance
   e. to remove and replace the flagstaff at each hole; and when doing so to be careful not to injure the holes by standing close to them, when the ground is soft
   f. to refrain from walking through bunkers.

5. Caddies shall not talk while a stroke is being played, and they must at all times be respectful and attentive.

6. Caddies are specially instructed to draw the player's attention, when necessary, to the following rules, and if requested to show their card of instructions to the player viz:- Rule I, General and Through the Green, Rule III, Priority on the Course, and Rule V Etiquette of Golf.'

In 1934 the Club offered the hotel owners £200 towards providing a *'caddie shack'* for the comfort and shelter of the caddies, and in 1936 organised a golf competition for regular caddies, with prizes donated by the Captain, Vice Captain and by many members. This competition was again held in 1937 and 1938, when there was a prize fund of £10, a considerable sum of money in those days. However the competition was not held in 1939 and reservations were expressed about continuing it in view of there being some doubt as to whether or not the winning scores returned were genuine! It is interesting and perhaps surprising to note that there were 59 entries in 1937, comprising 48 men and 11 women, with separate prizes for each group.

It was not all plain sailing between the Club and the caddies, because in 1922 there was a complaint about many balls being lost at hidden holes, apparently in most cases when caddies had been seen in the vicinity! Then in 1931 it was reported in Committee that several members had drawn attention to the common practice of caddies of *'both sexes, squatting on the course in the vicinity of the clubhouse in unseemly positions in full view of players'*. The Committee agreed to instruct the caddie master not to employ *'objectionable girls'* and to ensure that the caddies kept to their shelter when not caddying!

The job of caddie has changed much since those days, with some of the top caddies earning a fortune if they are lucky enough to get *'the bag'* of a successful tournament professional, and forge a partnership with him. Some of the caddies from Turnberry have caddied for world famous players and celebrities. Jim (*'Tats'*) McGill, who died in 2002, caddied for Jessie Anderson when she won the Ladies' British Open Championship at Turnberry in 1937 and for the Prince of Wales when he visited in the 1950's. A few have become full or part time tournament caddies, travelling world wide to ply their trade. One such was the late Willie Hill who sadly died quite young in 2001. Past Captain Jack Boyd remembers representing Turnberry at the Ganton Centenary celebrations in 1991 and watching the semi-final of the Amateur Championship between two Americans, one of whom was called David Duval. Duval's caddie seemed familiar looking, but it was only when he smiled and nodded that Jack realised it was Willie from Turnberry. Duval went on to become for a time the number one player in the World Ranking of professional golfers.

Former Turnberry professional Bob Jamieson, the late caddiemaster Rab Boyd and the present caddiemaster Willie McDines could all tell countless true stories about the caddies at Turnberry. Rab used to tell how one day an American player asked for a first class caddie who could give him all the distances. The appointed caddie had recently been before the local Burgh Court charged with theft for breaking into his prepayment electricity meter. When they got to the American's drive on the first hole, the player asked him for the distance to the green and enquired if he worked in yards or metres. The caddie replied honestly: *'Meters, sir, gas and electricity!'*

Willie recalls some stories about a caddie known as *'Big John'* Cavens, who was at the ninth tee from where the lighthouse comes into full view, and his player asked him if the light was still working. Big John replied: *'Aye, sir, but only at night'*. On another occasion Big John's player had hooked his ball towards the beach at the tenth where there was particularly wild terrain of rocks and long grass. After a long unsuccessful search for the ball the player told Big John to give up, but he was strangely reluctant to do. When the player pressed him to move on he admitted: *'It's no' the ba' I'm looking for, sir, it's yer clubs'*.

When Turnberry was owned by a Japanese company there were many visitors from Japan. One day two of the Turnberry members witnessed a Japanese gentleman trapped in the deep bunker on the front right of the sixth green on the Ailsa course, in which the player proceeded to take a dozen shots or more without success. At that point his caddie advised him to play out backwards over the low back lip. This he did successfully in one stroke, only to fluff it back into the bunker with his next shot. He looked apologetically at the caddie who by way of encouragement said *'Don't worry sir, we refill the bunkers every night'*.

Bob Jamieson had a close relationship with the caddies at Turnberry and recalled with affection many of the characters among them. There was '*Grunch*' Galloway who caddied regularly for many years for late Past Captain Graeme McCulloch, and who picked up particularly good tips because he always looked so ill; then there was *'Rip'* McDines who handed back tips if he thought they were not substantial enough with the words *'Your need must be greater than mine, sir'*; and then there were *'Preel'* Wilson, *'Hoppy'* Hopkins, *'Herky'* Speirs, *'Tango'* McGarva, *'Snooks'* Kelly and many others. The stories are never-ending about such characters,

Chapter V - The Modern Era Begins - 1972-1980

illustrating their ingenuity and resourcefulness in dealing with the varied people they served and the situations that arose on the golf course. Tango was a regular caddie for late Past Captain Stanley Morrison and the story is told of Mr. Morrison playing in a mixed foursomes competition on the Ailsa, when he suffered rather badly from his lady partner putting the ball into some weird and wonderful places he was not in the habit of visiting. So he was rather tired when they reached the 18th tee and he couldn't bear to watch his partner trying to play the tee shot over the big rough valley in front of the tee. Inevitably she duffed her shot into a horrendous spot down in the valley. Mr. Morrison turned and said:- *'Well Tango where are we?',* and Tango replied:- *'Well there's one thing for certain, sir, you're no' in a divot'.*

Bob recalls a caddie who fell into the burn at the 16th, but who managed to keep the clubs dry by holding them over his head as he went under; and the one who abandoned his player at the sixth because he objected to the player's foul language. He told the caddiemaster there were times and places for swearing but a golf course was not one of them! Caddies may be fairly rough diamonds but they share an understanding of the spirit of the game and of what is correct conduct on the course. There is also a caddie camaraderie. When *'Big John'* died the rest of the caddies at Turnberry subscribed to buy a seat inscribed in his memory, which sits at the back of the tee for the 4th hole on the Ailsa Course. There is also a seat in memory of Willie McDines' father Sam, at the 9th tee. Sam was a caddie at Turnberry for over fifty years.

Caddies may sometimes quite wrongly be looked upon simply as lowly manual workers, but they can aspire to participate with honour and importance in the highest echelons of the game as well as greatly enhance the pleasure of a round of golf for the ordinary golfer. They have certainly been an interesting and sometimes puzzling element of life at Turnberry, for members and visitors alike. Two Americans were overheard in the clubhouse one day after their round. One was saying to the other: *'Hank, one of the reasons we came to Scotland to play golf was because we share a common language, but do you know something, I couldn't understand a word that caddie said!*

John Player Classics and Other Tournaments

John Player Classic 1972

AFTER eight years without a major tournament, either amateur or professional since the Braemar 7-Club Tournament in 1964, Turnberry was chosen to host a major professional event in September 1972 – The John Player Classic. It attracted a very good quality international field, including Arnold Palmer, Doug Sanders, Tom Weiskopf, Gay Brewer and Billy Casper from America, Peter Thomson of Australia, Roberto Di Vicenzo of Argentina, Gary Player of South Africa, Bob Charles of New Zealand, as well as the best of the British professionals.

Play was over the full length of the 7060 yards Ailsa Course, for which the course record stood at 68, held jointly by John Panton of Glenbervie and Willie McDonald of Prestwick St. Nicholas, set in the Scottish Professional Championship in 1954. On the first day the weather was calm and little Brian Hugget of Wales, who had withdrawn from the Welsh team for the World Cup due to 'exhaustion', showed little sign of it when he reduced the record by four shots to 64. He had earlier complained about his drives being, on average, 15 yards shorter than they used to be, but he hit nearly every green in regulation, using fairway woods for his second shot on seven holes. He was closely followed by Peter Townsend of England on 65, Billy Casper on 67, Peter Oosterhuis of England on 68 and Bob Charles, Tony Jacklin and Doug Saunders on 69.

The second round, played on a day with a fresh wind, saw Townsend scoring 70 and taking the lead by one shot from Hugget with for a half way total of 135, whilst Oosterhuis and Jacklin moved up to third equal, two shots behind the leader, after 69 and 68 respectively. Bob Charles stayed well in contention with 138 after two 69's, despite his complaining that his game was in a poor state.

On the third day the players had to cope with a very strong wind and heavy rain and scores generally suffered as the round became a *'grim battle with the elements'*, as described in the *Glasgow Herald*. This saw Charles take the lead on 209, after a 71, with Townsend dropping to second on 210, after a 75. Harry Bannerman, the extrovert cigar-smoking reigning Scottish Professional

Bob Charles with his wife and the John Player Classic trophy in 1972 at Turnberry in atrocious conditions.

Champion, made an astonishing advance up the field with a remarkable 67, to lie fifth on 214. For perhaps the first and only time at a major championship there were on-course bookmakers and it was reported that Bannerman won £1,750 from a bet on himself to have the lowest round that day.

140

Chapter V - The Modern Era Begins - 1972-1980

On the final day the players again had to cope with a very strong wind and Bob Charles hung on to win the first prize of £15,000 with a 76 for a total of 285. Gay Brewer and Peter Oosterhuis were second equal on 286 and Tony Jacklin third on 287. This was Charles' third victory in a major European tournament, having won the Open in 1963 and the Piccadilly Match Play tournament in 1969. Despite the wild weather encountered at Turnberry there was speculation that Turnberry might become the permanent home for this tournament. Little did the organisers know what was in store for their event weatherwise when it returned the following year.

John Player Classic 1973

If the sponsors of this event had hoped for more clement weather at Turnberry than the wild winds which affected it in 1972, they were to be sadly disappointed. On the opening day however there was cause for some optimism on that score as the competitors set out in pursuit of the contents of a bulging prize purse, contending only with a fresh westerly wind. The members at Turnberry, being used to gales in September, considered those conditions positively benign and indeed there were some excellent scores produced by the select international field of 36 competitors. They were headed by Neil Coles of England and Johnny Miller of America on 66, with Tony Jacklin of England and Charles Coody of America both two behind on 68. Two other Americans, Gay Brewer and Tom Weiskopf, were on 69 and Norman Wood of Turnberry was on 70, along with Christy O'Connor of Ireland.

For the rest of the tournament the wind just got stronger and stronger and its unrelenting hostility turned the tournament into a battle for survival, not only for the players but also for the tented village. The latter, completely defeated, was flattened and blown away. So far as the players were concerned, it seemed at times that the man who could stay upright and finish the tournament would be declared the winner. Going into the last round only Tony Jacklin of the British players seemed to have any chance of preventing the American players once again plundering one of the richest British tournaments. Along with Tom Weiskopf he was on 216 and four behind the unlikely leader, Charles Coody, who was without a victory in his own country since winning the Masters over two years previously. Jacklin played well on the final round and at one point, on the eighth green, he had a 12 feet putt to draw level. He missed it and, after that, Coody stayed out of trouble and holed out solidly despite the gale force winds which threatened at times to move stationery balls on the green whenever a putter blade was put behind them. His winning total

The devastated tented village blown apart by the gale-force winds during the final round of the 1973 John Player Classic at Turnberry.

was 289, three ahead of Jacklin who finished second. Tom Weiskopf was third on 294 and O'Connor, Player and Tommy Horton of England, finished fourth equal, one shot further back.

Bobby Cole of South Africa managed to score a magnificent lowest last round score of 71 in the atrocious conditions, but there were many scores in the 80s, including an 84 by Neil Coles which was the highest score on the last day. He had a sequence of 11 holes in which bogey was his best score, and his 66 on the opening day must have seemed like a half-remembered dream.

After the tournament the sponsors announced that they would consult weather reports for the South Ayrshire coast for 20 years back, to see if there was a history of such bad conditions for this particular week in September. The conclusion must have been unfavourable, for the tournament never returned to Turnberry and, in some ways, the Club was not sorry about this. As usual the Club had organised the voluntary stewarding for both of the John Player tournaments, under the leadership of Charlie Jack assisted by David Logan. In November 1973 Charlie reported to the Club Committee his dissatisfaction with the sponsors in having delayed reimbursing the Club for certain outlays and for not having the courtesy to convey a spontaneous 'thank you' for all the hard work put in by the volunteers in the dreadful conditions, described by the *Glasgow Herald* as *'a purgatory'*, making *'the eyes water, the hands freeze and the brain run round the head like a pea in a drum'*.

Double Diamond Tournament 1975

The 5th annual Double Diamond International Team Tournament was held at Turnberry in September 1975 – sponsored by Allied Breweries. In the team event there were six teams of five professionals, representing the four home countries, the Americas, (comprising players from North and South America) and the Rest of the World.

Preceding the team tournament there was an individual championship over 36 holes and, after their 21-11 defeat in the Ryder cup, 7 members of the British team arrived at Prestwick at 6.30 a.m. to join the other players competing in this on the Tuesday. They found a great contrast between the warm air and lushness of Laurel Valley, Pennsylvania, and the painful driving rain and tight lies which met them on the Ailsa Course at Turnberry. Lionel Platts led after the first round with a 71 and 23 year old Eamonn Darcy of Ireland – fresh from his first Ryder cup cap – was second equal on 72 along with Roberto de Vicenzo, 29 years his senior and one of the world's most popular golfers of that era. De Vicenzo had at last been the Open Champion in 1967 at Hoylake after several high finishes over a number of years and the whole golfing world rejoiced for the victory which crowned an outstanding career. A few months later at Augusta he was most cruelly deprived of the chance to win the Masters and hold those two great titles at the same time. In the final round at Augusta he shot a brilliant 65 to tie with the American Bob Goalby. The total was correct but his playing partner had entered a four for his score on the 17th, instead of the birdie three which the spectators and television viewers had all witnessed. No way could be found round the rule that he had nevertheless signed for a four and it had to stand with his total altered to 66. De Vincenzo accepted his fate with dignity, blamed only himself and in so doing won the affections of the whole golfing world.

On the Wednesday the weather was even worse than on the Tuesday and a number of players failed to complete their rounds, whilst only 7 broke 40 for the inward half and only 14 bettered 80 for the round. Lionel Platts finished with 89, Darcy with 88 and de Vicenzo with 86. The combined score of the 35 players who completed both rounds was 1043 over par. Peter Dawson, a young left-hander from Yorkshire, had an early start when the rain was not quite so severe and won the tournament with a total of 153 – nine over par. Raymond Jacobs described the weather in his report in the *Glasgow Herald* as *'a day stolen from the mind of a mad meteorologist when no self-respecting seagull should have ventured out, let alone a professional golfer'*.

The International Team Tournament consisted of three days of round-robin matches of six teams playing four singles in each match. The weather improved for the first two days but then on the final day reverted to a bitter wind with driving rain making the 7th and 9th fairways out of reach from the championship tees. It was so bad that Gary Player at one point wanted to walk in but was persuaded to continue. Nevertheless some of the scoring was exceptionally good and the matches were

Chapter V - The Modern Era Begins - 1972-1980

The Winning Americas' Team

Billy Casper 44 (Captain)
U.S...5' 11"...13st. 13lb...established as one of the game's great players... twice U.S. Open Champion 1959 and in 1966 after memorable play-off with Arnold Palmer...U.S. Masters Champion 1970 again after play-off this time with Gene Littler...five times winner of U.S. Vardon Trophy for Tour's low stroke average...member of every U.S. Ryder Cup Team since 1961...became second person to win $1 million in professional golf in 1970... winner of 1975 New Orleans Open... Captain of Rest of World Team in last year's Double Diamond International.

Jim Colbert 34
U.S...5' 9"...11st. 11lb...Pro since 1965...winner of four U.S. Tour titles since 1969 including 1974 American Golf Classic...has won almost $500,000 during U.S. Tour career to date...is member of U.S. T.P.D. Policy Board...has outstanding record in major championships...best year to date was 1974 when including his victory in American Golf Classic he totalled almost $100,000 in official prize money.

Lou Graham 37
U.S...6'...12st. 7lb...U.S. Open Champion 1975...Lou claimed one of the world's top two titles after an exciting play-off with young John Mahaffey in June this year...joined the U.S. Tour in 1964 and won the Minnesota Classic in 1967 and the Liggett & Myers Tournament in 1972...has won over $600,000 in Tour earnings and makes his first appearance in Double Diamond International...while enlisted in army duty had the distinction of serving in the President's Guard of Honour.

Hale Irwin 30
U.S...6'...11st. 11lb...the 1974 U.S. Open Champion makes a welcome first appearance in the Double Diamond International...having another outstanding season with victories in the Atlanta Classic and the Western Open Championship...Hale is the current Piccadilly World Match-Play Champion having defeated Piccadilly Master Gary Player at Wentworth last autumn.

Roberto de Vicenzo 52
Argentina...6' 2"...12st. 12lb...British Open Champion 1967...runner-up U.S. Masters 1968...one of the world's most popular golfers...has over 130 tournament successes including 30 national open championships of 14 countries...plays for the first time in the Double Diamond International...World Cup individual winner 1970.

excitingly close. The players, by their perseverance, did well by the tournament. The teams were:-

Scotland	- Brian Barnes (Captain), Bernard Gallacher, David Huish, Ronnie Shade, Norman Wood.
England	- Neil Coles (Captain), Maurice Bembridge, Malcolm Gregson, Tommy Horton, Guy Hunt.
Ireland	- Christy O'Connor (Captain), Eamonn Darcy, Christy O'Connor junior, John O'Leary, Eddie Polland.
Wales	- Dai Rees (Captain), Craig DeFoy, Brian Huggett, David Llewellyn, David Vaughan.
Americas	- Billy Casper (Captain), Jim Colbert, Lou Graham, Hale Irwin, Roberto de Vicenzo.
Rest of the World	- Gary Player (Captain), Severiano Ballesteros, Bob Charles, Dale Hayes, Jack Newton.

The final score was Americas 26, Rest of the World 22, Scotland 20, Ireland 18, Wales 17, England 17. Of the Scots, Brian Barnes and David Huish scored $3^{1}/_{2}$ out of a possible 5, but former Turnberry assistant Norman Wood failed to win a point in his three matches.

The Turnberry Club had treated the tournament as a test for the stewarding arrangements in the run up to the Open due to take place in 1977, but the weather rendered stewarding almost unnecessary as only a few hundred spectators braved the elements. The press headlines were about the hazards of holding tournaments at Turnberry in September when the weather could be so severe, praise for the players for producing wonderful head to head matches in the adverse conditions and for the members who had stood by their task in such conditions. Captain Tommy Armstrong was presented with a crystal decanter by the organisers as a thank you for the Club's efforts.

European Open 1979

This tournament came to Turnberry in the week before the Ryder Cup was due to be held at the Greenbriar Club in America. Severiano Ballesteros of Spain had won The

---

143

Open at Lytham just two months previously and Sandy Lyle of Scotland had been named Rookie of the Year in 1978 and had won the Scottish Professional Championship just eight days before the start of the tournament. Lyle was only in his second year as a professional but had won the Scandinavian Open by three strokes from Ballesteros earlier that year. At Turnberry the stage was set for a showdown between the charismatic Spaniard with his flashing cavalier swing and the big solid Scot with his very individual poker-backed one.

For the last three days of the tournament the weather was as contrasting as the styles of Ballesteros and Lyle, switching from raining buckets to sun splitting the skies. The fairways were very narrow and bordered by thick rough and the lowest score on the first day was 68 by little known Tony Charnley, followed by Ballesteros on 69, Bob Charles of New Zealand on 70 and Lyle on 71. The second day was that rare event at Turnberry – an almost complete calm – but the course's defences held firm against the skills of the top quality field and only 13 out of 130 players broke par. Lyle shot 67 and Ballesteros shot another 69 to be halfway leaders on 138 along with Ken Brown. Peter Townsend, Bob Charles and Jose Maria Canizares of Spain followed on 140. On the third day Neil Coles of England shot a fine 66 to lead on 209 from Lyle and Townsend, both on 210, while Ballesteros slipped back after a 75 left him on 213. On the final day Sandy Lyle gave the Scottish crowd plenty to cheer about when he showed the field a clean pair of heels, taking only 21 shots for the first seven holes and 30 for the outward nine. He finished with a 65 to win by seven shots on 275 from Peter Townsend and Dale Hayes of South Africa. Ballesteros was a distant 284.

Sandy's win made him the first Scot to win a major tournament on home soil since Eric Brown won the

Sandy Lyle & Dale Hayes with the European Open Trophy.

PGA Match Play Championship, also at Turnberry, in 1960. He was rewarded with a first prize of £17,500 and the championship trophy presented by Prince Bernhart of The Netherlands.

A former assistant at Turnberry, Robin Fyfe, finished creditably on 289 and earlier that year, in June, Bob Jamieson's five assistants had finished in the first five places in the West of Scotland Assistants' Championship. It was won by Alastair McLean, with Niall Cameron second, Mark McDiarmid and Gregor Jamieson third equal and Brian Gunson, fifth. It was a period of great success for Bob's *'Stable'* of assistants. In that same year Niall Cameron won the Scottish Assistants' Championship by a huge margin. Many of Bob's assistants went on to secure very good positions at prestigious clubs. To be trained at Turnberry by Bob was the equivalent on an assistant professional's *curriculum vitae* of getting a first class university degree.

CHAPTER V - THE MODERN ERA BEGINS - 1972-1980

THE 1977 OPEN CHAMPIONSHIP

BY THE mid-1970's Turnberry had hosted numerous important tournaments, amateur and professional, including the Walker Cup, the Home Internationals, the Amateur Championship, two P.G.A. Match Play Championships, Scottish and British Ladies' Championships and three Scottish Professional Championships, but had never been chosen to host the most prestigious championship of them all, The Open. As a venue it was loved and revered by all who had experienced its charms, including many of the most distinguished golf commentators. In a brochure for Turnberry Henry Longhurst declared *'in those long periods inseparable from war-time service when there is nothing to do but 'sit and think', I used often to find myself sitting and thinking of the time when once again we might be playing golf at Turnberry'.* Henry was to get his wish and moreover was destined to commentate on television in his own incomparable way on many important tournaments at Turnberry before he died in 1978. It no doubt gave him great satisfaction to know that his beloved Turnberry had at last achieved the crowning glory of hosting the Open Championship, when it came there for the first time in 1977.

The Club's Championship Committee for The 1977 Open
From left to right: Ronnie Faulds, Bob Scott, Ritchie Hannah, Raymond McGuire, Alex Scott, Anne Fraser, Tommy Armstrong, Sylvia Scott, James Tinley, Bill Judge, David Logan, Charlie Jack and Hector McConachie

145

Turnberry Ladies' Championship Committee for the 1977 Open
Back row from left:- Janie Thomson, Margaret Hayter, Isobel Tinley, Anne Fraser, Shirley McGill,
Betty Hannah, Edith Anderson
First row from left:- Madge Walker, Jean Wilson, Isobel Cook, Rosemary Dykes, Margaret Faulds,
Sylvia Scott, Agnes McCall, Jessie Boyd, Isobel McFadzean

R. & A.'s Brave Decision

Donald Steel, writing in the 1977 Open championship programme, observed *'If anywhere could challenge Robert Louis Stevenson's description of Carmel Bay in California, the setting of Pebble Beach, as 'the greatest meeting place of land and water in the world', Turnberry must be a contender.'* It is no wonder that for one hundred years the members of Turnberry Golf Club have counted themselves uniquely privileged to play out their golfing lives on a course and at a place so special as Turnberry. Nor should it be any wonder that the Royal & Ancient Golf Club at last bravely took the risk in 1977 of choosing Turnberry as a new venue for The Open, despite worries about access and accommodation. They were rewarded with a then record crowd for an Open in Scotland and perhaps the most memorable finish of any Open Championship, before or since.

P.A. Ward-Thomas, in an article in *Country Life*, captured the essence of the occasion when he wrote:- *'The decision to hold the Open at Turnberry, taken with some foreboding, was richly justified. The superb weather was a great factor, the setting has few, if any, peers in championship golf, and the hotel, proud and gleaming on its hill, made possible a gathering together unlike any previous Open. I shall not forget the joy of looking down on the links each morning and knowing that the coming hours would produce the substance of indelible memory. Every Open Championship, in recent times, has been memorable for its stirring deeds, but a generation and more may pass before we see anything to compare with the marvellous contest at Turnberry which brought a great victory to Tom Watson and yet another disappointment to Jack Nicklaus. It will never perish from the memories or the chronicles of the game.'*

Chapter V - The Modern Era Begins - 1972-1980

Ailsa Course passes its test

After a period of years when the condition of Turnberry left something to be desired, great efforts had been made by Jimmy McCubbin, the head greenkeeper, and his staff in producing the course in excellent condition and some welcome rain just before the championship, after a dry Spring, softened and greened it up for the start of the tournament. Nevertheless the rough was light and almost negligible, fortunately rendering ineffective the absurd narrowness of the fairways (only 15 paces wide in places). Conditions were benign with only gentle winds all week and greens which mostly held well and had an even pace. The course's main defences were the difficult pin positions and the subtleties and challenges of its wonderful contours and layout. As the sun continued unabated every day, the ball ran further and further on the hardening fairways and only the dog-legged 7th played anything like a par 5. Yet only Nicklaus and Watson finished the tournament with an aggregate under par, albeit that Watson's aggregate of 268 was eight shots lower than the previous record aggregate of 276 by Palmer at Troon in 1962. Third, eleven shots behind, was another American, Hubert Green, who acknowledged how outclassed the field was by Watson and Nicklaus, by declaring that he had won the tournament he was playing in. Indeed Americans filled eleven of the first twelve places, with only Tommy Horton, then captain elect of the P.G.A., finishing in that group at 9th equal. David Ingram, a former assistant at Turnberry, finished top Scot and fourth amongst the U.K. players on 289. Arnold Palmer acquitted himself well, finishing 7th and an outstanding memory of the week was the participation of Henry Cotton, forty years after he had won at Carnoustie. Palmer and Cotton played together in the first two rounds and drew warm applause from the knowledgeable crowd, no doubt appreciating both of their tremendous contributions to the professional game. Mark Hayes, one of the up and coming young Americans, playing for the first time on a course without a single tree, shot a 63, beating Cotton's famous record 65 at Sandwich in 1934.

Henry Cotton on the 5th green

Donald Steel's report

Donald Steel's account in the *Sunday Telegraph* of the final day of the championship describes Watson's glorious and dramatic victory wonderfully well and no apology is necessary for repeating it here.

'Turnberry's first Open championship will not be its last, but it will never see anything more eventful, more dramatic, more stimulating and – for Jack Nicklaus – more cruel than Tom Watson's glorious victory yesterday. Nothing more could have been added to a sequence of final events which ran the full range of emotion, skill and bravery, as arguably the two best players in the world's oldest championship fought a sustained battle of epic proportions. They had been the dominating figures for two days, watched by a record crowd for an Open in Scotland.

Crowds began assembling at Turnberry from early morning, but they waited impatiently for the supporting bouts to finish. For them the bell didn't ring until Nicklaus, Watson, Crenshaw and Horton answered their calls to the first tee, where the flags stretched out for the first time in a wind from the north. The spectacle was a return fight of the one at Augusta earlier in the year won by Watson, and was every bit as enthralling. If anyone else was to get in on the act, it was vital to serve notice early. In such company there was no shortage of candidates. There was, for instance, Johnny Miller, the defending champion, capable of startling charges;

Jack Nicklaus on the practice ground in 1977

there was Crenshaw whose first major title must come soon; and there was Roger Maltbie, whose unspectacular approach hides his efficiency. Hubert Green showed the up and down nature of his game with five 3s in an outward half of 32, but Nicklaus, not the world's leading player for nothing, as he did on Friday, opened with two birdies in the first four holes which this time Watson could not match. They took him three strokes ahead of Watson, five ahead of Crenshaw and, by the time he headed up the 5th, nobody else seemed to have a chance. It seemed the perfect shut-out.

On the second, however, it was Watson who was better placed to set up the chance of a birdie. Nicklaus, down the bank on the left of the fairway, needed to produce one of his best shots of the week in order to prompt Watson to miss the green with his second on the left. Watson failed to get down in two. Nicklaus holed from about 12 ft. to the first of the enormous roars which punctuated his progress, and Watson was behind instead of in front. Although the third hole was

playing almost twice as short as it was last Saturday, Watson had to save his 4 from a bunker there, and it was significant that Nicklaus's other birdie in his opening barrage came against the wind at the 4th, the short hole on the edge of the shore. Here Nicklaus holed from 20 feet, but Watson, missing from a good deal closer and sensing that he could not slip any further, replied immediately with a beautiful 3 at the 5th. This heralded a definite revival and it was the turn of Nicklaus who holed an awkward putt on the same green to save his 4, to hang on. Watson gained another stroke on the par 5 7th, where he was well home in two, and he drew level with another birdie at the 8th. By the turn, which Nicklaus reached in 33 to edge one ahead again, they were to all intents and purposes playing a match.

A few holes later Nicklaus was nine strokes clear of everyone except his partner, and on the early homeward holes had a decided advantage in his personal duel with Watson, who was short of the 10th and 12th greens, and bunkered at the short 11th, doing very well not to drop a stroke to par. Nicklaus, however, having missed birdie putts on the 10th and 11th, finally holed one of six yards on the 12th, where he drove into the right-hand rough. The question then became simply whether Watson could give him two strokes and catch him over six holes. The answer, and the manner in which it was achieved, will be recalled as long as the game is played. At his best Nicklaus is invincible, but Watson's miracle began to unfold with a modest putt for a birdie on the 13th and really came alive with one of an altogether more indecent length from the left edge of the 15th green. At the 17th, his confidence fairly bristling, he went ahead for the first time with a long iron to the green which an understandably jolted Nicklaus could not match. After a deft little pitch and run, he missed from 4 ft., but even then the story was only beginning. Whereas Watson hugged the corner of the dog-leg of the 18th with an iron from the tee, Nicklaus reached for his driver for the first time on the hole in four rounds. In the words of Peter Thomson, five times Open champion, quoting an old Australian sheep-shearer in a game of poker, it was "Sydney or the Bush". It was doubly apt, because another roll or two and it would literally have been the bush. As it was, Nicklaus manufactured some sort of shot from the edge of the whins with an eight iron. It carried the ball to the front of the green and, amid unbelievable scenes, he proceeded to hole it. But it availed him nothing. Watson, playing his second shot first, had already hit a seven iron to no more than 2 ft. and while maybe not expecting to hole it was composed enough to finish a memorable task. Nicklaus, as generous in defeat as ever in victory, conceded afterwards that "he played better than I did and didn't allow himself to make any mistakes." With third and fourth rounds of 65, in itself

Chapter V - The Modern Era Begins - 1972-1980

another record, there is no denying the fact and Watson, the Masters champion, accepted the old trophy with an obvious sense of pride at a job well done and almost certainly the feeling that he will never be involved in anything quite like that again.'

Both Turnberry and Watson emerged from the 1977 Open with enhanced reputations. No one could surely again label Watson a 'choker', as American golf writers had done in April that year. With Nicklaus breathing down his neck at the Masters in the spring of that year and then again at Turnberry, he had triumphed on both occasions. His talent had blossomed in two greatly contrasting environments; amongst the magnolias of Rae's Creek and Amen Corner at Augusta and then again on the hard bare seaside links amongst the sand dunes of Turnberry in the shadow of the ancient castle and the famous lighthouse. The course had proved itself a worthy test for the greatest golfers in the world and played its part in producing a finish of classic proportions. Nicklaus was magnificent, even in defeat, and the names of Turnberry, Watson and Nicklaus will be forever linked. The Turnberry Club is now honoured to number Tom Watson and Jack Nicklaus amongst its members, the two great men having been offered and having accepted honorary membership on the occasion of the next Open at Turnberry in 1986.

Tom Watson holing the winning putt.

149

*Above: Jack Nicklaus and Tom Watson on the 10th tee in the final round.
Below: Tom Watson holds the trophy aloft.
Captain Hamilton Mitchell (far left) and Championship Committee Chairman Tommy Armstrong (2nd from right) look on.*

CHAPTER V - THE MODERN ERA BEGINS - 1972-1980

PROFESSIONALS AT TURNBERRY

WILLIE FERNIE

There doesn't seem to have been any appointment of a professional golfer at Turnberry until 1905, although Willie Fernie, of Troon, who laid out the course, certainly continued to be employed by the Marquis of Ailsa to supervise and oversee the development and maintenance of the course from its opening in 1901 till 1905 when Alex Weir became the first Turnberry professional. Fernie was still the professional at Troon during that period and there is no evidence of him having performed any other professional duties at Turnberry.

A.N. WEIR

It has sometimes been said and thought that Tom Fernie from Troon was the first golf professional at Turnberry, but this was not in fact so. The very first was Mr. Alex N. Weir, who came from Cruden Bay Golf Club where he had been the professional since 1899. He took up his duties at Turnberry on 4th December 1905, having been appointed by Glasgow and South Western Railway Company, when they took over the management of the golf course. His wages were paid by the Company and he was charged with keeping the golf course in proper order with *the men under his orders*. Mr. Weir obviously got down to his work on the course very speedily, because by May 1906, a newspaper report credited him with supervising considerable improvements to the main course and also with laying out a nine hole 'Ladies' Course'. In 1909 Weir was also responsible for a major re-design which created two full 18-hole courses This featured for the first time many of the most important features which can still be seen on the Ailsa Course today, including the basic layout of the first three holes and the positioning of a new green (now the sixth) on the high plateau overlooking Turnberry Bay. When he first arrived the Club were asked to endeavour to find workshop accommodation for him until other arrangements could be made when the railway opened. One of the rooms in the clubhouse was made available by the Club for use as a professional's shop. There is a reference in the Club minutes in April 1908 to the Club granting an *'honorarium of £3-3/- to A.N. Weir, golf professional'*, and to his being responsible for attending to the supply of caddies. He is one of the characters depicted in the cartoon of *'The Turnberry Golf Tournament'* held in 1908, which designates him *'The Turnberry Champion'*. The only other reference to him in the Club minutes was on 7th January 1911, indicating the Club's sincere sympathy about his sudden death. It was the recollection of one of our oldest members that he may have committed suicide, and the tone of the minute seems consistent with that possibility. The circumstances are not known, nor is much known about Mr. Weir's golfing abilities, but it is fitting to set the record straight about him being the first Turnberry professional and also to acknowledge his achievements as a golf course architect whose hand contributed not insignificantly to the development of the course.

TOM R. FERNIE

After Alex Weir's death several applications were received by the Club for the position of golf professional and these were passed on to the Railway Company as the prospective employer. On 4th February, 1911, Tom Fernie, of Troon, was appointed. He was one of the sons of Willie Fernie of Troon, so it was a fitting appointment and was to prove to be a long and happy one. He had received his early training with his father and was for a time private professional to the Duke of Portland. He was a fine stylish player and, before being appointed to Turnberry, he had already won the Scottish Professional Championship (instituted in 1907) for two years in succession, in 1909 and 1910 at Montrose and Lossiemouth respectively. The championship was held at Turnberry in 1911 and there were great expectations that Fernie, playing on his then home course, would win again for the third successive time. The arrangements for the tournament were made by the Secretary of the Scottish Professional Golfers Union and Robert McConnell, the Secretary of Turnberry Golf Club.

Tom Fernie on 18th tee at Turnberry in 1919 - the year in which he was the Scottish Professional Champion.

However perhaps the pressure on Tom Fernie to win was too great, for he could only finish eighth on that occasion, the winner being Edwin Sinclair, a fairly unknown professional from Leith, who had been in America.

As mentioned elsewhere Tom Fernie's golfing career was interrupted by the First World War in which he fought in the trenches in France and was severely wounded. Having survived that he again won the Scottish Professional Championship in both 1919 and 1920 at Monifieth and Gleneagles respectively. He was also several times both Ayrshire and West of Scotland Professional Champion and finished fourth in the Open Championship at Troon in 1923. Like his father before him he was also known as a golf course architect and he laid out the new course at Memorial Park, Maybole, which was opened on 17th May, 1924. On that occasion an exhibition match was played between Fernie and Willie Harvey (described as professionals at Turnberry) and amateurs R. Mitchell of Girvan and James Houston of Maybole. Harvey may have been an assistant to Fernie at Turnberry.

Tom Fernie gave up his post at Turnberry in 1926, having occupied it for 15 years, with a break during the war years. He was apparently well liked by the Club and its members and played an active part in designing and agreeing various alterations and improvements to the courses. After the first world war the second course at Turnberry was not re-opened until 1923, after being re-designed by the legendary James Braid and laid out under the supervision of Tom Fernie. When he married in 1921 the Club organised a subscription from members to buy him a wedding present. The sum of £28-4-6d. was collected, being the equivalent of almost 27 times the then annual subscription of £1-1/-! When he left to take up a new post at Royal Lytham St. Annes Golf Club a meeting of the Club was held, at which Captain J.R. Richmond presided and stated that *'they were met to do honour to their esteemed friend Tom Fernie who had a long list of achievements in the realm of golf, had won many trophies and whose name was likely to become historical in the annals of golf'*. He was presented with a handsome wristlet watch suitably inscribed and a wallet of banknotes, as a token of the respect and esteem in which he was held by the members of the Club.

JAMES McDOWALL

Jimmy McDowall succeeded Tom Fernie in 1927 after being professional at Prestwick for five years. The position had attracted applications from many of the best known professional golfers in Britain. According to reports at the time he had by then already become a notable player and had won the Ayrshire Professional Championship in 1925. The *Ayrshire Post* reported that he had *'startled the professional golfing world in a competition at Galashiels shortly after the war when he led the British Championship field against 'The Big Four', Taylor, Vardon, Braid and Herd and went on from that to tie for third place in the Glasgow Herald competition at Gleneagles'*. We also know that he won the Scottish Professional Championship in 1935 at Longniddry with a score of 280, which at that time was the lowest winning aggregate in the history of that tournament. It wasn't

Chapter V - The Modern Era Begins - 1972-1980

bettered until 1950, when John Panton won, also at Longniddry, with a score of 276.

Donald Henderson, one of the Club's Honorary Members, remembered the McDowall family well and used to play golf with Jimmy's son Stewart between 1935 and 1939, when they were both in their teens. The family had local connections in Maybole and district, and Jimmy was apparently a very fine clubmaker. There are still examples of McDowall limber (whippy) shafted clubs to be found in households in the area, but kept now as antiques and which the modern player would find very difficult to handle. Jimmy McDowall himself was a small man but Donald recalled that he could hit the ball a long way with a big draw, using a slow backswing with wonderful tempo through the ball. Apparently he was the old style of courteous and deferential professional and was very well respected for his skills both as a golfer and as a clubmaker and held in high esteem by the Club, its members and his fellow professionals. He held the post at Turnberry till the course closed on its conversion to an aerodrome during the Second World War.

STEWART McDOWALL

When the courses opened again in 1951 James McDowall's son Stewart was appointed professional at Turnberry and held the post till 1958, when he moved on to Hallamshire Golf Club, near Sheffield. Not a lot of information is available concerning Stewart McDowall, but the minutes of the Club note in March 1953 that Mr. McDowall supported the Club's effort to encourage young golfers. In particular he offered to give free lessons to younger members and to provide old clubs for them, if required. When he left in 1958 to take up his new post, the Club presented him with a handsome gift purchased by subscriptions from Members.

IAN MARCHBANK

In February 1958, Ian Marchbank succeeded Stewart McDowall. He had been the head assistant professional at Gleneagles under Jack McLean, from 1952 to 1958. Both Gleneagles and Turnberry were at that time owned by British Transport Hotels, and so the move was by way of a promotion within the Company. Ian remembers his time at Turnberry with affection, and recalls that he was and still is made very welcome there. He recalls particularly such good players and outstanding characters as Tommy Armstrong, Walter Linton, Alex C. Mitchell, Robbie Stevenson, Stanley Morrison and Graeme McCulloch. He also recalls playing several times with the American President General Dwight Eisenhower around 1959, when Mr. Eisenhower visited Scotland to stay in his flat at Culzean Castle (donated to him for his lifetime by the National Trust for Scotland in appreciation of his great contribution to victory in the Second World War). He describes the great man as being a very nice genuine person and a very keen golfer, playing off a handicap of 12. Ian, by his own admission, did not win much of note in the game, being fully occupied with his many management and professional duties and with running a very successful shop. When he left Turnberry in April 1962, it was to take over as professional at Gleneagles after the death of Jack McLean. His son Brian became a very notable tournament professional and won the Scottish Professional Championship.

BOB JAMIESON

In 32 years as the head professional at Turnberry Bob played golf with the rich and famous from all walks of life, including royalty, heads of state and sports stars. Amongst the film stars he welcomed were Sean Connery, Charlie Chaplin, Paul Newman, Bing Crosby and Burt Lancaster. He included amongst his friends Arnold Palmer, Gary Player and Jack Nicklaus and nearly all the top modern golfers visited his shop at Turnberry over those 32 years. Yet one of Bob's fondest memories was of playing a round of golf at Luffness Golf Club at the age of 16 with the legendary James Braid, who was one of the 'Great Triumvirate' of Taylor, Vardon and Braid who dominated golf in the late 19th and early 20th centuries and, amongst them, won 16 Open Championships between 1894 and 1914. Bob recalled that Braid was a very quiet spoken man and at the end of the round he said *'Aye laddie you'll no play the game until you keep that mashie-niblick in your bag'*. Bob explained that this was a reference to his desire at that age to smash every drive and hit every green with a lofted club instead of learning to play a variety of more effective shots. He also remembered with pleasure, that same year at Luffness, playing with the great American lady golfer Babe Zaharias just before she won the British Ladies' Championship at nearly Gullane. He said that her length off the tee was formidable.

Bob's way over the years at Turnberry was always that of the old style professional, who both gave and demanded respect. He always addressed members as

'Mr.' and and of course his assistants would address him in the same way. Indeed even Nick Price, the Open Champion of 1994, addressed him as 'Mr. Jamieson'. That was the way Bob was raised, first as the son of a father who was the steward at Luffness Golf Club, and then as an assistant to Bobby Halsall at Birkdale.

He was born in America in 1931, while his father was working in Philadelphia as a salesman for Anderson Tweeds of Galashiels. The family returned to Galashiels in 1935 and his father took up the job of steward at Luffness and in doing so he unwittingly laid down the pattern for his son's life. After watching the Scottish Boys Championship in 1946, Bob took up golf and got lessons from the local postman, who doubled as professional. He entered the Scottish Boys' Championship in 1947, but recalls that he was soundly trounced 4 and 3 in the first round. The next year however he did better, reaching the semi-final, and also getting to the quarter final of the British Boys at Kilmarnock Barassie. His reward was a place in the Scottish Boys' Team and he was chosen by the late Leonard Crawley to have special tuition at Rye from professionals Bobby Halsall and Willie Anderson. This led to him being offered a job as an apprentice professional at Birkdale under Bobby Halsall, at the age of 17. He accepted and spent a year there before doing two years National Service in the Royal Air Force and then returning to Birkdale for a further summer. He was then offered the job at Crieff, becoming probably the youngest full professional in Britain at that time at the age of 20. His retainer was £180 a year and he charged 35p per hour for lessons.

After ten years at Crieff, in 1962 he was appointed to Turnberry to replace Ian Marchbank, who had moved to Gleneagles. It was a good time to join, for Turnberry was just beginning to be accepted again on the world circuit, holding the Amateur in 1961, the Walker Cup and the P.G.A. Match Play Championship in 1963, and going on from there to host many other notable championships, to be crowned at last in 1977 with the Open Championship itself, for the first of three Opens there to date.

Open Week July 1986. Pro Shop Staff. Left to right: Gregor Jamieson, Simon Coulls, Graham Mackintosh, Calum Innes, Bob Jamieson, Guy Maxwell, Michael Moore and Colin Campbell.

Chapter V - The Modern Era Begins - 1972-1980

Perhaps the greatest testament to Bob's successful years at Turnberry is seen in the assistants who have passed through his hands. He undoubtedly had a gift for picking young hopefuls to learn their trade at Turnberry and a training at Turnberry under Bob invariably stood them in good stead in finding success in their future careers. Norman Wood became the pro at Royal Guernsay, won the Italian Open and became a Ryder Cup player; Ross Drummond won the Scottish Professional Championship five times and went on to have a successful career on the European Tour; Robin Liddle, won the Scottish Assistants' Championship and Northern Open and became the pro at Penina in Portugal; David Ingram won several Scottish tournaments and played for Scotland in the World Cup. Others such as Renton Doig, Douglas Smart, Robin Fyfe, Niall Cameron and Colin Campbell went on to become successful club pros.

Bob himself won the East of Scotland Professional Championship while he was at Crieff and finished fifth in the Scottish Professional Championship at Machrihanish in 1969 but, due to poor health in the 1980's, he played very little golf thereafter. He concentrated on his many other duties and interests at Turnberry, including teaching, running one of the most impressive golf shops in Scotland, managing his staff, keeping an eye on the caddies and starters and generally being a public relations asset to his employers, Turnberry Hotel.

Over the years Bob was a senior lecturer for the British and Scottish P.G.A. training schools and was influential along with his son Gregor in coaching Fiona and Mhairi McKay in their formative years as members of Turnberry. They went on to win numerous amateur championships and both became Scottish internationalists, and Mhairi of course is presently forging a very successful tournament career for herself in America.

In 1993, the Professional Golfers Association bestowed one of its highest accolades on Bob when he was made an Honorary Member, and he retired from Turnberry in 1994, after 32 years service. He always said that Turnberry was one of the most compellingly

August 1992. First winners of 1892 Trophy.
From left to right:- N. Cruikshank, Brian Gunson (Head Professional), Jack Boyd (Captain) Tom Paterson (Secretary).

being produced in the Ayrshire town of Mauchline, about 15 miles north of Turnberry. Ailsa Craig is almost as much a trademark of Turnberry as the famous lighthouse and the first hole on the championship course bears its name.

Sea Birds

At any major tournament hosted at Turnberry the cameramen are inevitably drawn to the seascape to complement the golf coverage, and the Firth of Clyde rarely lets them down. Predominant among the traffic of seabirds to be seen are the northern gannets, often seen folding their wings and plunging spectacularly into the sea in pursuit of mackerel and herring. More than 35,000 pairs of gannets nest on the granite ledges of Ailsa Craig, forming one of the largest colonies in Britain. This breeding station has been established for centuries and is referred to in ornithological literature as early as 1526. In mediaeval times the gugas (plump brown young birds about to leave the nest) were harvested for the table of the monks at Crossraguel Abbey nearby to Turnberry. The Reverend William Abercrombie, the Curate of Maybole, wrote in 1695 of gannets being sold to the lower classes who could not afford mutton or beef, but after 1880 there was virtually no demand for this type of food. The last thirty years has seen a steady increase in breeding pairs on Ailsa Craig and other birds such as puffin, shelduck and black guillemots have also returned since a plague of rats originating from visiting boats has been eradicated. Razorbills, fulmars and kittiwakes also breed on the island and are joined by numerous visitors from further afield. Turnberry Point is a favoured sea watching point and in spring and autumn there is usually a major passage of birds. In spring it is the build up of divers, predominantly red throated, but by far the most spectacular sight is the movement of up to 6,000 manx shearwaters between July and September. These pelagic birds only come onto shore to breed, and spend the rest of their lives out at sea. Their characteristic flap and glide flight and the miraculous way in which they skim the wavetops makes identification easy.

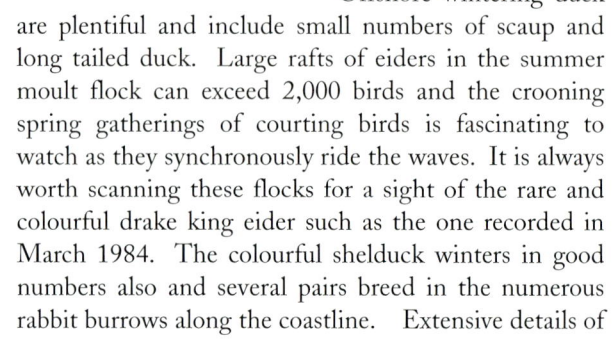

A Gannet in flight

Eider ducks in sea off Turnberry

Rarities too can repay patient observation. Pomerine skua, Leaches petrel and Sabine's gull turn up occasionally. Small numbers of the distinctive storm petrel, the smallest European sea bird, measuring barely six inches in length, come past and have been lured onto the shore at Turnberry to be ringed. Offshore wintering duck are plentiful and include small numbers of scaup and long tailed duck. Large rafts of eiders in the summer moult flock can exceed 2,000 birds and the crooning spring gatherings of courting birds is fascinating to watch as they synchronously ride the waves. It is always worth scanning these flocks for a sight of the rare and colourful drake king eider such as the one recorded in March 1984. The colourful shelduck winters in good numbers also and several pairs breed in the numerous rabbit burrows along the coastline. Extensive details of the seabirds off Turnberry have been compiled by Angus Hogg, the local bird recorder, and the total of species for the golf course stands at over 180.

Sea Creatures

Birds are by no means the only wildlife to be seen offshore. Although sightings of humpback and minke whales are rare, pods of porpoises and dolphins regularly grace the seas off Turnberry as they move up and down the Firth. Grey seals haul up on the rocks or come close inshore, their natural curiosity often giving the watcher great pleasure at seeing them at close hand. Many are to be seen, especially at low tide on the rocks and in the tidal lagoon at the south end of Turnberry Bay.

Calm days in mid-summer are when you are likely to spot the basking sharks cruising up and down from Turnberry to Culzean. These gentle giants which grow up to 35 feet in length, feed only on plankton, though to see them cutting through the water is an intimidating sight to anyone in a small boat. These sharks were hunted locally between 1982 and 1993, generating much anger from conservationists, but fortunately no licences have been issued since then.

Butterflies and Flora

The front line pioneers in the world of flowers are the sea orache, sea rocket and sea sandwort which manage to survive in the inhospitable tidal foredune area. Marram grass dominates and stabilises the dune structure and vegetation but flashes of colour are provided by ladies bedstraw, hawkweed, rest harrow and encroaching ragwort. On top of the dunes the true Scottish bluebell, the harebell, flowers in profusion in the sandy soil. Low bushy patches of burnet rose are also widespread and attract a variety of insects including not surprisingly the burnet moth, whose caterpillar stage feeds on the equally common birdsfoot trefoil [or 'ham and eggs'].

Scottish Bluebell

Red Admiral Butterfly

Butterflies abound, drawn by the dune flora and are a feature through March to October. Species such as the small tortoishell, green veined white, common blue,

Stoat in its winter coat in whins at Turnberry

grayling, small heath and the ringlet are common among the courses' grassy habitats. Irruptive species such as the clouded yellow and the painted lady do not appear every year but do breed irregularly. Another migratory species, the red admiral, which hails from North Africa, arrives in late spring and produces a home grown generation in late summer which does not usually survive the winter.

100 to 250 Years Ago

The golf courses as we see them today, though very open in character, are nonetheless a much more varied landscape than 250 years ago. Turnberry Park, as the area was then known, is portrayed on a Culzean estate map of 1750 as featureless, grass dominated farmland with 'good swamping pasture' adjacent to the dunes and 'fine light sandy pasture' inland on the low flat part of the new Kintyre course. The underlying geology is from the Devonian period, a well drained sandstone base to the south of the Lighthouse and rocky Devonian lavas stretching from this beacon north to Port Murray at the north end of the Kintyre course [now a geological Site of Special Scientific Interest]. You can speculate that this environment would have supported snipe, curlew, lapwings and other waders. Skylarks would have been thick on the ground and hares plentiful. By the time the first Ordnance Survey Map was published in 1857 the area still lacked tree and scrub cover, but the land was enclosed. The field pattern was small units to the north and large tracts, described as 'bents' to the seaward. Just inland from Turnberry Castle a small collection of farm buildings was shown on the 1857 map and referred to as the 'Turnberry Warren'. The name may derive from Turnberry being one of the locations in Ayrshire where rabbits were introduced in the late eighteenth century, the stock being a valuable source of food and fur.

Photographs in the book 'The Kingdom of Carrick and its Capital', by John Millar and John Latta, published in 1904, depict an almost uniform terrain of closely cropped bent grass and not a bush or tree in sight. They also show a long stone dyke [wall] which would at some time have separated the bents land from the inland pasture. The range of habitats and associated wildlife at that time would have been much more limited compared to the rich mosaic which has evolved naturally or been designed or helped by the hand of man since that time.

Wild Purple Orchids which grow in early Summer on parts of the Ailsa Course.

Chapter V - The Modern Era Begins - 1972-1980

Today

Although you tend to imagine that the golf course is a very open area, the interior of the course has an amazing amount of cover and this suits the mammal population quite well. The gorse and bramble thickets and small stands of pine afford enough cover to encourage small numbers of roe deer, seen mostly at the earlier part of the day and at dusk. The preponderance of grassland, be it light mown rough or the impenetrable heavier variety which penalises wayward shots, is ideal for rabbits. The local stoat population is kept busy keeping the numbers down and transient foxes also prey on the greenkeepers' foe.

Yellowhammer merges with golden gorse.

For the golfers there is one hazardous stream, straddling four holes, but for the naturalist this represents yet another piece in the biodiversity jigsaw with its own distinct community of plants. The lucky or very observant may catch a glimpse of an otter using the stream as a route inland from the sea, as otters have recently re-established themselves on the Ayrshire coast and are doing very well.

All year round you will see the kestrel quartering the grassland, hovering intently, eyes only on the ground below where the movement of a field vole will initiate the final dive. In winter the rarer short eared owl may also be seen silently hunting the same prey. The hare is well outside the capability of either of these predators and they thrive at Turnberry. They are among several creatures which are very common on this and other golf courses but whose declining numbers in many other parts of Britain are giving cause for concern. Joining the hare in this category is the grey partridge, of which there are several coveys at Turnberry each year, and the delightful skylark which is suffering serious decline nationally.

In natural history terms Turnberry golf courses cannot be seen in isolation as they are part of the rich mosaic of habitats on the south Ayrshire coast. To the south lies the Dipple shore at Girvan, a narrow but important ribbon of raised beaches and rocky shoreline used extensively by ducks, gulls and waders in winter. To the north the Maidenhead Bay is also a seabird haunt and the rich wooded cliff line of Culzean Castle & Country Park, managed by The National Trust for Scotland, adds the final dimension. Together they form a critical corridor for wildlife.

This wealth of wildlife is recognised by Turnberry Golf Club and the owners of Turnberry and also by the Royal and Ancient Golf Club of St. Andrews who take a great interest in the welfare of their Open venues. Wildlife records are kept by George Brown, the Golf Course and Estate Manager at Turnberry, and his enthusiasm for the flora and fauna ensures that every effort is made to accommodate the natural aspect of the links environment.

Imagine a round of golf without the skylark hanging in the air above the fairways, without the yellow hammer calling from the ranks of golden gorse, or without marsh orchids adding a splash of colour to the rough. Enjoy your golf, and the supporting cast.

Stonechat on the whins

Seapink on the seaside rocks

Chapter VI

Centenary - The Closing Years

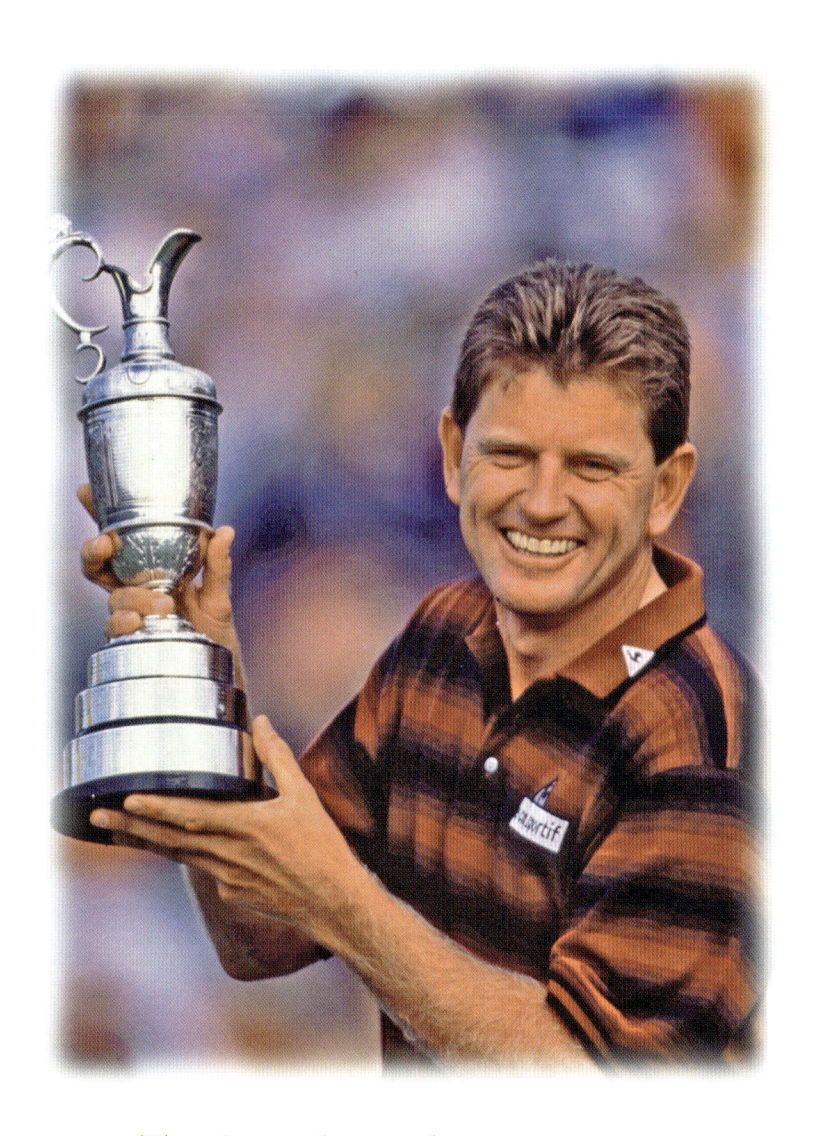

Turnberry hosts the top events

THE FINAL PERIOD - 1980-2002

Outstanding Players

THE 1980s were a very active period for the core activities of the Club. The competitions were all keenly contested and there were many very good low handicap players to ensure that no one player dominated the principal scratch awards. In 1980 the Stanley P. Morrison Salver for the Club Championship was won by C.W.F. (Bill) Judge who was Captain of the Club from 1982 till 1984. Bill was an Ayrshire County player and his outstanding record included winning the Club Championship on four occasions, in 1968, 1973, 1979 and 1980, the Sir James Bell Match Play Trophy four times, in 1976, 1977, 1983 and 1992 and the Bargany Cup in 1963, 1964, 1966 and 1967. During his captaincy in 1983 he also won the D.J. Logan Trophy which was donated to the Club in 1981 by Captain David Logan for a 72 hole scratch stroke play championship.

John A. Jones was another fine player at that time. He won the Club Championship three times in 1981, 1986 and 1989 and in 1981 he also won the D.J. Logan Trophy and Club Gold Medal for the lowest scratch score of the qualifiers for the Club Championship.

Brian Bain, a diminutive Girvan school teacher, proved that height is not essential to play the game well and he won the Club Championship twice, in 1982 and 1988, the Gold Medal three times, in 1983, 1984 and 1987 and the D.J. Logan twice, in 1987 and 1988.

Other notable players who won the Club Championship in the period included Gordon Rodger, John Wilson and Barry Forsyth. Gordon was subsequently to serve as Captain in 2000-2002 and he is one of only five Captains who were also Club Champions, the others being Robbie Stevenson, Graeme McCulloch, Stanley Morrison and Bill Judge, though none of them managed it during their period of captaincy.

The outstanding player in the 1990s was undoubtedly Allan Thomson whose exploits are described later.

Others who won the Club Championship during that period included Ian Rorison, John Hodge and Alastair Kidd, a Maybole man who spent his early life as a golf professional in New Zealand before returning to his native land and being re-instated as an amateur at Turnberry. Ronnie McLellan was the champion for two years in succession in 2000 and 2001 and John Broadfoot won the centenary year championship in 2002. John's was a particularly popular and long overdue victory, he having won the D.J. Logan Stoke Play Championship for four years in succession from 1999 to 2002.

John Broadfoot – Club Champion in Centenary Year 2002.

Special mention is also made of George Brown, Turnberry's popular and excellent Golf Course Superintendent since 1985, who won the D.J. Logan three times in 1990, 1993 and 1997, and John Dauthieu another former professional golfer re-instated to the amateur ranks, who won the Club Championship in 1983 and the D.J. Logan three times, in 1989, 1991 and 1994.

Chapter VI - Centenary - The Closing Years

In addition to the overall Club Championship for the Stanley P. Morrison Salver, Turnberry has another scratch championship to encourage and recognise merit without the distortion of handicaps. This is the C.L. Jack Championship for players with handicaps of 12 and over and Bill Slattery deserves a special mention as the winner on four occasions – 1988, 1996, 1997 and 1998. Bill's couthy description of a match played without handicaps is *'A man's game'*.

Allan Thomson

James Allan Thomson was born in May 1958, educated at Belmont Academy, Ayr, and became a member of Turnberry Golf Club in 1976. Prior to that he had been a junior member of Belleisle Golf Club, Ayr, from the age of 8. He continued to be a member of Belleisle as a senior and was made an honorary member of that club in 1981 in recognition of his golfing achievements. Indeed, throughout a distinguished golfing career he has always shown his loyalty to Belleisle Golf Club by giving that as his club when entering open competitions and championships. Nevertheless he loved playing at Turnberry, enjoyed his membership there, and Turnberry Golf Club is also very proud of his achievements. He was the Club Champion at Turnberry for five years in succession from 1995 till 1999, being every year that he entered that Championship. He has also been the Belleisle Club Champion on seven occasions.

Allan says that he didn't win much in boys' golf, but then getting him to talk about his feats is a bit like getting blood from a stone. In Ayrshire he won the county stroke play title at Loudoun in 1979 and the county match play championship at Troon in 1985. He also won many 36 hole scratch opens including the Viking Krus Trophy at Largs, the West Kilbride Open and the Belleisle Cup on no fewer than seven occasions. Further afield he won the Newlands Trophy at Lanark in 1988, the Shamash Trophy at Southerness in 1987, and the Edward Trophy at Glasgow Gailes in its centenary year in 1991.

On the wider stage of regional and national championships Allan has also performed with distinction, winning the West of Scotland stroke play championship over 72 holes at Paisley in 1985 and the Scottish Amateur Championship at Moray Golf Club, Lossiemouth, in 1989, beating fellow Ayrshireman Alan Tait in the final. Before that he was twice beaten in the final of the Scottish Championship, in 1981 by Colin Dalgleish at Western Gailes and in 1986 by Colin Brooks at Monifieth. He also was a beaten semi-finalist on three occasions in 1983, 1988 and 1998. In 1983 he reached the Quarter Final of the Amateur Championship at Turnberry when he was beaten by the eventual winner Philip Parkin, and in that same year he was third in the Brabazon Trophy, the English Open Amateur Stroke Play Championship.

From 1981 till 1992 he represented Scotland in the Home Internationals on eleven occasions, which was every year during that period, except 1990 which he missed due to a family illness, although he was selected. During this series he played at Woodhall Spa, Ganton and Formby in England; Portmarnock, Sligo and Lahinch in Ireland; Muirfield, Troon and Prestwick in Scotland; and Harlech and Porthcawl in Wales. No-one has represented Scotland on more occasions, except Charlie Green and George McGregor. One big disappointment for Allan was not being picked for the Walker Cup team in 1984, despite his really good form in 1983 which must surely have put him in contention.

One of Allan's treasured memories is qualifying for the Open Championship in 1982 and playing at Royal Troon in the Championship proper in the company of Bruce Leitske of U.S.A. Unfortunately he didn't make the 36 hole cut, but many of his friends remember the excitement they experienced when, on the first day, his name appeared briefly on the leader board, with a score of two under par after five holes. He played with Bernard Gallacher in a practice round for that Open, and found him to be an absolute gentleman. He reckons Gallacher had one of the finest short games he has ever seen. He recalls Gallacher in practice playing 6 balls from a pot bunker on the left of the fifth green to a pin position on a downslope very close to the bunker, and stopping each ball short of the pin. Allan then tried the same shot several times but each time the ball ran at least ten feet past the pin.

In the course of his career Allan played with and against most of the top amateurs of the day, some of whom have subsequently become successful professionals. Such people include Colin Dalgleish, Barclay Howard, Lindsay Mann, Charlie Green, George McGregor, Padraig Harrington, Peter McEvoy,

— 165 —

Raymond Russell, Warren Humphreys, Ian Carslaw, Andrew Coltart, Dean Robertson and Colin Montgomery. His handicap has been scratch or better since 1981 and as low as plus 2. Moreover this is despite consistently playing in club competitions even in poor weather, unlike some low handicap players who prefer to protect their handicaps by not playing in club events when the weather makes scoring difficult. The writer remembers playing with him in a Spring Meeting at Turnberry in bad conditions. At the sixth hole on the Ailsa Course Allan pulled his tee shot left and lost the ball. He went back to the tee and, with a penalty shot playing three off the tee, he proceeded to hole that tee shot through a strong head wind to this difficult 220 yard par three. His gross score that day was 73.

Allan Thomson – Scottish Amateur Champion 1989.

Sadly for Turnberry Golf Club, Allan now plays most of his golf at Old Prestwick, but he is a valued member wherever he plays, and is always prepared to play with any other members of whatever handicap. It is a great pleasure to play a round of golf with him, not only to watch such a fine golfer in action, but also because he is a fine courteous companion with a mischievous sense of humour, and who makes you feel that he has enjoyed the game, even if you have inevitably taken at least 10 strokes more than him.

Matches

There were numerous official matches with other clubs during the period, including Ayr Belleisle, Barassie, Prestwick St. Nicholas, Royal St. Georges, Loch Lomond and Gleneagles, and also with teams from the universities of Strathclyde, Glasgow and Dublin and the People to People Organisation of America. Regular unofficial matches on a home and away basis in alternate years were established in 1999, between teams from Turnberry and the Greenbrier Club of Lewisburg, West Virginia, USA. From Turnberry the enthusiastic organiser of these matches is Ian Brown and the honorary captain of the Greenbrier team for the first two years of the series was Sam Snead, the great American golfer who won our Open Championship at St. Andrews in 1946. When he came to Turnberry in 2000 with the Greenbrier team that was his first trip back to Britain since that occasion. He told Ian Brown that the prize money on this side of the Atlantic was too little to tempt him back. It was also his last trip back to these shores for he died that year, after his trip to Turnberry. Junior matches were held against Royal Mid-Surrey Golf Club in 1992 and Bruntsfield Golf Club of Edinburgh and Fettes College, Edinburgh, in 1994 and an annual home and away Seniors' match series with Bruntsfield of Edinburgh was established in 2000. Several invitations to play matches were declined including from Yale University, Cambridge University Stymie Club, Portmarnock Golf Club, Merion Golf Club, Pennsylvania and Grahamston Golf Club, Cape Province, South Africa, Newport Golf Club, California and Westin Resort, Sardinia. It seems a great pity that some of these could not be accommodated, with the prospect of away games in some very exotic places, but the schedule of matches was already almost too busy to be fulfilled by a Club with less than 300 members. There are also references in the Club minutes to a six-a-side match at Turnberry in 1987 with a representative Scottish Ladies' Team, and to a proposed match in 1986 at the old Musselburgh course between the Turnberry Club and the Honourable Company of Edinburgh Golfers, to commemorate the original championship course at Musselburgh where The Open was held five times in the nineteenth century.

Celebrations

The latter part of the nineteenth century was a time

Chapter VI - Centenary - The Closing Years

when many of today's famous golf clubs and championships were founded and Turnberry Golf Club was honoured to receive invitations to send representatives to a number of their centenary celebrations, including the following:-

Centenary of the Amateur Championship
at Royal Liverpool Golf Club in 1985.
Royal St. George's Golf Club at Sandwich in 1987.
Kilmarnock Barassie Golf Club, Ayrshire in 1987.
Ganton Golf Club, Yorkshire, in 1991.
Portmarnock Golf Club, Northern Ireland, in 1994.
Centenary of first Open Golf Championship held in England at Royal St. George's Golf Club, in 1994.
Royal Liverpool Golf Club in 1996.

The Club was also privileged to be invited in 1994 to send a representative to the 260th anniversary celebrations at Muirfield of The Honourable Company of Edinburgh Golfers (originally the Gentlemen Golfers of Leith), which is claimed to be the earliest formal golf club in the history of the game, there being definite proof of it having been instituted in 1744. Turnberry does not rival or even get close to claiming that kind of antiquity but it is fascinating to think that the *'Girvan Gang'* (referred to in Chapter I) were playing their regular games only 10 years later, in 1754, just across the Turnberry Bay and within sight of Turnberry.

Social Events

The Turnberry Club has survived in the face of great adversity ever since its inception but the members have always been able to celebrate the good times. In 1977 celebrations of the Club's 75th anniversary coincided with Turnberry hosting the most memorable Open Championship ever held. There was a wonderful feeling of jubilation and achievement amongst the members that year, but without conceit or stuffy elitism. Along with the hotel management they had thrown themselves wholeheartedly and enthusiastically into the tasks and challenges faced by any Club hosting the Open, with the extra pressure of being the first new venue for that great championship in 23 years. The result was a spectacular success. Watson and Nicklaus were of course the stars but the stage was Turnberry and each and every member felt a part of that success. For the Open that year there was a large temporary wooden building erected in the car park to accommodate visiting greenkeepers and, on the week after the Championship, the Club commandeered it, hired a jazz band and held an impromptu 'hooly' which no-one present will ever forget. The walls were literally going out and in as people danced and gyrated in the flimsy building. At one point a member whose name shall remain confidential but who has since left and joined another famous Ayrshire club, actually swung from a rafter causing fears that the whole structure would collapse inwards on top of the company.

Earlier that year there had been a more formal celebration in nearby Malin Court Hotel, by way of marking the Club's 75th anniversary. Over 200 people attended a dinner followed by a dance in a specially erected marquee. At the dinner the minute of the first general meeting of the Club was read out, which referred to an old railway waggon serving as the first clubhouse and expressed fears about obtaining adequate rights to the tee-off times on the newly laid out course. The continuing relevance of the latter problem 75 years later was not lost on the company but did not dampen their enjoyment of the occasion.

The main annual social events for many years have been the dinners and presentation of prizes held respectively by both the Gentlemen's Section and the Ladies' Section and the annual dinner dance in Turnberry Hotel. There have also been many special events over the years including informal buffet and dinner dances, film shows, race and gaming nights and even, one year, a St. Valentine's dance. Two mixed foursome competitions for the Sir John Tait Salver and the Cockburn Cup usually have a social function afterwards, and the Tri or Quad-Ams, Texas Scramble and Captain – v – Vice Captain match are always followed by a meal and presentation of prizes. The Social Committee and its conveners are kept busy organising such events and, since 1983, the conveners who have worked hard at this have been Ken MacKenzie, David Stobie, Eric Smeeton, Ronnie Gaw, Stuart Holmes, Bill Clare and Charles Tait.

One idiosyncracy of the Turnberry Club members which has persisted for as long as anyone can remember is an enthusiasm for playing dominoes after the game of golf. The Club minutes contain many references to this, from complaints about the noise made by the domino players to complaints by the participants about missing or poor domino sets. In the old clubhouse prior to 1993 special fitted felt table covers were purchased to deaden the sound of dominoes being slapped down on hard surfaces, but this did nothing to deaden the frustrated or triumphant bellowing of the players themselves, who become completely enrapt in the excitement which is surprisingly generated by this pastime. Since the new clubhouse opened the domino players have been banished to the lounge area of the men's changing rooms, though some, notably Douglas Dunlop and Maurice Sommerville, also play in the Half-Way house on the Ailsa Course, overlooking the sea and the lighthouse. Their concentration on the game is so intense that it is doubtful if they are aware of what must be the most spectacular outlook in the world for participants in their less than Olympic sport.

Douglas Dunlop and Maurice Sommerville – Domino Champions 2002.

Some Characters

Like most golf clubs Turnberry has produced its fair share of 'characters'. There was Tommy Girvan who died in 1993, a cigar smoking businessman from Ayr, who used to turn up at every annual general meeting and question why the Club was accumulating a healthy cash balance in its capital account and then propose that the money be spent immediately on the members. His proposal never ever found a seconder but was always received with good humour and tolerance. Tommy would surely have been delighted had he lived to enjoy the Club's centenary in 2002 when at last a large part of the Club's reserves were spent to ensure the members' enjoyment of the various special celebrations and competitions held to mark the occasion. Tommy's pals included Hector McConnachie, Willie Harkiss and Wallace Skilling and the story is told that, on one occasion when they were playing their usual four ball game on the Arran course on a rainy day, Tommy didn't feel too well at the seventh hole. The others were reluctant to abandon their round so they made Tommy comfortable under a whin bush and a brolly with a hip flask of some good stuff as medicine. They played on and checked on his condition when they got round to the thirteenth green which was near his sanctuary. Apparently the medicine had worked wonders and Tommy was able to join them again and complete the round.

Sadly Tommy and many of his friends are now gone to the great golf course in the skies. Douglas Dunlop knew them all well and he was entrusted by the Girvan family with scatterng Tommy's ashes at Turnberry. He has been retired for some time now but he was, by profession, a trader in the fruit and vegetable market in Glasgow, an institution where a quick mind and a ready wit are essential qualities for success and Douglas is particularly gifted in those. He was playing one day in a three ball game with Alex Wilson and David Struthers when a large seagull flew over and deposited the contents of its bowels on David's back. Alex told David what had happened and what a mess was on his jacket. David replied that it was O.K., as he had some toilet paper in his bag, to which Douglas immediately retorted *'You will never catch that bird'*. On another occasion somebody was telling of a news item about a parrot which was claimed to have a vocabulary of over 600 words and could tell jokes, at which Douglas immediately and irreverently commented *'That's more than most club captains'*.

Chapter VI - Centenary - The Closing Years

Some Senior Members 2002. From left – R. Faulds, H. Dykes, W. Bennet, D. Muir, W. Tait and D. Logan (behind).

A slightly younger member, Ian Gardiner, an Ayr solicitor, could be said to be a bit of an eccentric. He likes to play at the crack of dawn and go for a swim afterwards in the sea off Turnberry Bay. He doesn't believe in playing with new balls and only uses iron clubs. When he acted as a marshall at the Women's British Open Championship in 2002 he was given six new Titliest balls each day for his services, collecting 24 in all and he immediately swopped them with past Captain Stewart Jardine for a bag of 200 second-hand balls. It is falsely alleged that, when he plays a bounce game where the stake is a ball, he hands over a second-hand ball. This is not true but there have been occasions when he has paid up with a 10 year old new ball still wrapped in its original paper. His perks as a marshall included four lunch vouchers to a total value of £30, which he took to the hospitality tent and exchanged for 60 muesli bars which he carried around the course offering to all and sundry.

Turnberry Resort – Owners and Developments.

In August 1980 press reports and a statement in Parliament indicated that British Transport Hotels were to consider selling various hotels and golf courses belonging to them. In September of that year it was confirmed by Chris Rouse, the Hotel Manager, that a sale seemed likely and the Club entered into correspondence with George Younger, Secretary of State for Scotland, to ascertain the position. The reply indicated that the Government wished to see private capital playing a part in certain businesses till then wholly owned by the nationalised British Railways Board, including their subsidiary British Transport Hotels Limited, who were responsible for various hotel businesses including Turnberry Hotel and golf courses. At that time British Railways Board were considering options which included possible outright disposal of assets or floating one or more hotels or groups of hotels as joint ventures with other operators. The Turnberry resort and courses existed due to the entrepreneurial foresight of the Third Marquess of Ailsa and Glasgow and South West of Scotland Railway Company at the beginning of the 20th century and had been successfully managed anddeveloped by private capital until all the British railway companies were nationalised after the war in 1950. In 1980 it seemed that the future of Turnberry was to be entrusted once again into private hands and the Club was naturally apprehensive of its position in the scheme of things. The nationalised company deserved great credit during its thirty year stewardship, particularly for having rebuilt the courses after the war. It also played an essential part in ensuring that the Ailsa Course became a true championship course, not only because of its intrinsic quality but because it hosted during that period many of the most important tournaments in Britain, climaxing with The Open in 1977.

Nothing further happened regarding the sale of Turnberry until October 1982 when it was finally put on the market for sale by British Transport Hotels. The Club obtained a prospectus and a tender form from the Department of Transport, and there was a great deal of speculation amongst the members as to whether or not it would be feasible for the Club to submit an offer to purchase. The hurdles, both financial and logistical, of submitting a serious offer and, if successful, then managing a hotel and golfing resort, were really too great. The Club's efforts were channelled instead into trying to survive and negotiate reasonable playing conditions from the new owners, Sea Containers Ltd., who took over in March 1983.

There followed a period of upgrading of the hotel by Sea Containers Limited, an international company with many and varied interests which included operating the famous Orient Express. They commenced a £12m. programme of refurbishment of bedrooms and public rooms which was not completed until 1989. This was rewarded in 1986 when the hotel was awarded 5 star rating by the Automobile Association and the Royal Automobile Club and was elected to membership of the prestigious *'Leading Hotels of the World'*. In the same year Turnberry hosted The Open for the second time and a year later, in 1987, Sea Containers Limited sold Turnberry to a Japanese company, Nitto Kogyo Co., of Tokyo, which specialised in owning and managing golf courses and golf resorts throughout the world and who remained the owners until 1998. Turnberry had indeed come a long way from its humble beginnings before the hotel was built and a humble railway waggon without heat or water served as a temporary clubhouse for those braving the elements on the rough links still shared with the sheep.

Nitto Kogyo proved themselves generous stewards of Turnberry and their period of ownership saw momentous events for both the hotel and courses. On the golfing front the first three Senior British Open Championships were held in 1988, 1989 and 1990, The Open returned for the third time in 1994 and The Amateur, also for the third time, in 1996. In 1989 the

Jessie Boyd, wife of the Club Captain, is introduced to Prince Andrew, Duke of York, at opening of new clubhouse.

Chapter VI - Centenary - The Closing Years

hotel won the title of *'5 star Hotel of the Year'* chosen by the Automobile Association and in 1990 hosted the spring NATO Council Meeting attended by the British Prime Minister Margaret Thatcher, the American Secretary of State, James Baker and the Heads of State of all other member countries. This event coincided with the opening of a new £1.5m. conference suite and a year later, in 1991, a new £7m. Health Spa, with restaurant and 17 bedrooms was opened by H.R.H. Prince Edward. The Ailsa course was voted in various polls in 1992 as 19th best course in the world and 3rd best in the U.K., and the hotel won an award in 1993 as *'Hotel of the Year'*.

Having been invited in 1989 by the R. & A. to host The Open again in 1994, Nitto Kogyo commenced the construction of a new £4m. clubhouse and a £1m. golf course improvement project in 1991 and the new clubhouse was opened on 15th June, 1993, by H.R.H. Prince Andrew, Duke of York, a very keen golfer. There was a luncheon following the opening ceremony and the Prince could hardly wait to escape to the practice ground prior to taking part in a four ball match over the Ailsa course. He was partnered by the R. & A. Secretary, Michael Bonallack against the Turnberry Captain, Jack Boyd and a former British ambassador to Japan, representing Nitto Kogyo. It was a close match with no deference to Royalty by way of conceding missable putts, but the visitors just scraped home due to the enduring talents of the five-times Amateur Champion Bonallack, very capably supported by his Royal partner.

Credit must be given to Chris T. Rouse who was the General Manager of Turnberry Hotel and Golf Courses during the whole period from 1978 till 1998, serving under three different owners during that time. His post-graduate management training had been done with British Transport Hotels Limited, including secondments in France, Germany and Spain gaining experience in prestigious hotels in Paris, Weisbaden and Madrid. Before coming to Turnberry he had been Deputy General Manager of Gleneagles Hotel, Perthshire, General Manager of the Old Course Hotel, St. Andrews, and General Manager of Welcombe Hotel, Stratford-upon-Avon. At Turnberry his career covered the ownerships by British Transport Hotels from 1978 to 1983, Sea Containers Limited from 1983 to 1987 and Nitto Kogyo from 1987 till 1998. He retired from Turnberry in 1998 after an agreed hand-over period following its acquisition by Starwood Hotels & Resorts (USA). For 20 years his involvement covered a period of great development and enhancement of Turnberry's reputation as a world-class golfing resort and he also provided a certain continuity in the relationship between the Club and the various owners. Inevitably this was not always a happy relationship, involving the balancing of the Club's interests with the ambitious commercial ones of the hotel and the aims of the international companies which had taken over ownership. Chris Rouse drove a very hard bargain and the Club's minutes are full of references to difficult negotiations and General Meetings at which successive embattled Captains sought, on the one hand, to maintain the Club's position on the best possible terms achievable and on the other hand, to face the wrath and frustration of members if the results were not to their satisfaction. Throughout it all Chris Rouse did appreciate the commercial and public relations importance of having the historic Club as part of the Turnberry set-up, and the continued existence of the Club in good heart bears testimony to the effectiveness of its leadership, the patience and loyalty of its members and the understanding and acceptance of Turnberry's many owners.

The present owners Starwood are amongst the biggest global players in the hotel industry and their portfolio contains six large brand names, Sheraton, Luxury Collection, St. Regis, Four Points, W. Hotels and Westin. Turnberry comes within the Westin Group and, since 1998, they have spent in the region of £20m. on the development and improvement of the resort. The former staff blocks and cottages along the roadside below the hotel have been converted and extended to provide 12 self-contained lodges and 9 cottages supplementing the hotel accommodation of 132 bedrooms. Eighty per cent of the bedrooms have been completely refurbished, a larger conference centre has been added to the hotel and the Health Club and Spa have received further investment and have been expanded to provide a further 5 treatment rooms. An outdoor activity centre has been established which includes facilities for fishing, riding, archery, off-road driving and falconry. A magnificent golf academy has been built with all the latest technical teaching facilities, a driving range with covered bays and landing areas featuring landscaped greens and bunkers, for long and short game practice and a large new 18-hole practice putting green. Finally and notably, the old Arran course plus a large area of higher ground at Bain's Hill to the north have been used to create the scenically spectacular new championship length Kintyre course and a new nine-hole Arran course.

British Club Professionals' Championship

The Slazenger PGA British Club Professionals' Championship was held over the 6430 yard long Arran course from 29th July till 1st August 1980. It was won by David Jagger of West Selby, on the second hole of a sudden death play-off, after a tie with David Huish of North Berwick, on 286, which was six over par. Brian Waites of England was third on 288 and John McTear of Scotland, who has since become a member of the Turnberry Club, was fourth on 290.

Amateur International Matches

The year 2000 saw the hosting by Turnberry of both the Jacques Leglise Trophy and the St. Andrews Trophy matches. Both are amateur international matches played between two selected teams representing Great Britain and Ireland and the Continent of Europe. The Jacques Leglise Trophy is restricted to boy golfers and has been held annually since 1977, the previous venues having all been in Great Britain apart from 1998 when it was held at Villa D'Este in Italy. In the 23 matches prior to Turnberry, Great Britain and Ireland led the series by 18 matches to 5 and came to Turnberry as the holders. The St. Andrews Trophy has been held biennially since 1956 at alternating home and away venues, starting with the first match at Wentworth, England and with away venues including courses in France, Sweden, Spain, Belgium, Italy, Germany and Holland. Prior to Turnberry, Great Britain and Ireland led the series by 19 matches to 3 but the Continent of Europe came to Turnberry as the holders, having won in Italy in 1998.

At Turnberry both matches were held on Friday, 30th June, and Saturday, 1st July, and each match comprised four morning foursomes followed by eight afternoon singles on the two days. Both matches were won by Great Britain and Ireland, the Jacques Leglise Trophy by 16 wins to 8 and the St. Andrews Trophy by 13 wins to 11. The teams and captains were as follows:-

Jacques Leglise Trophy

Great Britain & Ireland

Yasin Ali (England)
Stephen Buckley (Scotland)
Jack Doherty (Scotland)
David Inglis (Scotland)
Derek McNamara (Ireland)
David Porter (England)
Richard Scott (Wales)
Josh Simons (England)
Player/Captain – Zane Scotland (England)

Continent of Europe

Rafael Cabrera (Spain)
Nicolas Colsaerts (Belgium)
Eduardo de la Riva (Spain)
Raphael De Sousa (Switzerland)
Tim Ellis (Germany)
Andreas Hogberg (Sweden)
Alexander Noren (Sweden)
Erik Stenman (Finland)
Andrea Zanini (Italy)
Captain – Charlie Westrup

St. Andrews Trophy

Great Britain & Ireland

Paul Casey (England)
Luke Donald (England)
Jamie Donaldson (Wales)
Nick Dougherty (England)
Noel Fox (Ireland)
Max Harris (England)
Mark Loftus (Scotland)
Steven O'Hara (Scotland)
Gary Wolstenholme (England)
Captain – Peter McEvoy

Continent of Europe

Thomas Besancenez (France)
Mikko Honen (Finland)
Panu Kylliainen (Finland)
Jochen Lupprian (Germany)
Stefano Reale (Italy)
Tino Schuster (Germany)
Jacques Thalamy (France)
Michael Thannhauser (Germany)
Rafael Vera (Spain)
Captain – Conzaga Escauriaza

Chapter VI - Centenary - The Closing Years

Secretaries

The Club has been well served by its Secretaries in the modern era, starting with the late J.B. Gordon Stewart who held the post from 1972 till 1978. His droopy moustache belied his cheerful personality and he was ably assisted from 1974 till 1977 by Ronnie Thomson. Together they fostered a good friendly spirit amongst the members and between the men's and ladies' sections, and it was a period of particular enthusiasm for the mixed competitions. In 1983 Gordon donated a silver salver to the Club as a trophy to be played for annually in a match between the Ladies and the Gentlemen.

After Gordon Stewart, Charlie Reid served as Secretary for four years from 1978 till 1982 assisted by a number of others including Jimmy Struthers, David Gourlay, Jimmy Steel and Bernard Shilling. For six years from 1983 till 1989 Matthew Lawson took over and introduced a much needed consistent and professional approach to the task. Tom Paterson became Assistant Secretary in 1984 and, when Matthew retired in 1989, Tom took over, with Jim Crawford as his Assistant. These two have been in office since then and have worked well together, ensuring that the Club's business and activities proceed smoothly. Tom, a chemistry teacher by profession until he retired in 2000, has a no nonsense phlegmatic approach to his tasks. He does not suffer fools gladly but he is invariably helpful and always efficient. On the course he can be recognised by a distinctive naval style cap and by his equally distinctive golf action which owes more to economy of movement than to a classic technique. However he is a formidable opponent, especially in match play. Jim Crawford is a Girvan man born and bred and, until he retired in 1987, he was the manager of two factories operated by Alginate Industries, a company which processes by-products from seaweed and has one of its plants on the coast just south of Turnberry. He is a cheery extrovert with previous golf club experience as an official and past captain of Girvan Golf Club. At one time his hobby was folk-singing and he certainly looks the part with his full beard. Jim was exactly the right man to take over the duties of match secretary in 1989, as his expertise with computers enabled him to set up the Club's first computer programme for recording scores and calculating handicaps at that time and thereafter for keeping the Club up to date in such matters. He looks after the competitions, matches and handicapping while Tom Paterson deals with meetings, minutes, finance, functions and correspondence. Together they make an excellent and efficient secretariat and the Club benefits from the continuity of their long service in their positions.

Some long-serving Members

Having a rough time. David Gray, Gordon Erskine and Malcolm Bowden

More long-serving Members

Saturday Regulars.   Rear – Ian Hutchison, John Davidson, Bill Manson
Front – Jim Smith, Rob Alexander, David Stobie.

The Two Ians.   Rorison and Passant.

Which one models for Pringle?
Gordon Rodger, George Brown, Jim Wilson.

Traditional Trio.
Ken MacKenzie, Alan Brown, Alan Boyd.

Chapter VI - Centenary - The Closing Years

Turnberry Ladies

THE Ladies' Section of the Club has always been virtually autonomous, as far as running its own competitions and financial affairs were concerned. Certain matters such as discipline and the arrangements with the owners of Turnberry were dealt with by the 'parent' Club. In effect the 'parent' Club was the Gentlemen's Section, with ladies only having a watching brief at general meetings through the guest attendance of the Captain and Secretary of their Section. By and large these arrangements worked well and amicably most of the time, mainly because there was no discrimination against the ladies in respect of their access to the courses and this was reflected in the latter part of the century by the ladies' subscriptions being virtually the same as those of the gentlemen. Then in 1997 a new constitution was adopted which put ladies and gentlemen on an exactly equal footing in relation to the general business and meetings of the Club, whilst delegating to separate Ladies' and Gentlemen's Sections the functions of administration of their separate activities. A joint liaison group representing both Sections was set up to deal with matters of joint concern.

Honorary Presidents

The Ladies' Section have traditionally had their own Honorary President and also at the outset an Honorary Vice-President. Their President from the Section's formation in 1912 until she died in 1945 was Lady Isabella Kennedy, Marchioness of Ailsa, the second wife of the 3rd Marquess of Ailsa. The minutes of meetings of the Ladies' Section between 1941 and 1972 are missing and it is not clear whether anyone was appointed to fill the vacancy arising from her death in 1945. Indeed this is probably unlikely as the Club did not resume its activities after the war until 1951. It is known however that Mrs. Ruth Hughes Onslow, the wife of Captain Oliver Hughes Onslow, served as the Ladies' Honorary President for a period after the war, possibly from 1957 till 1965.

In 1962 Lady Mary Kennedy, Marchioness of Ailsa, the wife of the seventh Marquess of Ailsa, joined Mrs. Hughes Onslow as joint Honorary President of the Ladies' Section and after 1965 she held the post on her own until she retired from it in 1999. During those 37 years she conscientiously attended general meetings and prizegiving dinners at which she regularly extolled the virtues of good old-fashioned standards of behaviour. She also took delight in enjoying the strawberry tarts traditionally served on these occasions. In 1972 she donated a silver rosebowl to the ladies for annual competition and, in 1987, she donated a further trophy named the Lady Ailsa Silver Jubilee Bowl for medal play over 36 holes, to mark the silver jubilee of her presidency. As a past President of the Ladies' Section but also as a senior member of the Kennedy family which played such an essential part in establishing golf at Turnberry, it is particularly appropriate that she has graciously written the Foreword to this publication.

Competitions and Trophies

The Ladies' Section has a strong tradition of friendship and conviviality amongst its members and with the men's Section of the Club. The Ladies enjoy their friendly social golf but also are keen and serious competitors and the Section has many handsome trophies to be competed for annually, including the Margaret Kinloch Trophy dating from 1960, for their club championship. From then until 2002 (43 years) the championship has been won by only twelve ladies due mainly to the pre-eminence of Mrs. Marion Wilson who won fifteen times between 1969 and 1990, and Karen Fitzgerald, who won twelve consecutive championships from 1991 till 2002. The winner in 1974 was Mrs. Rosemary Dykes who was Captain of the Ladies' Section and also Captain of the Ladies' Golf Union. The Ladies hold an annual outing to other courses and one particularly memorable one was when Margaret Morrison was Captain in 1987 and they flew from Glasgow to the Island of Islay off the West Coast of

Another of the Ladies' Section Trophies which merits special mention is an oval shaped gold medal with a dark blue enamel scroll across the top on which are the words *'Turnberry Golf Club'* in gold block lettering. In the centre is a hand-painted shield-shaped enamel picture of Turnberry lighthouse on the rocks with a blue background of sea and sky set between gold laurel leaves. Above the shield are crossed golf clubs and a golf ball in gold. On the back it is inscribed *'Scratch Gold Medal won by W.A. Templeton'* and the hallmark dates it to 1908. It seems likely that the winner was the Club's longest serving Honorary Secretary of that name who held office from 1920 till 1958. It is not an exact replica but it is very similar in design to the Club Gold Medal purchased by the Club in 1903 for the princely sum of £7 (over 6 times the amount of the annual subscription at that time), which was originally for the best scratch score in the Autumn Meeting. However it is only about one half of the size of that medal and it may be that winners of the Club Gold Medal were given smaller replicas to keep and that this was the replica given to Mr. Templeton. If so it is surprising that no other replicas have come to light and also that the Club was prepared to provide such a fine and valuable replica each year if that indeed was the practice.

Some years ago this Templeton medal was purchased at an auction by someone who realised its significance to Turnberry Golf Club and took it to Past Captain David T. Logan who has a jeweller's business in Ayr. Both the gold and the ceramic centre were damaged but David acquired the medal from his customer and had it repaired. He then had it set in a silver plate within a wooden casket and in 1996 he presented it to Turnberry Ladies' Section to be played for annually in a scratch stroke play competition. The first winner was Karen Fitzgerald in 1996, followed by Elizabeth Brown in 1997, Elizabeth Cosh for four years in succession from 1998 till 2001, and Angela Sharp in 2002.

Fiona and Mhairi McKay

Fiona (born 1971) and Mhairi (born 1975) are members of a keen golfing family, originally from the Glasgow area, but now resident in Girvan. Their father Peter, a well known Glasgow lawyer and former Sheriff, plays off a single figure handicap and their mother has played off as low as 8, while their brother Kenneth plays off 6. They were both encouraged to play golf at very early ages by their parents, starting off with cut-down clubs. Initially they were members of Bothwell Castle and Girvan Golf Clubs, and then joined Turnberry Golf Club as junior members in 1985.

Fiona has followed her father into the legal profession, is now happily married with a family and her golf activities have to take second place to career and family. Her lowest handicap has been +3 and she was capped at international level for Scottish Schools, Scottish Girls, Scottish Girls Under 21, and Scottish Ladies. She also played twice in the British Universities World Team Championships and her individual wins include the Lanarkshire Ladies' Championship in 1988 and 1992, the Riccarton Rosebowl in 1990 and 1991 and Mackie Bowl in 1992. She holds the ladies' course record of 68 at Gullane No. 1 course and was twice runner-up in both the Scottish Girls Championship and the Scottish Under 21 Championship. At an administrative level she has been non-playing captain of a Scottish Girls' Team and a Scottish Under 21 Ladies' Team in the European Championships. In 2003 she was Manager of the Great Britain and Ireland Team in the Vagliano Trophy ladies' amateur team contest with the Continent of Europe and has been appointed Manager of the Great Britain and Ireland Team for the Curtis Cup ladies' amateur team contest with the USA to be held in 2004.

Mhairi had an outstanding amateur record and her handicap was as low as +5. She was Scottish Girls' Champion in 1990 and 1992, British Girls' Champion in 1992 and 1993, West of Scotland Girls' Champion and Belgium Under 21 Ladies' Champion in 1992. She was also a beaten finalist in the Scottish Ladies' Championship in 1993 and in the British Ladies' Championship in 1997. In internationals she represented Scotland at girls, schools, under 21 and senior levels on many occasions, from 1989 till 1996 inclusive; was in the Curtis Cup team in 1994 and 1996 and also played in the Vagliano Trophy, the Espirito Santo Trophy (an international world championship for national teams of 3) and the Commonwealth Trophy (a championship for national teams of 5 from Commonwealth countries). While on a golf scholarship at Stanford University, California, from 1994 to 1997 she was a National Collegiate Athletic Association All American golf team member each year, and she met and practiced with Tiger Woods. She was also the Daily

Chapter VI - Centenary - The Closing Years

Telegraph Junior Golfer of the Year in 1991 and won the Lady Heathcoat Amory Award for her overall career achievements in both golf and for getting her degree in economics and politics at Stanford University, California. Mhairi turned professional in 1997, plays full time on the LPGA Tour in USA, and is making steady and sometimes spectacular progress. In 1998 she led the U.S. Ladies' Open by three strokes after five holes of the final round, ultimately finishing seventh, and in 2003 she led it by five strokes at the half-way stage before finishing sixth. She has had several second place finishes in top Tour events in the USA including in the 'Kellogs' Keebler Classic in Chicago in 2002 and 2003, on both occasions being runner-up to Annika Sorenstam of Sweden. In 2003 she won the Australian Women's Open Championship at Terry Hills, Sydney, and represented Great Britain and Ireland in the Solheim Cup at Interlachen, Minnesota, USA, in 2002 and Barsebach, Sweden, in 2003.

Both Fiona and Mhairi were coached at Turnberry by Gregor Jamieson, who is now based at Lake Nona Golf Club in Florida and still continued to coach Mhairi for some years into her professional career. In 2003 Mhairi was made an honorary member of Turnberry Golf Club.

Mhairi McKay and Fiona McKay.

179

TROPHIES

TURNBERRY Golf Club possesses an extensive and wonderful collection of trophies which are on display in a secure showcase in the entrance hall of the new clubhouse, which opened in 1993. At that time it was agreed with the owners of the hotel that the trophies would be put on permanent display there, for the interest and enjoyment of members and visitors alike. Each year they are removed for presentation to the winners at the annual dinner and presentation of prizes held by the Club in the hotel. Previously they were kept by the individual winners till the next prize-giving, but this sometimes resulted in damage to and even loss of trophies and bases. Now the winners hand back their trophies at the end of the dinner, for return to the showcase, having had the privilege of filling them with champagne or whisky and having a photograph taken with their trophies. The present arrangement keeps the trophies safe and in good condition, enhances the clubhouse entrance and is a fitting reminder of the history of Turnberry and the Club. A brief history of some of the oldest and most notable trophies is as follows:-

Tom Paterson, the Club's Honorary Secretary, stands guard over the Trophies laid out for presentation.

Chapter VI - Centenary - The Closing Years

Ailsa Challenge Cup

Presented to the Club by Lord Archibald Kennedy the Third Marquess of Ailsa, in February 1903. Lord Ailsa was the first President of the Club and of course was also the man who constructed the first course at Turnberry. This large beautiful silver trophy is inscribed with a scene of Turnberry Castle and the lighthouse, and is awarded for the best first class handicap score in the Summer Meeting.

Adam Wood Trophy

This was presented to the Club in 1903 by Adam Wood, esquire, one of the original members of the Club. He was also a member of Troon Golf Club and he was Captain of Troon in 1915. Apparently he was a keen collector of curios and in 1915 he gifted to the Troon Club a very old set of eight wooden clubs which are thought to be the oldest golf clubs in existence, perhaps dating back to the times of the Stuart Kings of Scotland. These clubs are now housed in the British Golf Museum in St. Andrews, with copies in the clubhouse of Royal Troon Golf Club. Adam Wood was obviously a man of importance and influence and played a very active part in promoting the young Turnberry Club and introducing many prominent and important persons as members. His cup is awarded each year for the best first class handicap score in the Spring Meeting.

Club Gold Medal

On 14th April, 1903 the minutes record that a sketch for a medal was approved and an order was given to Mr. John Templeton a local watchmaker and jeweller to provide this medal as a club prize, at an estimated price of £7. Originally the medal was won by the player with the best scratch score in the Autumn Meeting, but subsequently was awarded to the player with the best qualifying score for the Club Championship. It is a fine gold medal with a ceramic insert showing a scene of Turnberry Castle and the lighthouse.

Sir James Bell Trophy

Sir James Bell, of Montgreenan, Kilwinning, Ayrshire, lived from 1850 till 1928 and became a baronet in 1895. He was a Director of Clydesdale and Midland Banks, was twice the Lord Provost of Glasgow and Lord Lieutenant of the City of Glasgow. He contested the Americas Cup with his yacht "Thistle" and then again with "Comet" owned by the Emperor of Germany. He became a member of the Club on 17th September, 1903, proposed by Lord Ailsa and seconded by Adam Wood. This trophy was presented to the Club by him and it was first played for in 1905, originally as a "hole competition", a form of knock-out match play, with each round balloted and both persons going forward in the event of a tie. It is now awarded to the winner of an individual knock-out match play tournament which always attracts a large entry.

Bargany Cup

This elegant trophy of surprisingly modern design on curved tripod legs, was presented to the Club in 1909 by Captain North Dalrymple Hamilton, of Bargany Estate. The estate included extensive land and property in Dailly, Girvan, and South Ayrshire, and the donor stipulated that it was to be for a competition at Turnberry open to members of Turnberry, Girvan and Ballantrae Golf Clubs. However Ballantrae Golf Club ceased to exist when its course was taken over for agriculture during the Second World War and thereafter the competition was confined to members of Turnberry and Girvan Golf Clubs. The format originally agreed on was an individual match play tournament. In 1936 the cup was won outright by Mr. A.C. Mitchell, a member of Turnberry Golf Club, by winning it for three consecutive years. Colonel Dalrymple Hamilton, the son of the original donor provided a substitute miniature cup and the competition continued as before. In 1990 Mr. A. Mitchell, the son of A.C. Mitchell, graciously handed the original cup back to the Club after his father's death. Latterly the format has been changed to stroke play under handicap over 36 holes.

Weir Trophy

William Douglas Weir, LL.D., G.C.B., was one of the members who responded to a request by the Club for donations of prizes and trophies. He donated this trophy in 1905 for annual competition and it is awarded for the best handicap score of competitors with handicaps of 14 and upwards in the Summer Meeting. William Weir of Cathcart, as he is described on the trophy, was born in 1877 and he became the Honorary President and a Director of G. & J. Weir Ltd. of Cathcart. In 1938 he became the First Viscount of Eastwood. He had a distinguished career in both private industry and public service. During the first world war he was the Director of Munitions in Scotland and Director General of Aircraft Production and became a Secretary of State and President of the Air Council in 1918. In 1939 he was made the Director General of Explosives at the Ministry of Supply and after the war he was made a Commander of the Legion of Honours and a Freeman of the City of London. His honorary doctorate was from Glasgow University.

Richmond Cup

On 10th February, 1923, Mr. John R. Richmond of Blanefield, Kirkoswald, wrote to the Club and offered a prize *"in the form of a cup, a sum of money and possibly a set of clubs"*. The Secretary acknowledged the offer and suggested that a small cup be given for a *'bogey'* competition. This was a competition when the player matched his score at each hole against the *'bogey'* for that hole. Eighteen holes were played and the winner was the player who finished most holes up (or least holes down) on bogey. At that time *'bogey'* was the par for the hole. It was only subsequently due to American influence, that *'bogey'* came to mean a score of one over par at a hole. Nowadays the Richmond Cup is played for in a handicap Stableford competition. The donor subsequently became a Baronet and his full description was Sir John Ritchie Richmond (1869/1963) K.B.E., LL.D., C.B.E. He was the elder half-brother of Lord William Douglas Weir and was a director and vice-chairman of G. & J. Weir of Cathcart (today the Weir Group). He was Captain of the Club for 10 years from 1925 to 1936, and also held the post of Honorary President of Glasgow School of Art.

Fenton Trophy

At the Club's A.G.M. in April 1932 this trophy was offered to the Captain by Mr. J.L. Fenton, of Edinburgh, and it was resolved by the Committee that it should be competed for in an annual two-ball foursome medal competition, with teams drawn by ballot and to comprise one player with first class handicap and one with second class handicap.

Onslow Cup

This was donated by Oliver Hughes Onslow who was the Club's Captain for 20 years from 1936 to 1957. It was presented in 1937 for competition in match play by two-ball foursomes competition, with competitors selecting their own partners, and each pair comprising one first and one second class player. Captain Hughes Onslow also donated to the Club the water colour painting of "The Puddock" hole by J. Drummond Fish, which hangs in the Gallery of the clubhouse.

Colin Clark Memorial Trophy

Colin Clark of Currah, near Girvan, was a very early member, having joined on 18th June, 1903. At a meeting of Committee on 7th November, 1925, a letter was received from Mr. Scott Valentine, Solicitor, Girvan, stating that a few friends of the late Colin Clark wished to gift a silver cup in his memory to Turnberry Golf Club. He suggested that it be played for annually and be open to all members irrespective of handicap. The Club agreed to accept the cup and decided that it should be played for over 36 holes handicap stroke play, with the first round on the first Saturday in May and the second round on the first Saturday in June. Apart from a slight alteration in dates, this format continues to the present day. However the original cup was lost and a replacement was purchased in April 1961.

Stanley P. Morrison Salver

Donated by Stanley P. Morrison, who was Club Captain from 1965 till 1967. He stipulated that it was to be for annual competition by match play, off scratch over 18 holes with the final over 36 holes. The qualifiers were to be the 16 players with the lowest scratch aggregate of two scores from the Spring, Summer and Autumn Meetings. It is a fine silver salver and each winner's signature is engraved on the trophy. It was first played for in 1938 when the winner was R.H.U. Stevenson, qualifying with an aggregate scratch score of 144 for 36 holes, including a 70 in the Spring Meeting. The Competition Book notes this as equalling the course record. In 1958 it was agreed to recognise the winner of this trophy as the Club Champion.

Crawford Cup

In 1937 the then Vice Captain, John Crawford, donated this trophy for annual competition and suggested that it be for mixed foursomes. However it was felt that a large enough entry might not be forthcoming and most

Chapter VI - Centenary - The Closing Years

unusually it was decided that it should be played for by individual stroke play under handicap over the Ailsa Course and open to both ladies and gentlemen members. The ladies play off the LGU tees and their handicaps are adjusted for the difference in standard scratch scores. To date there have been 34 gentlemen winners and only 21 lady winners. In defence of the ladies' performance it has to be said that there are many more entries from amongst the gentlemen than from the ladies.

Trophy Winners 1987:-
Standing (left to right): D. McFarlane, A. Dunlop, S. McCann, D. Muir,
M. Birtwhistle, T. Smith, T. Paterson, W. Manson, R. Hindmarsh,
S. Guthrie, R. MacGregor, G. Rodger, M. Wilkinson, W. Marshall, J. Jones.
Front Row (left to right): D. Gray, W. Slattery, R. McGarvie, B. Bain,
G. Brown, C. Milligan, R. Grassom, G. Erskine.

THE AMATEUR CHAMPIONSHIP 1983

THE Walker Cup match between Great Britain and Ireland and the U.S.A. had just finished at Hoylake, the home of Royal Liverpool Golf Club, the week before the Amateur Championship took place at Turnberry from 30th May till 4th June, 1983. Almost the entire American and British teams headed north to Turnberry after a splendid match won by America by 13½ games to 10½. The Club members were asked by the Club to offer team members accommodation for the week, bearing in mind their amateur status. The usual arrangements were made for members to assist with the control and organisation of the event and afterwards a letter of thanks was received from the Royal and Ancient for their support, together with a donation to the Club's funds to show appreciation of this.

There was a new format for the Championship that year involving a 36-hole stroke play qualifying competition, comprising one round over the Ailsa course and one over the Arran, to reduce the field from 288 to 64 for the final match-play stage. Philip Parkin of Wales, one of the British Walker Cup team, led the qualifiers on 139, with 73 on the Ailsa and 66 on the Arran. Fifty players were on 149 or better and 22 others had a qualifying score of 150 and had to play off for the 14 remaining places. The play-off was by sudden-death and was decided at the first play-off hole when eight players failed to score par four or better. Casualties in the qualifying included Walker Cup players Rick Fehr of America and David Carrick and Lindsay Mann of Great Britain.

The first round matches were played in continuous rain and the course was only playable due to the use of special moto-mops which worked from 2 a.m. till 11 a.m. removing an estimated 7000

Philip Parkin, winner of the Amateur Championship 1983 at Turnberry - beating J. Holtgrieve of USA in the final.

Chapter VI - Centenary - The Closing Years

gallons of water from the course. The holder of the title, Martin S. Thompson of Middlesborough went out in the first round, as did Andrew Oldcorn of Ratho Park who had been undefeated in the Walker Cup contest. By the quarter-finals five Walker Cup players still remained and two Anglo-American battles were won by Englishmen Peter Deeble of Alnmouth and Simon Keppler of Walton Heath who respectively beat Jay Sigal and David Tentis. Allan Thomson, the solitary remaining Scot and a member of Turnberry Golf Club, went down by one hole to Philip Parkin and Jim Holtgrieve of America eliminated his compatriot Terry Foreman.

In the semi-finals Holtgrieve beat Deeble, whose game was wild, and Parkin beat Keppler, his Walker Cup team-mate, after being one down after 10 holes, which was the only time he had been down on the back nine in the whole Championship. Parkin was a popular finalist with his bubbly personality and stylish golf and had won the British Youth's Championship in 1983, whilst Holtgrieve of St. Louis was a comparative veteran in his mid-30s. In the 36-hole final Holtgrieve's driving was erratic but he did well to be only two down after 18 holes. Before the start of the afternoon round Parkin was on the tee long before his opponent, restlessly pacing about and eager to get on with the job. He then proceeded to win four of the first six holes and won the match and the title convincingly by five and four.

As a footnote it is interesting to mention that this Championship saw the 28th and last appearance in the event of Michael Bonallack before taking up his duties as the new secretary of the Royal and Ancient Golf Club. He won the Championship five times in all, the first being at Turnberry in 1961, then again in 1965 and then three times in succession from 1968 to 1970, a record unrivalled in modern times and only surpassed by John Ball, who won eight times between 1888 and 1912.

The 1986 Open Championship

ONE of the greatest fascinations of the game of golf is its infinite variety. Every course is different in layout, terrain and character from every other one and, particularly on Scottish links courses, the weather conditions can change radically from day to day and even from hour to hour. Anyone anticipating that conditions for the second Open Championship to be held at Turnberry would resemble the benign ones of 1977 was certainly to be disappointed, despite there being a spell of very calm weather for the first two practice days. This changed dramatically on the third and final practice day when a half gale suddenly blew in from the south and players found themselves playing one irons and even drivers for shots which had required only nine irons and wedges the day before. A suspicion that the fairways were too narrow and the rough too penal, became a 'conviction' in the minds of many players.

There was talk of the risk of injuries being suffered by players trying to escape the rough and suggestions that the fairways should be widened. Twenty five to thirty yards of fairway width at landing areas demanded a degree of accuracy which could not consistently be achieved in the sort of winds experienced on the Wednesday.

The R. & A. called a press conference and their spokesman was their Secretary, Michael Bonallack. He spoke with the authority of a man who had won the Amateur championship at Turnberry in 1961 as well as being a member of the Walker Cup team there in 1963, and declared that the Championship Committee regarded the course to be a fair test. The height and thickness of the rough and the overhead conditions were under the control of nature, and were part of the challenge for those who aspired to winning the claret jug.

Turnberry Open Championship Committee 1986.
Left to right – R. Grassom, D. Logan, G. Brown, B. Shilling, D. Stobie, M. Lawson, J. Carrick (Captain), C. Bather, A. Todd (Chairman), R. Dykes, S. Guthrie, T. Paterson, S. Jardine, R. Jamieson (Professional), C. Rouse (Hotel Manager).

Chapter VI - Centenary - The Closing Years

Turnberry in 1977 had produced a low record winning margin of 268 by Tom Watson and a record low round of 63 by Mark Hayes. It was played in brilliant sunshine with light winds drying out the fairways to such an extent that length was meaningless, and the course had no defences on that score. In the week following the Open even the members were driving the 350 yard first green along a fairway burned till it was as hard as concrete. Nevertheless only Watson, Nicklaus and Hubert Green, a distant third on 279, finished under par, but in many people's minds there was created a misconception that Turnberry was a low-scoring course. Turnberry, 1986, was to correct that misconception.

The First Round – A Matter of Survival

A cold westerly wind of up to thirty five miles an hour blew all during the first day, fortunately without rain. Everybody tangled with the savage rough at some point in their round, some more often and more damagingly than others. Lee Trevino, along with forty six others, fell victim to his own forecast that scores of 80 or worse were possible. Craig Stadler, former U.S. Masters winner, damaged a wrist playing from heavy rough, shot 82, and had to withdraw, due to the injury. Raymond Floyd, U.S. Open champion, scored 78, having taken an 8 at the 440 yard fourteenth, after losing a ball. There were many heart-rending stories of misfortune and a general feeling of injustice amongst the many who had not coped well with the conditions. Only the windsurfers in Turnberry Bay seemed truly happy with their lot. The members of Turnberry Golf Club, who turned out in great numbers, and suffered the atrocious conditions to

Jack Nicklaus playing from 9th tee.

keep the show on the road attending to scoring, stewarding, tented village and even litter control, did not have a great deal of sympathy for those who complained most. They themselves had suffered even narrower fairways for weeks in monthly medals and competitions before they were finally widened and semi-rough cut and manicured for the championship itself. So far as the members were concerned the players were only experiencing a normal hazard of golf on a tough links course in Scotland, but with the advantage of markers and spectators to ensure that they seldom lost a ball, a course honed to perfection in respect of green and fairway condition and a liberal area of semi-rough to prevent balls running into the really heavy stuff. They appreciated the views of the wiser heads amongst the players, like Jack Nicklaus, who opined that, although it was a case of survival in that first round, there was nothing wrong with that so long as it was the same for all. Then there was Raymond Floyd who declared that the conditions had been the hardest he had ever experienced but accepted this philosophically saying *'that's the way it is'*. He even joked about finding four balls in place of the one he lost at the fourteenth.

Greg Norman, out in the worst of the early morning weather with Floyd, found the conditions brutal but stuck to the task and managed to get round in 74, which might have been better, considering that he went to the turn in 35. Star of the day however was Welsh braveheart, Ian Woosnam, who scored 70 to be the only man to match par that day and whose inward half of 31 was nothing short of miraculous. Put Norman's 35 out to

Woosnam's 31 in and you see what was theoretically possible despite the conditions. This does not take account however of the limitations of one individual to cope both physically and mentally over five hours in such conditions. As Norman said *'You can feel a non-entity out there, hacking around the rough, shooting a 74 that feels like a 64 at the finish'*.

Others who coped well on the first day were Gordon J. Brand, Nick Faldo and Robert Lee, of England, and Anders Forsbrand of Sweden, who all scored 71. The enduring and diligent Bernard Langer of Germany, came in with a 72, and was joined on that mark by Andrew Brooks, a home based Scot, Derek Cooper of England, Ian Stanley of Australia and two virtually unknown Americans. Seve Ballesteros, the favourite, complaining bitterly of the slowness of play, took 76.

Tom Watson, the first champion at Turnberry in 1977, took 77, and Jack Nicklaus, his vanquished 'duellest' in 1977, took 78, as did a young Jose Maria Olazabal, of Spain, in his first season on the European pro circuit, and Brian Marchbank of Scotland, son of Ian Marchbank who had been the professional at Turnberry from 1958 till 1962. Tsuneyuki (Tommy) Nakajima of Japan, who was to figure prominently later in the championship, scored 74.

The Second Round –
The Great White Shark Shows His Teeth

Greg Norman came to Turnberry as the leader of the American money list and had also in previous years topped the European and Australian money lists. With the possible exception of Palmer and Nicklaus no other golfer had surely been a bigger success in terms of winnings

Jack Nicklaus and Tom Watson with Turnberry members in 1986 after accepting honorary membership of the Club.

and earnings. His charismatic and easy going charm added to his good looks had made him a favourite with the media and no doubt also with sponsors. Just as Nicklaus had turned his nickname of 'the Bear' into a profitable trademark, Norman, with his perfect white teeth and flashing smile, was to do the same as 'the Great White Shark'. The one thing missing from his curriculum vitae was a major championship and the press would not let him or the public forget this. It didn't help that he had been found wanting on previous occasions when he had real chances, such as in the play-off for the 1984 U.S. Open or when he couldn't hold on to a one-stroke lead in the final round of the 1986 U.S. Open. As such wonderful golfers as Colin Montgomerie and Phil Mickelson have since found out, it can get to the stage where it appears that, no matter how much they prove themselves in other championships, the only thing the press wants to ask them is about their lack of success in majors.

For all this Norman came to the championship in confident mood and excellent form. He held things together on the first day when others were faltering and was well pleased with his opening 74. His career had been full of very low rounds and he had always been capable of fantastic bursts of scoring when in the mood to go for everything. On the second day he tore the Ailsa course apart with a 63, in conditions which were easier but still very testing. He recalled afterwards *'The ball was coming off the middle of the club and I felt really confident and comfortable with my swing. I was totally involved with each shot and that is when I am at my most dangerous'*. His 63 included an eagle and eight birdies, and his huge gallery loved it. Only Mark Hayes at Turnberry in 1977 and Isao Aoki, of Japan, at Muirfield in 1980, had matched that score before in an Open championship and no-one had ever bettered it. But for three putts on the last green Norman might have done so. This wonderful round took him to the top of the leaderboard, giving him a two stroke lead over Gordon J. Brand, with Tommy Nakajima and Nick Faldo a further two strokes behind. The best placed Americans on equal tenth included Raymond Floyd and Payne Stewart, but Sandy Lyle, the defending champion, just made the cut along with Seve Ballesteros, the favourite and the great Jack Nicklaus, thrice the champion. Only fifteen players broke 70 that day and the nearest score to Norman's 63 was a 67 by Nakajima.

The Third Round –
Norman narrowly holds on

There was to be no respite from the weather. Saturday was almost but not quite as stormy as on the first day, but with the added difficulty of heavy rain from late morning. The wind however blew from a different quarter, helping on the outward half but hindering on the closing holes. The best weather was in the morning and the only round under par, a 69, was returned by Ho Ming Chung of Taiwan who was an early starter. Ian Woosnam again proved himself a very effective bad weather player by returning a par 70, as did four others, Sandy Lyle, the defending champion, Danny Edwards of America, Manual Pinero of Spain and David Graham of Australia. Greg Norman went to the turn in 32, but the wind took its toll on his inward half, for which he required 40 blows. It was sufficient to hold off his challengers, though on 211, his lead was cut from two to one, and Tommy Nakajima became his nearest challenger after an adventurous 71. Woosnam closed up to be only three behind alongside Gordon Brand, who shot 75. A distant six shots back in equal fourth place were Nick Faldo, Jose-Maria Canizares of Spain and the American Gary Koch, with Sam Torrance, Raymond Floyd, Bernard Langer and David Graham all one shot worse. Some very famous contenders who dropped out of contention were Sandy Lyle (70 for 221), Seve Ballesteros (73 for 224), Tom Watson (77 for 225) and Jack Nicklaus (76 for 227).

Norman had threatened to run away with the tournament in this round when he twice achieved a lead of five shots in the outward half, but at the end of the day he had to work very hard to hold on to the narrowest of leads. Those who have played the Ailsa course will be interested in some of his travails in the course of his round. For instance his five iron downwind at the 220 yard par three sixth hole finished in the deep bunker short right of the green. Close to the steep face he could only just get it on the green and three putted from there. He recovered well from this with birdies downwind at the seventh and eighth, but from thereon in he could only manage five pars and six bogeys, playing into a very strong wind most of the way, in a downpour of horizontal rain. He needed two drives to try to reach the twelfth where he found the rough, and again at the eighteenth where he came up short despite two wonderful shots. He revealed afterwards that his hands were slipping on the grip of the club and he couldn't see through the wind and rain in his face. From a comfortable lead with almost one hand on the trophy, his day's work ended with only a one stroke lead to take into the final round. His mind surely must have wandered to the unsuccessful outcome to the same situation in the U.S. Open, only a month before.

Tommy Nakajima, his pursuer, had attained some fame, or perhaps notoriety might be a better word, when he took nine at the Road hole in the 1978 Open at St. Andrews, after being on the green in two and putting into the notorious Road bunker from which he took four more shots to return to the green. He avoided any such disaster at Turnberry however and, after his opening 74, a second round of 67 and a third of 71 put him right in contention. In Japan he had won over £2m. and was beginning to rival Jumbo Osaki and Isao Aoki. This was his great opportunity to surpass them and become a Japanese national hero.

The Final Round –
Norman silences the Doubters

As the sun rose on the final day Ailsa Craig, that great granite rock rising out of the Firth of Clyde on the sea route to Ireland, had a sliver of mist floating across it like a bow tie, but the top was clear. The locals say *'if Ailsa Craig puts on its tie you may be sure it's gonna be dry'*, and sure enough it was soon evident that at last the weather was going to be kind, and would permit a more even contest between the players and the course.

Seve Ballesteros was first to take advantage by shooting a 64 and leap frogging from thirty-eighth place to finish equal sixth. Gary Koch tied with him after a 71 and he was the leading American. So the American dominance in 1977, when the first eight players were all American, was not repeated on this occasion. Another American, Fuzzy Zoeller, a firm favourite with the crowd for his good humour and unfailingly pleasant demeanour, whistled his way to a 69 and finished equal eighth along with the Scot Brian Marchbank (69) and Tommy Nakajima who had a disappointing last round of 77.

Norman and Nakajima, the leaders after the third round, were paired in the last game, as is the way in the Open. Nakajima had outscored Norman by three shots in the third round with 71 to 74, but to do so, had scrambled brilliantly and bravely to keep his score going despite the handicap of playing in glasses in driving rain. At the twelfth hole for instance a wild second shot with a four iron finished in heavy rough on the wrong side of the hill which is topped by a war memorial, from where he couldn't even see the green. Miraculously he somehow managed to dig the ball out and over the hill on to the green and then proceeded to hole a sixteen foot put for his par four. Such heroics were not repeated on the final day however and, at the very first hole he allowed Norman's lead to increase by two when he took three to reach the green and then three putted from no more than six feet. Then at the third hole Norman seemed to have closed the door on his opponent when he holed a bunker shot for a birdie three to increase his lead to four. Apart from a bogey five at the fifth, Norman played immaculately thereafter and finished a convincing winner by five shots from the Englishman, Gordon J. Brand. Bernard Langer of Germany learned the night before that his wife, Vicki, had given birth to their first child and the main scoreboard read *'Congratulations'*, as he putted on the last green, for a 68 and equal third place with Ian Woosnam of Wales. Langer's score was the only one lower than Norman's 69. Nick Faldo finished with a 70 for fifth place on his own, declaring himself delighted with his performance with his 'reconstructed' swing.

Surely there was never a more popular victory. Everyone who loved the game of golf was delighted to have a champion who had already proved himself to be one of the all time greats of the game. His win at Turnberry was an overdue confirmation of this fact and erased any remaining doubt about his ultimate talent. What is more, Norman himself considered the Open to be the most special of all the majors, as well as being the oldest and most historic. Support for his cause had come however not just from the golfing public. His resolve had been strengthened before the final round by words of encouragement from great players such as Jack Nicklaus, Hubert Green and Fuzzy Zoeller, who all knew personally the pressures of his situation. They and others like them welcomed his victory. It is to his everlasting credit that he shouldered the burden of the expectations and hopes of his peers as well as those the golfing public, and at last won his first and most coveted major title. The Royal and Ancient Golf Club, and Turnberry Golf Club were quietly satisfied that once again the championship had produced a champion of unchallenged pedigree.

Chapter VI - Centenary - The Closing Years

Greg Norman, the 1986 Champion, proudly holds the Open Trophy.

On the administrative side the Club's Championship Committee was chaired by Past Captain Alex Todd, and dealt with crowd control, scoring and recording, as well as less obvious but essential tasks of recruiting and managing an army of volunteers and temporary employees engaged for such things as ball spotting, score boards, tented village, messengers and litter control. Experience gained at The Open in 1977 was invaluable. Many of the members had been stewards and marshalls in 1977 and again formed the backbone of the crowd control team led by David Logan, Depute in 1977 and Chief Marshall on this occasion. Similarly the Ladies had an experienced team of scorers under the charge of their Captain, Rosemary Dykes. The week of The Open involves each member of the Championship Committee being at Turnberry each day from dawn till dusk, but this is only the culmination of much hard work of preparation and planning for the whole of the preceding year. There are, of course, some perks, such as invitations to a few formal dinners and golf matches and the chance to meet or rub shoulders with some of the competitors. In 1986 a particularly enjoyable such latter occasion was when Jack Nicklaus and Tom Watson accepted honorary membership of the Club.

The Senior British Open Championships

AT a time when senior tournaments were still in their infancy the first Senior British Open Championship was launched at Turnberry in 1987 by International Management Group, The European Tour and the Royal and Ancient Golf Club of St. Andrews. This was to be the first of four successive such Championships held at Turnberry from 1987 till 1990 and Turnberry Golf Club and its members provided hospitality and enthusiastic and expert support and assistance in running these prestigious events. From the start the Championship was well supported and became highly regarded by players and public alike. Starting the first four years of its existence on one of the best and most beautiful links venues in Britain, no doubt contributed to it getting off to a flying start.

The Club's championship committee for the inaugural event comprised Captain Jim Carrick, Vice-Captain Stewart Jardine, Secretary Matthew Lawson, Bernard Shilling, Tom Paterson, Bill Manson and Ladies' Captain Margaret Morrison, with Stewart Jardine acting as Chief Marshall. Coming the year after The Open had been at Turnberry in 1986 and being held for four years in succession, these Championships were an enormous commitment for the Club in terms of the procurement and organisation of the many voluntary personnel required for crowd control, scoring, recording and many other tasks. They also inevitably involved considerable disruption to normal play on the course. However fairly satisfactory arrangements were made with International Management Group for a financial benefit to the Club in recognition of this.

1987 Championship - 23rd – 26th July

Play was over the Ailsa course shortened by some 400 yards from the 6957 yards used at the 1986 Open. Neil Coles, of England, a prime candidate for the title of most enduring player in the history of European golf, led by one shot after the first round, with a bogey-free four under par 66 played on a day of warm sunshine with a fresh breeze. Hard on his heels was New Zealand's great left-hander Bob Charles with 67 and the legendary Arnold Palmer on 68. Coles increased his lead over Charles and Palmer to two after a second round 73 and spreadeagled the field with a 67 in the third round, which left him five shots ahead of Palmer, and seven ahead of Charles and the Englishman Peter Butler. A closing 73 gave Coles the title and the first prize of £25,000 with an aggregate of one under par 279. Bob

Neil Coles, winner of the 1987 Senior British Open Championship at Turnberry

Chapter VI - Centenary - The Closing Years

Gary Player with the Senior British Open Championship Trophy - won by him at Turnberry on both 1988 and 1990.

Charles made up six shots with a round of 67 on the last rain-sodden day, to finish only one behind, with Arnold Palmer third on 285. John Panton of Scotland was the leading player in the age category over 60.

After 1987 Neil Coles went on to have a brilliant senior career and, when he won the Jersey Seniors Open in 2000 it was his 45th career victory making him the first golfer in history to win a professional tournament in six different decades, starting with the 1956 Gor-Ray Tournament as a 22-year old.

1988 Championship - 21st – 26th July

This was to be Gary Player's first of three wins in this event. Along with Gene Sarazen, Ben Hogan, Jack Nicklaus and Tiger Woods, Player is one of only five players to have won the *'Grand Slam'* of all four Major Championships:- the Open at Carnoustie in 1968 and at Royal Lytham and St. Annes in 1974, the US Open in 1965, the USPGA Championship in 1962 and 1972 and The Masters in 1961, 1974 and 1978. He was to have an equally distinguished senior career.

At Turnberry in 1988, over a 6480 yard Ailsa course, he opened with a first round 65 for a three stroke lead over Billy Casper of America. He followed this with a 66 to stay two ahead of Casper and four ahead of the defending champion Neil Coles. The weather was placid on the first day but deteriorated as the tournament progressed, with rain squalls and a strong southerly wind on the final day. Nevertheless Player completed his four rounds at eight under par (65, 66, 72 and 69 for an aggregate of 272) to win the second Senior British Open and become the first man to complete the Senior Grand Slam (UK and US Opens, US PGA and Tournament Players Championship). Second was Billy Casper (273), third was Harold Henning of South Africa (274) and fourth was Bob Charles (277). Neil Coles finished sixth tied with Arnold Palmer on 283 and Christy O'Connor was the leading player over 60, finishing ninth on 286.

1989 Championship - 27th – 30th July

Bob Charles, the Open Champion in 1963 and the only left-hander ever to win The Open, had finished second in the Senior British Open in 1987 in its inaugural year and fourth in 1988. He is a great lover of links courses and the Senior British Open shares with The Open the tradition of being played on great seaside links courses, having started at Turnberry and thereafter continued at Royal Lytham, Royal Portrush and Royal County Down. Charles has been quoted as saying *'Playing in the Senior British Open Championship on links courses is one of the traditions of the event that makes it so enjoyable. I hope that the tradition remains forever. The sheer joy of walking the links alongside the ocean with barely a tree in sight makes a wonderful change to the real estate developments we often play on in the States.'* Charles began playing seniors golf in 1986 and by 2003 had won 26 senior titles. In the first ten years of the Senior British Open he was never worse than sixth, came second four times and won twice.

His first victory was at Turnberry in 1989. On the first day in a fresh westerly breeze Billy Casper led with

193

a 67, three ahead of Neil Coles and four ahead of Gary Player. Overnight rain slowed the course and perhaps aided Ronald Nicol (Scottish Boys Champion in 1948) to hole a 6-iron at the first hole for a second round eagle 2. Sixty seven professionals and three amateurs made the 36-hole cut of 155, with Billy Casper leading on 136, by two from Bob Charles. Casper still led by two after three rounds, but on the last day, in bright sunshine but with a cold wind, Charles forged ahead to win the £25,000 first prize with an aggregate of 269 (70, 68, 65, 66), seven ahead of Billy Casper. This set a tournament record which stood until the tournament returned to Turnberry in 2003, when Tom Watson won and set a new record of 263 on his dream return as a senior to the venue of his unforgettable Open victory in 1977.

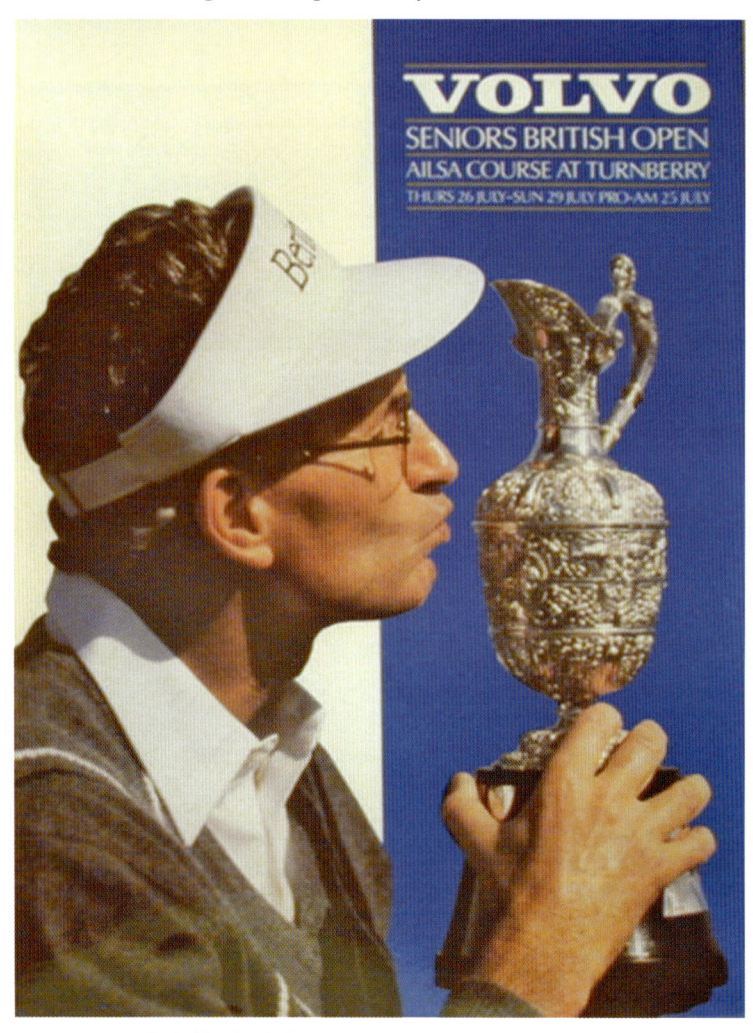

Bob Charles, left-handed New Zealander who won the Senior British Open Championship at Turnberry in 1989.

Again Christy O'Connor won the prize (£2,000) for the leading player over 60; and Charlie Green of Scotland and Gordon Clark, respectively the British and English senior amateur champions, shared the top amateur spot on 299.

1990 Championship - 26th – 29th July

Gary Player won in 1990 at Turnberry and was to go on to be the first player to win the Championship three times when he won again at Royal Portrush in 1997. When he came back to play in the Championship at Turnberry in 2003 he wrote in the programme *'What an honour it is to come back to Turnberry. It's unique – one of my favourite golf courses anywhere in the world. It's a magical place that brings back so many memories for me: The sheer grandeur of the links, the ambiance of the hotel, the exceptional food, the legendary friendliness of the Scots and the breathtaking views in every direction.'* Turnberry and its members also have many memories of Gary Player over the years, including seeing him keep fit by running up the steps from the clubhouse to the hotel and his generosity in giving the Club prizes for junior members' competitions. On the course stewarding of the spectators round Gary Player always had to be perfectly controlled and if his fierce competitive concentration was disturbed, he was not slow to complain.

The play in 1990 began in warm sunshine. Arnold Palmer and Brian Waites led the first day with 66s, followed by Simon Hobday and Deane Beman on 67. Conditions on the second day were 'turbulent', with rain in the afternoon, Deane Beman adding a 66 to his first round 67 to be one ahead of Arnold Palmer (66, 68) and Gary Player (69, 65) with Bob Charles a further stroke behind (68, 67). 67 professionals and 5 amateurs (including two Scots, Charlie Green and Gordon Murray) made the cut. Deane Beman (67) was five shots ahead of Gary Player (71) after the third round; Harold Henning shot 62 in that round. Play on the final day was in tempestuous conditions, with a south east gale and occasional rain, which changed the course dramatically – the 17th which had been within reach of a

194

Chapter VI - Centenary - The Closing Years

drive and a short iron, that day required three full shots. Only 21 of the 72 players broke 80: Deane Beman fell away to an 81, while Gary Player edged ahead with a 75 to take his second Seniors British Open with a total of 280. Second equal were Deane Beman and Brian Waites on 281, and Charlie Green was the top amateur on 295. Arnold Palmer, at the age of 60, finished fourth only two strokes behind the winner, and impressed everyone who followed him, not only with the enduring quality and strength of his play but also with his sportsmanship and lovely friendly demeanour. He patiently signed autographs for young fans for longer than anyone else and, on the final day in dreadful wind and rain at the 17th hole, whilst very much in contention, he showed remarkable patience and calm with an over enthusiastic youngster. Palmer had put his tee shot into the right hand rough and a ring of stewards and spectators were gathered round the ball as the great man approached. Just as Palmer arrived a small boy squeezed into the ring and was in danger of stepping on the ball when Arnie's two huge hands were gently laid on him and he was lifted clear, as easily as if he were a small loose impediment. After playing his shot Palmer took time to have a kindly word with the lad before moving on. It is to be hoped the youngster remembers his experience and appreciates that he had that day a close encounter with one of the greatest ever figures in golf.

195

THE 1994 OPEN CHAMPIONSHIP

NOTHING is ever simple or unremarkable about Turnberry. Situated in a comparatively remote corner of Scotland it has nevertheless witnessed turbulent and heroic times going back to the birth of the great 14th century King of Scotland, Robert the Bruce, in the castle in whose ruins is built the famous lighthouse overlooking the ninth fairway. It was fitting that, when two previous opens were held at Turnberry, they produced heroic golfing deeds by Tom Watson and Jack Nicklaus in 1977 and Greg Norman in 1986. Could it be the scene in 1994 for yet another outstanding championship? As on both of those earlier occasions, the championship had the previous year been held at Sandwich, where Greg Norman had won with a fabulous last round of 64, and the prospect of Watson, Norman and Nicklaus all returning to Turnberry was mouth watering. In the final practice round Watson and Nicklaus played a money game against Norman and Nick Price, first and third respectively in the Sony World Ranking. Reputedly they had a better ball score of 60 and enhanced their bank balances at the expense of the younger men. Could they defy the years and re-capture the magic of 1977, was the question being asked. Jack Nicklaus was realistic in his assessment. He said *A lot of people think you're going to be around for ever, but that can't happen. Out there today people thought it was 1977. It isn't'*.

Low Scoring Sets Scene on First Day

The course was in wonderful condition with greens soft and holding due to recent rains and fairways significantly wider than in 1986. The best conditions prevailed for the early starters and the rain, which began in early afternoon, also brought a strong breeze from the south and plunging temperatures. Nevertheless the first day's play saw an abundance of low scoring led by 31 year old Greg Turner of New Zealand, with a 65, despite being out in the worst of the weather. He was followed on 66 by Jonathan Lomas of England, a young rookie on the European Tour, playing in his first Open. In all, thirty players broke 70 including Andrew Magee of the U.S.A., who took 67 but missed the 36 hole cut after taking 80 in the second round. Jesper Parnevik of Sweden and David Feherty of Northern Ireland both took 68, as did Tom Watson, who was to mount a serious challenge, as if to turn back the clock and prove Nicklaus wrong. Nick Price of Zimbabwe, Brad Faxon, Jeff Maggert and Peter Jacobson, all of USA, Frank Nobilo of New Zealand and Ernie Els of South Africa were the most notable of a group of 16 players who all shot 69.

Watson Chases Vardon Record on Second Day

On day two the skies were blue and there was a stiff breeze from the northwest which completely changed the clubbing from day one, making the outward half play much longer and the home nine shorter. The scoring reflected the easier conditions, with 47 players shooting in the sixties. It was a day for nostalgia, with Tom Watson matching his final round score of 65 in 1977 and ending the day at the head of the field on 133. Parnevik and Faxon shared second place, a stroke behind after scoring respectively 66 and 65. Nick Price also shot a solid 66 to lie fourth on 135 and Greg Norman came into contention on 138 after a 67 with a birdie-birdie finish.

At the end of the day however, the big story was about the possibility of Tom Watson winning a sixth Open Championship and thus matching the record of Harry Vardon, the only man to have done so. Vardon had been one of the first true superstars of golf, dominating the game along with James Braid and J.H. Taylor (collectively named the Great Triumvirate) with an outstanding championship career stretching over 18 years from his first Open title in 1886 till his sixth in 1914. James Braid and J.H. Taylor each won five times, but in modern times only Peter Thomson of Australia and Tom Watson had come close to equalling Vardon's record of six. Watson had won his first title at Carnoustie in 1975

Chapter VI - Centenary - The Closing Years

and his fifth at Royal Birkdale in 1983 thus winning five times in eight years. Now, after a gap of eleven years, here he was at Turnberry again and in the lead at the half-way point, with Parnevik and Faxon, both young enough to be his sons, snapping at his heels. Could he emulate Vardon?

Zoeller Whistles into the Lead

On the third day the weather was perfect both for the golfers and to display the course at its most majestic and beautiful. The sun reflected from a tranquil sea, ruffled into contrasting blues by a pleasant fresh breeze and shimmering all the way to the wonderful backdrop of Ailsa Craig, Kintyre and the island of Arran. Visibility was so good that even the coast of Ireland could be seen in the distance behind the end of the Kintyre peninsula. The 81 players who had made the cut went about their work enthusiastically and to great effect with 42 of them shooting scores in the 60's. These included Tom Watson who, with a 69, achieved his third consecutive round under 70, but nevertheless found himself, at the end of the day, demoted to equal third, tied on 202 with three others, Nick Price with a 67, Jesper Parnevik of the eccentric dress, with 68 and Ronan Rafferty of Ireland with 66. The day belonged however to that most likeable of Americans, Fuzzy Zoeller, always ready with a quip to the crowd or a joke for the score recorders when others, less placid, were tetchy and up-tight. One of the most memorable actions in golf, ranking along with Nicklaus conceding Jacklin's putt to half the Ryder Cup match at Royal Birkdale in 1969, must surely be that of Zoeller at Winged Foot in the 1984 United States Open. Having witnessed Greg Norman hole a long putt up ahead on the 18th green and, believing that Norman had beaten him for the title, he took a white towel from his bag and waved it above his head as a gesture of magnanimous surrender. As it happens the putt ensured Norman only a tie and Zoeller was an easy victor by eight strokes in a play-off next day. Now, ten years later, Zoeller whistled his way round Turnberry for a third round 64 to take a share of the lead on 201 along with former American Walker Cup player Brad Faxon who shot 67.

Nick Price birdies the 12th in his final round.

Mother Nature takes a hand

When the final day dawned warm and with a light wind from the north-east it was obvious that there would be more low scoring. All links courses need a strong wind to stiffen their challenge, particularly in July when the fairways are running fast. Moreover a dry spring had ensured that the rough was not nearly as heavy as it had been in 1986 and the Royal & Ancient Golf Club, wisely preferring Mother Nature to have a hand in things, did not seek to trick up the course artificially for the Open. If low scores result from this due to benign conditions and the wonderful talents of the top players, so be it. What better entertainment could the public enjoy than to watch the stars get the chance to use their exceptional skills, allied to equipment fashioned by the latest technology, to produce prodigiously low scores on a course that is beautifully prepared and fairly presented. The Ailsa course is over 7000 yards long off the tiger tees with an abundance of challenging shots required. In the Championship Tees Competition held yearly by Turnberry Golf Club, even the low handicap players struggle to break 80 and scores over 100 are not uncommon. Nevertheless, after missing the 36-hole cut, Lee Trevino claimed that the Ailsa course was too easy and blamed the watering system for destroying the true links nature of the course. The truth is that George Brown, the Course Superintendent, had only used the watering system very sparingly, and one always has to view somewhat cautiously the views of a disappointed golfer.

In their interviews after the third round both Zoeller and Faxon opined that, if the next day was fine it would take at least three or four under par in the final round to win. Neither was able to achieve that, with Zoeller taking 70 to finish third, three shots behind, and Faxon taking 73 to finish sixth, six shots back. Tom Watson, with his sights set on equalling Vardon's six win record, hoped for a 40 mile per hour wind saying *'Nature has produced an easy course for us this year. Without wind it's going to take something in the middle 60's to win'*. He didn't get his wind and his closing 74 left him on equal eleventh, his dream in tatters. Mark James, of England with 68, and Anders Forsbrand of Sweden with a wonderful 64, finished fourth equal on 273, five shots adrift along with David Feherty, who shot 70.

A Skip and a Fringe of Brown Curls

The championship however was fought out between a Swede and a Zimbabwean. Jesper Parnevik, the Swede, ranked No. 37 in the Sony World Ranking, was one of an increasing number of fine Swedish golfers competing in the pro-ranks, all products of the forward

Nick Price plays his second shot to the 18th.

Chapter VI - Centenary - The Closing Years

looking policies of the Swedish Golf Federation, which encouraged junior golfers and helped the most promising ones to graduate to the P.G.A. European Tour. The best previous finish of a Swede in the Open was the fifth place of Robert Carlsson in 1992, and now Forsbrand had gone one place better with his closing 64 being just one shot off the Open record for one round. The young Parnevik, wearing the skip of his golf cap turned up and with a fringe of brown curls escaping down his forehead, looked more like a candidate for a lollipop than the claret jug, but appearances were certainly deceptive. He upstaged both of his compatriots and came very close also to upstaging the whole field. He was defeated only by a remarkable finish by Nick Price of Zimbabwe and perhaps, after all, by his own immaturity. Standing on the 18th tee for the final time, having birdied both the 16th and 17th holes, Parnevik was 12 under par, two ahead of Price, but deliberately did not look at the scoreboards all around him. The frequent cheers from behind him led him to believe that he needed a birdie at the last to clinch the title and foolishly, or perhaps in an effort not to confront the pressure of knowing exactly what he needed to do, he did not check. Instead of going for the middle of the green with his pitching wedge second shot, he played directly at the flagstick situated on the front left corner, just beyond a grassy hollow. The ball fell short in a difficult lie in the hollow and he was unable to get up and down for his par, leaving the door unexpectedly open for Price.

Both Hands On The Trophy

Nick Price himself had been a nearly man on two occasions in the Open. The first was in 1982 when he was only 25 years old and led by three shots at Royal Troon with six holes to play, only to let it slip away to lose to Tom Watson by one shot. Then in 1988 he led by two shots at Royal Lytham after three rounds, but, despite a closing round of 69, he had once again to play second fiddle, this time to Seve Ballesteros of Spain, who

The new Open Champion with the Turnberry Captains and some members of the Turnberry Championship Committee. (Left to right): Jack Boyd, Captain Charlie Jack, Ladies Captain Claire Stevenson, Nick Price, Gordon Rodger, Peter Wiseman, David Stobie.

snatched victory with a final round of 65. His career had blossomed in the 1990's, and he came to Turnberry as the most successful player in the world at that time. In 1992 he had won the USPGA Championship and, between then and Turnberry, he had won seven tournaments, including The Players Championship in 1993, a year in which he earned nearly $1.5 million and was voted Player of the Year.

It would be a mistake to think of the 1994 Open at Turnberry as the one which Jesper Parnevik threw away. Rather it was the one in which Nick Price proved himself to be a truly great champion. It was his second major win and the manner of his winning proved that he was the one prepared and determined enough to succeed at the highest level. On the sixteenth green he was three strokes behind Parnevik who was about to drive at the eighteenth and final hole. Price holed his birdie putt and the deficit was reduced to two. Then, whilst Parnevik was making bogey at the last, he nailed a four iron to the 17th green, albeit almost 50 feet from the hole. He considered the putt carefully from all angles before setting it off briskly along a right hand borrow. As it got nearer the hole the crowd held their breath and it seemed as if the ball was in slow motion on its perfect line, before it fell into the middle of the hole. Meanwhile Price had started running after it and jumped three feet in the air as the ball dropped and the crowd roared with delight, a thousand fists punching the air along with his own.

Price took no chances down the last, hitting the middle of the fairway with a three iron from the tee and then the middle of the green with a seven iron. Two safe putts gave him the title. When presented with the famous claret jug by Charlie Jack, the Captain of Turnberry Golf Club, he declared emotionally *'In 1982 I had my left hand on the trophy. In 1988 I had my right hand on the trophy. Now finally I have both hands on it'*.

The new Champion with some of the Turnberry marshalls.

THE AMATEUR CHAMPIONSHIP 1996

THERE were 288 entrants for the Championship and, as in 1983, a qualifying 36-hole stroke play competition, comprising one round on the Ailsa course and one on the Arrran course, was held to reduce the field to 64 for the final match-play stage. The competitors came from many countries, including USA, Argentina, France, Belgium, Denmark, Netherlands, Sweden, Canada, Norway, Australia, New Zealand, South Africa, Finland, Germany and Spain. This illustrated particularly a tremendous rise in the status of and interest in golf in the Continental European countries which would have been hardly credible even a decade earlier. Scotland was well represented with 55 entrants including some local hopefuls, notably Gavin Lawrie of Prestwick St. Nicholas for his ninth appearance, Hugh McKibbin of Troon Welbeck and Allan Thomson of Ayr Belleisle and of Turnberry who had been a quarter finalist in 1983. Of these Gavin Lawrie did best but went down at the 19th in the second round to Colin Rodgers of Royal Mid Surrey, having beaten Craig Watson of East Renfrewshire 3 and 2 in the first round.

By his own admission, Warren Bladon of Kenilworth, England, arrived without any great ambitions other than to qualify for the match play stages. He certainly did that for he set a blistering pace and led the qualifiers with an aggregate of 138. Only 15 Scots reached the match play and of these only 7 survived the first round and only 3 reached the third round, namely Fraser McLaughlan of Wishaw, Roger Beames of Wick and R. Clark of Erskine.

Fraser McLaughlan, the youngest competitor at age 17 and an impressive figure at 6'3" tall and 13 stones in weight, made it all the way to the quarter finals, having won at the 23rd in the third round against Ian Ferrie of Alnmouth, never having been up till then. However he lost at the 18th to the burly Bladon in his quarter final, mainly due to his opponent's amazing short game. Clark had also been a victim of Bladon in the previous (third) round, losing narrowly at the 19th.

Roger Beames, a 21 year old highlander from Wick and the first golfer from north of Inverness to represent his country, played solidly throughout the championship, beating Ivo Giner of Spain in the quarter finals and Steve Bodenheimer of USA in the semi finals.

After his victory over McLaughlan, Warren Bladon beat Robert Wiggins of Slaley Hall, England, by one hole in the semi finals. On the first nine of that match he pitched in twice and required only 10 putts. In the final against Beames it all came down to the last hole which they came to all square. Beames pulled his 5-iron approach shot slightly left and it kicked off into the hollow beside the green. He then chipped dead, leaving his opponent with a 12 foot birdie putt for the title, which Bladon duly slotted. Beames, who reckoned it had cost him £4,500 that season to travel and play in a modest number of tournaments, was disconsolate. He admitted *'I am gutted – I don't know if I can get much sadder than this'*. Bladon was delighted with his unexpected win but declared that he had no intention of following the previous year's winner, Gordon Sherry, into the professional ranks – *'not yet at least'*.

The weather for the Championship was excellent and, from the quarter finals, the temperatures were reminiscent of the Mediterranean Costas. One man who arrived on the Saturday to enjoy the weather and watch the final was Ewan Frazer, the husband of Ann Frazer, a past Captain of Turnberry Golf Club Ladies' Section. Mr. Frazer, holder of the D.S.O. and a veteran of the battle of El Alamein and the Second World War, was confined to a wheelchair as a result of contracting polio in North Africa during the war. He nevertheless didn't anticipate any problem. After all he himself had devised the wheelchair route for the 1994 Open Championship at Turnberry for the R. & A., and his wheelchair was equipped with wide low pressure tyres. Unfortunately an over-zealous security man refused him admission much to the subsequent embarrassment of the R. & A. and Turnberry Hotel when the story emerged too late for the injustice to be righted. Apart from that the organisation of the Championship had been excellent.

Warren Bladon and his caddy celebrate his winning putt on the 36th green in the final of the Amateur Championship in 1993.

CHAPTER VI - CENTENARY - THE CLOSING YEARS

WEETABIX WOMEN'S BRITISH OPEN CHAMPIONSHIP 2002

SOME years ago when Turnberry Golf Club started planning for the celebration of its Centenary, there was inevitably speculation about the possibility of the Open returning to Turnberry for the fourth time, in the Club's centenary year. There was a gap of nine years between the first Open at Turnberry in 1977 and the second in 1986, and one of eight years between that and the third one in 1994; and so there seemed a reasonable chance that 2002 would see the fourth visit of the world's oldest major championship. It was not to be however, for reasons related to local road and rail access problems according to the official release from the Royal & Ancient Golf Club Instead the year was marked, tournament-wise, by hosting the Women's British Open Championship sponsored by Weetabix. This turned out to be not only a very enjoyable event, but one which was a wonderful advertisement for the quality of women's golf at the highest level. The inaugural championship was held at Fulford in 1976 and had always been held at English venues until it came to Turnberry. At Turnberry it was in its second year of being recognised as the fourth of the world's Major tournaments for women, the other three being the LPGA Championship, the US Open and the Nabisco Championship.

The entry included all the top women golfers in the world, including Annika Sorenstam of Sweden who arrived as favourite, having already that season won six titles on the American LPGA Tour, including the Nabisco Championship, plus the Australian Masters; Julie Inkster of America, holder of the US Open title; Si Ri Pak of Korea, the LPGA Champion and holder of the British title, and Laura Davies of England who won the title in 1986 and had recently become the first foreigner to earn a place in the US LPGA Hall of Fame. Scotland was strongly represented by Kathryn Marshall, Janice Moodie, Catriona Matthew and Mhairi McKay, all of whom had been playing well on the US women's tour and were strong contenders for selection for the Solheim Cup team to meet the USA later in the year. In particular local interest was of course centred on Mhairi McKay, a member of Turnberry Golf Club since she was just a tot, and whose father and mother Peter and Mary, brother Kevin and sister Fiona are all members of the Club. Interviewed for the press before the start of the tournament she commented: *'Playing over Turnberry, my home course, in a Major, is pretty special and I just hope I can do well. I know I'm biased, but this is the No. 1 course for me and I feel very privileged and spoilt to have played it so many times. Winning a Major Championship is your dream but to win here would be the ultimate'.* She was no doubt nervous and under special pressure, playing under the burden of the great expectations of the predominantly Scottish crowd. Nevertheless in the first round she shot a fine 68 which she declared her *'best round ever over the Ailsa course'*. The leader was Candie King of Thailand with a magnificent 65, followed by Karrie Webb of Australia on 66, and Si Ri Pak of Korea, Rachel Teske, another Australian, American Tina Barrat and Germany's Elisabeth Esterl, all on 67. Altogether that day twenty two players bettered 70 on a layout measuring over 6400 yards. Even allowing for the almost perfect conditions and a course in immaculate condition, that illustrates how high is the standard of play on the women's tour. The spectators were delighted and astonished to witness both the accuracy and the distance achieved by the women who, for the most part, were not at all Amazonian, but on the contrary, were mostly femininely attractive in both figure and action. They achieved distance allied to accuracy by dint of excellent and graceful technique rather than by muscle power. It brought to mind the motto of Royal Troon Golf Club: *'Tam arte quam marte'*, meaning *'As much by skill as by strength'*, although in the case of the ladies this could more appropriately be *'More by skill than by strength'*.

On the second day the wind was blowing and the rain pouring down for the early starters, who included Mhairi McKay, but she still managed a very creditable even par 72. When the last players finished about 9 p.m., this left her four shots under par and only four shots off the lead held jointly by Karin Koch of Sweden and the rookie, 21 year old, Candie King of Taiwan. The ever dangerous Karrie Webb of Australia added a 71 to her opening 66 and was in a threatening position, only one shot behind the leaders.

A lot of interest on the second day centred on Karin Koch, both for her immaculate golf and for her Scandinavian good looks. She was the girl who holed the winning putt for Europe in the Solheim Cup Match with the USA, at Loch Lomond in 2000, and gained some notoriety in 2002 by being picked in a *Playboy* web-site as the sexiest player on the LPGA Tour, an *'honour'* she took in good humour.

Notables who missed the cut included world no. 1 Annika Sorenstam, Julie Inkster and Laura Davies who had arrived in optimistic mood, having won the Norwegian Masters the previous week. Davies was close to tears in the press tent when she admitted to massive disappointment. Sorenstam ended a run of 74 tournaments without missing a cut on the US-based LPGA Tour. She had arrived in Scotland the previous week and, by way of practice on links courses, had played Troon, Glasgow Gailes and Prestwick, at each of which she was welcomed as an honoured guest.

The third day was warm and sunny, showing Turnberry at its best, making it the perfect setting to showcase women's golf, and the women proved worthy of the task. Karin Koch produced a third successive 68 to be joint leader on 204, along with 23 year old Jennifer Rosales of the Phillipines who shot 65, the lowest score of the day. Koch had already won tournaments on both

The Winner, Carrie Webb, strides over the 18th green to the prizegiving, followed by her fellow-Aussie Michelle Ellis and Spaniard Paula Marti; who were 2nd equal.

Chapter VI - Centenary - The Closing Years

The prizewinners and the presentation party, await the start of the prizegiving.

sides of the Atlantic, but not a Major; whereas Rosales, in her third year as a professional, had never before led an LPGA event, let alone a Major championship. She looked as if she weighed only about seven stone and stood no more than five foot tall, but she hit the ball an enormous distance from the tee with her long graceful swing generating whiplash-like speed through the ball.

The leaderboard was full of foreign born players, with Natalie Gulbis of the United States (after a 67) and Spain's Paula Marti, both two shots off the lead; and Karrie Webb of Australia, a further shot back in a group of five more foreigners. Of the 66 strong home players in the starting field, only eight made the cut and not one of those was close to the lead. Mhairi McKay got to six under par at one point, with two early birdies, to raise Scottish hopes, but subsequently dropped five shots for a 75 and one under 215. Catriona Matthew and Kathryn Marshall, like McKay strong contenders for a wild card pick for the European Solheim Cup team to defend the trophy in Minnesota, later that year, both made the cut, but well down the field.

The final day dawned grey and dreich with wind and rain, but that didn't prevent the players producing some sparkling golf in the difficult conditions. The most sparkling of all was Karrie Webb, who again scored four under par 66, as she had done on day one, and claimed the championship and a place in the history books. Her 15-under par total of 273 won her the first prize of £155,000, by two shots, making her the first three times winner of the title. She had previously won at Woburn in 1995 in her rookie season and again at Sunningdale in 1997. She had already achieved a career grand slam of the four Majors at the LPGA Championship in 2001, when the now defunct Du Maurier Classic was one of the Majors. This win made her the first to achieve a career grand slam of the five different Major championships available in her career, and was her sixth Major in just four years.

For Webb there was also the special thrill of following in the footsteps of her childhood idol, Greg Norman, who won his first Open Championship over the same Ailsa Course in 1986. His winning aggregate was 280, seven strokes more than her winning score, but over a layout 600 yards longer and in much more difficult weather conditions. Nevertheless the comparison gives some idea of the high quality of her play. She herself declared *'This is one of my greatest moments. Turnberry is a great course and has produced many great champions'*.

One disappointment for the Scottish fans was the lack of home interest in the last 36 holes. Catriona Matthew and Kathryn Marshall finished top Scots and also the leading British players, in joint 35th, 16 shots behind the winner. Mhairi McKay, with a closing 76, was two shots further back.

As always the Turnberry Club organised the marshalls and the match scorers recruited from members of the Club and from neighbouring clubs. Past Captain Stewart Jardine was Chief Marshall, assisted by Past Captain Gordon Rodger, and the Ladies' Captain, Karen Fitzgerald was in charge of the scorers. At the prizegiving the LPGA presented a framed tapestry to Turnberry Golf Club as Official Host of the tournament and this was handed over by Karrie Webb to Club Captain Tim Morrison.

Carrie Webb hands over a commemorative gift from the LPGA, to Club Captain Tim Morrison.

Chapter VII

Reflections of Past Captains

Memories of Friends and Events

DAVID LOGAN
1980-1982

IF you asked me what Turnberry has meant to me since I became a junior member 48 years ago, the first thing I would think of is the friendship and companionship of the other members. The Club has always been one where there is no snobbery and there are no cliques. There is a general goodwill amongst the members, which makes it a great pleasure to play golf there, whether with my own special friends or with others when the opportunity arises. Because the membership numbers are limited to about half of the numbers of many other clubs, it is possible to know almost all the other members and the social occasions are always a great success.

I remember many particular characters with great pleasure and affection. There was John L. Walker, a draper from Girvan, whose own dapper appearance was always a perfect advertisement for his gents' outfitters business. He joined the Club in 1919 and was made an honorary member fifty years later in 1969. He was also a smart little golfer. In 1929 he won the Bell Trophy, the premier individual match play competition at Turnberry, and one of the most difficult trophies to win, involving 8 or 9 rounds of knock-out games. Forty three years on from that win he again reached the final in 1972, unfortunately losing to a much younger member, though only at the 20th hole.

James P.K. McDowall, Captain in 1961-63, was another I remember with great affection. Always a perfect gentleman, he took a great interest in the golf of his fellow members, congratulating good performances and encouraging those who were not playing so well. He was a great one for arranging games and ensuring that no-one was without one and he was usually known as 'Mr. James'. He had a dry sense of humour at times and I remember him following games in the Bargany Cup and remarking mischievously that *'there have been a lot of 'Warwick' balls found on the course since the Girvan boys got in to the Bargany'*.

When the European Open was played at Turnberry in 1979, on the eve of the preceding Pro-Am I was asked to provide a few low handicap members to make up numbers. I phoned Robin Ross, one of Turnberry's best players at that time, and eventually located him at the Abbotsford Hotel in Ayr, his favourite watering hole. When I asked him if he would play with Sandy Lyle the next day at first he thought I was pulling his leg. Robin duly played with Sandy and helped him with his clubbing during the round. When Sandy went on to win the European Open, Robin claimed that his advice had formed the basis for his victory.

At the 1977 Open Charlie Jack was Chief Marshall in charge of crowd control and I was his Depute. When Charlie had a heart attack a few months before the big event, I realised what an awesome responsibility could be resting solely on my shoulders and so it was much to my relief when Charlie recovered in time to fulfil his duties.

In preparation for 1977 we had been to Carnoustie and Birkdale to see how things were done at the two previous Opens, so we had a blueprint to work from. It was our first Open and we wanted to get it right. The excellent weather throughout the tournament helped to put the crowds in a good mood. We were lucky in a way

Chapter VII - Reflections of Past Captains

because I reckon it was the last of the 'garden party' Opens, with a very relaxed atmosphere.

There was no problem with people getting in, as Keith Mackenzie of the R. & A. made sure there were plenty of ticket booths. We were nevertheless almost caught out when some people disembarked straight on to the course from a boat which landed them at the old pier below the lighthouse. They were very honest, however, and asked a steward to direct them to a ticket booth. They were quickly transported in buggies to buy their tickets.

1977 was a very special Open – perhaps the most memorable of them all. Everyone remembers the sun and how hot it was that week. What everyone forgets is that there was a violent thunderstorm during the third round, which caused play to be suspended but didn't prevent both Watson and Nicklaus scoring 65, leaving them three shots clear of the field.

On the final day our main problem was keeping the crowd calm and preventing them running for position, as the final game passed through. By that time the course was so dry from the sun and the excitement was so great that there was a particular problem at the ninth after Watson and Nicklaus hit their second shots. The crowd were allowed to follow the match up the fairway to get a good view and a huge cloud of what looked like smoke rose into the air. This caused a certain amount of alarm to both the players and the crowd, before anyone realised that it was just dust caused by thousands of feet moving quickly along the bone dry ground.

It was strangely quiet at first during the final round and there was an almost tangible feeling amongst the spectators that we were about to witness something very special in golfing history. The reality was even more remarkable than the expectation and the excitement and the applause just built and built to the finish. After Nicklaus holed his long birdie putt on the 18th, Watson took no time at all over his two footer for victory. He just walked up and knocked it in. I thought he was trying to make sure the moment wouldn't get to him. I can only guess at how Watson felt, but I felt completely drained and yet I did not want the day to end. It will remain in my memory forever.

When the European Open came to Turnberry in 1979 Charlie Jack was again in charge of crowd control and I was his deputy. The experience which I gained in 1977 and 1979 stood me in good stead some years later when I was Chief Marshall when the Open again came to Turnberry in 1986.

Club prizewinners 1977. Back row from left: T. Smith, I Brown, R. Grassom, A. Coutts, A. Todd, C. Kirkwood, H. Mitchell, C. Ross, G. McCallum, J. Hogarth, M. Elliot, R. Ross
Front row from left: D. Logan, H McCylmont, L. Whitehead, N. Bain, D. Henderson, J. Boyd, S. Jardine, W. Judge

BILL JUDGE
1982-1984

IT was overcast but pleasantly warm for an early May morning. Arran was cloaked with low cloud and Ailsa Craig had disappeared altogether as the small group made its way from the cars parked on the rough track leading to the beach across the elevated tee and down to the exposed and dramatic championship tee at the ninth hole of the Ailsa course at Turnberry. It was rumoured that more than one professional golfer had to be led blindfolded to play from this tee!

My mind drifted back to the late 1960's, when as a relatively new member of Turnberry Golf Club, I had listened enthralled to the tales of an elderly gentleman, as he sat by the fire in what has come to be known as the old clubhouse. It was a small, congenial place, of wooden construction and the members' room had seating for about 20. Willie Campbell was often to be found on a winter's afternoon sitting at the fire with a group of eager listeners as he reminisced over his experiences and told stories of golfers he knew or had played with in his years as an international competitor. My favourite was about another legend of Scottish golf.

Mrs. A.M. (Helen) Holm was one of Scotland's finest lady golfers; she was also tall and imposing, very often dressed in black and seemed rarely to smile on the golf course. She was playing in the Scottish Ladies' Championship over the Ailsa course at Turnberry in 1930, a tournament she subsequently won. Although she had successfully negotiated the first couple of rounds, she was having difficulty with her club selection at the 6th hole and in each of the first two rounds had played a spoon, finishing short in the greenside bunker. On the morning of the third round, standing on the first tee, she said to her caddie – *'Alec, you know the trouble I've had with my tee-shot at the 6th; well I was lying in bed thinking about it last night. I've been playing the wrong club – it's a driver, so no matter what happens when we reach the 6th, give me my driver'.*

'Right, Mrs. Holm', said Alec.

However the wind had freshened from the South overnight and Mrs. Holm was striking the ball very well. So well, in fact, that by the time she reached the 6th she had changed her mind about the driver and turning to the caddie as she reached the tee,

'Spoon, Alec' she said.

'Now Mrs. Holm' replied Alec, *'remember what we were thinking in bed last night!'*

Now there were three of us who had undertaken to perform a last rite for one of the finest amateur golfers to join Turnberry Golf Club. Willie Campbell had been a member of the Walker Cup team in 1930 and had represented a victorious Scottish side in successive Home Internationals from 1933 to 1936. He died in 1970. After cremation, his ashes were to be scattered by his great friend Stanley P. Morrison. Unfortunately Stanley died before the job was done and the casket containing Willie's ashes wasn't discovered until some time later. Stanley's son Brian found it when clearing the house for sale, realised what it was and sought my help in making the proper arrangements. We had enlisted the help of the minister, as both Brian and I felt it

Chapter VII - Reflections of Past Captains

appropriate that the golfing reverend, a member of the Club and a keen golfer, should be present. We had reached the Championship tee and the minister broke the silence. *'Well gentlemen, let's get started'*. *'I can't get the lid off,'* said Brian. *'I'll have to go back to the car for a screwdriver'*. I was left holding the casket while Brian returned to the car. After a lengthy delay he returned with a screwdriver. The screws were rapidly removed, and we agreed on a few moments meditation after the ashes had been scattered. Brian inverted the casket after checking the wind direction and gave it a gentle shake. Absolutely nothing happened; a more vigorous shake but Willie, firmly wedged, was not to be moved; a smart tap on the bottom of the box produced no effect whatsoever. We had hoped to have the proceedings concluded before any golfers reached this part of the course; but time was overtaking us and a group of players had reached the eighth tee. Willie was still firmly stuck in the bottom of the box. Brian and I exchanged glances. There was only one course of action and Willie was assisted from the casket with the aid of the screwdriver while we reverently smoothed his lumpier bits into the hallowed turf!

As we hurried back to the car the group of golfers had reached the eighth green and instantly recognised the three furtive figures as members who would not normally be seen on this part of the course without clubs. *'Morning, boys'* one called. *'It's a fine morning for the purpose!'*

CAPTAIN and PAST CAPTAINS at Centenary Dinner.
Left to Right Back Row: Alex Todd, Charlie Jack, Stewart Jardine, Jim Smith, David McDowall
Front Row: Gordon Rodger, David Logan, Bill Judge, Captain Tim Morrison, Bill Manson, Jack Boyd

ALEX TODD
1984-1986

In my report to the A.G.M. of 1985 I made mention that the season of 1985 would be remembered as the long dry summer of discontent. The courses carried a very heavy burden of visitors which resulted in the members experiencing great difficulty in getting tee-off times, particularly on the Ailsa course and at weekends. This epitomises the main problem faced by most Captains of the Club since 1976/77. Given the ever increasing popularity of Turnberry their endeavour has always been to strike a happy balance between the need for the hotel management to maximise profitability and the playing requirements of the Club members. There has always to be a measure of give and take and, during 1984/86, a better system of prior booking for members came into force and this along with a drop of 50 in the membership improved things considerably.

On the personal side I was privileged to become the Chairman of the Club's Championship Committee for the 1986 Open, with responsibility for setting up the convenorship for the many functions which the Club had to undertake The convenors, in turn, chose their own teams and the whole operation went very smoothly and efficiently, drawing high praise from R. & A. after the Open for a job very well done. The lighter side of being Captain was having the opportunity to play and officiate at inter-club matches, the Pro-Am, the People to People matches and dinners and to meet with various celebrities at the Pro-Celebrity functions. Following a match with a group from Atlanta I did receive an invitation to play Augusta; sadly never taken up.

A visit to Hoylake to represent the Club at the centenary celebrations of the Amateur Championship had a rather strange outcome. The night before the event I was invited to join a group of Hoylake members for dinner at the hotel where I was staying and on my return to Turnberry I sent a small selection of Turnberry golf items to the gentleman who had hosted the dinner. Some weeks passed before I had a letter apologising for the delay in replying and saying that my unidentified little parcel had been viewed with some suspicion and examined by the bomb squad! My final memory is of playing the Ailsa Course on a wet, cold and miserable morning in a fourball with Michael and Angela Bonallack and Rosemary Dykes. In my weakened physical state that morning after a jovial evening the night before, my golf was very undistinguished, but the company is to be long remembered.

CHAPTER VII - REFLECTIONS OF PAST CAPTAINS

STEWART JARDINE
1988-1990

For 35 years it has been my joy and delight to play golf on Turnberry's links and to be a member of Turnberry Golf Club. Many words more eloquent than mine have been written about the pleasures and challenges of the courses, particularly the Ailsa, and of the natural beauty of the Turnberry landscape. Even after all these years, the views from the seventh tee along the sandy beach, over to Ailsa Craig and Arran and north to Holy Loch still take my breath away.

Each hole presents a different challenge and holds personal memories for me of both good shots and disastrous ones. I remember some good rounds and many others not so good, when over-ambition, lack of ability or the unbearable injustice of a bad lie or bounce, has snatched defeat from the jaws of victory or turned a potential sub-par round into one outside the buffer zone. That is not to say that the Turnberry courses are unfair for they are not and they seldom punish a good shot. Moreover, whatever the outcome, the sheer delight of playing at Turnberry always overcame my disappointments and made my successes more satisfying.

Yet, above all, my greatest pleasure has come from the lasting friendships that have been formed playing golf at Turnberry. It is a game which is essentially a battle between the player and the course but is at its most enjoyable when played with companions in friendly but earnest competition. There is nothing more satisfying than victory in a good four ball game, having given your all with a trusty partner to win a pound or two, and then, if at Turnberry, to be out of pocket buying the drinks or the coffees! Over the years it has been my good fortune to play with regular partners, who were competitive, loved golf, always gave one hundred percent effort and were excellent company both on and off the course.

I was very fortunate in my early years after joining Turnberry Golf Club to play regularly with two of Turnberry's golfing greats, Alex Thomson and Walter Linton. Alex, in particular, was a regular Sunday fourball partner and I always hoped that the sweetness and rhythm of his swing would transfer to mine and suddenly transform me overnight into a better golfer. While this may have been a forlorn hope, I know that watching Alex from close at hand benefited everyone who played with him.

Alex and Walter were champions of both Turnberry and Girvan Golf Clubs on many occasions. Alex was Turnberry Club champion on three occasions in 1960, 1969 and 1974 while Walter was champion six times, 1954, 1955, 1956, 1959, 1961 and 1963. Although both were fierce competitors, they also enjoyed their social golf and were excellent companions. Alex was a scratch golfer who was seriously contemplating turning professional when war broke out in 1939. He joined the Royal Air Force and became a physical training instructor and saw active war service, being amongst the last of the Allied troops evacuated from Dunkirk in 1940. On his return home in 1945 he felt that he was then too old to take up professional golf and instead he started his own business in Girvan as a gents' outfitter and took up golf again as an amateur. The trophies and championships soon followed. The strength he gained from physical training was obvious in his striking powers with his driver and long irons. He had strong wrists and an easy rhythmical swing which remained the same with all his clubs from driver to wedge.

Walter Linton, a dentist in Girvan, was the thinking man's golfer. He had a consistent swing that kept the ball very straight and he was also superb in his course management. He was always aware of the percentage of success likely in each shot and would often play for position with an iron rather than take on an over-ambitious shot. This combined with a superb short game meant that he made very few mistakes.

Both Alex and Walter gave great encouragement to others and enjoyed the success of their friends just as much as their own. Perhaps this was their best legacy to Turnberry Golf Club. That is not to say that they were above the usual friendly banter and gamesmanship which is part and parcel of bounce games. Alex could try to sell you a suit or Walter could remind you of your next dental appointment, just as you were facing a difficult putt. In those days, after the golf, it was always a delight to go into the clubhouse and enjoy a cup of coffee and one or two of Mrs. McCallum's scones and cheese and replay all the successes and misfortunes of the round.

Perhaps my greatest satisfaction is that my two sons are now full members of the Club and have learned to enjoy and respect the great game of golf. Like me they have made many friends in the Club and their lives have been enriched by lasting friendships and enjoyment of the challenge of the Turnberry links. Golf is fortunately a game with a handicapping system which gives everyone an equal chance of winning. Even as the handicaps creep inexorably upwards as we get older, on our day we may still win a match or a trophy if we play well and, even if we do not win, we will be the better and the happier for playing golf at Turnberry with good friends.

Stewart Jardine and Jack Boyd on 9th tee during the Centenary Team Competition

BILL MANSON
1990-1992

My memories of Turnberry Golf Club are many and varied as may be judged from what follows. My first contact with the Club was with its then Secretary/Treasurer, a man whose considerable geniality was equalled only by his efficiency. He had written to inform me that, my application for membership having been accepted, my entrance fee and subscription were now due. He further suggested that since it was his habit to be present in the Clubhouse on a Thursday afternoon I might wish to meet him to pay my fees and to be introduced into the workings of the Club. And so it was that I found myself seated in front of a blazing coal fire in the Clubhouse, for this purpose. I handed the Secretary my subscription and entrance fee separately as he had requested. The subscription he tucked away in a right-hand hip pocket of his trousers which he informed me accommodated new and late subscriptions, while my entrance fee was destined for a left-hand hip pocket reserved for casual items of income. This done he accepted my offer of a celebratory drink and I in turn accepted a scone with cheese freshly baked in the Clubhouse kitchen. The genuine warmth of the welcome to the Club accorded to me then and its informality was to be repeated many times by my fellow members.

Regarding the apparently unorthodox financial procedure which I had witnessed it should perhaps be remembered that the entrance fee amounted to two guineas and the subscription to seven which rendered the process highly practical.

This introduction heralded the enjoyment which I have received ever since from my membership of this Club. I will always remember such pleasures as playing on the Ailsa course in the serenity of a summer evening with fellow members and more particularly from their company. One such member and there have been many was my late friend Tom Smith an individual for whom the term gentleman might have been invented. He was a highly competent golfer with a disarming enthusiasm for the game, an enthusiasm which on more than one occasion, but on one in particular, brought him into close contact with an equal enthusiast, Arnold Palmer. This occurred on a Saturday morning when our usual four-ball found itself sharing the fourth tee of the Ailsa course with the great man and three of his friends. He had failed to qualify for the last two days' play at the Open Championship being played at Troon. He declined our offer for his party to play through our match but suggested that we all play the hole together and then he would move on. This we did, some of us with more assurance than others. Tom's tee shot landed on the left level with the flag about half way down the rough slope from the green to the beach as did that of our American friend. The two balls were about four feet apart. Palmer played first but thinned his shot across the green and up the opposite bank. As he made to walk after his ball Tom laid a gentle restraining arm on him. He proceeded to explain to the ex-Open Champion, in some detail, how he could prevent himself from making

215

the same mistake again and suggested that this would be immediately apparent from watching Tom hit his almost identical shot. This he did and his ball finished up about six inches from the hole. Whereupon Arnold Palmer removed his cap and in great good humour shook Tom by the hand adding that Tom should have been at Troon instead of himself.

Turnberry during the past 100 years has not always been a centre for relaxation and especially so during two World Wars. The monument placed in the middle of the Ailsa course commemorates those who died in wartime operations at Turnberry but until relatively recently only the names of those lost in the first World War were inscribed on the memorial. I attended the open air service held on the 13th tee on a grey November afternoon in 1990 when the names of those who perished during the use of Turnberry as an R.A.F. airfield in the second World War were commemorated. The service concluded with aircraft from the flying school at Prestwick flying slowly overhead in a formation shaped like a cross. It was a timely and lasting reminder that not everyone who had visited Turnberry and in particular the 170 men and women whose names are inscribed on the monument had enjoyed the good fortune accorded to me.

From left – Stewart Jardine, Alan Stevenson, John O'Leary (Professional) and Bill Manson in Pro-Am team competition proceding British Seniors' Open

Chapter VII - Reflections of Past Captains

Charlie Jack
1994-1996

I took over the office of Captain of Turnberry at a most exciting time for the Club and a most fortuitous time for myself as we were about to host the now renowned 1994 Open Championship. That Open provided a finish which easily matched the 1977 "Duel in the Sun" between Watson and Nicklaus seventeen years earlier. I stood behind the eighteenth green on the Sunday afternoon as Jesper Parnevik walked on to the tee holding a three shot lead over Nick Price who was playing the sixteenth. Along with thousands of others I was convinced that the young Swedish golfer was going to be lifting the Claret Jug. I decided to go into the cool of the locker room for ten minutes to settle my nerves before making the presentation. Watching the golf on the locker room television was Mats Willander, who was thrilled at the prospect of his fellow countryman winning the title and he offered to teach me a few words of Swedish to congratulate Jesper. The next few minutes were spent rehearsing my Swedish until I felt it was time to head outside for the presentation. I made my way through the clubhouse going over the unfamiliar Swedish words in my head and walked out towards the eighteenth green. As I looked up at the giant scoreboard I discovered that the Open had been won by Nick Price from Zimbabwe. He didn't understand a word of Swedish!

Prior to the Open being played at Turnberry I had been invited along with past-captain Jack Boyd, and our wives, to attend the Portmarnock Golf Club centenary celebrations just outside Dublin. I would like to give you a small flavour of that delightful Irish trip.

The happy party of four had set off from Glasgow Airport to represent Turnberry at Portmarnock. I had already experienced the local logic when I phoned a Portmarnock Hotel to book rooms for Jack and Jessie and my wife Shauna and myself. This story has since come back to me as a joke but it did originate on our trip. I asked the receptionist if they had two twin or double rooms available for the time in question. She told me they had two grades of room available, one had a bath and the other had a shower. I replied that I was sure either would be suitable but out of interest asked what was the difference. *'Oh'* she said *'you stand up in the shower'*. I knew then that I was going to enjoy our trip.

We were greeted on our arrival at Dublin Airport by Ben Naughton, a senior member of the golf club, who along with his wife Jessie were to be our social hosts for the weekend and of whom we all quickly grew very fond. Ben took us to his car in front of the terminal building along with our cases and golf clubs. He opened the boot, only to discover his own full set of golf clubs, motorised caddy car, hold-all and practice balls with barely enough room for a pair of shoes. *'Ah'* said Ben *'now I remember what I forgot to do'*. After much thought we decided the girls would travel with Ben while Jack and I would go by taxi with the luggage. On the way, I asked the driver the best way to get from Portmarnock to Dublin city centre. He started to tell me all sorts of road directions. *'Sorry'* I interrupted *'I meant is there a bus service or local train'. 'Ah'* said the driver *'did you not bring your car?'* This from the man who had picked us up at the airport terminal. That evening Ben and Jessie were taking us to the centenary flag raising ceremony, an event which for me captured the atmosphere of our whole weekend. The City of Dublin Police silver band tuned up as members and guests assembled on the lawn in front of the clubhouse. The band leader was introduced to us and we were told he was also a Chief Inspector in the force and that, should the weekend go without any embarrassing incidents, he would be a Superintendent on Monday! The band struck up with the national anthem as the Irish flag was run up the pole. Everyone felt the formality of the occasion and stood sombrely to attention. The next flag to be raised was that of the R. & A. To our delight the band gave an excellent rendering of "Flower of Scotland" and many of the crowd joined in song, well led by ourselves and the delegation from Royal Troon. We sensed that those from the R. & A. and some other of the guests were not quite as impressed by the choice of music! The third flag was that of the Irish Golf Union. By now the band was in full swing and they gave a hearty rendering of "If you're Irish, come into the parlour". Suddenly the lawn looked like a mass audition for Riverdance, with feet and knees going in all directions, encouraged no doubt by the generous champagne reception we had all just left. The fourth and final flag was the Portmarnock Club's centenary flag. As it rose the band played a beautiful and haunting Irish air called "Misha Eire" and as I looked around, it was hard to find an eye not holding back a tear.

The weekend continued with wonderful and incomparable Irish hospitality and "crack", providing stories to be told and memories to be cherished for years to come. Long may golf clubs celebrate their tradition and heritage with such events and if the opportunity comes your way to attend one of these celebrations, don't miss it for the world!

Charlie Jack presents The Open Trophy to Nick Price in 1994.

CHAPTER VII - REFLECTIONS OF PAST CAPTAINS

JIM SMITH
1996-1998

The person who proposed me for membership of Turnberry Golf Club in 1961 was a man of many parts, who was at the time the Honorary President of the Club. His name was Oliver Hughes-Onslow. He was known to his family and friends as 'Tim' but to most other people including the members of Turnberry Golf Club he was 'the Captain'. I am proud to be able to give this brief biography, assisted by the Captain's grandson James Hughes-Onslow, who has provided many of the details.

For 21 years Oliver Hughes-Onslow was Captain of Turnberry Golf Club from 1936 till 1957 and when he retired he was made Honorary President, a position he held until his death in 1972.

He was born in 1893 at Ballantrae, not far from his family's estate at Laggan, famed for its pheasant and woodcock shooting, and for its salmon and trout fishing on the Stinchar. He became a keen shot, said to have a deadly reflex with rabbits in bracken, and an ace salmon caster. He went to Eton, where he excelled at sport, especially rugby and the Wall Game. As Keeper of the Oppidan Wall (a position his oldest son Andrew was also to hold), he helped modernise the rules of this arcane and brutal sport, making them almost comprehensible and humane. Perhaps it was this early experience of committee chairmanship which made him so effective at Turnberry, and as a member of the local and county councils.

After school, he went to the Royal Military College at Sandhurst and was then commissioned into the Irish Guards. He was one of the first to see action in France and, with so many of his friends losing their lives, this was an experience that affected him for the rest of his life. His uncle Arthur was killed in 1914, and his father Denzil in 1916.

In June 1916, a month before his father was killed, the Captain, or Lieutenant as he then was, was married to Ruth, daughter of Rev. George Dods, the minister at Barr. The wedding took place at Barr Parish Church. Having married into a religious family, he was to become increasingly involved in church affairs, eventually serving for 12 years as an elder at Kirkoswald. The Captain and his wife had a daughter and three sons, and subsequently 12 grandchildren and 30 great grandchildren.

He remained in the Irish Guards until 1922, when he was invalided out, but he was later to serve in the Second World War with the King's Own Scottish Borderers. Indeed he received injuries in the Second World War which caused him to suffer from arthritis and made it difficult for him to play golf. Between the wars he studied law at the Middle Temple and was called to the Bar in 1926, but partly because of family pressures and partly because of voluntary public works, he never practised as a barrister.

Hughes-Onslow's mother Marion was a rich woman, with a string of Bentleys, chauffeurs and other servants, so he and his two younger brothers had independent means. It was this that enabled him to give tireless service to a variety of local causes, in Maybole, Ayr, Kirkoswald and, of course, Turnberry. Unlike his two younger brothers the Captain never took to the metropolitan high life, indeed he loathed travelling. In 1926 he bought Craig, a windswept cottage which had been the Turnberry post office until it was struck by lightning in 1909, and it was here that he spent the rest of his life until his death in 1972. When his mother died in 1933, the Captain could have lived on the family estate but preferred to stay at Turnberry next to the golf course. The drawing room window at Craig offered a fine panorama across the first green towards Ailsa Craig, with the clubhouse and the lighthouse also in view.

The Captain was content to busy himself with his family, his golf and his enthusiasm for the new technology of cars, including rally driving, and photography. But it was on the committees which he served with good humour, humility and wisdom that he made his greatest contribution to Ayrshire life. He was a member of Maybole District Council for 34 years and a member of the education sub-committee. He became chairman of the council in 1938 and was chairman of Maybole Juvenile Court in 1958. After serving as an elder of Kirkoswald Parish Church for 12 years from 1944 he became the session clerk for 11 years from 1957. In 1962 he was much photographed in the press welcoming Dwight and Mamie Eisenhower to the church at Kirkoswald while they were staying at Culzean. He represented Kirkoswald on Ayr County Council for more than 30 years and was chairman of the Board of Management of Southern Ayrshire Hospitals, and chairman of the Carrick District Licensing Court until 1968.

He became a J.P. in 1936 and served on the Ayrshire Joint Probation Committee and on the Advisory Committee for J.P.s for South Ayrshire. He and his three sons were members of the Queen's Bodyguard for Scotland (the Royal Company of Archers).

He was a man of great enthusiasms and he had an abundance of time and energy to pursue them. Always fond of motoring, in the early 1930's he took up rally driving, but in those days the sport took a more gentle, amateur form than it does today. In the early 1950's he enthusiastically welcomed the young Stirling Moss to Turnberry to race and test his famously unreliable BRM racing car on the concrete runways left over from the wartime military airfield. It broke down!

His wife Ruth was a lady with a very strong personality and impeccable social sense, but above all with a very warm heart. The Captain also had these qualities and also great dignity. Both had a good sense of humour but with a hint of intolerance which did not 'suffer fools gladly'. My abiding picture of the Captain is of him wearing a jacket and matching plus fours in a large check pattern, with brogue shoes and a bold checked shirt and tie. On anyone else his dress might have looked loud and outlandish; on him with his size and impressive bearing, it looked perfectly normal.

His presence at the Club's general meetings and annual prize givings, which he loved to attend, added a certain dignity and sense of importance to those occasions. He was large not only in stature but also in patience, spirit and generosity but with a mischievous sense of humour. A truly gentle giant.

CHAPTER VII - REFLECTIONS OF PAST CAPTAINS

DAVID MCDOWALL
1998-2000

The one constant in our lives as Turnberry Golf Club members is having to live with change!. And so it was as my term of vice captaincy drew to a close. At the end of December 1997 the then Japanese owners of the hotel sold out to the present American owners, Westin Hotels, and the Club were faced with some uncertainty. For years we had dealt with Chris Rouse, as Manager of the hotel for three successive owners. As he departed the scene my big challenge as I prepared to take office, was to establish a rapport with the new owners. I feel that this was satisfactorily achieved and indeed that a good working relationship is now in place.

In 1997 the Japanese owners of the hotel had put plans in place for the improvement of the golf practice facilities. However by the summer of 1998, as my captaincy began, the new American owners had more ambitious plans in mind. The golf academy was constructed and the Arran course, with the new ground to the north, was completely redesigned into the new Kintyre course.

It is much tougher than its Arran predecessor. Length has been added but with narrow fairways retained, arguably it is now a sterner test than the Ailsa championship course. The inward nine holes are particularly difficult. I recently asked a member how he had fared in a medal competition over the Kintyre. He replied that it had been like the Second World War, out in 39 and back in 45! The course has knitted together very quickly and our members now have two superb courses and practice facilities second to none, and a 9-hole academy course.

The Arran was a shorter course than the Ailsa but its gorse lined fairways meant accuracy was at a premium and where competitions were "course optional" members would deliberate long and hard on the choice. So it was that the late Colin McDonald, faced with a home tie against a Royal Troon member, agonised for a few weeks as to which course to choose to give himself an advantage! He spoke with his regular playing partners and eventually came to the view that, since his opponent was a bigger hitter than him but more erratic, the Arran should be the venue. On the day of the big match Colin was delayed in the office and had to drive furiously to Turnberry, arriving with only minutes to spare. His opponent was standing fully prepared, relaxed and ready to play. Colin threw open the boot of his car only to discover that he had arrived without clubs, shoes or any gear at all! He had to borrow everything from the steward and the golf professional and needless to say he was comprehensively beaten. Having the choice of course had been of no avail.

I particularly enjoyed inter-club matches but soon learned not to take them too seriously. My very first such match as Vice-Captain was against Kilmarnock Barassie at their course. There were seven games and the then Captain, Jim Smith and I had recorded a victory in the top game. As each of the remaining games finished the Barassie Vice-Captain checked the result with his

221

players and informed his Captain of the state of the match. I was sure that he was having problems with simple arithmetic as he had his team a game better than I calculated. However I said nothing as I recounted the scores in my head and continued to enjoy the company and hospitality of our hosts. As the final game came off the course the players signalled a Barassie win and the Vice-Captain said to his Captain that the overall match had been drawn. I could not contain myself at this point and I claimed a Turnberry victory by four games to three. The Barassie Captain then politely explained that the top game was purely a social game and it did not count towards the result! The match had ended with three wins apiece. Our Captain, Jim Smith, knew the format but, amused at my competitive instincts, he let me walk right into the situation. He had a great laugh at my expense, as did our hosts!

In 1998 we added to our tally of inter-club matches with an annual match against the Glenearn Club at Gleneagles. The inaugural match took place at Gleneagles on 29th August 1998 on what I recall was probably the best day of that summer. Captain Ken Wilburn and the Glenearn team made us very welcome. One of our opponents had a hole-in-one, but overall the Turnberry members played exceptionally well in securing an opening victory. Importantly, our team made new friends and subsequent matches have been well enjoyed. The 2000 trip to Gleneagles, by minibus, seems to have been a particularly good day by all accounts although many of the recollections were somewhat impaired by the apres-golf.

Relaxing and socialising after the golf can sometimes seem more important than the golf itself! During my captaincy I was fortunate to be invited by Nairn West Golf Club to participate in their hosting of the 1999 Walker Cup. The invitation had gone out to all clubs who had previously hosted the event and of course Turnberry had played host in 1963. The Nairn Club arranged golf for their guests and it was a wonderful experience playing with and meeting captains and representatives of other clubs from all over Britain and Ireland, from various parts of the U.S.A. and from the R. and A. and U.S.G.A. At Royal Dornoch a bus was laid on to take players and caddies from the clubhouse to the far reaches of the course for a shot-gun start. It was about 8.30 a.m. and a dishevelled looking man sat down beside me on the bus. He looked as if he had been sleeping rough and he was carrying a four pack of beer. From my own caddying days at Turnberry I assumed that he was one of the caddies. As we talked I discovered that he was, in fact, the President of one of the districts of the Irish Golf Union and he had been partying well into the morning. I was in his company and that of his Irish colleagues a few times over that weekend and they knew how to enjoy themselves! Some of them came down to play the Ayrshire courses on their way back to Ireland and then, just for good measure, they were off the next week to Brookline to watch the Ryder Cup!

The Walker Cup on Saturday and Sunday was contested in a wonderful sporting and friendly manner worthy of the great game of golf and surely providing a lesson that the professionals could have done well to follow more closely a year later in the Ryder Cup in America. The win by the Great Britain and Ireland team was magnificent to witness, and I was also privileged to witness a fine match at Turnberry the following summer when Great Britain and Ireland beat a European team in the St. Andrews Trophy.

In closing these few reminiscences, I just hope that the next one hundred years at Turnberry are as eventful for our Captains and members as the first one hundred have been. We have often been at the centre of the golfing stage, both in amateur and professional championships. As a venue for these Turnberry provides an unrivalled setting, magnificent courses and the willing personnel and facilities to hold the top events. It has an important place in the history of the game and I am sure that it will figure prominently in its future.

GORDON RODGER
2000-2002

IS there anywhere more spectacular than Turnberry? The views over the Firth of Clyde and north towards Bute are unparalleled no matter what the season. To be elected Captain of Turnberry Golf Club was an honour – a long way from being a caddie at the club while a student in the 70's. Rab Boyd was the caddie master at that time and he commanded the respect of his charges with a combination of invective, good humour and a never-ending supply of jokes. Between games of cards he divided his men into caddies and bag-carriers and then sub-divided them into clean and dirty! I graduated from sweeping out the caddie shack to bag-carrier and finally to caddie (clean). I was taught the ropes by characters like Tam Kiltie from Maybole and Big John Cavens from Girvan.

There is always change at Turnberry, most of it for the good. Hotel Managers and Directors of Golf come and go and Ken Millar and Brian Gunson were the respective incumbents for part of my tenure. Many a good laugh was enjoyed during a round with them. Ken left the Hotel before he could put into practice his novel idea of having a telephone on the 9th tee to enable players to order a large brandy (or even a soft drink) from Brian at the 'Halfway House'. It is probably a good job this never materialised as Douglas Dunlop would have requested a telephone be put in at the car park at the lighthouse road as well!

Turnberry has staged many amateur and professional events in its life. In July 2000 the Club hosted an international match for the St. Andrews Trophy and a boys' international match for the Jacques Leglise Trophy between Great Britain and Ireland and The Continent of Europe. Many of those who played in the event are now making a living in the professional ranks – Luke Donald, Paul Casey, Mikko Illonen and Steven O'Hara to name a few. I remember the booming drives and the unusual sight of players playing their ball out of the burn surrounding the 16th green. I also remember Past Captain David McDowall, acting as starter for the event. With his straw hat firmly on his head, his pronunciation of the German, Spanish and Finnish surnames bought a smile to everyone's faces. If Ivor Robson ever wants a week off the European Tour, David would make an excellent substitute.

The Club plays a number of interclub matches each year, some at home and some away. Many friendships have been created through these games and none more so than on trips to Gleneagles. On one of these trips to play Glenearn Golf Club a mini bus was hired to take us there and back, though I don't remember much of the return journey. Donald Love, the match convener, organised the day and entertained us with his usual round of funny stories. Jim Nicol, one of our staunchest members and a fine tenor singer, gave us a live version of his No. 1 CD 'The Last Rose of Summer' and Bells and Gordons did the rest. It was a wonderful day never to be forgotten. I don't remember the result of the match but, if it was like most of the others in my period of Captaincy, we lost. Well, it's only a game!

My final months of Captaincy co-incided with the first three months of the Club's centenary year, with a flag raising ceremony taking place on a bright sunny day in early January following the traditional match between the Captain's and Vice-Captain's teams. It was wonderful to see Campbell Hicks and Donald Henderson, our two longest serving members, raise the flag with a little help from the caddie master Willie McDines.

The Hotel continues to improve the already excellent facilities at the resort and, while the Ailsa has remained virtually unchanged, the Arran course was re-designed by Donald Steel and re-named the Kintyre. The new course is an excellent test of golf with the closing holes being as difficult as any of those on an Open Championship course. A new nine hole Academy course – named Arran – was created to supplement the teaching facilities at the Colin Montgomerie Links Golf Academy.

One constant factor at Turnberry since 1986 deserves specific mention, namely George Brown, the Head Grass-cutter (sorry, 'Course Superintendent')! Throughout his period in charge George has kept the courses in fantastic condition all year round, whatever the weather. As a member of the Club he has also been one of our best players over the years, winning many of the trophies and shooting many low scores including a 64 scratch over the Arran course in 1995. George's professional expertise has been much in demand and he has travelled the world gaining and dispensing it and often, in the process, meeting the rich and famous. His stories are priceless but not always repeatable. After a game of golf with ex-President Clinton, George told an American TV company that what is said on the course stays on the course.

No matter what the weather or the standard of your golf there is no finer place to be than Turnberry. If you are playing well the course will reward you with memories of your good shots made spectacular by the setting and, if you are playing badly, you will at least have the consolation of doing it on the most beautiful links course in the world.

Some of the members at the front of the clubhouse on 5th January 2002, to witness the raising of the Club's Centenary Flag.

CHAPTER VII - REFLECTIONS OF PAST CAPTAINS

TIM MORRISON
2002-2003

A new book about Shell's Wonderful World of Golf has been produced and in it there are published letters that Gene Sarazen wrote to the dying Bobby Jones. One letter is dated 8th June, 1965, and reads:- *'I sure enjoyed my visit to Turnberry. My last day there I played with Stanley Morrison, Captain of the Club and owner of a malt whiskey distillery. That night he had his boy deliver a bottle of Scotch, 35 years old. I'm not drinking it, just sniffing it. It's too good to drink.'*

Thirty-seven years later that 'boy' was proud to be elected Captain of Turnberry Golf Club during its centenary year, following in his father's footsteps. It has indeed been a privilege to be Captain during that year and, along with many other members I have spoken to, I found the raising of the centenary flag on 5th January, 2002, to be not only an historic but also a very emotional occasion.

It is impossible to know what dreams and aspirations the founders and original members of Turnberry Golf Club had in 1902 for their new club and for the exciting new links just laid out on the Turnberry peninsula. Perhaps they dreamt of hosting The Open which had its origin at nearby Prestwick in 1860 and was being held there again in 1903. No doubt they envisaged having great matches on the new course but could not have foreseen a Walker Cup – it had not even been conceived. However, would even the most ambitious of those early pioneers have pursued such dreams if they had known that, within forty years, the links would be virtually destroyed by conversion to military uses, not just once but twice? They persisted however and the existence of the Club became a constant in the ever-changing history of Turnberry. Perhaps the Club's most notable achievement has been to survive and thrive in a highly commercial, ever-changing environment and at the same time provide Turnberry with a historic link to its beginnings, to the local communities and to the best trad-itions of golf in Scotland. The celebration of this with some justifiable pride in the Club's centenary year would no doubt have been approved by the 22 gentlemen who met in Maybole Town Hall on 24th April 1902, to found the Club.

To judge by the feedback from many members it seems that the year and its special events were a great success, and this was due to the work and assistance of many people. First of all there was excellent pre-planning by the Centenary Committee under Stewart Jardine, whose imagination and understanding of the Club gave us a wide and varied programme of events. Then there was the actual organisation by all the conveners. Ken Mackenzie put in hours behind the scenes with the hotel management and staff, arranging the social functions and catering, and Donald Love and Jim Crawford made admirably efficient arrangements for all the golf events. Support came from Turnberry Hotel who not only provided a first class service and quality of fare but were most generous hosts on a number of occasions. Stewart Selbie, Mark Ancram and Paul Burley worked very closely with the Club as a team and deserve enormous thanks for their support during the year. George Brown, the Course Superintendent, as always, consistently provided us with outstanding golf courses appreciated by members and visitors alike. Finally the enthusiastic participation and involvement of the members at all the events and competitions ensured a very successful and special centenary year.

My sincere thanks go to all the conveners and members of Committee not specifically mentioned by me but who all devoted so much time and effort to the Club's preparations for the centenary year. However I wish to make special mention of two individuals, the first of whom is Greg Jardine, Convener of the Junior Section. Greg has carried on the good work of Ian Lawson, his predecessor, in advancing the Club's policy of encouraging the training and development of our junior members. He has given an enormous amount of his time to this crucial area of the Club and, with his own fine golfing and communication skills, he has been an inspirational role model to his young charges. The second is Tom Paterson, our Secretary, who was a guiding light throughout my year in office. The Club is fortunate to have had his services since he took over as Assistant Secretary in 1984 and as Secretary and Treasurer in 1989. His experience and knowledge of Club affairs are invaluable and the Club is very fortunate having him guiding its more transitory office bearers and looking after its assets.

The centenary year began with the traditional match between the Captain's team and the Vice-Captain's team on 5th January. It was played in glorious dry and sunny conditions followed by a ceremony at which the centenary flag of the Club was raised by the two most senior and long-standing members, Donald Henderson and Campbell Hicks, who could each boast a membership of 64 years.

Then followed the customary annual dinner dance on 9th February in Turnberry Hotel attended by 240 people, comprising only members and their partners. Every room in the Hotel was occupied by those attending, making it a wonderful, relaxed 'family' occasion with a minimum of formality and without speeches apart from a toast to the Club proposed by one of the Club's own, Past Captain Jack Boyd, the author of this book.

The main centenary celebrations were held over the weekend of 5th/6th April. Golf competitions were held on both the Ailsa and Kintyre courses on the Friday and Saturday in which 142 members and invited guests took part and two excellent days of golf were enjoyed in beautiful weather. The winning teams on Friday were Graeme Simmers (Captain of the R. & A.), Andrew Dinwoodie and myself on the Ailsa course, and Ian McDonald, Stewart Hay and Bryce McQuiston on the Kintyre course. On Saturday the winning Ailsa team consisted of James Rait (Captain of Royal Troon), Ian Lawson and John Watt, whilst the winners on the Kintyre were Jim Byers, Michael Brown and David Kidd. The highlight of the weekend was the formal dinner held on the Friday evening in the Hotel, attended by 143 members and 30 guests. Representatives came from clubs which, like Turnberry, have had the honour of hosting The Open or major amateur championships namely the Royal & Ancient Golf Club of St. Andrews, Royal Troon, Prestwick, Muirfield, Royal Birkdale, Carnoustie, Royal Liverpool, Royal Lytham, Nairn, Ganton, and Royal Porthcawl; and of course from those local Ayrshire clubs with which Turnberry Golf Club has established a rapport over the years, namely Kilmarnock Barassie, Prestwick St. Nicholas, Ayr Belleisle and Brunston Castle. In addition there were guests from Gleneagles, Portmarnock, the Scottish Golf Union and the Scottish Region of the Professional Golfers Association. The principal guest speakers were Graeme Simmers, the Captain of the R. & A. who proposed the toast of Turnberry Golf Club, and Donald Steel, eminent author, journalist and golf course architect, who replied on behalf of the guests. It was a truly memorable evening and the Club was presented by its various guests with a number of very personal and thoughtful gifts (now displayed in the Clubhouse) to commemorate the occasion.

The season continued with all the usual competitions but also with many special centenary events:- a cocktail party on 24th April, 2002 (the 100th anniversary date), a team competition in May, an expanded Quad-Am in August and a Texas Scramble in October, all enthusiastically supported.

The Club Championship is always of special importance and there was keen competition to win it in the centenary year. The finalists were John Broadfoot and Chris McHugh and it was a pleasure for me to referee a very sporting match. John played outstanding golf to become the champion and holder of the silver salver presented to the Club by my father in 1937.

Chapter VII - Reflections of Past Captains

The Past Captains' day took place in October and was attended by nine Past Captains and, considering that our Captains spend two years in office, two years as Vice Captain and at least four years on Committee, this represents seventy-two years service that they have collectively devoted to the Club. We owe them an enormous debt of gratitude. During that day we had as our principal guest Harry McCaw, Past Captain of both the Royal and Ancient Golf Club and Royal County Down Golf Club, who proposed the toast to the Club. Other guests were Jeremy Caplan, a member of the General Committee of the R. & A., and Neil Crichton, the Chairman of that Committee.

Whether the Open Championship will return to Turnberry for a fourth time and if so, when, is not yet known but it will surely not be postponed for too long. It is unthinkable that the course which has produced three of the best Champions and most dramatic of contests in the history of The Open should be passed over for too long, once the logistics of transport to the course are satisfactory. The hosting instead of the Women's British Open Championship during the centenary year proved to be a delightful substitute without being as disruptive to other events as an Open would have been.

The final event of the centenary year was a mixed quad-am team competition on Saturday, 21st December, 2002, when 98 members teed off at 9.00 a.m. in a shot-gun start over the Ailsa course, and this was followed by the lowering of the centenary flag, performed by Campbell Hicks. It was a matter of much regret that Donald Henderson, who along with Campbell, had raised the flag some twelve months earlier, was too ill to attend. A new Club flag was raised in its place as a symbol of hope and expectation for the next 100 years of good golfing and companionship over the bonnie links of Turnberry.

Winners of Centenary Team Competition
Left to right: Graeme Simmers (Captain of R. & A.), Tim Morrison and Andrew Dinwoodie

227

HISTORY OF TURNBERRY GOLF CLUB

Turnberry Golf Club's Centenary Committee and Officials
Back from left: Charles Tait, Alex Ingram, Greg Jardine, Ian Brown, John Hodge, Jim Crawford and Ian Lawson.
Front from left: Donald Love, Tom Paterson, Tim Morrison (Captain), Alan McKinlay (Vice-Captain) and Ken MacKenzie

The Captain with some of the guests at the Centenary Dinner on 4th April 2002

Appendix 1

Description of Willie Fernie's Original Course At Turnberry Which Appeared in Golf Illustrated on 21st June, 1901

'The Glasgow and South Western Railway Company have chosen the face of the rising ground overlooking the course at the south end for their hotel, and it is from this point, nearest Girvan, that the last hole and the first tee are situated. The following description, taken from the Glasgow Evening Times, will give the reader some idea of the nature of the course. First hole (300 yards). The drive is from the level towards the sea, and is into the bent, and thence into a deep and extensive rather marshy hollow, where the first green will have to be formed from the foundation. Second hole (350) yards. The drive is over a steep bent-covered hill, which it is proposed to form into a bunker, facing the tee, and the lie is on a depressed plateau inclining towards the hole. The green is situated in a hollow, open at both ends. Third hole (370 yards). The approach is across a burn of some size, with clear water, and the present green (there being an alternative one) is in the hollow just beyond the burn. There is a large bed of yellow iris on the tee side of the burn, but it is proposed to alter the course of the burn, and probably do away with the flags. Fourth hole (280 yards). The course is still among the sand hills, and the green is in a deep round hollow, open only on the side of a straight approach, forming, in fact, a cul de sac. Fifth hole (400 yards). Through the sand hills, the green being again in a hollow, but of large extent. This concludes the course in the sand hills, and from the second tee it has been parallel, coming north, with the coast. Sixth hole (200 yards). The tee is on a rocky eminence with the sea on both hands, and the lighthouse and its precincts in full view across a rocky inlet of the sea. Play is rather inland, across an elevation with a cairn on the top of it, the green being on the near side of the road to the lighthouse. Seventh hole (160 yards). At the tee to this hole a very fine view of the rocky coast to the north of the lighthouse is obtained, and here the outcropping rocks are encountered on the course. The green is below the Warren farm house. The eighth (290 yards). The course is still as near the rocky beach as it can be, and a marshy ditch formed by the water from Bruce's well, forms a hazard from the tee. This hole is the most northerly point of the course, and the player turns south in an inland direction to the ninth. Ninth hole (360 yards). The green has been placed in a slight depression, with a bunker in front and a bunker on the left, both close to the green. Tenth hole (450 yards). A marsh and a bunker have to be crossed from the tee, but once over these all the player has to do is to get as much length out of his second as possible. The approach is very tricky, however, for unless the player has got well up with his second he encounters a telegraph wire which runs along the road to the lighthouse, and there is also a telegraph post to deal with, and, in any case, the public road and a turf dyke, just beyond which the green lies. Eleventh (500 yards). This hole goes across the course toward the sea again, on ground which has been partly reclaimed from the bent, and the hole is over a stone wall on a plateau short of the sand hills, where the fifth green is. Twelfth hole (360 yards). The drive is diagonally across the wall back again in a southerly direction through the reclaimed ground, there being a bunker to the right, partly in the line of the green. Thirteenth hole (280 yards). The drive includes the recrossing of the burn. Fourteenth hole (260 yards). The green is situated on the near side of the wall, which here runs at right angles to the direction it has at the eleventh hole. This hole, curiously enough, occupies the same position as the fourteenth green at Prestwick, being the nearest point to the starting place which a player reaches in the course of the round. It has this further resemblance to the Prestwick green in that it is situated close to the west of another green, only in this case it is the seventeenth hole, where at Prestwick it is the eighteenth. Fifteenth hole (370 yards). The player turns back again across smooth ground and again recrosses the burn, the green being situated just beyond the stream. It is a fine hole, having a bunker between it and the burn, and a bunker running along the left side. The approach, which is a comparatively long one, must be very accurate. Sixteenth hole (240 yards). This hole is across a perfect piece of flat turf, the trend being slightly further inland than at any previous part of the course. Seventeenth hole (570 yards). The burn is recrossed *once more going to this very long hole, which in ordinary circumstances will require three full drives to reach it. With the exception of the burn there is no hazard, the course being along a level expanse of perfectly smooth turf till the neighbourhood of the green is reached, where a marsh is in front of the green and a bunker to the right. The green is just short of the wall, and, as already indicated, in the neighbourhood of the fourteenth hole. Eighteenth hole (300 yards). The tee can here be made on the near side of the wall to form a hazard, or on the opposite side of the wall to avoid it. In any case a considerable extent of sand hills and rough ground has to be crossed to get on to the flat, ground beyond.'*

Appendix 2

Open Championships - Statistics

OPEN CHAMPIONSHIP 1977

Name	Score					Name	Score				
T Watson (USA)	68	70	65	65	268	R Maltbie (USA)	71	66	72	80	289
J Nicklaus (USA)	68	70	65	66	269	E Darcy (Ire)	74	71	74	71	290
H Green (USA)	72	66	74	67	279	K I Brown (Sco)	74	73	71	72	290
L Trevino (USA)	68	70	72	70	280	M Pinero (Spn)	74	75	71	71	291
G Burns (USA)	70	70	72	69	281	B Dassu (Ita)	72	74	72	73	291
B Crenshaw (USA)	71	69	66	75	281	M N Hseih (Tai)	72	73	73	73	291
A Palmer (USA)	73	73	67	69	282	B W Barnes (Sco)	79	69	69	74	291
R Floyd (USA)	70	73	68	72	283	J Morgan (Wal)	72	71	71	77	291
J Schrooeder (USA)	66	74	73	71	284	N C Coles (Eng)	74	74	71	73	292
M Hayes (USA)	76	63	72	73	284	D I Vaughan (Wal)	71	74	73	74	292
T Horton (Eng)	70	74	65	75	284	J Gonzales (USA)	78	72	71	72	293
J Miller (USA)	69	74	72	74	284	A Jacklin (Eng)	72	70	74	77	293
P W Thomson (Aus)	74	72	67	73	286	R J Charles (NZ)	73	72	70	78	293
H K Clark (Eng)	72	68	72	74	286	S Ginn (Aus)	75	72	72	75	294
G L Hunt (Eng)	73	71	71	72	287	H Irwin (USA)	70	71	73	80	294
J Pate (USA)	74	70	70	73	287	B G Huggett (Wal)	72	77	72	74	295
R Cole (SA)	72	71	71	73	287	V Fernandez (Arg)	75	73	73	74	295
P J Butler (Eng)	71	68	75	73	287	M G King (Eng)	73	75	72	75	295
G V Marsh (Aus)	73	69	71	74	287	R de Vicenzo (Arg)	76	71	70	78	295
R Shearer (Aus)	72	69	72	74	287	C O'Connor (Ire)	75	73	71	77	296
S Ballesteros (Spn)	69	71	73	74	287	J C Farmer (Sco)	72	74	72	78	296
G Player (SA)	71	74	74	69	288	B J Waites (Eng)	78	70	69	79	296
T Weiskopf (USA)	71	71	71	72	288	R Davies (Aus)	77	70	70	79	296
P Dawson (Eng)	74	68	73	73	288	M Bembridge (Eng)	76	69	75	77	297
J Fourie (SA)	74	69	70	75	288	V Tshabalala (SA)	71	73	72	81	297
R Massengale (USA)	73	71	74	71	289	I Mosey (Eng)	75	73	73	77	298
D Ingram (Sco)	73	74	70	72	289	D Jones (N Ire)	73	71	73	78	298
M F Foster (Eng)	67	74	75	73	289	C S Hsu (Tai)	70	70	77	81	298
J O'Leary (Ire)	74	73	68	74	289	G D Jacobson (USA)	74	73	70	81	298
A Gallardo (Spn)	78	65	72	74	289	N A Faldo (Eng)	71	76	74	78	299
N Suzuki (Jpn)	74	71	69	75	289	S Locatelli (Ita)	72	72	76	79	299
G Burrows (USA)	69	72	68	80	289	V Baker (SA)	77	70	73	79	299

OPEN CHAMPIONSHIP 1986

Name	Score					Name	Score				
G Norman (Aus)	74	63	74	69	280	P Stewart (USA)	76	69	75	76	296
G J Brand (Eng)	71	68	75	71	285	G Player (SA)	75	72	73	76	296
B Langer (Ger)	72	70	76	68	286	G Turner (NZ)	73	71	75	77	296
I Woosnam (Wal)	70	74	70	72	286	R Maltbie (USA)	78	71	76	72	297
N Faldo (Eng)	71	70	76	70	287	M O'Meara (USA)	80	69	74	74	297
S Ballesteros (Spn)	76	75	73	64	288	H M Chung (Tai)	77	74	69	77	297
G Koch (USA)	75	72	72	70	289	M O'Grady (USA)	76	75	77	70	298
F Zoeller (USA)	75	73	72	69	289	A Charnley (Eng)	77	73	76	72	298
B Marchbank (Sco)	78	70	72	69	289	F Couples (USA)	78	73	75	72	298
T Nakajima (Jpn)	74	67	71	77	289	M Clayton (Aus)	76	74	75	73	298
C O'Connor (Ire)	75	71	75	69	290	L Mize (USA)	79	69	75	75	298
D Graham (Aus)	75	73	70	72	290	J Hawkes (SA)	78	73	72	75	298
J M Canizares (Spn)	76	68	73	73	290	Lu Hsi Chuen (Tai)	80	69	73	76	298
C Strange (USA)	79	69	74	69	291	R Tway (USA)	74	71	76	77	298
A Bean (USA)	74	73	73	71	291	T Armour III (USA)	76	70	75	77	298
A Forsbrand (Swe)	71	73	77	71	292	S Randolph (USA)	72	76	77	75	300
J M Olazabal (Spn)	78	69	72	73	292	G Marsh (Aus)	79	71	75	75	300
R Floyd (USA)	78	67	73	74	292	C Mason (Eng)	76	73	73	78	300
R J Charles (NZ)	76	72	73	72	293	M McNulty (Zim)	80	71	79	71	301
M Pinero (Spn)	78	71	70	74	293	M Mackenzie (Eng)	70	70	77	75	301
R Rafferty (N Ire)	75	74	75	70	294	L Trevino (USA)	80	71	75	75	301
D Cooper (Eng)	72	79	72	71	294	E Darcy (Ire)	76	75	75	75	301
V Somers (Aus)	73	77	72	72	294	T Lamore (USA)	76	71	77	77	301
B Crenshaw (USA)	77	69	75	73	294	F Nobilo (NZ)	76	75	71	79	301
R Lee (Eng)	71	75	75	73	294	A Chandler (Eng)	78	72	78	74	302
P Parkin (Wal)	78	70	72	74	294	J Heggarty (N Ire)	75	72	80	75	302
D Edwards (USA)	77	73	70	74	294	M Gray (Sco)	75	76	76	75	302
V Fernandez (Arg)	78	70	71	75	294	D Hammond (USA)	74	71	79	78	302
S Torrance (Sco)	78	69	71	76	294	S Simpson (USA)	78	71	75	78	302
I Stanley (Aus)	72	74	78	71	295	O Moore (Aus)	76	74	79	74	303
J Mahaffey (USA)	75	73	75	72	295	P Fowler (Aus)	80	71	77	75	303
M Kuramoto (Jpn)	77	73	73	72	295	D Jones (N Ire)	75	76	79	75	305
D A Weibring (USA)	75	70	76	74	295	R Drummond (Sco)	76	74	77	78	305
A W Lyle (Sco)	78	73	70	74	295	T Watson (USA)	77	71	77	71	296
M James (Eng)	75	73	73	75	296	R Chapman (Eng)	74	71	78	73	296
A Brooks (Sco)	72	73	77	74	296	G Weir (Sco)	78	69	80	80	307
R Commans (USA)	72	77	73	74	296	K Moe (USA)	76	74	82	82	314
T Horton (Eng)	77	73	82	74	306	H Green (USA)	77	73	81		Retd

OPEN CHAMPIONSHIP 1994

Name	Score					Name	Score				
N Price (Zim)	69	66	67	66	268	D Clarke (Ire)	73	68	69	70	280
J Parnevik (Swe)	68	66	68	67	269	J Van De Velde (Fra)	68	70	71	71	280
F Zoeller (USA)	71	66	64	70	271	D Love III (USA)	71	67	68	74	280
A Forsbrand (Swe)	72	71	66	64	273	M Ozaki (Jpn)	69	71	66	74	280
M James (Eng)	72	67	68	66	273	J Gallagher Jnr (USA)	73	68	69	71	281
D Feherty (Ire)	68	69	66	70	273	T Edwards (USA)	68	68	73	72	281
B Faxon (USA)	69	65	67	73	274	G Kraft (USA)	69	74	66	72	281
N Faldo (Eng)	75	66	70	64	275	H Twitty (USA)	71	72	66	72	281
T Kite (USA)	71	69	66	69	275	D Frost (SA)	70	71	71	70	282
C Montgomerie (Sco)	72	69	65	69	275	M Lanner (Swe)	69	74	69	70	282
R Claydon (Eng)	72	71	68	65	276	K Tomori (Jpn)	69	69	73	71	282
M McNulty (Zim)	71	70	68	67	276	T Watanabe (Jpn)	72	71	68	71	282
F Nobilo (NZ)	69	67	72	68	276	P Baker (Eng)	71	72	70	70	283
J Lomas (Eng)	66	70	72	68	276	J Cook (USA)	73	69	70	73	283
M Calcavecchia (USA)	71	70	67	68	276	T Nakajima (Jpn)	73	67	70	73	283
G Norman (Aus)	71	67	69	69	276	B Watts (USA)	68	70	71	74	283
L Mize (USA)	73	69	64	70	276	R McFarlane (Eng)	68	74	67	74	283
T Watson (USA)	68	65	69	74	276	G Brand Jnr (Sco)	72	71	73	68	284
R Rafferty (Ire)	71	66	65	74	276	H Meshiai (Jpn)	72	71	71	70	284
M Brooks (USA)	74	64	71	68	277	B Langer (Ger)	72	70	70	72	284
V Singh (Fiji)	70	68	69	70	277	C O'Connor (Ire)	71	69	71	73	284
G Turner (NZ)	65	71	70	71	277	P-U Johansson (Swe)	73	69	69	73	284
P Senior (Aus)	68	71	67	71	277	R Allenby (Aus)	72	69	68	75	284
R Estes (USA)	72	68	72	66	278	W Grady (Aus)	68	74	67	75	284
T Price (Aus)	74	65	71	68	278	S Elkington (Aus)	71	72	73	69	285
P Lawrie (Sco0	71	69	70	68	278	M Roe (Eng)	74	68	73	70	285
J Maggert (USA)	69	74	67	68	278	L Clements (USA)	72	71	72	70	285
T Lehman (USA)	70	69	70	69	278	C Mason (Eng)	69	71	73	72	285
E Els (SA)	69	66	69	71	278	R Alvarez (Arg)	70	72	71	72	285
M Springer (USA)	72	67	68	71	278	W Bennett (Eng) *	72	67	74	73	286
L Roberts (USA)	68	69	69	72	278	W Riley (Aus)	77	66	70	73	286
P Jacobsen (USA)	69	70	67	72	278	A Lyle (Sco)	71	72	72	72	287
C Stadler (USA)	71	69	66	72	278	C Ronald (Sco)	71	72	72	73	288
A Coltart (Sco)	71	69	66	72	278	M Davis (Eng)	75	68	69	67	279
B Marchbank (Sco)	71	70	70	69	280	L Janzen (USA)	74	69	69	67	279
G Evans (Eng)	69	69	73	68	279	B Crenshaw (USA)	70	73	73	73	289
D Gilford (Eng)	72	68	72	68	280	C Parry (Aus)	72	68	73	76	289
D Hospital (Spn)	72	69	71	68	280	J Haeggman (Swe)	71	72	69	77	289
J M Olazabal (Spn)	72	71	69	68	280	N Henning (SA)	70	73	70	78	291
S Ballesteros (Spn)	70	70	71	69	280	J Daly (USA)	68	72	72	80	292
C Gillies (Sco)	71	70	72	75	288						

* denotes Amateur

APPENDIX 3

RESULTS OF AMATEUR CHAMPIONSHIPS AT TURNBERRY

1961 AMATEUR CHAMPIONSHIP
(from Third Round)

Third Round

L G Ranells (Prestbury)	beat	A Frazer (Drumpellier)	4 & 3
J B Carr (Sutton)	beat	C W Green (Dumbarton)	21st
R J Jamieson (Cawder)	beat	G G Emerson (Ralston)	4 & 2
J Winning (Loudoun Gowf)	beat	K P Walker (Kilmacolm	7 & 6
R D B M Shade (Duddingston)	beat	F Bostock (USA)	4 & 3
C Lawrie (Royal & Ancient)	beat	R D Davies (USA)	2 & 1
J Walker (Irvine)	beat	J J Penrose (USA)	4 & 3
L G Taylor (Ranfurly Castle)	beat	M P Korich (France)	5 & 4
H V S Thomson (Troon)	beat	W I Turnbull (Innerleithen)	3 & 2
H M Campbell (Falkirk Tryst)	beat	B Gogan (Douglas Park)	3 & 1
G R Dixon (Ravensworth)	beat	G Huddy (Lindrick)	3 & 2
G B Cosh (Cowglen)	beat	F F Sugden (Switzerland)	3 & 1
D Moffat (Newcastle)	beat	Maj D A Blair (Nairn)	19th
D G Neech (Eltham Warren)	beat	A Sinclair (Drumpellier)	2 & 1
R L Morrow (Troon St Meddans)	beat	J B McHale (USA)	4 & 3
R A G Munro (Erskine)	beat	R T Gardiner-Hill ((Royal & Ancient)	3 & 2
I G F Lee (Cathkin Braes)	beat	D J Hamilton (Craigmillar Park)	4 & 2
M C Douglas (Thornhill)	beat	M D Mitchella (Temple)	4 & 2
J R Young (Cathcart Castle)	beat	B H G Chapman (Porters Bar)	2 & 1
I Wright (Aboyne)	beat	D St J Brew (Sandy Lodge)	3 & 2
A D Crafts (Coxmoor)	beat	Dr D J C Cameron (Bothwell Castle)	4 & 3
J C Beharrell (Little Aston)	beat	D D Cameron (Erskine)	5 & 4
M J Christmas (West Sussex)	beat	J Pirie (Milngavie)	4 & 3
B Stockdale (Royal Lytham & St Annes)	beat	J H Morrison (West Kilbride)	7 & 5
H Tinbrook (USA)	beat	R L Renfrew (Glasgow)	2 & 1
A Kyle (Royal & Ancient)	beat	I Caldwell (Sunningdale)	2 & 1
J Glover (Clitheroe)	beat	W A Slark (Walton Heath)	19th
L S Foster (Prestwick)	beat	D P Davidson (Tynemouth)	3 & 2
W A Stewart (Erskine)	beat	D W Alexander (Dalmahoy)	3 & 2
M F Bonallack (Thorpe Hall)	beat	P J Binns (Royal Mid Surrey)	6 & 5
J M Sharp (Caldwell)	beat	Dr D M Marsh (Southport & Ainsdale)	20th
D W Frame (Worplesdon)	beat	J Wilson (Kilmarnock Barassie)	3 & 2

Fourth Round

Carr	beat	Ranells	2 & 1
Jamieson	beat	Winning	2 & 1
Shade	beat	Lawrie	2 & 1
Walker	beat	Taylor	5 & 3
Campbell	beat	Thomson	2 & 1
Dixon	beat	Cosh	2 holes
Moffat	beat	Neech	2 & 1
Morrow	beat	Munro	2 & 1
Douglas	beat	Lee	1 hole
Wright	beat	Young	4 & 3
Beharrell	beat	Crafts	3 & 1
Christmas	beat	Stockdale	1 hole
Kyle	beat	Tinbrook	4 & 3
Foster	beat	Glover	1 hole
Bonallack	beat	Stewart	3 & 2
Frame	beat	Sharp	1 hole

Fifth Round

Carr	beat	Jamieson	8 & 7
Walker	beat	Shade	2 & 1
Dixon	beat	Campbell	4 & 3
Morrow	beat	Moffat	3 & 2
Wright	beat	Douglas	1 hole
Christmas	beat	Beharrell	3 & 2
Foster	beat	Kyle	2 & 1
Bonallack	beat	Frame	3 & 2

Quarter Finals

Walker	beat	Carr	19th
Morrow	beat	Dixon	3 & 2
Christmas	beat	Wright	5 & 3
Bonallack	beat	Foster	5 & 4

Semi Finals

Walker	beat	Morrow	1 hole
Bonallack	beat	Christmas	6 & 4

Final

Bonallack	beat	Walker	6 & 4

1983 AMATEUR CHAMPIONSHIP

First Round

A Martinez (Leicestershire)	beat	J S Thomson (Kirkcudbright)	4 & 3
A S Oldcorn (Ratho Park)	beat	I R Brotherston (Dumfries & County)	6 & 4
T Philpot (USA)	beat	E V McGoldrick (USA)	5 & 4
A P Parkin (Newtown)	beat	S Campbell (Cawder)	4 & 2
J L Plaxton (Fulford)	beat	J D Hallett (USA)	1 hole
A D Pierse (Tipperary)	beat	D Suddards (South Africa)	3 & 2
C Laurence (Warren)	beat	S Morrison (Gullane)	1 hole
J A Thomson (Ayr Belleisle)	beat	S J King (Holywood)	1 hole
J B Dunlop (Broomieknowe)	beat	I A Carslaw (Williamwood)	3 & 2
D Tentis (USA)	beat	G Bell (Hartlepool)	5 & 4
G K MacDonald (Callander)	beat	B Hoffer (USA)	3 & 2
M P D Walls (Hillside)	beat	P B Malone (Belvoir Park)	6 & 5
J F Hawksworth (Royal Lytham & St Annes)	beat	V N Gavalas (USA)	6 & 4
K Frandsen (USA)	beat	G H Murray (Fereneze)	5 & 4
W Case (USA)	beat	B Tuten (USA)	3 & 1
S D Keppler (Walton Heath)	beat	A Rose (John o' Gaunt)	1 hole
W L Malley (USA)	beat	A Godillot (France)	2 holes
G Starkman (USA)	beat	D V Banke (USA)	5 & 4
P Deeble (Alnmouth)	beat	J Veghte (USA)	1 hole
A J Currie (Irvine Ravenspark)	beat	P McEvoy (Copt Heath)	2 & 1
J T Moffat (West Kilbride)	beat	R Sommier (USA)	2 & 1
P J Hedges (Langley Park)	beat	P Snowden (Altringham)	3 & 2
J Sigal (USA)	beat	W Musto (USA)	6 & 5
R Van Niekerk (South Africa)	beat	L G Carbonetti (Argentine)	3 & 2
B Lewis (USA)	beat	J L Schneider (France)	3 & 2
J Holtgrieve (USA)	beat	N D Kelly (Hilton Park)	6 & 5
R H Willox (Deeside)	beat	J W Milligan (Loudoun Gowf)	19th
A G Pickles (Alloa)	beat	N G Webber (Goring & Streetley)	1 hole
T P Foreman (USA)	beat	D James (USA)	3 & 2
G Shaw (Haggs Castle)	beat	B Wylie (Canada)	Retd hurt
C Bufton (Shifnal)	beat	G B Benett (USA)	6 & 5
M S Thompson (Middlesbrough)	beat	E Pery (France)	7 & 6

Second Round

Martinez	beat	Oldcorn	4 & 2
Parkin	beat	Philpot	6 & 5
Pierse	beat	Plaxton	3 & 2
Thomson	beat	Laurence	7 & 6
Tentis	beat	Dunlop	3 & 2
Walls	beat	MacDonald	4 & 3
Hawksworth	beat	Frandsen	2 & 1
Keppler	beat	Case	4 & 3
Malley	beat	Starkman	3 & 2
Deeble	beat	Currie	2 & 1
Moffat	beat	Hedges	2 & 1
Sigal	beat	Van Niekerk	19th
Holtgrieve	beat	Lewis	1 hole
Pickles	beat	Willox	19th
Foreman	beat	Shaw	19th
Thompson	beat	Bufton	5 & 4

Third Round

Parkin	beat	Martinez	3 & 2
Thomson	beat	Pierse	4 & 3
Tentis	beat	Walls	3 & 2
Keppler	beat	Hawksworth	4 & 3
Deeble	beat	Malley	1 hole
Sigal	beat	Moffat	4 & 3
Holtgrieve	beat	Pickles	2 & 1
Foreman	beat	Thompson	2 & 1

Fourth Round

Parkin	beat	Thomson	2 & 1
Keppler	beat	Tentis	3 & 1
Deeble	beat	Sigal	1 hole
Holtgrieve	beat	Foreman	19th

Semi Finals

Parkin	beat	Keppler	2 & 1
Holtgrieve	beat	Deeble	7 & 5

Final

Parkin	beat	Holtgrieve	5 & 4

1996 AMATEUR CHAMPIONSHIP (from Second Round)

Second Round

W Bladon (Kenilworth)	beat	P Lawrie (University College, Dublin)	3 & 1
R Clark (Erskine)	beat	S McCarthy (Royal North Devon)	3 & 1
I Ferrie (Alnmouth)	beat	E Little (Portpatrick Dunskey)	4 & 3
F McLaughlan (Wishaw)	beat	R J Derksen (Netherlands)	6 & 5
R Wiggins (Slaley Hall)	beat	C Aronsen (Norway)	2 & 1
P Purhonen (Finland)	beat	D Dupin (France)	3 & 2
N Boysen (Netherlands)	beat	D Orr (East Renfrewshire)	1 hole
M Eliasson (Sewden)	beat	D Patrick (Mortonhall)	1 hole
M Erlandsson (Sweden)	beat	R Porter (Germany)	2 & 1
S Boddenheimer (USA)	beat	C Brauner (USA)	2 & 1
R Geilenberg (Germany)	beat	Y Taylor (Brynhill)	2 & 1
C Rodgers (Royal Mid Surrey)	beat	G Lawrie (Prestwick St Nicholas)	19th
M Brooks (Carluke)	beat	M Ellis (Wrexham)	3 & 2
I Griner (Spain)	beat	P Bolton (Chorlton-cum-Hardy)	19th
S Philipson (Prudhoe)	beat	K Ferrie (Alnmouth)	5 & 4
R Beames (Wick)	beat	J Fanagan (Milltown)	3 & 1

Third Round

Bladon	beat	Clark	19th
McLaughlan	beat	Ferrie	23rd
Wiggins	beat	Purhonen	19th
Boysen	beat	Eliasson	2 & 1
Boddenheimer	beat	Erlandsson	4 & 3
Rodgers	beat	Geilenberg	1 hole
Griner	beat	Brooks	2 & 1
Beames	beat	Philipson	3 & 2

Quarter Finals

Bladon	beat	McLaughlan	1 hole
Wiggins	beat	Boysen	4 & 3
Boddenheimer	beat	Rodgers	5 & 4
Beames	beat	Griner	19th

Semi Finals

Bladon	beat	Wiggins	1 hole
Beames	beat	Boddenheimer	3 & 2

Final

Bladon	beat	Beames	1 hole

Appendix 4

Turnberry Golf Club - Captains

1902-06	J. Marshall	1976-78	W.H. Mitchell
1907-08	D. Templeton	1978-80	A.M.Y. Scott
1908-22	R. Niven	1980-82	D.J. Logan
1922-25	Lt.Col. North Dalrymple Hamilton	1982-84	C.W.F. Judge
1925-36	J.R. Richmond C.B.E.	1884-86	W.A. Tod
1936-57	Capt. O. Hughes-Onslow	1986-88	J.A. Carrick
1957-58	R. Black	1988-90	S. Jardine
1958-61	W. Graeme McCulloch	1990-92	W. Manson
1961-63	Jas. P.K. McDowall	1992-94	J.R. Boyd
1963-65	J. Grindlay	1994-96	C.L. Jack
1965-67	S.P. Morrison	1996-98	J.W. Smith
1967-69	A.C. Cockburn	1998-00	D.R. McDowall
1969-71	D.K.D. Gourlay	2000-02	D.G. Rodger
1971-73	R.H.U. Stevenson	2002-03	S.W. Morrison
1973-76	T. Armstrong		

Turnberry Golf Club - Champions

1937	W.G. McCulloch	1967	J. Mackenzie	1986	J.A. Jones
1938	R.H.U. Stevenson	1968	C.W.F. Judge	1987	B. Bain
1939	S.P. Morrison	1969	A. Thomson	1988	B. Bain
1940	R.H.U. Stevenson	1970	R.G. Ross	1989	J.A. Jones
1952	W.G. McCulloch	1971	S. Reid	1990	B. Forsyth
1953	S.P. Morrison	1972	S. Reid	1991	A.J.W. Kidd
1954	W.S. Linton	1973	C.W.F. Judge	1992	B. Forsyth
1955	W.S. Linton	1974	A. Thomson	1993	I.B. Rorison
1956	W.S. Linton	1975	R.G. Ross	1994	J.A. Thomson
1957	T.R. Callan	1976	A.N. Sturrock	1995	J.A. Thomson
1958	T. Armstrong	1977	N.M. Bain	1996	J.A. Thomson
1959	W.S. Linton	1978	D.C. Braid	1997	J.A. Thomson
1960	A. Thomson	1979	C.W.F. Judge	1998	J.A. Thomson
1961	W.S. Linton	1980	C.W.F. Judge	1999	J.J.R. Hodge
1962	J. Mackenzie	1981	J.A. Jones	2000	R. McLellan
1963	W.S. Linton	1982	D.G. Rodger	2001	R. McLellan
1964	W. Cairns	1983	J.A. Dauthieu	2002	J.C. Broadfoot
1965	W.A. Wilson	1984	J.D.S. Wilson		
1966	A.N. Sturrock	1985	J.B. Morrison		

Appendix 5
Ladies Section - Captains

1912-19	Mrs. A. Dunlop	1981-83	Mrs. W. Boags
1906-07	A. Dunlop	1983-84	Mrs. W. Gray
1919-24	Miss M.G. Milroy	1984-85	Mrs. L. Hogarth
1924-32	Miss W. Strain	1985-86	Mrs. R. Dykes
1932-33	Miss A.W.H. Kennedy	1987-88	Mrs. S.W. Morrison
1933-34	Mrs. Q.M. McCall	1988-89	Mrs. S. Murray
1934-35	Mrs. J. Paterson	1989-90	Mrs. E. Munro
1935-37	Mrs. W.T. MacKay	1990-91	Mrs. J.G. Lackie
1937-39	Mrs. R.S. MacKintosh	1991-92	Mrs. M. Hunter
1939-58	Mrs. J. Kinloch	1992-93	Mrs. M.M. Duncan
1958-59	Mrs. A. Craddock	1993-94	Mrs. M.S. Goudie
1959-61	Mrs. A.L. Dunlop	1994-95	Mrs. C.E. Stevenson
1961-63	Mrs. A.C. Cockburn	1995-96	Mrs. S.L. Farquhar
1963-65	Mrs. W.S. Lanham	1995-97	Mrs. B.E. Beckett
1965-67	Mrs. R. Cowan	1997-98	Mrs. E.A. Smith
1967-69	Miss M. Wyllie	1998	Mrs. F.J. McKellar
1969-71	Mrs. G. Gordon	1998-99	Mrs. I. McFadzean
1971-73	Mrs. H.R.C. Wilson	1999-00	Mrs. C. McCrindle
1973-75	Mrs. E.F. Frazer	2000-01	Mrs. S. Hamilton
1975-77	Mrs. R.W. Scott	2001-02	Miss K. Fitzgerald
1977-79	Mrs. R.T. Faulds	2002-03	Mrs. L. Smith
1979-81	Mrs. W. Cameron		

Ladies Section - Champions

1960	Mrs. R. Cowan	1982	Mrs. A.T.F. Wilson
1961	Miss S. McKinven	1983	Miss J. Leishman
1962	Mrs. H.R.C. Wilson	1984	Miss J. Leishman
1963	Mrs. R. Cowan	1985	Mrs. M. Wilson
1964	Mrs. A.C. Cockburn	1986	Mrs. M. Wilson
1965	Mrs. A.C. Cockburn	1997	Mrs. M. Wilson
1966	Mrs. G. Gordon	1988	Miss Fiona McKay
1967	Mrs. A.C. Cockburn	1989	Miss Fiona McKay
1968	Mrs. R. Fairbairn	1990	Mrs. M. Wilson
1969	Miss Marion Fairbairn	1991	Miss K. Fitzgerald
1970	Mrs. A.T.F. Wilson	1992	Miss K. Fitzgerald
1971	Mrs. A.T.F. Wilson	1993	Miss K. Fitzgerald
1972	Mrs. A.T.F. Wilson	1994	Miss K. Fitzgerald
1973	Mrs. A.T.F. Wilson	1995	Miss K. Fitzgerald
1974	Mrs. H. Dykes	1996	Miss K. Fitzgerald
1975	Mrs. A.T.F. Wilson	1997	Miss K. Fitzgerald
1976	Mrs. A.T.F. Wilson	1998	Miss K. Fitzgerald
1977	Mrs. A.T.F. Wilson	1999	Miss K. Fitzgerald
1978	Mrs. A.T.F. Wilson	2000	Miss K. Fitzgerald
1979	Miss J. Leishman	2001	Miss K. Fitzgerald
1980	Miss J. Leishman	2002	Miss K. Fitzgerald
1981	Mrs. A.T.F. Wilson	2003	Miss K. Fitzgerald

Appendix 6
Acknowledgements

In addition to those mentioned in my Preface many people have assisted in providing information, material, memories and photographs. First of all thanks are due to many Club members including Campbell Hicks, Douglas Dunlop, the late Donald Henderson, Ian Maxwell, Peter McKay, Stewart Jardine, Secretary Tom Paterson, Assistant Secretary Jim Crawford, Ladies' Captain Sarah Finnie, Ladies' past Captains Anne Fraser, Lily Hogarth, Margaret Hunter, Rosemary Dykes, Isobel McFadzean, Mary Goudie, Margaret Morrison and Karen Fitzgerald, as well as Nan Macdonald, Kathleen Andrew, Mary McKay, Myra Cameron, the late Agnes McCall and Secretary Sheila Pickles and also many others too numerous to mention.

Particular thanks are also due to the families of Captain Oliver Hughes Onslow, David Gourlay, Walter Linton, Alex Thomson, Robbie Stevenson, Graeme McCulloch, Stanley Morrison and Willie Templeton, who all kindly provided information and photographs from their family records.

For other photographs we are indebted to Turnberry Hotel for allowing the use of those from the collection in the clubhouse gallery and from their publications; to the Ladies' Golf Union for making available the albums from their archives; to photographer John McEwan of Girvan for his collection of The 1977 Open; to Mrs. Margaret Morrell for the aerial wartime photographs; to Bill Cotton of PPL Sport & Leisure for photographs of The 1986 and 1994 Opens; to 'Golf Illustrated', 'Fairway & Hazard Magazine', 'The Kingdom of Carrick and its Capital', and 'The Illustrated Sporting and Dramatic News' for photographs reproduced from their publications, and to Club member Mike Blair for photographs of past Captains. Thanks also to Tim Morrison for allowing the use of his painting of Turnberry which appears on the cover. Some photographs of views and of members were taken by myself over the past few years and I would have liked to have included more, if space had permitted.

There follows a list of credits which is as accurate and comprehensive as possible but, should I have used other source material which has not been acknowledged due to oversight or difficulty in tracing source, then I tender my apologies.

JACK BOYD.

Photographic and Document Credits

(1) **The Kingdom of Carrick and its Capital** – Views and Verse' published 1904 by John Latta and William Miller:- Lighthouse – p.2: 3 of Course – p.20: 3 of Course – p.21: 3 of Course – p. 22; 2 of Maybole – p.29: Clubhouse – p.36.

(2) **Royal & Ancient Golf Club.** 1740 painting of St. Andrews - p.6.

(3) **Trustees of Culzean Estate.** 1892 Notice - p.7: 1982 letter from Murray - p.8: 1892 letter from Lord Ailsa – p.9: 1897 public notice – p.9: 1900 letter from W. Fernie – p.17: 1903 letter from Girvan G.C. – p.25: Membership card – p28.

(4) **Turnberry Hotel Collection.** Menu - p.56: Plane - p.57: 17th green 1957 – Heading page Ch. IV: Bonallack/Walker 1963 – p. 113: Bob Charles – p.140: Tented village – p.141: Programme – p.143: photos – ps. 144, 170, 184, 186, 192, 193, 194, 195, 202.

(5) **Railway Archives.** 1915 GSWR Guide – p.13: Turnberry Station – ps. 11 and 15: Scorecard – p.44: Advert – p.51.

(6) **Gordon Riddle.** 3rd Marquess – p.12: Wildlife – ps. 157, 158, 159, 160, 162.

(7) **Royal Troon G.C.** Fernies – p.18.

(8) **John McMillan.** Layout plans of courses – ps. 19, 26, 50, 53, 69, 91.

(9) **Unknown.** Photo of 1905 Golfers – Heading page Chapter II.

(10) **A.D. Henderson.** Postcard of Hotel – p.34.

(11) **Tony Kerrigan.** Photo of John Marshall – p.39.

(12) **Collectors World, Glasgow.** Postcard of great golfers – p.41.

(13) **Ladies' Golf Union.** Ladies Championships – ps. 45, 46, 47, 54, Heading page Ch. III, ps. 65, 71, 72, 73, 74, 75, 81, 82.

(14) **A.C. Hicks.** Postcard of 5th green – p.53.

(15) **W. Ralston, Glasgow.** Hotel and course – p.55.

(16) **Cartoon by Doyle.** P.77.

(17) **Mrs. Margaret Morrell.** Aerial views ps. 84, 93.

(18) **Sutton's *'Turf for Sport'*.** Photos – ps. 90, 94, 95, 96, 97.

(19) **Fairway and Hazard Magazine.** Mrs. Peel – p.106.

(20) **Illustrated Sporting and Dramatic News.** H. Cotton lesson – p.135.

(21) **Golf Illustrated.** O'Connor/ Black – p.107.

(22) **John F. Brown.** Ailsa Craig – Heading page Ch. V, Ladies - ps. 204 and 205.

(23) **John McEwan.** 1997 Open – ps. 145, 146, 147, 148, 149, 150.

(24) **Bob Jamieson Collection.** p. 154.

(25) **Fred Westcott, Maybole.** Ducks – p.158, Stoat – p. 160, Yellowhammer – p. 161.

(26) **PPL Sport & Leisure (Bill Cotton).** Aerial View - p88: N. Price on Heading page Ch. VI, G. Norman – p.191, N. Price – ps. 197 and 198.

(27) **Pamela McGill, Girvan.** ps. 164, 169.

(28) **Scottish Golf Union.** A. Thomson – p. 166.

(29) **George Young Photography.** 1994 Open – ps. 199, 200 and 218.

Bibliography

Ayr Advertiser 1900-2002

Ayr Observer & Galloway Gazette 1902

Ayrshire Post 1900-2000

A Corner of Carrick – James A. Guthrie 1979

Ailsa Craig – Rev. R. Lawson 1895

Carrick Gazette

Carrick Herald

Cassillis & Culzean Estates Records

Country Life 1964-1977

Doyle Cartoon – 1933

Fairway & Hazard Magazine 1912 – 1924 – 1937 – 1954

Glasgow Herald and The Herald

Glasgow Evening Times

Golf Illustrated 1904, 1957 - The Bailie Cartoon Supplement 1908

Golf – Scotland's Game – David Hamilton

Golf between the Wars – Bernard Darwin

Glasgow & South-Western Railway Company, Booklet on Golfing Resorts 1915

Glasgow & South-Western Railway Company - The Carrick Coast Tourist Guide 1915

Guinness Book of Golf Records Facts and Champions – Donald Steel 1987

Ladies' Golf Union, St. Andrews – Library & Archives

Prestwick Golf Club – Birthplace of The Open 1989

Rail and Travel Monthly Magazine 1910

Royal and Ancient Golf Club Open Programmes and Official Annuals

Royal Troon Golf Club History

Sunday Telegraph 1977

The Dawn of Professional Golf – Peter N. Lewis 1995

The Illustrated Sporting & Dramatic News 1938

The Girvan Gang – Golf in Ayrshire in 1851 – David Hamilton

Turf for Sport Magazine 1950 – Suttons Consumer Products Ltd.

The Kingdom of Carrick and its Capital – Miller & Latta 1904

Turnberry Golf Club Records and Archives

Turnberry Hotel publications

The Golfers Handbook – Various editions

The Magnificent Castle of Culzean and the Kennedy Family – Professor Michael Moss